Contemporary Biographies
in Communications
& Media

Contemporary Biographies in Communications & Media

SALEM PRESS

A Division of EBSCO Information Services, Inc.

Ipswich, Massachusetts

GREY HOUSE PUBLISHING

Copyright © 2014, by Salem Press, A Division of EBSCO Information Services, Inc. and Grey House Publishing, Inc.

∞ The paper used in these volumes conforms to the American National Standard for Permanence of Paper for Printed Library Materials, Z39.48-1992 (R1997).

Library of Congress Cataloging-in-Publication Data

Contemporary biographies in communications & media. -- [1st ed.].

   p. : ill. ; cm. -- (Contemporary biographies in--)

Includes bibliographical references and index.

Part of a series that is supplemental to the Salem Press series: Careers in--

Contents extracted from the monthly magazine: Current biography.

ISBN: 978-1-61925-234-9

   1. Mass media specialists--Biography. 2. Mass media--Biography. 3. Communication--Biography. I. Title: Contemporary biographies in communications and media II. Title: Careers in-- III. Title: Current biography.

P92.5.A1 C66 2014

302.23/092

Contents

Publisher's Note

Contemporary Biographies in Communications & Media is a collection of twenty-nine biographical sketches of "living leaders" in the fields of communications and media. All of these articles come from the pages of *Current Biography*, the monthly magazine renowned for its unfailing accuracy, insightful selection, and the wide scope of influence of its subjects. These up-to-date profiles draw from a variety of sources and are an invaluable resource for researchers, teachers, students, and librarians. Students will gain a better understanding of the educational development and career pathways of the contemporary communications and media specialist to better prepare themselves for a career in these industries.

The geographical scope of *Contemporary Biographies in Communications & Media* is broad; selections span the Eastern and Western Hemispheres, covering numerous major geographical and cultural regions. All of the figures profiled are still working at one or more of their specialties, including writing, directing, leading major corporations, hosting television and radio programs, consulting, inventing, and publishing.

Articles in *Contemporary Biographies in Communications* range in length from 1,000 to 4,000 words and follow a standard format. All articles begin with ready-reference listings that include birth details and concise identifications. The article then generally divide into several parts, including Early Life and Education, and Later Career, a core section that provides straightforward accounts of the periods in which the profiled subjects made their most significant contributions to the communications and media industries. Essays are supplemented by bibliographies, which provide starting points for further research.

As with other Salem Press biographical reference works, these articles combine breadth of coverage with a format that offers users quick access to the particular information needed. Articles are arranged alphabetically by last name. A general Bibliography offers a comprehensive list of works for students seeking out more information on a particular individual or subject, while a separate bibliography of Selected Works highlights the significant published works of the professionals profiled. A Profession Index lists the 58 professions covered in this volume and the individuals associated with each.

An appendix consisting of nine historical biographies culled from the Salem Press *Great Lives* series introduces readers to professionals in communications and media of historical significance integral to the work and research that revolutionized these industries.

The editors of Salem Press wish to extend their appreciation to all those involved in the development and production of this work; without their expert contribution, projects of this nature would not be possible. A list of contributors follows.

Contributors List

Barratt, David
Broadus, Matt
Cullen, Christopher
Dewey, Joseph
Dvorak, William
Ewing, Jack
Hagan, Molly
Hartig, Sean
Johnson, Judy A.
Larson, Eugene
Malinowski, Nicholas W.
Mari, Christopher
Muteba, Bertha
Neumann, Caryn E.
Orens, Geoff
Padovano, Joanna
Peck, Jamie E.
Rasmussen, R. Kent
Rolls, Albert
Segura, Liliana
Shin, Ji-Hye
Stern, Kate
Thomas, Cullen F.

Contemporary Biographies in Communications & Media

Abrams, Jonathan

Serial entrepreneur, software engineer

Born: 1970(?), Toronto, Ontario, Canada

When Jonathan Abrams founded the on-line social network Friendster, in 2002, he envisioned it as a safer, more appealing alternative to existing dating sites, one on which members would register, free of charge and by invitation only, to meet people through friends rather than total strangers. In designing the site, Abrams had in mind the concept of "six degrees of separation" (the theory that anyone on Earth can be linked to any other person anywhere in the world through a chain of acquaintances that has no more than five intermediaries); he aimed to give users access to the personal profiles of their friends, friends of friends, the friends of those people, and so on, thus making it possible for them to try to establish new personal or business relationships. By early 2003 Friendster's membership was growing at a weekly rate of 20 percent; by the following July, the number of registered users had reached one million. In October 2003 Abrams declined a $30 million acquisition offer from Google, chosing instead to try to build Friendster using venture capital. Around that time the demand for Friendster began to decline, partly because of server troubles and lack of innovation and partly because of increasing competition from rival social-networking sites. In 2004 Abrams stepped down as Friendster's CEO while retaining the title of company chairman. Friendster attempted to attract more customers by offering an array of multi-media features, emulating competitor MySpace's emphasis on music as a "community" focus. In 2005 Abrams lost his chairmanship as well as most of his equity in Friendster in a company recapitalization. He became co-owner of a San Francisco nightclub, Slide, in September 2006 and in late 2006 founded Socializr, a social event-planning and management Web site. Events management proved to be a difficult market, and Socializr was acquired by competitor Punchbowl in November 2010.

In January 2011 Abrams became cofounder and managing partner of Founders Den, a "co-working space" and private club for entrepreneurs. In mid-2012 he founded Nuzzel, a social news sharing site that integrates links-sharing among friends on Facebook and Twitter, among other sites; Nuzzel currently is in beta testing. Before launching Friendster, Abrams had started and later sold another company, called HotLinks; earlier, he worked in senior engineering roles at Bell-Northern Research, Nortel Networks, Netscape, and Bitfone.

In 2003 Abrams was named *Entertainment Weekly*'s "breakout star," while *Time* listed Friendster as one of the "coolest inventions" of the year. In 2004 *Technology Review* named Abrams one of the world's top young innovators. Also in that year he was listed among *Advertising Age* magazine's entertainment marketers of the year and nominated in the software-designer category for the *Wired* Rave Awards.

Education and Early Career

Jonathan Abrams was born in about 1970 in Toronto, in the province of Ontario, Canada, and was raised in Thornhill, just north of Toronto. He told an interviewer for the Conference Guru Web site that his interest in computers and business began during his childhood. He attended McMaster University, in Hamilton, Ontario, where he majored in computer science. During summer breaks he worked in Ottawa, Canada's capital, as an intern for Bell-Northern Research, a telecommunications-equipment manufacturer. He earned a B.S. degree with honors from McMaster in 1995. After his graduation Bell-Northern hired him to write telecommunications software. Later, after Bell-Northern became Nortel Networks Corp., he worked on Internet software at the company's computing-technology laboratory. "After six months, I decided I wanted to move to where the action was, I wanted to move to where all the Internet stuff was being created. I was more interested in the Internet stuff than the telecom stuff," he told Kate Heartfield for the *Ottawa Citizen* (July 31, 2003). In 1996—at the height of the boom in Internet technology stocks—Abrams left Canada to accept a job as a senior software engineer at the Netscape Communications Corp. in Mountain View, California, in the heart of so-called Silicon Valley. "I wanted to be where I considered then to be the center of the universe," he told Todd Inoue for Metroactive, the on-line site of *Metro Silicon Valley* newspaper (October 9, 2003). His responsibilities at Netscape involved managing the company's Web browsers and working on projects to promote open standards for Internet protocols. In 1998, after less than two years with Netscape, he lost his job—apparently for economic reasons, not poor performance.

In 1999 Abrams launched a business of his own—HotLinks Network, an on-line bookmark and Web directory service that enabled users to share their preferred Web sites with others. "We're trying to recapture the original idea behind the Internet—to bring people together in a spirit of discovery," he told Jayson Matthews for siliconvalley.internet.com (November 6, 2000). He funded the $2 million venture primarily with capital from an affiliate of CMGI, an investor in technology companies, and staffed it with former co-workers of his from Nortel. Along with many other Internet start-ups, his business (based in Mountain View) suffered during the dot-com downturn (the so-called dot-com bubble "officially" burst in 2000), and he was forced to reduce his payroll. "My greatest challenge was trying to run my first company in hypercompetitive 1999 with very limited business experience," Abrams told the Conference Guru interviewer, after admitting, "In many ways, I ended up in over my head. . . . Naturally, I made many mistakes, and while HotLinks was not a complete failure, it was a real disappointment for me to have had to lay off valued members of our team, and not provide a better outcome for the people who built the company with me." In 2001 Abrams sold HotLinks. Later that year he was hired to head the engineering group of Bitfone Corp., in Palo Alto, California, a fledgling wireless software company. Within nine months he found himself unemployed again, following Bitfone's merger with Digital Transit. He soon joined Ryze.com, a networking community, founded by Adrian Scott, whose members were categorized according to interests, location, and current and past employers.

At around that time Abrams broke up with his girlfriend of two years, and he began to explore the possibility of meeting single females through on-line dating sites. "But when I checked out these sites, I found that they were kind of anonymous and random and creepy, and I didn't find it very appealing," as he recalled to Robert Siegel for the National Public Radio (NPR) news magazine *All Things Considered* (July 10, 2003). "The other thing was that I noticed in real life, my friends preferred to meet people through their friends. So I kind of looked at those two things and thought it would be cool if there was a Web site where you could meet people through your friends online." As Abrams later explained to Jason Calacanis of the online program This Week in Startups (November 6, 2012), "I started coming up with the idea of: what if online, instead of being anonymous, instead of being Cyberdude307, I'd be Jonathan, and I'd bring the real-world social context that I had with me, online."

Inspired by the positive response he received from friends regarding his idea for an invitation-only online social network, Abrams left Ryze.com and, working from his apartment in Silicon Valley, created the software needed to launch the project. He decided against approaching venture capitalists for start-up funds; as he told Kate Heartfield, such investors "push you to spend a lot of money right away and in this economy, that didn't seem wise. I thought it would be more impressive to raise a small amount of money and go further with it." He raised $400,000 from friends and other investors, including Mark Pincus and Reid Hoffman, the founders of the networking sites Tribe and LinkedIn, respectively, whose combined investment was $310,000, as reported by Victoria Murphy in *Forbes* magazine (December 8, 2003).

"I started coming up with the idea of: what if online, instead of being anonymous, instead of being Cyberdude307, I'd be Jonathan, and I'd bring the real-world social context that I had with me, online."

In August 2002, rather than actively promoting the service, Abrams tested Friendster by having 20 of his friends use it, in the hope that those people would invite 20 of their friends to join the site and the network would thus grow through word of mouth. "It was really like that old shampoo commercial where you tell two friends and then they tell two friends and so on," he told T. L. Stanley for *Advertising Age* (March 1, 2004). By the end of the year, although the site was still private, membership was growing at the rate of 4 percent to 7 percent daily, forcing Abrams to switch from a friend's server to a commercial server in January 2003.

Later Career

In March 2003 Abrams offered a free trial version of Friendster to the public. Within three months the number of members registered to the site was increasing by about 20 percent every week, reaching a peak of 1.75 million in October 2003. The company's main sources of revenue initially were advertisements at the site and the sale of Friendster merchandise (T-shirts, hats, and mugs). Although Abrams had ruled out asking registered users to pay a subscription fee for basic service, in August 2003 he instituted an $8 per month charge for premium features, among them a chat room and a mechanism through which e-mail or instant messages could be sent to potential new friends outside the Friendster network. (By comparison, such online services as Match.com and Yahoo! Personals charged $20 to $25 monthly subscription fees.)

Friendster was approaching a million members by July 2003, when Abrams raised investments totaling $1 million from Tim Koogle, who was then CEO of Yahoo! and a member of the Friendster board of directors; Peter Thiel, the former chief executive of PayPal; and Ram Shriram, the former vice president of business development of Amazon.com and a former member of the executive team at Netscape Communications. According to Matt Marshall, writing for the *San Jose Mercury News* (October 3, 2003) Abrams turned down a $30 million acquisition offer from Google. He chose instead to accept venture-capital investments from Kleiner Perkins Caulfield & Byers and Benchmark Capital that totaled $13 million and reportedly raised the value of Friendster to an estimated $53 million, according to Ann Grimes in the *Wall Street Journal.* Abrams retained about a third of Friendster's stock but relinquished control over its board, which proved to be a costly error. He used the venture capital money to expand the company's staff and to purchase additional servers, routers, and other hardware to speed the network's processing time. The extra equipment had become vital with the surge in traffic, which had caused slowdowns. Contributing to that increase in usage was the registration at Friendster.com of imposters (commonly known as Fakesters), people posing as fictitious characters (the cartoon character Homer Simpson, for example) or as well-known personages (the actor Kevin Bacon was a popular choice).

In October 2003 Friendster switched the site's architecture from Java to the open-source Web server Apache (which costs nothing and allows users to modify software to fit their particular needs) and to the programming language PHP, thus enabling the company to add more features. That month only 1.75 million of its 7 million registered users visited Friendster.com. In a conversation with Natalie Hanman for the London *Guardian* (April 28, 2005), Clay Shirky, a specialist on Internet technologies who teaches at New York University, attributed the decline in usage to a lack of technological innovation. In an attempt to make Friendster not merely a social networking site but also a for-profit company, Abrams had also agreed to step down from his chief-executive role; he was replaced by Tim Koogle in March 2004. Koogle served as interim CEO until June 2004, when Scott Sassa, a former NBC head of entertainment, assumed the position. Sassa intended to generate most of Friendster's revenue through advertising on the site. "Friendster's mass appeal, viral growth and stickiness will make it one of the brands that will redefine the media landscape," he stated in a press release, as quoted by Elizabeth Millard on the CRM Web site. Besides posting horoscopes and news headlines at the site, Sassa made promotional tie-in agreements with DreamWorks and Sony Pictures. In March 2005 Sassa offered members of Friendster, for a fee, the opportunity to create and update their own blogs.

While Friendster was attempting to appeal to a mass audience, similar social networking sites were having greater success targeting niche audiences. MySpace.com, for example, a social network (launched in October 2004) connected with the Los Angeles music scene, attracted 24.3 million unique visitors (visitors counted only once) in October 2005, according to ComScore Networks (on-line), while ComScore Media Metrix, a division of ComScore Networks, reported that Facebook.com (founded in February 2004), which quickly became especially popular among college students, attracted 9.5 million unique visitors in October 2005. According to ComScore Media Metrix, that same month Friendster drew only 1.4 million unique visitors. Another competitor, Orkut, was launched by Google in January 2004.

In May 2005 Friendster announced (without making its financial records public) that it expected its annual sales to total $10 million. The next month Sassa resigned. He was succeeded by Taek Kwon, formerly the executive vice president of product and technology for Citysearch.com, who believed that the solution to Friendster's problems lay in enhancing the site. In October 2005 Friendster launched a redesigned site that offered new features including extra photo storage space, free blogs, photo slideshows, classifieds, movie and music reviews, and, thanks to a so-called distribution partnership with Grouper Networks, new file-sharing capabilities. In March 2006, in partnership with Pandora and its Music Genome Project, Friendster offered its members the capability of creating playlists containing their favorite music. Earlier, Stefanie Olsen had reported for CNET News.com (November 14, 2005) that Friendster had hired Montgomery & Co., an investment bank in Santa Monica, California, to find a buyer for the company. In August 2006, however, Friendster procured $10 million in funding in a round led by DAG Ventures, and Kent Lindstrom became CEO. Yet domestically, once surpassed by MySpace (called by some a copycat site), it never succeeded in challenging its competitors' dominance. Gary Rivlin, writing for the *New York Times* (October 15, 2006), gave an account of Friendster's sinking fortunes, describing the site as "the iconic case of failure" and noting that it was receiving less than 2 percent of the number of domestic visitors to MySpace each month. According to Max Chafkin in *Inc.* (June 1, 2007), in March 2007, "Friendster fell to thirteenth place among social networks in the U.S. and saw its market share decline to 0.3 percent."

As early as spring 2004, however, the company had become aware that while it was slowing domestically, it was seeing dramatic growth in Asia, especially in the Philippines. Half the site's traffic was already originating in southeastern Asia. By the time Richard Kimber (formerly of Google) replaced Lindstrom as CEO in 2008, Friendster had received $20 million in another round of funding (from IDG Ventures) and was strongly focused on Asia, where it had become the preeminent social networking site. In December 2009 Friendster was purchased by MOL Global, a Malaysian payment platform firm with which it was already partnering for its e-commerce operations. The purchase price was $39.5 million (of which just $26.4 million remained for shareholders after a variety of deductions). In June 2011 Friendster ended its social networking operations and became an online gaming site.

Abrams came to see his company's flameout, as Chafkin wrote, as "not simply a singular failure, but a systematic one" owing to the basic workings of the venture capital system. By Abrams's own account, he "brought on experienced investors to help Friendster fulfill its potential. But the all-star team was the curse of death." Frequent changes in management and direction left the company reeling. In all, as Abrams himself told interviewer Jason Calacanis of This Week in Startups (#303, November 6, 2012), "From the venture financing, in the fall of '03, to the company being sold in '09, the company went through six C.E.O.s in those six years. Six years, six C.E.O.s. … Friendster was sold for, around, $40 million, in '09. The Malaysian company that bought it, then, promptly sold the patents, that I'm the inventor of, to Facebook, for more than they paid to buy the company. Which was, like, the final chapter of the mismanagement of that company."

Abrams is co-owner of Slide—"San Francisco's first retro-ultralounge," according to *San Francisco* magazine (August 2007)—which opened on the site of a former Mason Street speakeasy in September 2006. By then Abrams had been working for some time on an event-planning and management Web site called Socializr, which launched in late 2006. Built by Abrams himself, Socializr—initially with "angel" funding from Rembrandt Ventures, David Samuel, and others and later with venture capital ($1.5 million) from Rembrandt Ventures (September 2007)—improved on competitor Evite by tapping users' existing social networking presences and integrating music and videos. Despite attempting to stay "lean," Abrams was compelled to lay off staff in September 2009, "probably," as analyst Michael Arrington speculated, owing to "competitive pressure from Facebook and others" rather than from its ostensible rival Evite (TechCrunch, September 16, 2009). Socializr was acquired by competitor Punchbowl in November 2010.

Abrams moved on to other ventures. In January 2011 he became cofounder (with Jason Johnson, Michael Levit, and Zachary Bogue) and managing partner (with Bogue) of Founders Den, an invitation-only "curated, co-working space," in Abrams's words, and private club for "serial entrepreneurs" located in San Francisco's South of Market (SoMA) district. Coveted space at Founders Den typically is rented for relatively short terms by established entrepreneurs working on start-ups. In mid-2012 Abrams founded Nuzzel, a social news-sharing site that integrates friends' news links postings on Facebook and Twitter; Nuzzel, currently in beta testing, faces an array of competitors but has won praise from initially somewhat skeptical critics for its elegance, ease of use, and contextual features, such as friends' tweets on a given story and relevant links to other news aggregators. As with Abrams's other concepts, it draws on a given user's on-line circle of friends, in this case to gather links to news and stories presumably of interest to the user, keeping the user apprised of what friends are reading and sharing. Asked about the genesis of Nuzzel, Abrams told Ellen Lee, in an interview posted at the *San Francisco Chronicle*'s on-line site SFGate (October 23, 2012), that "The idea of Nuzzel was to help manage the social overload" created by the on-line welter of "friends," "followers," and ever-expanding networks of connections. "It's not some sort of silly faddish thing," he continued. "It's a utility." Abrams's experience with Socializr led him to return to the development model he had used, by necessity, with Friendster: "[W]hen I had the idea for Nuzzel, I went back to basics. I built a prototype … [to] see the reaction and see if this idea really had potential before I raised money and hired a team. That worked well with Friendster, and it's why I decided to build something first." Nuzzel went on to raise more than $1.7 million in seed funding from investors and venture capital firms, including IDG Ventures, 500 Startups, Charles River Ventures, SoftTech VC, and Andreessen Horowitz.

Abrams has long been active in the Silicon Valley tech community. He is a mentor in Steve Blank's entrepreneurship classes at Stanford and Berkeley, a top-rated mentor at the Founder Institute, and an advisor to AngelList and LeanLaunchLab. He was a long-time member of the advisory board of the Silicon Valley Association of Startup Entrepreneurs (SVASE), co-chair of the SDForum Venture Finance SIG, and moderator of the SVASE CTO Forum, and he has been a judge for the Business Association of Stanford Entrepreneurial Students (BASES) Entrepreneurs Challenge business plan contest; "bplan," the UC Berkeley Startup Competition; the Stanford-Berkeley Innovators' Challenge; the Intel Challenge; and Start-Up Chile.

Abrams is married and a father.

Further Reading:

Advertising Age S p8 Mar. 1, 2004

beta.nuzzel.com

Fortune p30 Jun. 28, 2004

Harvard Business School Case Study, Sep. 14, 2006. Prod. #: 707409-PDF-ENG

Inc. p84 Jun. 1, 2007

Los Angeles Times C p1 May 26, 2005

New York Times III p1 Oct. 15, 2006

Newsday B p3 Oct. 16, 2003

Ottawa Citizen F p2 Jul. 31, 2003

San Francisco Chronicle/SFGate Oct. 23, 2012

SF Weekly Aug.13, 2003

This Week in Startups #303 Nov. 6, 2012

www.jabrams.com

Abramson, Jill

Newspaper executive

Born: 1954, New York, New York, United States

On June 2, 2011, Jill Abramson was named executive editor of the *New York Times,* becoming the first woman to hold that post in the paper's 160-year history. After cutting her teeth as an investigative reporter in Washington, D.C., for the *Wall Street Journal* and the *Times,* Abramson became the *Times*'s Washington bureau chief in 2000 and managing editor of the paper in 2003. She was the first woman to occupy any of these positions in what many consider to be a male-dominated institution. On accepting her new post—which she assumed officially in September 2011—Abramson told the newsroom, as quoted by Jeremy W. Peters in the *New York Times* (June 2, 2011), that the appointment is "the honor of my life." "Every executive stands on the shoulders of others," she said, mentioning in particular and thanking her "sisters"—her female colleagues at the newspaper, including its chief executive officer, Janet L. Robinson, and the columnist Maureen Dowd, as well as the women who came before her there. Abramson told Ed Pilkington for the London *Guardian* (June 7, 2011), "I know I didn't get this job because I'm a woman; I got it because I'm the best qualified person. But nonetheless what it means to me is that the executive editor of the *New York Times* is such an important position in our society, the *Times* itself is indispensable to society, and a woman gets to run the newsroom, which is meaningful." Abramson replaced Bill Keller, who stepped down to become a contributing writer for the *Times*.

As the executive editor, Abramson is charged with balancing the interests of the business side of the newspaper and its publisher, Arthur Sulzberger Jr., with those of the newsroom. (She was the fourth executive editor appointed by Sulzberger since he took over as publisher in 1992.) Abramson sought to reconcile the printed newspaper's production, marketing, and advertising with those of the coexisting—and to some extent competitive—Web version of the *Times*. Abramson told Michael Kinsley of the *New Republic* (August 19, 2013), "We're pursuing a smart strategy that combines our core strengths and exploits the fact that we've never deviated from either a journalistic or business strategy that is rooted in a belief that quality journalism pays." Abramson remained committed to investigative reporting, and she credits *Times* publisher Sulzberger with a virtually unparalleled willingness to support such reporting: "He has continued to invest in what I think is the most important journalism of all, and that is having plenty of boots on the ground—journalists who are witnessing, and who are expert, and who are gathering the news in foreign countries and all across our country. By keeping up that investment, which the Sulzberger family sees as a mission, " Abramson told Kinsley, "he has put the *Times* in a position to expand internationally, which is one of the centerpieces of our current strategy: to push out the *New York Times* and make it the quality news source internationally, just as years ago he led the push to make the *New York Times* the predominant national news source. And I think he has been visionary in these things and that the Sulzberger family has fought a very brave fight to show that quality journalism pays."

In addition to her newspaper career, Abramson is the author or co-author of several books, including *Strange Justice: The Selling of Clarence Thomas* (1994). "There is no one I'd rather be in a foxhole with," Abramson's friend Jane Mayer, the co-author of *Strange Justice,* told Keach Hagey for Politico.com (June 2, 2011). "She is tough as nails. … She's a vigorous defender of the truth, and she's fearless."

Education and Early Career

The second of two daughters, Jill Ellen Abramson was born on March 19, 1954, and raised in an upper-middle-class Jewish home on the Upper West Side of Manhattan, in New York City. Her father, Norman Abramson, ran a textile-importing firm called Irish Looms Associates, and her mother, Dovie, was a homemaker; like their children, the elder Abramsons were Manhattanites by birth. Abramson's sister, Jane Abramson O'Connor, born in 1947, is the editor at large for Penguin USA Books for Young Readers. She is also the author of 46 books for young people, including the popular series *Fancy Nancy,* about a precocious girl with a fondness for things she considers "fancy," such as French words and feather boas; O'Connor has said that the character is based on herself and her sister during their younger years. The Abramsons were avid readers of the *New York Times.* Abramson told Pilkington that while she was growing up, her family's attitude toward the paper was that "what the *New York Times* said was absolute truth."

Abramson was educated at Ethical Culture schools: the Midtown School, in Manhattan, from kindergarten through sixth grade, and, from seventh through twelfth grades, the Fieldston School, an elite, private preparatory school in the New York City borough of the Bronx. Students at the schools received lessons in ethics in every grade. Abramson remembers her third-grade ethics teacher, Florence Klaber, posing the question, "Do the ends justify the means?" "We were constantly being pitched moral dilemmas by her and trying to separate the ends and the means, and answer that question, which for a small child is powerful," she told Josh Nathan-Kazis for the *Forward* (June 1, 2011). Abramson graduated from Fieldston in 1972 and enrolled at Harvard University, in Cambridge, Massachusetts. During her college years she became a stringer for *Time* magazine. She graduated magna cum laude with a B.A. degree in history and literature in 1976, the same year she covered the presidential-election campaign for *Time.* In an op-ed piece for the *New York Times* (March 21, 2010), Abramson recalled both the excitement and apprehension she felt at the time. "I remember being in the bar of the Sheraton Wayfarer [hotel] on the night of the New Hampshire primary, so proud of the press credentials dangling from my neck. I gazed at all the famous 'boys on the bus,' including [*Washington Star* and *Baltimore Sun* reporter] Jack Germond and ["Gonzo" journalist and *Rolling Stone* reporter] Hunter Thompson. But as a very young woman, I didn't dare belly up to the bar. Those days are over."

Abramson next worked at NBC News and then became an editorial consultant and staff reporter for *American Lawyer.* That publication's editor, Steven Brill, hired her along with a handful of other young journalists, including the future Reuters editor in chief Stephen Adler; James B. Stewart, later of the *New Yorker*; the future *Businessweek* editor Ellen Pollack; and Jim Cramer, later the host of the TV show *Mad Money.* Brill, a demanding editor, was impressed by Abramson's journalistic zeal. In 1986 he named Abramson, then 32, editor in chief of his Washington, D.C., legal-trade weekly the *Legal Times.* Two years later she met Al Hunt, who was then the Washington editor of the *Wall Street Journal.* Even though the *Journal* had put a freeze on hiring, Hunt interviewed Abramson in 1988. "It was the most dazzling interview I've ever had in my life," Hunt told Hagey. "She rattled off stories that she thought we should be doing right away. So I hired her. I've never made a better hire." For the *Journal* Abramson covered politics with her fellow Fieldston graduate and childhood friend Jane Mayer, who is currently a staff writer at the *New Yorker.* Abramson was named deputy to then-bureau chief Alan S. Murray in 1993.

Meanwhile, Abramson had published her first book, *Where They Are Now: The Story of the Women of Harvard Law, 1974* (1986), written with the former *American Lawyer* staff reporter Barbara Franklin. The 1974 class at Harvard University School of Law was the first at the school in which women had constituted more than 10 percent of the entering students. Of the 70 women Abramson and Franklin interviewed, fewer than a quarter had made partner in their respective firms, while over half of their male counterparts had; others had left the profession altogether to start families. The authors had looked for women who "had it all," or who they felt had managed to balance their professional and personal lives successfully, but they had been unable to find any; perhaps for that reason Linda Greenhouse, in her review of *Where They Are Now* for the *New York Times* (February 23, 1988), found the book to be "ultimately unsatisfying." "What remains unclear is the authors' stance toward their material," Greenhouse wrote. "The book is scarcely a celebration of the range of choices in women's lives. Rather, the emphasis is on the degree to which the women have strayed from the Harvard (male) model of success. … Are the women who left the partnership track victims? Failures? By whose standard?"

Where They Are Now reflected Abramson's interest in the plight of professional women looking to strike a balance between their personal and work lives while trying to navigate male-dominated fields. She was the editor of the *Legal Times* when, in 1988, she wrote a feature for the *New York Times Magazine* (March 6, 1988) profiling Peggy Kerr and Nancy Lieberman, who were among the first women to be named partners at one of the country's most prestigious law firms, Skadden, Arps, Slate, Meagher & Flom, in New York City. (Kerr was the firm's very first, in 1981.) "During the 1980's the overall progress of women at private law firms has been slow," Abramson wrote, "but dramatic gains have come in the last two years." At Skadden, Arps in 1988, she noted, women accounted for 184 of the 651 associates employed; 14 of the firm's 158 partners were women.

Abramson was also interested in another gender-related issue, one that would become a common refrain in her reportage—most notably in a *Times* article entitled (ironically, given future events), "When Will We Stop Saying 'First Woman to ____ '?" (April 9, 2006). Abramson noted that in the 1980s, when law firms were looking to diversify while bringing in more revenue, more lawyers were making partner than ever before, but she wondered if the increase in the number of female partners was a by-product of expanding business rather than a breakthrough for women. In the article Abramson also discussed varied reactions to Katie Couric's becoming the first solo female anchor of a network primetime news program, the *CBS Evening News.* "Surprisingly to me, in the immense coverage of [Couric's taking the job] … many stories did not lead with the 'first woman' angle," Abramson wrote, arguing that that perhaps indicated progress for women; on the other hand, she also noted, the anchor position had been devalued: "The network news shows are all suffering from declining, aging audiences. … With the fragmentation of television audiences and the advent of cable and on-demand services … the prestige of being an anchor is not what it was in the days of Walter Cronkite." Abramson concluded the article by writing, "This is yet another transitional moment for professional women. … But there are still few women successfully leading the cornerstone institutions of our society."

Abramson and Mayer's *Strange Justice: The Selling of Clarence Thomas* (1994) addressed events in 1991, after President George H. W. Bush nominated Clarence Thomas to serve on the U.S. Supreme Court. During the Senate confirmation hearings, Thomas's former colleague Anita Hill, a 35-year-old lawyer, testified under oath that he had sexually harassed her while he was her supervisor at the Equal Employment Opportunity Commission. Thomas also testified under oath, refuting Hill's claim. Due to the seriousness of the charge and the explicit nature of Hill's accusations, the story consumed headlines for months. Meanwhile, a smear campaign was mounted against Hill. Abramson and Mayer's book, researched over the course of three years, represented an attempt to set the record straight. "Clarence Thomas said that if he had ever behaved in the manner that Anita Hill had accused him of in the hearings, 'You would think that there would be bits and pieces of this elsewhere in my life that would have suggested some sort of pattern,'" Mayer told Nina Totenberg for the National Public Radio program *Morning Edition* (November 3, 1994). "And what we were able to do was to find the bits and pieces and put together the pattern." The two journalists found numerous women who supported Hill's claim and had stories of their own to share about Thomas. Abramson and Mayer also raised troubling questions about the inner workings of the confirmation process itself, and they blamed then-Senator Joseph R. Biden for refusing to call women whom he knew had raised similar claims against Thomas to testify and corroborate Hill's story. In a review of *Strange Justice,* Richard Lacayo wrote for *Time* (November 14, 1994): "The authors conclude that 'the preponderance of the evidence suggests' that Thomas lied under oath when he told the committee he had not harassed Hill. Their book doesn't quite nail that conclusion. Yet its portrait of Thomas as an id suffering in the role of a Republican superego is more detailed and convincing than anything that has appeared so far." (Thomas was narrowly confirmed by the Senate.) *Strange Justice* was nominated for a National Book Award.

On April 5, 1997, the *National Journal* featured Abramson on its cover, naming her one of the 25 most influential journalists in Washington. The magazine called her a "triple threat," adding about her work at the *Wall Street Journal,* where she was then deputy Washington bureau chief: "Abramson not only has a say in hiring decisions (she's pushed for more women) and a hand in shaping the bureau's coverage of Washington, but also weighs in with her own investigative reports on the money-in-politics front." That same year Abramson met the *New York Times* columnist Maureen Dowd (the two would become close friends); Dowd asked Abramson if she knew a female journalist who would be interested in working for the *Times.* Abramson suggested herself. By September of that year, Abramson was working for the Washington bureau of the *New York Times* as the new editor of investigative-reporting projects. Michael Oreskes, the *Times*'s incoming Washington bureau chief, told Paul Starobin for the *National Journal* (September 6, 1997) that Abramson's name was "at the top of everyone's list" of investigative reporters in Washington, thanks to *Strange Justice* and her illuminating reporting on the intersection of money and politics in the nation's capital. As for Abramson, she was very happy to join the *Times,* the newspaper that she had revered as a child, telling Starobin: "I had always harbored a desire to work there at some point." Abramson quickly rose through the ranks, becoming Washington editor in 1999 and bureau chief, in charge of a staff of 60, in 2000—a position she was the first female to hold.

Abramson's years at the helm of the *Times*'s Washington bureau coincided with several historic events. The year 2000 saw the Republican George W. Bush—following a protracted vote recount and a 5–4 Supreme Court decision—defeat the Democrat Al Gore for the U.S. presidency. Abramson had many run-ins with the Bush administration. "I'm a battle-scarred veteran in that regard," she recalled to Pilkington. "There were several national security stories that they asked us not to publish that we ended up publishing." In New York the reporter and former foreign correspondent Howell Raines was named executive editor of the *Times* five days before the September 11, 2001, terrorist attacks on the United States. The *Times* and Raines were praised for their in-depth coverage in the immediate aftermath of the tragedy; the *Times* won seven Pulitzer Prizes for that year.

Raines encouraged competition among his staff, including the Washington bureau, and continually pushed for bigger stories; "Hunt big game, not rabbits," he would say, as sources told Ken Auletta for the *New Yorker* (June 10, 2002). Many at the *Times* accused Raines of becoming too aggressive and of micromanaging the paper after his initial success, and he and Abramson often butted heads. She felt that he was trying to edge her out of her job (in fact, he tried to move her to the paper's book review section); he would try to tell her, rather than ask her, what the Washington reports would include. "It was humiliating," one reporter told Auletta. "It wasn't, 'Jill, what do you have in the Washington report?' It was, 'Jill, this is what we think should be in the Washington report.'" During this period, "She was," concluded Lloyd Grove of *Newsweek* (July 31, 2013), a "skilled and resilient bureaucratic infighter who tended to outlast and outwork her adversaries." It was not until Abramson threatened to quit that relations between the New York and Washington offices improved. Meanwhile, Raines's competitive attitude began to cause larger problems for the paper. Between 2001 and 2003 the Times reporter Judith Miller, citing unnamed sources, published many articles detailing the Iraqi leader Saddam Hussein's supposed production of weapons of mass destruction (WMD). That information, much of it cited by the Bush administration as justification for the 2003 invasion of Iraq, later proved to be false. Abramson revealed little publicly about the matter until 2008, when she assessed Bob Woodward's book *The War Within,* the fourth volume of his inside look at the Bush administration, for the *New York Times Book Review* (September 28, 2008). She wrote that in his second volume, *Plan of Attack,* Woodward "acknowledges an error of his own: he admits he should have pushed the *Washington Post* to publish a front-page article about the flimsiness of the intelligence on W.M.D. I was Washington bureau chief for the *Times* while this was happening, and I failed to push hard enough for an almost identical, skeptical article, written by [investigative reporter] James Risen. This was a period when there were too many credulous accounts of the administration's claims about Iraq's W.M.D. (including some published in the *Times* and the *Post*)."

Later Career

Howell Raines stepped down as executive editor in 2003, after Jayson Blair, a *Times* reporter, was discovered to have fabricated or plagiarized many of his stories, precipitating a scandal that was deeply embarrassing for the newspaper. When Bill Keller assumed the post of executive editor at the *Times,* he appointed an unprecedented two managing editors to address the complexities of a newsroom beginning to grapple with competition from the Internet. One of the editors was John M. Geddes, who dealt specifically with news operations; the other was Abramson, who dealt with news gathering. (At the age of 49, Abramson got a small tattoo of a New York subway token on her right shoulder to commemorate her return to the city.) Keller told Gabriel Sherman for *New York* magazine (September 26, 2010) that he (Keller) and Abramson were a perfect match. "She's an investigative reporter by temperament. The investigative reporter in you makes you alert to hidden agendas. I tend to see the good in people. Jill is more wary and suspicious—she's the perfect person to have my back." The two editors grew close as they worked hard to become, as Sherman wrote, "a stabilizing force after the tumultuous Raines era."

Tumult of another sort soon developed, however, as the *Times,* facing the worldwide economic recession that began in December 2007, fell victim to one of the most extensive cutbacks in advertising ever to hit the newspaper industry. Sales declined steadily. As Jason Horowitz and Paul Farhi reported in the *Washington Post* (June 2, 2011), "The paper eliminated 100 newsroom jobs in late 2009, or about 8 percent of its total. … Its newsroom staff of about 1,200 reporters, editors, photographers and digital journalists is the largest, by several hundred people, of any newspaper in America, and one of the largest of any news organization. Non-newsroom positions at the Times have been harder hit."

Still, Horowitz and Farhi noted when Abramson's selection was announced, "Abramson and Baquet will oversee a newspaper that has 917,000 daily print subscribers and a Web site that draws nearly 33 million unique visitors per month, one of the highest among news sites. In interviews, both Keller and Abramson said they believed that the newspaper could hold the line on future cuts. But, Keller said, … 'Do we have a business model that will support [the same level of news-gathering]?' … No one can answer that question with absolute certainty."

Many believe that digital journalism will mark the defining challenge of Abramson's tenure as executive editor, and her knowledge of digital journalism and social media proved to be an important factor in her selection for the post of executive editor. "She's going to be dealing with all the problems [Keller] dealt with but at an accelerated pace and with less resources," the media business blogger Alan Mutter told Horowitz and Farhi for the *Washington Post*. "He had the problem of rebuilding morale and credibility. … She has the problem of a broken business model."

"We've never deviated from either a journalistic or business strategy that is rooted in a belief that quality journalism pays."

Abramson had become familiar with such challenges in 2010, during a six-month stint of overseeing the *Times*'s on-line operation and researching and visiting other on-line news organizations, including the Huffington Post and Politico. "Her aim is to push our integration to the next level," Keller wrote to the *Times* staff in 2010, as quoted by Dylan Byers in *Adweek* (June 2, 2011), "which means mastering all aspects of our digital operation, not only the newsroom digital pipeline but also the company's digital strategy in all its ramifications." Abramson was one of the architects of the *New York Times* Web site "paywall," which was implemented in March 2011. Capitalizing on the popularity of the site, the *Times* began to allow readers to view 20 articles each month for free; to view more, readers pay subscription fees of between $15 and $35 per month. After almost three months, the *Times* paywall had garnered 100,000 on-line subscribers, which, Horowitz and Farhi reported, was regarded as "a promising start to a business model that could fundamentally change the news industry's financial base."

Nevertheless, Abramson told Sherman that digital revenues alone would not be enough to support the *Times*: "If you were digital only, you'd be talking about a smaller news organization." She added that the *Times* is different from on-line news sites such as the ones she visited, which, "with a few exceptions, [offer] surprisingly little original reporting of consequence," she told Sherman. "I don't want to belittle what Politico and others do. They do break real news, and they're quite enterprising. But they're not doing the Pentagon Papers"—a reference to the classified Vietnam War-era government documents made public in 1971 by the *New York Times.* Ideally, Abramson suggested, digital media will provide a new forum for long-form investigative journalism. "The long-form article isn't only alive, it's actually dancing to new music," she told Boston University students at a conference on June 9, 2011, alluding to the advent of personal electronic reading devices such as the Kindle and the iPhone.

Lloyd Grove, writing for *Newsweek,* commented that "Running the *New York Times* has never been for the faint of heart. Abramson's 23 months at the wheel have been punctuated by the death in Syria of Pulitzer Prize–winning foreign correspondent Anthony Shadid, a bitter contract dispute with the Newspaper Guild, and, seven months ago, forced buyouts of around 30 midlevel editors, including some of the *Times*' most beloved veterans." Bill Keller, Grove said, remarked that "'Some of these people were a serious loss—they carry institutional memory and good will and a sense of how the place works at a human level. But it was a smart choice for Jill to do a round [targeting highly paid managers] at least where you were not losing reporters and photographers and copy editors. It shows that everybody shares in the pain.' … Yet, unique in an industry plagued by cutbacks and shutdowns, Abramson's newsroom is staffed at the same level (around 1,100 employees) as it was a decade ago, and boasts 14 national and six regional bureaus, plus 25 foreign bureaus—more than at any moment in the paper's history. … Meanwhile, the *Times*' risky transition from free to metered online access appears to be working: the Web edition boasts more than 700,000 paying subscribers." As Abramson's tenure moved into its third year, the Times Co. divested itself of the *Boston Globe* and the *Worcester Telegram & Gazette* (at a mere fraction of their original purchase price). In the fall of 2013 the venerable Paris-based *International Herald Tribune* was renamed the *International New York Times.* "In the newsroom," Grove continued, "Abramson says she's been preaching the gospel of vivid writing, granular reporting, and what she calls 'the story behind the story,' instead of a traditional *Times* tendency to present news and analysis in the 'voice of God.'"

Abramson has taught a course in narrative journalism at Yale University, in New Haven, Connecticut, since 2006. She has also been a visiting professor at Princeton University, in Princeton, New Jersey.

In 2009 Abramson brought home a nine-week-old Golden Retriever. She then began writing *The Puppy Diaries,* which became a popular series in the *Times*'s House & Garden section. *The Puppy Diaries: Raising a Dog Named Scout*, adapted from her columns, was published in 2011. Abramson and her sister, Jane O'Connor, with Deborah Melmon, further adapted the series for two children's picture books.

When asked to describe Abramson, most friends and colleagues use the word *tough,* in both a mental and physical sense. In 2007 Abramson was hit by a refrigerated truck while walking across West 44th Street, near the *Times*'s building in New York City. She lost a great deal of blood and suffered a fractured leg; police told her that her life had been spared by inches. From her hospital bed, where she remained for three weeks, Abramson led the *Times* investigation of the media mogul Rupert Murdoch as he was finalizing the purchase of the *Wall Street Journal.* "Long before she got run over by the truck, people knew she had a lot of strength," Keller told Gabriel Sherman. Lloyd Grove of *Newsweek* quoted Abramson herself as saying, "with flagrant understatement," "I do think that almost being killed does help you keep in perspective small setbacks like a Politico story"—earlier in April Politico had published an article critical of Abramson—"or a difficult personnel issue. … Or maybe it's just part of the aging process that I've gotten better at that."

Abramson met her husband, Henry Little Griggs III, at Harvard University. They were married on March 14, 1981. They have a son, Will, who is the founder of the indie-rock label Cantora Records, and a daughter, Cornelia, a resident surgeon at Massachusetts General Hospital. Abramson and her husband live in the Tribeca neighborhood of New York City.

Further Reading:

Adweek Jun. 2, 2011

Forward Jun. 1, 2011

(London) *Guardian* Jun. 7, 2011

National Journal p650 Apr. 5, 1997, p1722 Sep. 6, 1997

National Public Radio *Morning Edition* (on-line transcript) Nov. 3, 1994

New Republic Aug. 19, 2013 (with photo) *New York* Sep. 26, 2010

New York Times Feb. 23, 1986, June 2, 2011

New York Times Book Review p6 Mar. 21, 2010

New Yorker p48 June 10, 2002, Oct. 24, 2011

Newsweek Jul. 31, 2013 (with photo)

Politico.com June 2, 2011, April 23, 2013

Time Nov. 14, 1994

Washington Post C p1 June 3, 2011

Selected Books:

Abramson, Jill, and Barbara Franklin, *Where They Are Now: The Story of the Women of Harvard Law, 1974,* 1986

Abramson, Jill, and Jane Mayer, *Strange Justice: The Selling of Clarence Thomas*, 1994

Obama: The Historic Journey, ed. Vincent Alabiso et al, introduction by Bill Keller, 2009 [biographical text by Abramson; collects coverage from the *New York Times*]

The Puppy Diaries: Raising a Dog Named Scout, 2011

Reeves, Richard, and Jill Abramson, comps., *The Kennedy Years: From the Pages of the New York Times,* 2013

Alterman, Eric

Journalist, historian, media critic, teacher

Born: 1960, New York City, New York, United States

The historian and media critic Eric Alterman has become a favorite target for conservatives because of his politically charged books, which have questioned the existence of the so-called liberal media bias, condemned the George W. Bush presidency, and attacked the obstructionism and dishonesty of Beltway politics, among other stands. A columnist ("The Liberal Media") for the *Nation* magazine, Alterman founded and is the primary author of Altercation, a blog at the *Nation* that began at MSNBC in May 2002 and moved to Media Matters in America in 2006 before taking its present shape at the *Nation* in January 2009. Alterman is a senior fellow at the liberal think tank Center for American Progress, for which he writes and edits the column "Think Again"; senior fellow of the World Policy Institute at the New School; and a fellow of the Nation Institute. In July 2007 he was named Distinguished Professor of English and Journalism at Brooklyn College, and he is a professor at the CUNY Graduate School of Journalism.

Alterman first came to widespread notice with the book *Sound and Fury* (1992), an indictment of the attention and authority granted right-wing pundits by the media and the public. He went on to write *What Liberal Media?* (2003), *When Presidents Lie* (2004), and *Kabuki Democracy: The System vs. Barack Obama* (2011), among other books. Alterman has garnered considerable attention himself, generating heated attacks from those on the right and equally passionate defenses by his supporters. "My audience is the universe of sensible people," he told Elisabeth Eaves for *Publishers Weekly* (January 27, 2003). "You don't have to see the world my way to agree with what I'm saying. I make the argument—I give you the evidence."

Education and Early Career

Eric Ross Alterman was born on January 14, 1960, in the New York City borough of Queens; he grew up in Scarsdale, New York, an upper-middle-class suburb of New York City. Alterman's mother, the former Ruth Weitzman, was a school psychologist, and his father, Carl, was a salesman and engineer. According to George Gurley, in an article for the *New York Observer* (April 14, 2003), Alterman worked at the Bronx Zoo for a time while a student. Alterman described himself in an article for the *Nation* (March 9, 2005, on-line) as "a pretty serious Jew—bar mitzvah, educated in Israel, lights candles on Friday night, goes to shul, sends the kid to Hebrew school, contributes to [the Jewish periodical] the *Forward*." Yet Alterman is frequently called on to defend himself against charges of anti-Semitism or anti-Israel bias, because of what has been construed as his strong support for Palestinian rights. He wrote to *Current Biography* that he is, rather, "a strong defender of the Israeli peace movement and of the necessity of a just peace between Israel and the Palestinians, rather than of Palestinian rights per se."

Alterman attended Cornell University, in Ithaca, New York, earning his B.A. degree in history and government in 1982. In 1986 he earned a master's degree in international relations from Yale University, in New Haven, Connecticut, and he then went on to study for a doctoral degree in U.S. history from Stanford University, in Palo Alto, California, earning his Ph.D. in 2003. During his student years he wrote on a freelance basis for such publications as *Mother Jones,* the *Nation,* the *New Republic, Harper's, Vanity Fair,* and the *New York Times.* While Alterman was at Stanford, his first book, *Sound and Fury: The Washington Punditocracy and the Collapse of American Politics,* was published. (In later editions the subtitle was *The Making of the Punditocracy.*) In *Sound and Fury,* Alterman described what he saw as a decline in the nation's public discourse, which he attributed to the rise of right-wing pundits—opinionated print and television personalities, including Pat Buchanan, Robert Novak, and George Will—and to an eclipse of journalistic values by what he described to *Current Biography* as "entertainment values." Alterman took as his starting point the year 1896, when the publisher Adolph S. Ochs championed a policy of objectivity at the *New York Times.* At that time such a policy was an exception; most papers freely featured the opinions of their writers. As objectivity progressively became the media standard, pundits appeared, according to Alterman, to supply the missing opinions. Unlike today's "talking heads," the early pundits, Alterman contended, used their positions not to argue endlessly but to champion bipartisan views. That changed in the 1960s, when many of the most influential political commentators began voicing their distrust of government officials. In order to balance its content in the face of criticism from President Richard M. Nixon's Republican administration, the *New York Times* hired such conservative op-ed writers as George Will and William Safire, and other publications followed suit. Those men, Alterman argued, had little background in journalism but were employed because they were the only conservatives available. That scenario eventually led to what Alterman saw as the control of the media by "the punditocracy," right-wing figures whose visibility and influence were detrimental to political discourse. Many reviewers of *Sound and Fury* noted Alterman's insightful points but complained about his angry tone and his exaggeration of the pundits' power. Alterman was invited to appear on several popular television talk shows to promote the book, which, he told Gurley, he had hoped would make at least some of the right-wing pundits "afraid to show their faces in public again, because I had so humiliated and revealed them for the charlatans that they were—but, in fact, nothing changed at all. Everything went back to the way it was."

Alterman began appearing as a regular commentator on the MSNBC cable channel in 1996. His association with the company—first as a television personality and columnist, then as a blogger—would last for a decade. In 2002 he was invited by MSNBC's Joan Connell to create what he later described in the *Nation* as the "first blog created for and sponsored by a mainstream media organization" (January 8, 2009), and his blog Altercation appeared at the cable channel's Web site from May 2002 until September 2006. Although the company claimed that his dismissal was purely a business decision, some of Alterman's supporters have theorized that it was actually an attempt by management to censor his viewpoints. He was promptly hired by Media Matters for America, which made him a senior fellow and hosted Altercation from mid-September 2006 until December 2008. Sportswriter Charlie Pierce and historian and military commander Robert Bateman contributed to Altercation at Media Matters, where the blog remained a daily. On January 8, 2009, Altercation debuted at the *Nation,* where Alterman's posts have appeared regularly but not daily, often in tandem with postings by Reed F. Richardson, a former Army officer and Alterman's former intern. Pierce, Bateman, and other guest columnists have often contributed to Altercation at the *Nation.*

In *Who Speaks for America? Why Democracy Matters in Foreign Policy,* published in 1998, Alterman argued that American foreign policy reflected too little participation on the part of the public. He contended that the country's system of diplomacy had become increasingly corrupt and ineffective, owing to the government's progressively sinister policy of expansionism, willingness to make covert deals that bypassed the Constitution, and susceptibility to the influence of special-interest groups. Alterman suggested that those problems could be remedied by calling on foreign-policy advisory committees composed of ordinary citizens to make recommendations to Congress and the White House. Many critics, while questioning whether the American public was as well suited and eager to guide the country's actions abroad as Alterman implied, still found the book valuable. Gregg Easterbrook wrote for *Washington Monthly* (December 1998), "*Who Speaks for America?* sits square in the tradition of the book that should be read precisely because it's full of material we think we do not need to read. Alterman has produced a volume that is well-written, vigorous and perceptive." In *Perspectives on Political Science* (Summer 1999), John Dumbrell wrote, "Alterman paints with a broad brush. … More a successful polemic than a judicious analysis, [the book] should nonetheless be widely read and its arguments heeded."

In 1999 Alterman, by then widely known as a regular columnist for the *Nation,* published the nonpolitical *It Ain't No Sin to Be Glad You're Alive: The Promise of Bruce Springsteen.* The book, which took its title from a line in the Springsteen song "Badlands," examined the iconic rock musician's New Jersey childhood and relationship with his father, his rise in the music industry, and his breakthrough success with the 1975 album *Born to Run.* Springsteen had been a powerful influence on Alterman's teenage years; Gurley quoted Alterman as writing that the title single of *Born to Run* "exploded in my home, in my mind and changed my life." Miriam Longino, in a review for the *Atlanta Journal-Constitution* (January 23, 2000), wrote that "as a 15-year-old ticked off at the world, Alterman hung out on the high school football field drinking Miller eight-packs, boom box turned up loud, shouting [Springsteen lyrics] to the sky." She continued (drawing on the lyrics of the song "Born to Run" herself), "[Alterman's] analytical, middle-aged mind, combined with an almost teenlike worship of Springsteen, makes this music bio much more than gossipy patter. For the Springsteen fan, it's an insightful, fuel-injected ride on a runaway American dream."

Later Career

Alterman returned to the familiar realm of politics for his next book. In the exhaustively footnoted *What Liberal Media? The Truth about Bias and the News* (2003), he countered the claims of left-wing bias in the media that had been made in such widely read titles as Bernard Goldberg's *Bias: A CBS Insider Exposes How the Media Distort the News* (2001) and Ann Coulter's *Slander: Liberal Lies about the American Right* (2002). Regarding the success of his opponents' books, Alterman told Elisabeth Eaves, "There's a conservative movement in this country and it's big. One of the opening quotes of [my] book is [the musician] Paul Simon's 'A man hears what he wants to hear and disregards the rest.' I think people like to buy books that confirm what they believe they already know, and there are a lot of them on the conservative side. They're very good at getting the word out." He explained to Eaves that he had written the book because of his "frustration at the power of a dangerous and destructive myth [of liberal media bias]. … You say the words 'liberal media' and it conjures up a whole host of images and alleged facts that make it possible to make a case without actually making the case. It's a kind of shorthand and substitute for careful thinking, to say nothing of actual journalistic proof." As evidence that the media more often tilted not to the left but to the right, Alterman pointed out that many journalists had called for the impeachment of Democratic president Bill Clinton, who had lied under oath about his extramarital affair, and largely remained silent in the wake of the Republican George W. Bush's controversial 2000 election victory after the Florida recount. Some critics saw Alterman's claims that the media favored the right to be the inevitable convictions of a passionate liberal, while others found the book a refreshing alternative to the right's rhetoric. Chauncey Mabe, in one representative review, wrote for the Fort Lauderdale, Florida, *Sun-Sentinel* (April 13, 2003), "While it comes as no surprise that an out-and-out liberal scribe like Alterman finds little liberal bias, he reaches his conclusions in ways that are difficult if not impossible to refute."

The Book on Bush: How George W. (Mis)Leads America (2004) is a broad critique of Bush's presidency, co-authored by Alterman and Mark Green (the former New York City Public Affairs Commissioner and later Public Advocate who had been the Democratic nominee against Michael Bloomberg in the city's 2001 mayoral election). The book attacked, among other things, the Bush administration's energy policy and the president's invocation of God to defend his foreign policy. The authors also exposed inconsistencies between the president's public image and his actions in office; they contended that Bush had presented himself as moderate in his 2000 campaign but, once elected, had introduced policies reflecting the interests of the extreme right. An anonymous critic for *Kirkus Reviews* (February 9, 2004) called the book "carefully researched and plenty passionate: a veritable bible for Bush-bashers." Other critics were impressed by the scope of the book, although they questioned whether that comprehensiveness helped the authors' case. While acknowledging that Alterman and Green "stay above ... the snobbish preoccupation with malapropisms that cheapen[s] so many critiques of the Oval Office occupant," James P. Pinkerton wrote for the *Washington Post* (February 1, 2004) that the book still failed to account for Bush's popularity.

Alterman's next book, *When Presidents Lie: A History of Official Deception and Its Consequences,* also published in 2004, examined four examples of presidential deception in the twentieth century. It covered Franklin Roosevelt's secretive deals with the Soviet dictator Joseph Stalin; John F. Kennedy's unpublicized compromises with Russia during the Cuban missile crisis; Lyndon B. Johnson's distortion of the Gulf of Tonkin incident, which led to the increased presence of the United States in Vietnam; and the Ronald Reagan administration's cover-up of arms sales in the Iran-Contra scandal. John W. Dean wrote for *Washington Monthly* (November 2004) that *When Presidents Lie* is "an astute study of presidential decision-making—if lying instead of telling the truth can be so dignified—along with critical examination of the news media's unfortunate but recurring role in facilitating presidential lying."

Alterman's *Why We're Liberals: A Political Handbook for Post-Bush America* (2008) took up the vilification of the term *liberal* by the conservative "punditocracy," asserting that the majority of Americans actually agreed with "liberal" positions while rejecting the "label." With even many prominent liberal politicians carefully avoiding the term, Alterman sought to reclaim it, proudly: "That liberals remain on the defensive regarding the accusation that their positions are out of step," he wrote, "is more the product of effective conservative propaganda and credulous reporting than of any genuinely identifiable trends in public opinion." Yet some reviewers, especially those identifying themselves as politically to Alterman's left, were disappointed that Alterman, in their view, then chose to demolish conservative pundits and rhetoric rather than to reassert a progressive and avowedly liberal agenda for the country. Scott McLemee wrote in the *New York Times,* "The challenge, then, is translating this durable but inchoate mass of left-leaning public sentiment into an effective political movement. Alterman is, as always, a capable polemicist. He has no trouble shooting every fish in the barrel. But after a while, the whole effort begins to seem like an exercise in identity politics for an ideological minority" (March 16, 2008).

In *Kabuki Democracy: The System vs. Barack Obama* (2011), Alterman took up themes explored in *The Book on Bush* and *Why We're Liberals* (and his *Nation* column and blog), inquiring into the reasons why the election as president of Barack Obama had thus far failed to transform American politics. Alterman compared President Obama to President John F. Kennedy: "Had the president been willing to make a stronger case for his core beliefs from the bully pulpit, his words might have had a salutary effect on the tone of American politics, just as John F. Kennedy's did during his presidency, despite a similar commitment to a dealmaker's style of politics." Yet, he continued, "The far more important fact for progressive purposes is simply this: The system is rigged, and it's rigged against us." Diagnosing some of the factors in a sclerotic political process, Alterman asserted: "For if our politicians cannot keep the promises they make as candidates, then our commitment to political democracy becomes a kind of Kabuki exercise; it resembles a democratic process at great distance, but mocks its genuine intentions in substance."

"You say the words 'liberal media' and it conjures up a whole host of images and alleged facts that make it possible to make a case without actually making the case. It's a kind of shorthand and substitute for careful thinking, to say nothing of actual journalistic proof."

The Cause: The Fight for American Liberalism from Franklin Roosevelt to Barack Obama (2012), which Alterman wrote with Kevin Mattson (Connor Study Professor of Contemporary History at Ohio University) is, as *New York Times* reviewer Jeff Shesol observed, "less a book about liberalism than it is a book about liberals." For Shesol the many and various portraits failed "to cohere" into a compelling history of liberalism, although "to be fair … It is hard to dissect a gestalt." (May 18, 2012). In their book Alterman (the primary author) and Mattson sought to reclaim the history of liberalism since Roosevelt from the narrative successfully promulgated by liberalism's opponents. Their own narrative replaced the right-wing caricature of welfare and socialism with a catalog of achievements in social justice and civil rights as well as New Deal and later policies that protected labor, helped the poor, and saw a dramatic postwar expansion of the middle class, while acknowledging the political costs and the divisions within liberalism that have threatened to sideline it as a political force. Writing in the *American Prospect,* Joan Walsh averred that, "The most important contribution of *The Cause* is to situate the recent predicaments of liberalism in a longer arc of history than we see it framed in in today's political debates" ("Our Battle Scars," May 7, 2012).

In 1992 Alterman won the George Orwell Award, given by the National Council of Teachers of English to honor honesty and clarity in the public use of language, for *Sound and Fury,* and in 1999 he received the Stephen Crane Literary Award *for It Ain't No Sin to Be Glad You're Alive.* For his work at the Center for American Progress, Alterman received the 2011 Mirror Award for Best Commentary, Digital Media, from Syracuse University's S. I. Newhouse School of Public Communications. Together, three of his pieces for the *Nation*—"How Low Will the 'Washington Post' Go?," "How Rupert Murdoch Buys Friends and Influences People," and "The Agony and Ecstasy—and 'Disgrace'—of Steve Jobs"—were finalists for the 2012 Mirror Award for Best Commentary, Traditional/Legacy Media, and in 2013 three more *Nation* articles—"The Mainstream Media's Trivial Pursuit of Campaign 2012," "Shut Up about the Jews Already …," and "The Washington Post's Problem"—were finalists in the same award category.

Alterman is a Distinguished Professor of English and Journalism at Brooklyn College, part of the City University of New York (CUNY). In addition to his fellowship at the Center for American Progress, Alterman holds fellowships at the New School's World Policy Institute and the Nation Institute.

In 2003 Alterman was asked to audition for the role of a reporter on the HBO series *The Sopranos,* but he did not win the part (which went to one of the show's writers). He was later hired as a historical consultant for HBO.

Alterman, whose first marriage ended in divorce, lives in Manhattan with Diana Silver, who teaches at New York University, where she also earned her doctorate in public administration. They have a daughter, Eve Rose. Alterman is sometimes reported to have a demanding, mercurial personality. "Eric is difficult," Katrina vanden Heuvel, one of Alterman's editors, told Gurley. "But behind that difficult, gruff exterior is someone who cares deeply about progressive ideas and democracy in this country."

Further Reading:

billmoyers.com/segment/eric-alterman-on-liberalisms-past-present-and-future/ Apr. 20, 2012

Nation Mar. 9, 2005

New York Observer p1+ Apr. 14, 2003

Publishers Weekly p247 Jan. 27, 2003

Who's Who in America, 2006

www.ericalterman.com

Selected Books:

Sound and Fury: The Washington Punditocracy and the Collapse of American Politics, 1992 (later editions subtitled *The Making of the Punditocracy*)

Who Speaks for America? Why Democracy Matters in Foreign Policy, 1998

It Ain't No Sin to Be Glad You're Alive: The Promise of Bruce Springsteen, 1999

What Liberal Media? The Truth about Bias and the News, 2003

Alterman, Eric, with Mark Green, *The Book on Bush: How George W. (Mis)Leads America,* 2004

When Presidents Lie: A History of Official Deception and Its Consequences, 2004

Why We're Liberals: A Handbook for Restoring America's Most Important Ideals, 2008

Kabuki Democracy: The System vs. Barack Obama, 2011

Alterman, Eric, with Kevin Mattson, *The Cause: The Fight for American Liberalism from Franklin Roosevelt to Barack Obama,* 2012

Baldauf, Sari

Finnish corporate director, former telecommunications executive

---

Born: 1955, Kotka, Finland

As chairman of the board of the Finnish energy firm Fortum, former executive vice president and general manager of the Finnish telecommunications giant Nokia, and board member for several prominent companies and foundations, Sari Baldauf is one of the most prominent businesswomen in Europe. She began her career at Nokia in 1983, when it was still a conglomerate of such varied products as toilet paper, rubber boots, and power cables. As a new management team at Nokia restructured it to more actively pursue its telecommunications ventures, Baldauf emerged as one of the companies most valued managers, and she shares credit with several other high-level executives for transforming the company into a global telecommunications powerhouse. In the October 12, 1998, edition of *Fortune* magazine, Baldauf was named one of five of the "most powerful businesswomen in Europe," and until she left Nokia in 2005, she was consistently cited on the magazine's annual list of the 50 most powerful businesswomen outside of the United States. (The yearly list began 2001; she was ranked sixteenth the first year, fifteenth in 2002, fourteenth in 2003, and twelfth in 2004.)

Baldauf credited the nonhierarchical corporate culture of Nokia as one of the reasons she was able to climb so high in the company's management. "If something is presented to the board, it's not done by the top guy in a group; it is the person who knows the most about it," she told Janet Guyon for *Fortune* (February 15, 1999). "If you bring value added, you get credit." At Nokia Baldauf was regarded as a supportive manager who could nevertheless be tough when necessary.

Education and Early Career

Sari Maritta Niiranen was born on August 10, 1955, in Kotka, Finland. She earned her B.S. degree at Aalto University School of Science and Technology in 1977 and went on to the Helsinki School of Economics and Business Administration, where she received a master's degree in Business Administration in 1979. She participated in the school's "Finland's International Business Operations" program, resulting in her employment as a training officer at the Finnish Institute of Exports for about a year after graduation. In 1981 she took a post for about one year as a marketing manager for the telecommunications company Falcon Communications in Abu Dhabi, the capital of the United Arab Emirates. Baldauf was hired by Nokia in 1983 as a strategic planning manager, part of a three-year research project on the company's prospects for expanding internationally. Two years later she was promoted to vice president of corporate planning at Nokia Electronics, and a year later she became the vice president of business development and venture capital in Nokia's New York office.

Shortly after Baldauf joined Nokia, the company underwent major restructuring. In the mid-1980s the conglomerate's chief executive, Kari Kairamo, bought out several technology companies, including four color-television manufacturers, a Swedish computer manufacturer, and the formerly state-owned Finnish telecommunications company. Baldauf became the vice president of business development for the telecommunications company, which was renamed "Telenokia" in 1987. That year Baldauf led a strategic task force that outlined how Nokia could utilize the digitalization of the cellular phone market. ("Digitalization" comprised the "second generation" of cellular phones, the first generation being "analog"; digitalization allowed phones to be smaller, lighter, cheaper, and imbued with longer battery life.) Telenokia was renamed Nokia Telecommunications in 1988, and Baldauf was named president of its cellular systems division, which provided infrastructure to cellular network operators. After Kari Kairamo's suicide, in December 1988, Nokia's management sold off many of its manufacturing businesses with limited growth potential (including the conglomerate's paper, rubber, chemicals, floorings, and ventilation system companies) as well as the computer division. Instead management concentrated on companies that showed significant signs of potential growth—telecommunications equipment and cellular telephones.

Nokia had been manufacturing telecommunications equipment for the Finnish army and the state-owned telephone company since the early 1960s, and in the late 1970s several nations' telecommunications authorities embarked on a project to build an inter-Nordic cellular phone system. "Some of the big telecommunications companies thought wireless was a pretty small niche," Baldauf told Fleming Meeks for Forbes (September 12, 1994). "But we saw it as an opportunity." The Nordic system began operating in 1981, and Nokia provided it with both telecommunications equipment and phones. Jorma Ollila, who had been promoted to the cellular phone division to determine whether it should be sold off, was appointed Nokia's CEO and president in 1992, and he continued the process of streamlining the company along the lines of its telecommunications interests. The moves were profitable but were also aided by a worldwide deregulation of many countries' telecommunications markets.

Baldauf was largely responsible for pitching Nokia's infrastructure products to a number of markets around the world, and by 1992 Nokia was among the top 10 global suppliers of telecommunications equipment. The mobile phone division of Nokia met with even more success during the 1990s cellular phone boom, selling nearly 15 percent of the world's cellular phones between 1981 and 1994. By September 1994 Nokia had a 20 percent market share of cellular phones sold in the world. (In 1998 Nokia overtook Motorola as the world's largest manufacturer of mobile phones, selling 37.4 million phones—a 22.9 percent market share—to Motorola's 32.3 million. The following year Nokia's market share was 27 percent, and by 2003 it was 40 percent.) In 1994 Nokia Group had net sales of $6.4 billion (U.S. dollars), 22 percent of which was generated by Nokia Telecommunications. On February 1, 1994, Baldauf became a Nokia Group executive board member. Baldauf remained president of Nokia Cellular Systems until 1996. She then took a half-year sabbatical, during which she traveled and became conversant with Asian cultures.

In the mid- and late 1990s, Nokia executives began to focus on emerging cellular markets beyond Europe and the United States. Jorma Ollila selected Baldauf to run the company's Asia-Pacific (APAC) operations, with the title of executive vice president of Nokia APAC. The region provided ample room for growth; it contained a particularly young demographic of cellular phone users who rapidly embraced new technology and innovations. Not only was Baldauf assigned to oversee the company's entrance into new markets but she was also charged with the task of investigating the possibility of introducing advanced, "third-generation" (3G) cellular technology in the Asia Pacific region, rather than building upon a steady clientele of "second-generation" cellular customers in Europe. Expected to be a vast improvement over the previous generation, 3G mobile phone technology was supposed to allow for the high-speed transference of digital data, allowing cellular phones to have a variety of new capabilities that included sending pictures and communicating through live, streaming video. "The unique demands of the discerning Asian consumers will dictate new products," Baldauf said at a launch of one of Nokia's phones in Beijing, as quoted by a reporter for the Jakarta Post (November 17, 1997). "More and more products and innovations are being launched first in Asia-Pacific." Baldauf drew praise within Nokia for attaining contracts from many of China's major network operators. From 1997 until 1999 she was also a member of the board of the Finland-China Trade Association. When Baldauf left Nokia APAC in July 1998 to return to her position heading the infrastructure arm of Nokia—her new position was officially the president of Nokia Networks—she stayed on as the member of the board responsible for operations in Japan and China.

"I am involved with organizations that work to improve the life prospects of young people as well as with those that enhance the quality of our life by the means of art and culture."

Later Career

Baldauf told Janet Guyon for *Fortune* (October 12, 1998) that during a trip to Nokia's German operations plant shortly after she began her presidency of Telenokia's Cellular Systems division in 1988, workers would "look at me and say, 'Fine, the secretary came. Where is the boss?'" By the late 1990s, however, Baldauf had emerged as one of the top female executives in Europe, and she was considered one of the five executives composing Nokia's inner circle. (The other four were Jorma Ollila, CEO; Pekka Ala-Pietelä, president; Matti Alahuhta, head of mobile phones; and Olli-Pekka Kallasvuo, CFO.) In 1999 Baldauf's division held the second-highest world market share for supplying network equipment for cellular operators (the Swedish company Ericsson was the leader). The division generated $6.5 billion in sales that year, nearly a quarter of Nokia's total sales.

Explaining Nokia's success, Baldauf told Ian Grayson for the Australian (March 13, 2001) that "Nokia has a strong market share and brand, and we are very good at supply chain management. It is about understanding market trends and then coming up with products that make it possible to do those things. As well as understanding technology, you have to understand the end user, and that is what we do. This, of course, is coupled with having very large volumes." The rise of Nokia's stock price in the late 1990s alone illustrates how trustworthy investors felt the company had quickly become: after opening on the New York Stock Exchange at a little more than a dollar per share in 1994, the stock had risen to more than $24 per share by July 1999. Nokia's first-quarter profits of 2000 were $822 million, 76 percent higher than the first quarter of 1999. Its stock market value by April 2000 was $250 billion, the most of any European company, and by the middle of that year, its closing share price had edged $60.

The introduction of third-generation cellular technology, touted heavily by the telecommunications industry in the late 1990s and 2000, was delayed after a telecommunications industry bust during 2000 and 2001, when a wide swath of cellular phone operators suffered high debt levels and licensing problems in a number of European nations. Such operators proved reluctant to invest in the new cellular technology that Nokia and other manufacturers of cellular phones and equipment were offering, the promise of which had partially informed their financial predictions. As a result investment in Nokia suffered. Its stock price was down to about $40 per share by August 2000 and was about half that a year later. Baldauf told Robert Clark for Telecom Asia (August 1, 2001) that the dip in stock price was owing to Nokia's not having "been very good at this hyping. Hyping! We're pragmatic people, we do more than we talk. So in that sense, about a year ago, I think we were not perceived as the most successful company in the marketplace. But if you look at the situation in the marketplace in Europe today, we have announced major contracts and we are now building the target market position that we have sought for ourselves; to have 35[percent] of the [3G systems] market of networks delivered. So my outlook on 3G is very positive." Despite the poor stock performance, Nokia's sales increased by more than $1 billion—to 7.7 billion euros (roughly $7.1 billion)—between 1999 and 2000. Instead of continuing to push 3G technology infrastructure, for which it had about a 30 percent market share, Baldauf told Ian Grayson that in 2001 Nokia's technical focus was on General Packet Radio Service (GPRS), a precursor to 3G that industry commentators call "2.5G," "because that brings the world of packet data into mobile networks." (While digital phones still rely on available airwaves individually divided among all users, 3G phones split information into coded parts—packets—that make more efficient use of the same space. The GPRS uses packet data, although it is not as fast as 3G.)

By 2002 the downturn of the telecommunications industry began to severely affect Baldauf's Networks division. Sales fells slightly in 2001 and again in 2002. In February 2003 Nokia Networks announced it was cutting 550 research and development jobs, splitting the cuts between its operations in the United States and those in Finland, Great Britain, and Sweden. (Of Nokia's 17,500 employees at the end of 2002, about one-third worked in the Networks division.) The following month Nokia announced that for the first time since 1996, Nokia Networks would experience an operating loss in its first quarter, partially because system sales were projected at declining 15- to 20 percent compared with the first three months of 2002. In April 2003 Nokia Networks announced that it was cutting another 1,800 jobs.

While Baldauf had tied for first place in the 2002 Wall Street Journal Europe (February 27, 2002) list of the most successful women in Europe, she was not featured on the 2003 list. In June 2003 Baldauf indicated at a Nokia mid-year strategy update that the entire infrastructure market would experience a fall of at least 15 percent in 2003, but expected the market to stabilize in 2004. "It's not a rosy picture for the infrastructure market," she said, as quoted by a reporter for AFX Financial News (June 11, 2003). "We don't expect any fast, sudden growth in the market, but we are growing the market in the long term through addressing different market segments." Several days later Baldauf indicated that she expected demand for 3G equipment and networks to recover in the second half of 2004.

In September 2003 Baldauf visited China with other top Nokia executives after rumors circulated that China was considering issuing 3G licenses. Baldauf and others at Nokia pushed the Chinese government to embrace 3G technology immediately. In an interview with Christopher Brown-Humes for the Financial Times (October 1, 2003), Baldauf indicated that 3G was definitely going to occur on a worldwide level, but that it still faced the obstacles of satisfying a wide range of customers with high expectations. "In fact, when I describe where we are now, I like to use a sea analogy," she told Brown-Humes. "When you come from a narrow gulf into the open sea, you get cross waves. It's always very difficult to sail there. You don't know how the boat will go. Our industry is in those cross waves right now."

Baldauf's title was officially changed on January 1, 2004, to executive vice president and general manager of networks, but she remained the most powerful executive in Nokia's networks division, which became profitable again in 2004. In October 2004 editors for the Financial Times named Baldauf the top woman in European business. In December 2004, however, Baldauf announced that she planned to leave Nokia in February 2005.

During and after her tenure at Nokia, Baldauf served on the board of directors of several Finnish and international companies. She was vice chairman of Sanoma, a Finnish media corporation (2003–2009), and a director of Hewlett-Packard (2006–2012) and CapMan Corporation (2008–2011). She joined the board of F-Secure, a Finnish security software developer, in 2005. Since 2008 she has been a member of the Supervisory Board at Daimler. Baldauf joined the board of the Finnish utility company Fortum in 2009; she has been board chairman since 2011, making her the first female chairman of a major Finnish company. In May 2012 Baldauf became a Supervisory Board member of AkzoNobel NV, and in October 2012 she was appointed to the Supervisory Board of Deutsche Telekom AG.

Baldauf is affiliated with several foundations and other organizations concerned with entrepreneurship, sustainable development, and promotion of new business enterprises, particularly those that support youth development. These organizations include the Finnish Business and Policy Forum (EVA); the John Nurminen Foundation, which sponsors Clean Baltic Sea projects; and the Startup Foundation, which Aalto University originated at Aalto University and promotes growth enterprises in Finland. She serves on the board of Finland's Children and Youth Foundation and was a director of the Baltimore-based International Youth Foundation, a charity focused impoverished children, from 2000 until 2009. Baldauf has a strong interest in culture and chairs the board of directors of the Savonlinna Opera Festival in the scenic lake district of Saimaa in eastern Finland, closer to St. Petersburg than to Helsinki.

In 1996 Baldauf became a Knight, first class, of the Order of the White Rose of Finland. She has received honorary doctorates from Aalto University School of Science and Technology, the Helsinki University of Technology, and the Turku School of Economics and Business Administration of the University of Turku.

Baldauf speaks Finnish, English, Swedish, German, and French. She is divorced and has no children. She enjoys hiking, skiing, and classical music and entertains family and friends at her country house on Finland's south coast.

Further Reading:

Australian p54 Mar. 13, 2001

Financial Times p2 Oct. 1, 2003, Oct. 1, 2004

Fortune p102 Oct. 12, 1998, p174 Oct. 16, 2000, with photo

New Straits Times p26 Nov. 21, 1995

SinoCast China IT Watch Sep. 5, 2003, Sep. 9, 2003

Telecom Asia p30 Aug. 1, 2001

Ball, Alan

Playwright; film and TV writer, director, and producer

Born: 1957, Atlanta, Georgia, United States

"I hate those arbitrary distinctions between comedy and drama," Alan Ball, who writes scripts for television, film, and the stage, told Marc Peyser for *Newsweek* (March 18, 2002). "My life seems to have a mixture of both, and I respond to entertainment that has both. Also, I think humor is a necessary tool for survival." A sometime director and producer as well as a scriptwriter, Ball served as a writer for the TV sitcoms *Grace under Fire* and *Cybill* before he rose to national prominence in 1999 with his screenplay for the widely admired feature film *American Beauty*. A tale of a dysfunctional suburban family, *American Beauty* won dozens of honors, among them five Academy Awards, including those for best picture and best screenplay.

Ball next produced, wrote the scripts for, and occasionally directed *Six Feet Under,* a critically acclaimed HBO TV series about a distinctive family of morticians. During its five-year run, each episode of *Six Feet Under* involved a death; the family's husband and father died in Episode One, then returned in ghostly fashion to comment on the behavior of his wife and children. "What grief can do for us is teach us that the ability to feel tremendous pain increases our capacity to feel joy," Ball commented to Sharon Waxman for the *Washington Post* (May 26, 2002). "You can't just have it one way. Life is filled with both." *Six Feet Under,* like *American Beauty,* blended tragic and comedic elements and won multiple awards. Ball also wrote the scripts for the TV series *Oh, Grow Up,* the feature film *Towelhead,* the full-length plays *Five Women Wearing the Same Dress* and *All That I Will Ever Be,* and the one-acters *Made for a Woman, Bachelor Holiday, Power Lunch, The M Word,* and *Your Mother's Butt.* He was the writer, executive producer, and showrunner of the TV series *True Blood,* which premiered in 2008 and which, according to Gina Piccalo, writing for the *Los Angeles Times* (July 18, 2010), "cemented Ball as the creative hero of HBO." Ball also developed and was an executive producer of the Cinemax "pulp" series *Banshee.* Of his varied professional experiences, Ball told Cynthia Lucia, in an interview reprinted in *Alan Ball: Conversations* (2008): "Theater is more language-oriented—you can luxuriate in words, in rhythms, in the music and poetry of language. Film is like a dream—you can tell a story visually, with really beautiful images and symbols and subconscious currents and mythic moments. TV for me is like a novel because you can continue to develop a story over hours and hours and hours. You can really get to know the characters and be with them and grow with them."

Education and Early Career

Alan Ball was born on May 13, 1957, in Atlanta, Georgia, and grew up in Marietta, an Atlanta suburb. His father, Frank Ball, was a quality-control manager for Lockheed Aircraft; his earlier, unsuccessful experience as a carpenter had left him permanently demoralized. Alan, the family's fourth and last child, was born when his mother, Mary Ball, a homemaker, was 44. His birth came about 20 years after those of his brothers and about nine years after that of his sister, Mary Ann, whom as a child he considered to be his best friend. Ball wrote his first play at age six, and he "constantly directed the kids in the neighborhood in little productions," according to Sharon Waxman in the Washington Post. One of his favorite activities—playing with other children in nearby woods—ended when all the trees were cleared to make way for construction of a four-lane highway; many homes were bulldozed, too, although not that of the Balls. "That was probably my first experience with a profound sense of loss," Ball told Bob Longino for the Atlanta Journal-Constitution (March 26, 2000). "You know, of something being really important that was suddenly gone. And it was weird and never the same after that."

When Ball was about eight years old, he became dimly aware of his homosexuality; for the next 25 years, he remained largely in denial about it. Nearly everyone he knew in his home town regarded homosexuality with hostility, so the idea of being gay was "terrifying" to him as a child and young adult, he told Waxman; he added, in reference to a popular sitcom (1998–2006) whose male title character was gay, "I didn't grow up watching Will & Grace." He told Bernard Weinraub for the New York Times (March 4, 2001), "The only images of gay people I saw on the screen were either villains or noble martyrs who usually died." Recognition of his homosexuality "threatened something in me," he said to Waxman. "I knew it was something I couldn't let anybody know." Ball came out of the closet when he was 33. Shedding the burden of his long-held secret, he told Waxman, "was the biggest step I ever took toward emotional well-being."

Earlier, when he was 13, on the day his sister, Mary Ann, turned 22, she was killed instantly when, while driving Ball to his piano lesson, she crashed into an oncoming car while rounding a blind curve. "That was like death just stuck its face right in mine and said, 'Uh, helloooo,' and I've been living with that ever since," Ball (who was unhurt in the collision) told Phil Rosenthal for the Chicago Sun-Times (May 31, 2001). His sister's death "separated my life into 'the life before' and 'the life after,'" Ball explained to Paul Clinton of the Advocate (July 3, 2001). After the accident, Ball recalled to Weinraub, sometimes— "at the worst of it"—he felt as if he was living "in a house with ghosts" as his family struggled to cope with the loss. "My mother got into a gothic end-of-the-world religion thing," he said, and his father became severely depressed. When Ball was 19, his father died of lung cancer. "It wasn't so much that I was unhappy [after those losses]," Ball told Waxman. "I was painfully aware of the ephemeral nature of life. No matter what you have, you can lose it in an instant, without warning. What that did for me for many, many years was, it kept me from committing to anything. It kept me from committing to myself, even, from really fully taking risks emotionally. From going after things."

Ball attended Marietta High School, where he served as senior-class president, editor of the student newspaper, and a drum major in the band. He told Bob Longino, of the Journal-Constitution, that he invented "this persona for myself of really being an overachiever, kind of an All-American guy that really wasn't me." With the goal of pursuing a career as an actor, Ball enrolled at the University of Georgia and then transferred to the School of Theatre at Florida State University, in Tallahassee. After he earned a bachelor's degree, in 1980, Ball moved to Sarasota, Florida, where he helped to set up a theater company called General Nonsense. In his late twenties, he moved to New York City, and with several friends he formed the Alarm Dog Repertory Company. Between 1986 and 1994, the group performed at such New York venues as the Public Theater, the Westbeth Theater Center, and the West Bank Cafe. To support his acting and writing, Ball worked as an art director at the magazines Inside PR and Adweek.\

During that period several of Ball's plays were mounted Off-Off-Broadway, including *Five Women Wearing the Same Dress.* That snarky comedy, the title of which refers to five gossipy bridesmaids (one of them portrayed by Allison Janney), debuted at the Manhattan Class Company in early 1993; it struck Mel Gussow, writing for *the New York Times* (February 18, 1993), as "frothy and frivolous," with the sorts of "one-liners and comebacks" characteristic of TV sitcoms. Those qualities impressed Tom Werner and Marcy Carsey, two of the executive producers of the ABC sitcom *Grace under Fire,* and won for Ball a position as a writer for that show. The title character of *Grace under Fire* was a single mother who, after leaving her abusive husband, becomes a hard-hat-wearing oil-refinery worker. Ball accepted the job, he told Weinraub, because "my theater company was sort of spinning its wheels," and his colleagues' "day jobs were turning into careers. People were starting to have kids." In addition, Brett Butler, the actress chosen to play Grace, was a native of Marietta. "I thought, 'How many times will this happen in my life?' I flew out on a Friday and began working Monday."

Ball wrote for *Grace under Fire* during its highly rated first year (1993–94), then left to write for the CBS sitcom *Cybill,* with Cybill Shepherd in the role of a twice-divorced mother who yearns to build a flourishing acting career. During *Cybill* 's three-year run (1995–98), Ball became the show's executive producer. "I had a meteoric rise at *Cybill,*" he told Weinraub. "[Shepherd] would have a big meltdown in the middle of every season and fire half the staff. And those of us who stuck around got big promotions." With both *Grace under Fire* and *Cybill,* Ball was frustrated by his bosses' seemingly never-ending demands for script changes. He told Rosenthal, "One of the things I've heard network executives say in a meeting is: 'Let's assume I'm the stupidest person in America. Am I going to get this?' And, you know, frankly I'm thinking: 'If you're the stupidest person in America, I don't care if you get it. I'm not writing for you.'" Furthermore, as he told Weinraub, "[Butler and Shepherd] looked on the shows as basically p.r. for their lives. It was like taking dictation. You'd hear, 'I have a bad haircut, so let's do a show about that.' It taught me a valuable lesson about television: not to be too proprietary about the material. Let it go. Find something else."

While working overtime on Cybill virtually every day, Ball would spend a couple of hours around midnight writing the story that became American Beauty. He told an Amazon.com (1999) interviewer that he "channeled" into its script the "anger and rage" his working situation provoked in him. "It's no mistake that American Beauty was about a man who was beaten down and lost interest in his life rediscovering his passion for living," he told Weinraub. The completed script was sold to DreamWorks, Steven Spielberg's studio, for $400,000; Sam Mendes, who previously had worked only in theater, signed on to direct.

The focus of American Beauty—"a tale of pain and dysfunction beneath the surface of suburban life, told through the eyes of a dead man," in Waxman's words—is a well-to-do couple, Lester Burnham (Kevin Spacey) and his wife, Carolyn (Annette Bening), and their teenage daughter, Janie (Thora Birch). As the film opens Lester speaks from beyond the grave; he is then shown several months before his death, when, feeling depressed, cynical, and burned-out over his profession and his home life, he quits his lucrative job in the advertising industry, finds work with a fast-food outlet, and becomes infatuated with Janie's friend Angela (Mena Suvari), a would-be femme fatale. Lester then undergoes a transformation, passing up a chance to have sex with Angela and growing aware of the world's nonmonetary, mundane treasures. Carolyn, meanwhile, in a singleminded quest to succeed as a real-estate agent, has lost interest in her husband and daughter; in her drive to get ahead, she begins an affair with one of her competitors. The morose Janie, who seems to despise her parents, becomes friendly with her teenage neighbor, Ricky Fitts (Wes Bentley), a Peeping Tom often seen with a video camera. Circumventing the cold, rigid discipline of his father, Ricky uses and sells marijuana—to Lester, among others. Ricky's father, a retired Marine colonel, hides his attraction to men behind a fierce homophobia; his wife, Barbara (Allison Janney), has become nearly catatonic.

A plastic bag wafting in the breeze is a recurring image in American Beauty. The image was inspired by an experience Ball had years earlier, in which a plastic bag floating in the air seemed to circle him, triggering in him a "completely unexpected sense of peace and wonder," he recalled to Longino. He told the Amazon.com (1999) interviewer, "When you first see the title [of the film] you think 'American Beauty plus rose,' and then you see the movie and you think that Angela's the American Beauty—the blond cheerleader that is the secretive object of lust. But it's not Angela—it's that plastic bag. It's the way of looking at the world and seeing what incredible beauty there is in the world. And I think that's something that we're born with that gets ironed out of us by our culture and by experience and by conformity. I think there's a part of everybody that yearns to get that back."

American Beauty earned virtually unanimous praise. In a representative review for TV Guide (1999, on-line), Maitland McDonagh described the film as "black comedy of the deepest, richest darkness laid over an aching meditation on the atrophy of dreams not so much deferred as unformed, unarticulated and lost in the shuffle." "This chronicle of suburban families imploding in slow motion contains genuine laughs," he continued, "but they escape through clenched teeth. … First-time screenwriter Alan Ball … pulls off his satirical jibes with pitch-perfect aplomb, weaving them into a plot that oozes menace" and "keeps you spell-bound." "As a thumbnail analysis of the middle-class American psyche, Alan Ball's script is a devastating attack," Angus Wolfe Murray wrote for the British Web site Eye for Film (1999). "It is also extremely funny. … The movie astonishes with its breadth of scope, covering every aspect of dysfunction—from voyeurism to stalking to homophobic rage to role playing to unlawful killing. … Films like this save Hollywood from atrophy."

Ball did not expect American Beauty to become a hit, and shortly before its release, he had agreed to write a sitcom for ABC. The show, Oh, Grow Up, about a gay man and his two straight roommates, was partly autobiographical. "The [final product] was not at all what I intended when I pitched it," Ball told Waxman. "But you talk yourself into believing it's good. Otherwise how do you justify going to work every day?" The series was canceled after 7 of its planned 13 episodes had aired.

Later Career

Ball had become much sought-after in Hollywood and had received many lucrative film proposals.

"I was offered everything, but I didn't want to become a hired gun, I didn't want to be hired to write other people's ideas," he told Weinraub. A suggestion from the HBO executive Caroline Strauss that Ball create a show about a family of undertakers drew him back to TV. "What interested me is what it would be like to live with death on a daily basis," Ball told Drew Jubera for the Atlanta Journal-Constitution (June 3, 2001). "What do these people do: Embalm somebody and then go to their Little League game? Well, yes. That's what they do." Six Feet Under revolved around the Fishers—three siblings, Nate, David, and Claire, and their mother, Ruth—who own a Los Angeles, California, mortuary. "Like the characters in [American Beauty], the Fishers … are sardonic and screwed up," Tad Friend wrote for the New Yorker (May 14, 2001). "Nate is a soulful social dropout who sees marriage as the enemy; Claire spends much of the first episode high on crystal meth; and David, the middle child, is chalky-faced and remote, seemingly the ideal funeral-home director—but he's also a closeted gay man who is about to plunge into a night life of clubs, drugs, and one-night stands." The father, Nathaniel, is killed in a car crash in the first episode and reappears, in surreal sequences, to offer the family members "advice, support or, just as often, a sarcastic gibe," Sharon Waxman wrote. Ball told Waxman, "The show is about the loss I've felt in my life. The grief I've felt over loss, the people I've lost. … About greeting grief, and being able to move past it." Six Feet Under ran for five seasons (2001–05) and attracted a sizable following; it became "one of the flagship components, along with The Sopranos, Sex and the City, and Curb Your Enthusiasm, that have made [HBO] a critical favorite and powerhouse," Greg Braxton wrote for the Los Angeles Times (August 15, 2005). Six Feet Under won a Golden Globe Award for best dramatic series in 2001; the cast won the Screen Actors Guild Award for outstanding ensemble in a drama series in 2002 and 2003; and the series and those associated with it garnered a total of nine Emmy Awards, including one, in 2002, for Ball as outstanding director of a drama series. In a *New York Times* review of Brett Martin's *Difficult Men,* about the writer-creators and showrunners of the present "Golden Age ... of TV art," Lisa Schwarzman commented, "Under the guidance of the showrunner Alan Ball, the writers' room for *Six Feet Under* ... could lay plausible claim to being the happiest in TV" (July 12, 2013), despite the series's subject matter.

"Theater is more language-oriented—you can luxuriate in words, in rhythms, in the music and poetry of language. Film is like a dream—you can tell a story visually, with really beautiful images and symbols and subconscious currents and mythic moments. TV for me is like a novel because you can continue to develop a story over hours and hours and hours. You can really get to know the characters and be with them and grow with them."

Some critics have derided Ball's vision of the world as a cynical one, in which desperate people fail themselves and their loved ones," Sharon Waxman wrote. Ball does not dispute that description, but he has maintained that his work reflects real life more accurately than most other popular works for TV and Hollywood. "It's hard to have a brain in your head, keep your eyes open to the culture, and not be cynical," he told Waxman. "People who are the most cynical are the most romantic at heart. That's definitely true of me." Still, he said, "I'm completely not cynical about the characters in [*Six Feet Under*]. I believe in them as thinking beings struggling to find meaning in their lives. Failing sometimes. Succeeding sometimes. What's necessary, what's important, is not failing or succeeding, it's the struggle that's important. Our culture is so much about success, which I think is very—very—shallow. You learn more from failure."

Ball both wrote and directed *Towelhead* (2008), a controversial feature film, based on a novel by Alicia Erian, about the coming-of-age and identity struggles of 13-year-old Jasira, the daughter of a Lebanese-American father and his former wife, an American. The film starred Summer Bishil as Jasira; Peter Macdissi as her father; Maria Bello as her mother; and Toni Collette and Aaron Eckhart as neighbors. The story was set in Houston, Texas, during the first Persian Gulf War (1990–91), which triggered some anti-Muslim sentiment but far less, and of far less virulence, than the sort that followed the 9/11 terrorist attacks. The film generated mixed reviews. Its admirers included Carrie Rickey, who described it for the *Philadelphia Inquirer* (September 19, 2008) as a "brutally honest and edgily funny story" about "the many forms of social and sexual abuse that does not make the abusee a victim but victor." "Not since [the 1961 film] *Splendor in the Grass* has there been such a candid and sympathetic account of the mixed messages, double-standards, giddy highs and hormonal free falls experienced by teenage girls," Rickey asserted. By contrast, *Towelhead* struck Ruthe Stein, the reviewer for SFGate.com (September 19, 2008), as "so disturbing it makes you uncomfortable watching it. For the price of admission, you become an unwilling voyeur." "Towelhead" is a derogatory label derived from the fabric headwear traditional among many Arab men. According to Stein, "An Islamic civil rights group wanted the film's title to be changed because it is insulting to Arab Americans," and then added, "There is much else in *Towelhead* to take exception to."

Ball came up with the idea for the HBO show *True Blood* after he happened upon the first four novels in Charlaine Harris's best-selling Southern Vampire series in a Barnes and Noble outlet in 2005. The heroine of the book and HBO series is Sookie Stackhouse (played by Anna Paquin), a waitress who has telepathic powers; its hero—and Stackhouse's love interest—is the nearly 200-year-old vampire Bill Compton (Stephen Moyer). (Moyer and Paquin married in 2010.) "True Blood" refers to the synthetic blood marketed by a Japanese soft-drink company, which enables vampires to enter civilized society. Ball told Ed Potton for the *London Times* (April 1, 2006) that *True Blood*—which he has described as "popcorn for smart people"—is "very raucous, more entertaining, much, much funnier" than *Six Feet Under,* adding, "I'm done peering into the abyss for a while." Michael Lombardo, HBO's president of programming, told Gina Piccalo for the *Los Angeles Times* (July 18, 2010) that *True Blood* won the approval of HBO executives solely "because of [Ball's] creative vision." In a conversation with Dave Itzkoff of the *New York Times* (July 17, 2011), Ball recalled that when he was "called upon to give a one-sentence thematic pitch to the higher-ups at HBO as to what the show was about," he told them, "Well, ultimately at its heart, it's about the terrors of intimacy." "From the beginning, Ball has used *True Blood* vampires as stand-ins for every genre of the disenfranchised," according to Piccalo. "Nearly all the characters grapple with shame and struggle against their instincts." She added, "Occasionally, remnants of Ball's own Buddhist faith influence the plot." Ball commented to her, "Certainly, people's desires get them in trouble on the show. That's definitely a Buddhist concept."

True Blood debuted in 2008; its sixth season began in June 2013. Among its many honors, the show won the Television Critics Association Award for outstanding new program of 2008–09. After the show's fifth season, Ball stepped down as day-to-day showrunner, but he remained as executive producer. In September 2013 HBO announced that the seventh season (2014) would be the show's last. "*True Blood* has been nothing short of a defining show for HBO," said Michael Lombardo, HBO's president of programming.

After the end of Ball's day-to-day involvement in *True Blood,* he focused more intensively on development of *Banshee,* a "pulp thriller" series that debuted on Cinemax ("Skinemax") in January 2013. The series was originally developed for HBO. When HBO decided to pass on the series—it had also passed on another of Ball's series projects, *All Signs of Death,* based on Charlie Huston's noir novel *The Mystic Arts of Erasing All Signs of Death*—Cinemax picked it up. Ball told Merle Ginsberg and Gary Baum of the *Hollywood Reporter* (January 10, 2013), "I never felt like, 'Skinemax, that's a step down,' … When we were at HBO, we were dialing back on the pulp nature. At Cinemax, we went to our original pitch again: high-octane entertainment, violent and clever, yet complex. It also allows us to treat the sexuality in the show in a very frank and adult manner. We don't have to hold back." Like *True Blood, Banshee*—despite its small-town setting—is not family fare. Ball was showrunner as well as the executive producer of 12 episodes in the series's first season. At the same time Ball also worked on screenplays, and his *What's the Matter with Margie?*—starring Elizabeth Banks, directed by Daniel Minahan, and co-produced by Ball with Anthony Bregman—was scheduled for release in 2014.

The book *Considering Alan Ball: Essays on Sexuality, Death and America in the Television and Film Writings* (2006), edited by Thomas Fahy, contains essays by Fahy and nine others. The subtitle notwithstanding, it includes discussions of Ball's works for the theater. Fahy also edited *Alan Ball: Conversations* (University Press of Mississippi, 2013), which collects 13 interviews with Ball conducted over a 12-year period. Ball's screenwriting for *American Beauty* is analyzed in Mark Axelrod's *Constructing Dialogue: From Citizen Kane to Midnight in Paris* (2013). On an altogether more frivolous note, *True Blood: Eats,*

Drinks, and Bites from Bon Temps, by Gianna Sobol, Alan Ball, and Benjamin Hayes, with recipes by Dawn Yanagihara (2012) is, according to an anonymous *Publisher's Weekly* review (October 1, 2012), "part series scrapbook, with plenty of stills from the show … and part cookbook and cocktail guide."

Alan Ball lives in Los Angeles.

Further Reading:

Advocate p50+ Jul. 3, 2001

Atlanta Journal-Constitution L p1+ Mar. 26, 2000, L p1+ Jun. 3, 2001

Chicago Sun-Times p49 May 31, 2001

Los Angeles Times E p1+ Aug. 15, 2005

New York Times II p21 Mar. 4, 2001, Jun. 17, 2011

New Yorker p80+ May 14, 2001

Utne p51+ Sep./Oct. 2005

Washington Post G p1+ May 26, 2002

Books:

Thomas Fahy, ed., Alan Ball: Conversations (Univ. Press of Mississippi, 2013)

Thomas Fahy, ed., Considering Alan Ball: Essays on Sexuality, Death, and America in the Television and Film Writings (McFarland, 2006)

Brett Martin, Difficult Men: Behind the Scenes of a Creative Revolution (Penguin 2013), Chapter Thirteen: "The Happiest Room in Hollywood"

Selected Films:

American Beauty, 1999

Towelhead, 2008

Selected Television Programs:

Cybill, 1995–98

Six Feet Under, 2001–05

True Blood, 2008–

Banshee, 2013–

Bourdain, Anthony

Chef, writer, television host, editor

Born: 1956, New York City, New York, United States

"What Jean Genet was to the prison, what Tom Waits is to the lowlife bar, Anthony Bourdain is to the restaurant kitchen: a charmingly roguish guide to a tough, grimy underworld with its own peculiar rules and rituals," Adam Shatz wrote for the *New York Times* (May 13, 2001). A graduate of the Culinary Institute of America, Bourdain conquered a years'-long addiction to illegal drugs to gain respect as a chef in some of New York's most exclusive restaurants. With his best-selling book *Kitchen Confidential: Adventures in the Culinary Underbelly* (2000)—a brutally honest memoir and a "half-humorous, half-frightening expose of the restaurant industry," in the words of Bill Gibron, writing for popmatters.com (August 1, 2005)—Bourdain became a celebrity. On the strength of the enormous popularity of *Kitchen Confidential,* he launched another career, as the host of *A Cook's Tour: Global Adventures in Extreme Cuisines,* a short-lived television show for the Food Network. The book he wrote to accompany the program became another best-seller and won the 2002 Guild of Food Writers Award for Food Book of the Year. Bourdain returned to writing memoirs in *Medium Raw: A Bloody Valentine to the World of Food and the People Who Cook,* followed by a pocket-sized Insider's Edition of *Kitchen Confidential* updated with Bourdain's annotations and a new Afterword.

Well-known for his profane wit, Bourdain appeared from mid-2005 until November 2012 in a series for the Travel Channel called *No Reservations.* The success of *No Reservations* led to a second, "high-octane" Travel Channel series, *The Layover,* in each episode of which Bourdain had 24 to 48 hours—the time of an extended air-travel layover—to explore the food scene and construct a narrative about a given city. The strain of filming the two shows at the expense of his home life led Bourdain to leave the Travel Channel in 2012 for CNN, where he embarked on a new series, *Anthony Bourdain: Parts Unknown.* Bourdain published another, mostly nonfiction book, *The Nasty Bits: Collected Varietal Cuts, Usable Trim, Scraps, and Bones,* in 2006; the final chapter is a 30-page story, "A Chef's Christmas." During the fourth season of *No Reservations,* he came out with a tie-in book, *No Reservations: Around the World on an Empty Stomach* (2007), billed by its publisher, Bloomsbury, as an "illustrated, behind-the-scenes travel journal of Anthony Bourdain's global adventures." In his introduction to the book, Bourdain wrote, "If one thing is clear to me about traveling perpetually, it's that it's a great gift. … If I have a single virtue, it's curiosity. It's a big world."

Bourdain's books also include three novels—*Bone in the Throat, Gone Bamboo,* and *The Bobby Gold Stories*—and a book based on items on the menu of the Brasserie Les Halles, a New York City restaurant with which Bourdain has been associated since 1998: *Anthony Bourdain's Les Halles Cookbook: Strategies, Recipes, and Techniques of Classic Bistro Cooking.*

Education and Early Career

The first of the two sons of Pierre Bourdain, a Columbia Records executive who died in the late 1980s, and Gladys Bourdain, a *New York Times* editor, Anthony Bourdain was born on June 25, 1956, in New York City. He grew up with his brother, Christopher (who became a currency analyst), in Leonia, New Jersey. By his own account, he was a precocious child: as a preschooler, for example, he told Deborah Ross for the *London Independent* (June 11, 2001), he found a copy of Rudolf Flesch's book *Why Johnny Can't Read* (1955) in his parents' bedroom and proceeded to teach himself to read "way beyond what should have been my level." He has traced his love of food to a summer holiday in 1966, when he traveled with his family to France (his father's birthplace) to stay with relatives. In Paris some of what he had most enjoyed eating in New Jersey—hamburgers and peanut butter and jelly sandwiches—could not be found, so he was forced to taste other foods. Eating his first oyster, he recalled to Deirdre Donahue for *USA Today* (November 29, 2001), affected him "viscerally, instinctively, spiritually—even in some small … way, sexually—and there was no turning back. … My life as a cook, and as a chef, had begun. Food had power. It could inspire, astonish, shock, excite, delight and impress. It had the power to please me … and others." Reflecting on his relationship with his father, Bourdain wrote in *Bon Appétit* (May 31, 2012), "To experience joy, my father taught me, one has to leave oneself open to it."

During his teens in New Jersey, Bourdain has said, he often felt angry—although he has maintained that he cannot remember why—and he developed a drug habit, which became the focus of many fights he had with his parents. Nevertheless, in his high school (the Dwight-Englewood School, in Englewood, New Jersey), he performed well enough to gain admission to Vassar College, an elite institution in Poughkeepsie, New York, that had opened its doors to men in 1969 after more than 100 years as a women's college. He chose Vassar in order to be with his high-school girlfriend, Nancy Putkoski, who later became his wife.

Bourdain has claimed that at Vassar, which he entered in 1973, he did not attend any classes but wrote papers for other students so as to earn money to buy drugs. In the summer of 1974, he got a job as a dishwasher in a restaurant in Provincetown, on Cape Cod, Massachusetts. There, for the first time, he told Andrew Billen for the *London Times* (July 12, 2005), he felt respect for others—the people with whom he worked in the kitchen—and tried to gain their respect, although up until then he had never felt any for himself. After he completed his sophomore year at Vassar, he transferred to the Culinary Institute of America, in Hyde Park, New York, one of the most prestigious cooking schools in the United States. After his graduation in 1978, he began working in the kitchen of the Rainbow Room, a glamorous restaurant in Manhattan's Rockefeller Center, where he stayed for 18 months. During the next half-dozen years, Bourdain made his way up the hierarchy in New York's culinary world at a variety of restaurants, among them Chuck Howard's, Nicki & Kelly, and Gianni's. Then, in the mid-1980s, he again became a heavy user of drugs and alternately worked briefly in a series of restaurants or did not work at all. His stint as a short-order cook led him to hate such food as French toast or fried eggs, "because, to me, it smells of failure and defeat," as he told Ross. In time he developed an addiction to heroin and found himself with neither a job nor a home. In 1988 he entered a methadone program, "which got me off the street overnight," as he told Deborah Ross, "but three times a week I had to queue up with other hideous junkies"—in his view, an unbearable indignity. He thus tried to go cold turkey, suffering through withdrawals and substituting cocaine for heroin in the process. Eventually he succeeded in ending his drug habit and began to rebuild his career, first as a chef at the Supper Club in New York City, then at Vince and Linda Ghilarducci's Italian Affair in Santa Rosa, California, where he stayed for two years and one year, respectively. In 1996 he returned to New York and worked for a few months at Coco Pazzo Teatro before handing in his resignation.

While he was reestablishing himself in New York restaurants, Bourdain was also trying his hand at writing. During the mid-1980s, to pass the time, he had written notes for a novel. While the story was expanding, and after he had conquered his heroin habit, he had taken a creative-writing course at Columbia University, in New York. The book was still unfinished when, in 1992, Gordon Howard, his Vassar roommate, urged him to complete it. Indeed, Howard paid Bourdain's expenses for a ten-day vacation in Cozumel, Mexico, on the condition that Bourdain would do so. In 1993, within about six months of his return from Mexico, Bourdain had honored his pledge. Howard brought the novel to Random House, in New York City, which published it in 1995 with the title *Bone in the Throat.* Inspired in part by transcripts of the trial of the mobster John Gotti and by Bourdain's experiences as a restaurant worker, the book is a satiric thriller told from the perspective of Tommy Pagano, a chef at the Dreadnought Grill, a restaurant in the Little Italy section of Manhattan that is the cover for an FBI-financed mob sting operation. Marilyn Stasio, who reviews crime and mystery fiction for the *New York Times Book Review* (August 6, 1995), described *Bone in the Throat* as a "prodigiously self-assured" and "deliciously depraved" first novel whose author's "comic vision goes beyond original."

"If one thing is clear to me about traveling perpetually, it's that it's a great gift. … If I have a single virtue, it's curiosity. It's a big world."

When *Bone* was arriving in bookstores, Bourdain was busy creating the menu for the Italian Affair restaurant. He was also spending four hours a day working on his next novel, *Gone Bamboo* (1997), another satiric thriller involving mobsters, this time set on the Caribbean island of St. Martin. The year *Gone Bamboo* was published, according to various sources, Bourdain became the chef at Sullivan's, in the Ed Sullivan Theater (from which David Letterman broadcast his TV program, *The Late Show with David Letterman*). The following year Bourdain became the executive chef at Brasserie Les Halles, a New York restaurant specializing in French food; he currently holds the title "chef at large" there.

A major turning point for Bourdain came after he submitted a piece called "Don't Eat before Reading This" to the *New Yorker* magazine. Although the *New Yorker* rarely accepts unsolicited manuscripts, the magazine published Bourdain's brief article in its April 19, 1999 issue. "Don't Eat before Reading This," as Howard Seftel wrote for the Phoenix (Arizona) *New Times* (June 10, 1999), "exposed restaurant practices that chefs and restaurant owners would prefer the public didn't know"; for example, in it Bourdain warned diners to avoid ordering fish on Mondays, when it would be four days old, and revealed that when a customer orders a steak well-done, the chef chooses from among the worst cuts of meat. Only hours after the April 19 issue reached newsstands, Bourdain was offered a book deal. *Kitchen Confidential: Adventures in the Culinary Underbelly* was published in 2000. Going beyond simply telling readers unsavory details about restaurant kitchens, Bourdain took the opportunity to describe his alcohol and drug abuse, casual sexual encounters, and experiences in food preparation. Among those who expressed mixed feelings about the book was Sarah Billingsley, who wrote for the Pittsburgh, Pennsylvania, *Post-Gazette* (September 24, 2000) that the "richly described preparations and food references alone are enough to keep a reader entertained" but complained that "the chef's ego throbs on every page, even when Bourdain is self-deprecating. He is an unreliable and somewhat bitter narrator, with the limited writing skills of a college freshman who's been granted the 'literary' quarter to use profanity." More often, however, reviewers lavished *Kitchen Confidential* with praise. "In a style partaking of Hunter S. Thompson, Iggy Pop and a little Jonathan Swift," Thomas McNamee wrote for the *New York Times* (June 4, 2000), "Bourdain gleefully rips through the scenery to reveal private backstage horrors little dreamed of by the trusting public. He calls paying customers 'weekend rubes' and describes himself in an earlier, less enlightened incarnation as 'a shiftless, untrustworthy coke-sniffer, sneak thief and corner-cutting hack.' Thankfully, in his new life he has retained his brutal honesty."

Kitchen Confidential became a best-seller; by 2001, according to Deirdre Donahue, it had sold more than 700,000 copies, and it has been translated into 28 languages. A sitcom called *Kitchen Confidential,* inspired by Bourdain's book, debuted on the Fox network in September 2005. It starred Bradley Cooper as a chef named Jack Bourdain, who is determined to rebuild his career after being mired in drug addiction and experiencing homelessness. The series was canceled after 13 installments.

Meanwhile, Bourdain had become a celebrity. He immediately signed contracts for two more nonfiction books. The first, *Typhoid Mary: An Urban Historical* (2001), tells the story of Mary Mallon, a cook whom the New York City Department of Health, in 1906, determined was spreading typhoid fever and who became famous as the first healthy carrier of the disease in the United States. Despite the Health Department's insistence that she was spreading typhoid through her unwitting contamination of the food she prepared, she refused to stop cooking, even after she secured her release from a government-imposed quarantine by promising never to cook again. For Bourdain the "central question" regarding Mary was, as quoted by Adam Shatz, "Why did she go on cooking when she had every reason to believe she was spreading a possibly fatal disease?" Drawing on his own experiences, Bourdain suggested that Mary was simply a proud cook who wanted to work under any circumstances, even if she was sick or in pain. In an assessment for *Newsday* (April 15, 2001), Peg Tyre described Bourdain's retelling of the story as "competent" but felt that "his emphatic and sometimes coarse style … sometimes detracts from the story."

The second nonfiction book that Bourdain wrote to fulfill the terms of his contract was *A Cook's Tour: In Search of the Perfect Meal* (2001), which reached various best-seller lists. It was published as a companion to Bourdain's TV series *A Cook's Tour,* which aired for 22 weeks on the Food Network in 2001; among other glimpses of Bourdain overseas, installments showed him in Vietnam eating a still-beating cobra heart immediately after it had been cut out of the snake and consuming sheep's testicles in Morocco. *A Cook's Tour* earned the Guild of Food Writers Award for Food Book of the Year in 2002 and was shortlisted for the 2002 Thomas Cook Travel Book Award. It also impressed critics. "Bourdain swaggers where the rest of us fear to tread," Karen Stabiner wrote for the *Los Angeles Times* (December 23, 2001). "Having scorched his way through the New York restaurant scene, he turns his attention in *A Cook's Tour* to the rest of the world. This time around, Bourdain is off in search of the perfect meal. Not your idea of a perfect meal, which might revolve around such civilized thrills as a beautiful wine or a bottomless bowl of caviar. His idea … reads more like a catered screening of *Apocalypse Now.*" The book convinced some critics that Bourdain was, above anything else, a food writer. As Kathryn Hughes wrote for the *London Daily Telegraph* (December 29, 2001), "Take away the food, and Bourdain begins to sound like just one more middle-aged writer sent on assignment by a glossy American men's magazine to various hearts of darkness. But keep him close to the steam, the blood and the guts of everyday eating and he remains untouchable."

Bourdain's next book was the novel *The Bobby Gold Stories* (2003), about a mob-connected ex-convict who works in restaurants and clubs. In a review for the Palm Beach (Florida) *Post* (December 14, 2003), Scott Eyman wrote that *The Bobby Gold Stories* "isn't great, but it is good. It's all text and no subtext, which is why it's fun to read, but also why it doesn't hang in your head afterward." Jack Batten, a critic for the Toronto (Canada) *Star* (October 5, 2003), felt that the "tales of restaurant life behind the scenes radiate exotic authenticity" but complained, "Bourdain's touch is less convincing when he deals with the Mafia thugs who bring the violence to his books."

The Bobby Gold Stories was followed by Bourdain's *Les Halles Cookbook: Strategies, Recipes, and Techniques of Classic Bistro Cooking* (2004). Elliot Essman, reviewing the book at stylegourmet.com in 2005, commented, "Bourdain greatly respects top culinary artists like Alain Ducasse and Thomas Keller, but his subject is bistro cooking, 'the most beloved, old-school, typical and representative [French] cooking, the wellspring of all that came after.' He writes as executive chef of New York's Les Halles; a brash, Parisian-style bistro. … Bourdain's mission is to position bistro cooking as a truly accessible cuisine for the non-professional cook … He's chosen his sections and recipes with intelligence and care."

Bourdain's fourth nonfiction book, *The Nasty Bits: Collected Varietal Cuts, Usable Trim, Scraps, and Bones* (2006), contains essays about food, leisure, and travel that originally appeared in such publications as the *New Yorker, Rolling Stone,* and *Gourmet* and that, in some cases, Bourdain updated for the collection. Various pieces make clear the writer's disdain for "celebrity" chefs and media food personalities and his intolerance for veganism. Bruce Handy, in a review of *The Nasty Bits* for the *New York Times* (May 28, 2006), called it "a mix of the inspired, slightly less inspired … and the occasionally random or perfunctory" and concluded that overall Bourdain is a "vivid and witty writer" whose "greatest gift is his ability to convey his passion for professional cooking." After characterizing Bourdain as "the bad boy of the culinary world" and a knock-off of the cult hero and writer Hunter S. Thompson, Mia Stainsby, a *Vancouver Sun* (June 17, 2006) critic, described *The Nasty Bits* as "an entertaining, gritty, witty, nasty read."

Later Career

In July 2005 Bourdain began appearing in the weekly series *Anthony Bourdain: No Reservations*; in that show, which aired on the Travel Channel, he introduced viewers to cuisine in different parts of the world. In his review of *No Reservations* for popmatters.com, Bill Gibron wrote, "Tony Bourdain is angry—and he's not afraid to share it with the world. He hates processed and pre-packaged foods. He loathes TV chefs who reduce classic cuisine to a series of easy to follow steps and perky soundbites. He argues for the purity of ingredients and the classicism of cultural culinary expression. But mostly he is mad at us, for allowing our taste buds to be tainted by fast food and microwaved mediocrity." Gibron continued, "When Bourdain turns off the anger and enjoys the food, he's fabulous. His obvious love of whatever he is eating, bordering on the orgasmic in some instances, is complemented by a complete knowledge of why the food has this effect." According to Virginia Heffernan in the *New York Times* (July 25, 2005), he "indulges wanderlust and regular lust. Or rather," she added, "it's not clear whether he'll get into sex and drugs, the mainstays of … *Kitchen Confidential*. … But he's not saying no to anything here, and one of his many principles about food is that 'it does lead to sex, and it should.'" The series won the Critics' Choice Best Reality Series award in 2012. In 2009 and again in 2011, *Anthony Bourdain: No Reservations* won a Creative Arts Emmy Award for Outstanding Cinematography for Nonfiction Programming, for which it was also nominated in 2012. It garnered numerous additional Emmy nominations: best long form documentary (2007); best editing (2009); outstanding nonfiction series (2009, 2011, 2012); outstanding picture editing for nonfiction programming (2011, 2012); and outstanding writing for nonfiction programming (2010, 2011, 2012).

In July 2006, while Bourdain was filming an installment of *No Reservations* in Beirut, Lebanon, violence erupted there between members of Hezbollah, an Islamic terrorist paramilitary group, and the Israeli Defense Forces (IDF). "We were there because of the food, of course; I'm in love with mezze [a selection of appetizers], huge, groaning tables everywhere filled with these little, delicious treats," Bourdain told a reporter for the *London Independent* (September 30, 2006). At his Web site (jrisius.com), cinematographer Jerry Risius presents a video and recounts the experience: "We continued to film and document while waiting to be evacuated. The subsequent episode included footage of both Bourdain and our production staff, and included not only our initial attempts to film the episode, but also our firsthand encounters with Hezbollah supporters, days of waiting for news with other expatriates in a Beirut hotel, and their eventual escape aided by a "cleaner" (prohibited to shoot and unseen in the footage); and our eventual departure with the US Marines. The episode was nominated for an Emmy Award in 2007."

The success of *No Reservations* led to the creation of another TravelChannel series, a one-hour, ten-episode series entitled *The Layover,* which premiered in November 2011. The show's premise was the exploration of a city accomplished within the span of an air-travel layover of 24 to 48 hours. Bourdain found the shooting schedule of the second show "a burden," and he announced in April 2012 that he would do another season of *The Layover* but that it would be his last. He told Gabe Ulla of the "foodie" Web site Eater that, "*The Layover* was hard on me. It was hard with that much food and liquor in a two-day shooting period, back-to-back-to-back. And that's after shooting *No Reservations. No Reservations* is a pleasure most of the time. ... *Layover* has its utilitarian aspects" (April 9, 2012). In May 2012 Bourdain announced that he would be leaving the Travel Channel altogether to host a new series for CNN, again focusing on food and culture. For a finale season of *No Reservations,* the Travel Channel repackaged the last seven episodes of season 8 plus some re-edited older episodes—Bourdain called them "clip shows." *No Reservations*'s run concluded in November 2012. Bourdain's CNN series, entitled *Anthony Bourdain: Parts Unknown*, premiered on April 14, 2013. In its first season, it won four Emmy nominations for 2013, and it was renewed for another season.

With Joel Rose, Bourdain co-wrote the original graphic novel *Get Jiro!* (2012), with art by Langdon Foss, for DC Comics/Vertigo. He is also a consultant and writer for the HBO series *Treme.* Bourdain told Archana Ram of *Entertainment Weekly,* "I'm trying to write good television here. I had a one-month-long writing class years ago and my teacher's first rule was never settle personal hash in your writing if it's fiction. I feel free to do that in my non-fiction, but I'm writing a drama here" (March 1, 2011).

In 2011 Ecco Press, a division of HarperCollins, announced that Bourdain would have his own imprint at Ecco, Anthony Bourdain Books, publishing three- to five books per year. The first three were set to appear in 2013. In the Ecco press release (February 22, 2012), Bourdain commented, "This will be a line of books for people with strong voices who are good at something—who speak with authority. ... We are just as intent on crossing genres as we are enthusiastic about our first three authors." Bourdain took on a new role, executive producer, for *The Getaway,* a travel series that debuted in September 2013 on the Esquire television network.

Bourdain was inducted into the James Beard Foundation's Who's Who of Food and Beverage in America in 2008, and in 2010 he received an Honorary CLIO Award for Food and Travel. The CLIO Awards is international awards competition for advertising, design, interactive, and communications.

Bourdain has an apartment in Manhattan, although he spends much of his time traveling. He married Nancy Putkoski in 1985; they were divorced in 2005. Bourdain married Ottavia Busia in 2007, and their daughter Ariane was born that year.

Further Reading:

Bon Appétit, May 31, 2012; "Management by Fire: A Conversation with Chef Anthony Bourdain,"
Harvard Business Review, Vol. 80 No. 7 Jul. 2002
(London) *Independent* p34 Sep. 30, 2006
Los Angeles Times R p3 Dec. 23, 2001
Newsday May 31, 2000 B p15
New York Times C p1+ Sep. 10, 1997, IX p3 May 21, 2000, Jul. 25, 2005
New Zealand Listener Nov. 8–14, 2003; popmatters.com Aug. 1, 2005
(London) *Sunday Times* p3 Oct. 24, 2004
(London) *Times* p6 Jul. 12, 2005
USA Today Nov. 29, 2001; www.anthonybourdain.net/

Video:

Video filmed for the *No Reservations* episode in Beirut was posted at www.jrisius.com/television/anthony-bourdain-no-reservations-beirut/ by Jerry Risius, field producer and director of photography on the shoot for Zero Point Zero Productions

Selected Books:

Fiction

Bone in the Throat, 1995
Gone Bamboo, 1997
The Bobby Gold Stories, 2003

Nonfiction

Kitchen Confidential: Adventures in the Culinary Underbelly, 2000
A Cook's Tour: In Search of the Perfect Meal, 2001
Anthony Bourdain's Les Halles Cookbook, 2004
The Nasty Bits: Collected Varietal Cuts, Usable Trim, Scraps, and Bones, 2006

Brûlé, Tyler

Media entrepreneur, magazine founder

Born: 1968, Winnipeg, Manitoba, Canada

"Through the super-styled pages of Wallpaper* and Monocle," Ruaridh Nicoll wrote in the Observer, "Tyler Brûlé has turned his own life into a successful business" (March 17, 2012). Brûlé 's influence in the worlds of high-end fashion, design, travel, and leisure stems from the contents and look of Wallpaper*, the lifestyle magazine that he launched in 1996. It was reinforced by Monocle—described by Nicoll as a "compendium of global, newsy nuggets with a furious aversion to celebrity"—and the "hyper-curated Monocle empire," as it was called in a T Magazine feature (New York Times, May 10, 2013). The idea for Wallpaper* came to the Canadian-born Brûlé when he was forced to take a months-long break from work in 1994 after sustaining serious injuries in a sniper attack as a 25-year-old freelance journalist in Afghanistan. None of the dozens of fashion, design, and food magazines that he read while recuperating at his home in London, England, "talked to me," he recalled to Janet Izatt for PR Week (September 13, 1996), and they contained "very little that appealed. There were a lot of gaps in the market, but I thought I could fill them with one magazine." Still feeling the "lure of the road" but unwilling to put his life in jeopardy again, he told Izatt, "I thought, why not take foreign reportage, fashion and trends, art, and great travel and turn it into a magazine?" In 1997, after the publication of only four issues of Wallpaper*, Time Warner bought an 85 percent share in the magazine, making Brûlé a millionaire. Brûlé remained editor in chief of Wallpaper*, and in 2001, when he was only 32 years old, he earned a Lifetime Achievement Award from the British Society of Magazine Editors.

By that time Brûlé had started two other magazines, *Spruce* and *Line,* which did not survive, and the company Wink Media (later renamed Winkreative), which was set up to produce print ads that appeared in *Wallpaper*.* After his departure from *Wallpaper** in 2002, Brûlé hosted two television shows and expanded his reputation as an arbiter of good taste as a design consultant. In 2007 he founded the upscale *Monocle,* which its Web site identifies as a "global briefing on current affairs, business, culture, and design." According to Chris Daniels, writing for *Marketing Magazine* (July 30, 2007), Brûlé applied the same approach to *Monocle* as he had to *Wallpaper**: "Treat the planet as one massive marketplace." Brûlé is the chairman and editor in chief of *Monocle,* which has spawned radio and TV shows, a half-dozen retail shops around the world, and, thus far, two cafés. Brûlé also writes a column, "Fast Lane," for the *Financial Times.* According to James Silver, writing for the London *Guardian* (February 12, 2007), Brûlé is "one of a very few media personalities to have excelled in both the creative and business sides of the industry, as well as inspiring a generation of loft-dwelling, interiors-obsessed metrosexuals, who think nothing of popping over to Lisbon [Portugal] at the weekend to go trousers-shopping." Writing for *Bloomberg BusinessWeek* (July 5, 2010), Tim Adams described Brûlé as "combin[ing] no-holds-barred career momentum with an aesthete's playfulness, stubborn business judgment with an entrenched place on *The Independent on Sunday* 's annual Pink List of the most influential gay people in Britain."

Education and Early Career

An only child, Jayson Tyler Brûlé was born in Winnipeg, Manitoba, Canada, on November 25, 1968. His parents, Paul Brule and Virge Brule (who spell their surname without accent marks and later divorced), raised him in a series of Canadian cities. His mother, who is of Estonian descent, is an artist; his father, who is of French-Canadian and Irish descent, played with Canadian Football League teams (the Ottawa Rough Riders, the Winnipeg Blue Bombers, and the Montreal Alouettes) from 1968 to 1972 and then built a career in marketing. At a young age, Brûlé recalled to Sholto Byrnes for the London *Independent* (January 10, 2005), "I was quite clear that I wanted to go to New York and take Peter Jennings' job as the main anchor on ABC." When he was a ninth-grader in Quebec, a threatened teachers' strike led his parents to send him to live with his grandmother in Ottawa. He completed the ninth and tenth grades at Nepean High School, where he felt very happy. "I really found my groove there and it carries all my fondest school memories," he told Richard Starnes for the *Ottawa Citizen* (July 30, 1997). He later attended Humberside Collegiate and Etobicoke Collegiate, in Toronto, Ontario. "I became a delinquent when I went to Toronto and I hated all the schools I went to," he told Starnes.

"We've seen the creep of the consultant on to the editorial floor—and that brought on a certain crisis of confidence."

After he graduated from high school, Brûlé studied journalism and political science at Ryerson University, in Toronto; he worked as a waiter part-time as well. (James Silver reported that he also took classes at Bennington College in Vermont.) Brûlé dropped out of college in 1989 and then moved to England, where he landed a job as a researcher for the BBC Two television show *Reportage*. During the next few years, he held various positions with the TV show *Good Morning America*, Fox Television, and *Elle* magazine. "It was an amazing time to network," he told Janet Izatt. As a freelance writer, he also contributed pieces to publications including *Esquire, Vanity Fair,* the London *Sunday Times,* the German magazine *Stern,* and the Toronto *Globe and Mail*'s *Destinations* magazine.

In 1994, while in Afghanistan preparing to write a story for *Focus,* a German newsmagazine, Brûlé was shot in both of his arms during an ambush on the vehicle in which he was riding. (According to various sources, he was in Afghanistan under the auspices of the organization Médecins Sans Frontières (Doctors without Borders), the vehicle had a United Nations emblem on it, and he was shot in a shoulder as well.) "It looked like someone had thrown a bucket of blood across his chest," Zed Nelson, a photojournalist who was in the car with Brûlé and accompanied him to a hospital, told Fiona McClymont for the London *Independent on Sunday* (July 15, 2001). After medics removed Brûlé 's shirt, jewelry, and watch, Brule called Nelson to come close to him. "I thought he was going to say his last words. I said, 'What is it, Tyler?' and he said, 'Get my Rolex!' … Within an hour of that we were laughing. I was taking photos of him and he was saying, 'Check my hair.'"

Following his evacuation from Afghanistan, Brûlé spent about half a year recuperating in London. (Despite treatment, his left arm and hand have remained severely impaired.) "I recovered through a great, hot London summer, with cocktails in the garden all the time and cooking," he told Richard Starnes. He also read scores of magazines. "This is what life's about, I thought," he recalled to Starnes. "It's about living in a great house, wearing good clothes and seeing the world." He added, "The more I thought about it, the more I thought that's what everyone wants at the end of the day. These are primal needs. But traditionally magazines that deal with those primal pursuits are always aimed at people who are pushing 50 and the market never addresses younger readers. I want to go for younger readers." In January 1996 Brûlé visited the headquarters of the clothing and accessories company the Gap, in San Francisco, California, and signed the firm on as the first advertiser for his proposed magazine. He then secured a small business loan from the British government, backing from an Australian publisher, and funds from friends and family, including his mother (the last of whom he thanked in *Wallpaper**'s masthead in every issue).

Bearing the slogan "The stuff that surrounds you," *Wallpaper** debuted in September 1996 as a bimonthly. In 1997, after the fourth issue appeared, Time Warner paid Brûlé a rumored $1.63 million for 85 percent ownership of *Wallpaper**. In addition to holding the remaining 15 percent, Brûlé retained editorial control. "He's taken *Martha Stewart Living* and made it hip," Bronwyn Cosgrove, a former beauty editor for the British edition of *Cosmopolitan,* told Caroline Byrne of the *Globe and Mail* (November 1, 1997). Sam Whiting wrote for the *San Francisco Chronicle* (July 2, 1998), "With retro graphics reminiscent of the '60s, Brûlé 's creation has become a style reference for the urbane." Through news accounts of *Wallpaper**'s sale, Brûlé 's father deduced that his son was homosexual. "He called me up in a rage and said I was a disgrace, and he disowned me," Brûlé recalled to Jan Wong for the *Globe and Mail* (October 13, 1998). The long period of estrangement between father and son ended a few years ago.

After Time Warner bought *Wallpaper**—its first European acquisition—the company conducted a marketing campaign to introduce the brand to U.S. advertisers and readers. The magazine won the Art Direction Award from the New York division of the Society of Publication Designers and was declared the "best international launch" by the International Press Distributors. "Where the magazine is completely brilliant is that it's multidimensional," Mike Moore, a furniture-store owner who advertised in the magazine, said to Sam Whiting. "It talks about travel, it talks about home. It talks about architecture, food." The magazine did not please all its readers. "Tyler's definitely got a voice. But whether you like the sound of Tyler's voice or not is another thing," Bronwyn Cosgrove told Caroline Byrne, condemning the style of *Wallpaper** as "elitist, nauseating, grotesque." In response to such criticism, Brûlé told Byrne, "Look, this [magazine] is not going to change governments. This is about escaping and getting away." Now published 12 times a year, *Wallpaper** has a circulation of approximately 105,000, with 90 percent of its buyers in Europe, including Great Britain, and the United States.

In 2001 Brûlé became the youngest-ever recipient of the British Society of Magazine Editors Lifetime Achievement Award. The next year Time Warner fired him—reportedly over unauthorized expenses involving use of a London taxi, according to Brûlé, or use of a chartered plane, according to others—and he sold his share of *Wallpaper**. He also signed a noncompete agreement stipulating that he would not establish another magazine for two and a half years.

Later Career

Brûlé then devoted himself to developing Wink Media, a full-service design- and branding agency that he had established in 1998. Later renamed Winkreative, it is now a subsidiary of Winkorp AG ("AG" being equivalent to "Inc."), which Brûlé set up in 2002. Originally headquartered in Zürich, Switzerland, Winkreative worked with clients including Swiss International Air Lines (which, as Brûlé suggested, changed its stewards' uniforms, airport lounges, and logo to simply "SWISS"), Sky One, Marks & Spencer, BMW, Nokia, Adidas, Bally, B&B Italia, Spanair, James Perse, Pottery Barn, Stella McCartney, and Prada. Brûlé told Chris Daniels of *Marketing Magazine* that at that time (2007), Winkreative's annual billings totaled $20 million. In 2011 Winkreative relocated to a modernist brick building in London's Marylebone neighborhood, where its offices include an events space and recording studios. The agency added a number of prestigious Asian clients to its roster, including *China Daily,* Swire Properties, Mitsui Fudosan, Shinsegae, and Taoyuan Taiwan International Airport, as well as Metrolinx, formerly the Greater Toronto Transportation Authority. Winkorp, however, remains headquartered in Zürich.

In 2004 Brûlé began writing a column for the Weekend Life and Arts section of the *Financial Times,* an internationally distributed newspaper published in London. His column, "Fast Lane," discusses architecture, travel, fashion, and style as observed by Brûlé during his extensive global travels. "We wanted an expert on trends, and we decided he would be a very good trend-spotter," Richard Addis, a *Financial Times* editor, told Tony Lofaro for the *Ottawa Citizen* (January 15, 2004). In 2005–06, through Winkontent, Winkorp's editorial and TV-production division, Brûlé produced and hosted a show about the media, called *The Desk,* which aired on BBC Four; its failure to attract many viewers led to its being canceled after one season. "I loved the show and curiously if another [program about the media] had replaced it, then maybe I'd say something went wrong, but nothing has," Brûlé told James Silver. "We were never promised a second series. … I don't know whether the BBC really knew what they wanted from the programme." Concurrently, in another Winkontent project, he produced and hosted *Counter Culture,* a BBC Four series in which he investigated consumerism in Russia, Sweden, Italy, Libya, Japan, and the United States. According to one on-line blurb for the series, he aimed to examine the "cultures of six very different countries through their attitudes to retail."

Toward the end of 2006, Brûlé announced his intention to launch a magazine called *Monocle.*" I noticed a gap in the global market from watching consumer behaviour at airports," he explained to Justin Pearse for the British publication *New Media Age* (June 28, 2007). "I saw people buying a business news monthly and an interiors magazine, like the *Economist* and *Wallpaper*.* … So I thought, why do you have to divorce business and lifestyle?" He recruited investors from Spain, Sweden, Switzerland, Japan, and Australia, each of whom owns a flourishing family business and a 10 percent stake in *Monocle.* In publicity material released before its debut, according to Chris Daniels, *Monocle's* prospective readers were described as people "who probably don't live in their country of birth, whose work takes them to several different countries a week and who thought they had outgrown news and business magazines as we currently know them"— " in other words," Daniels commented, "a reader like Brûlé." The first issue of *Monocle* reached newsstands in February 2007. "There is page after page of dense yet enticing text, laced with savvy argument and writerly panache," Matthew DeBord wrote about *Monocle* for the *Los Angeles Times* (September 29, 2007). "By and large, the writers are not big names but rather versatile journalists who can get the job done." DeBord added, "Brûlé has managed to create—twice now—something of absorbing visual elegance that's also worth reading." Speaking with Ruaridh Nicoll of the London *Observer,* Brûlé commented on his own editorial perspective: "We've seen the creep of the consultant on to the editorial floor—and that brought on a certain crisis of confidence."

Monocle is published ten times a year in London, where it is headquartered, and maintains bureaus in New York, Zürich, Hong Kong, and Tokyo, Several different high-quality types of paper are used in each issue. "It's part of our mantra," Brûlé explained to Amy Larocca for *New York* magazine (Dec. 5, 2010). "If you deliver something that has an improved quality of paper and is collectible, it shouldn't come as a surprise that people want to pick it up, hold on to it, pay a premium on it." The magazine currently sells about 150,000 copies of each issue in more than 80 countries. Subscribers pay considerably more for their copies than those who pay the $10 newsstand price, although they also receive on-line access to the magazine's archive for the year as well as a merchandise discount and other benefits. "The editorial tone is the opposite of jaded, with a relentless optimism that suggests we can build a better world if we just think creatively about intractable global problems and buy the right stuff along the way," David Carr wrote for the *New York Times* (August 24, 2009). Fred Pawle wrote for the *Australian* (April 16, 2009), "While print publications around the world turn to technology to retain their readers, Tyler Brûlé has created a magazine with a distinctly old-fashioned tone and built it into a global phenomenon. … In a world of tightly defined demographic niches, *Monocle* is boldly diverse."

Monocle has retail stores in London, Hong Kong, Tokyo, Osaka, and New York as well as an e-commerce site. Each sells merchandise, including *Monocle* tie-ins as well as the magazine, and maintains bureau offices in back rooms. The brand also includes Monocle 24, a global, around-the-clock radio service; Monocle TV, which began airing on the Bloomberg Network in December 2010; and two Monocle cafés: the original, in Tokyo, which opened in September 2011, and another, close to Monocle's Midori House headquarters in Marylebone, which opened in April 2013. In the summer of 2010, Brûlé published the first issue of *Monocle Mediterraneo,* a summer-oriented tabloid newspaper offering news, interviews, essays, and fashion spreads; *Monocle Alpino* is a corresponding winter-themed tabloid newspaper. Both remain on the newsstands for six weeks and are available on-line. In 2011 *Advertising Age* magazine named Brûlé editor of the year.

"Tyler is a man with a brain that goes a mile a minute," Ben Boehm, an executive with Bombardier Aerospace, one of Winkreative's clients, told Chris Daniels. Ruaridh Nicoll commented, "Self-awareness is what he does. Art directing his life, his style is his business model … the painfully modern aesthetic that infuriates so many. Those programmes on his radio station and the section titles in his magazine reflect the man. He is an urbanist, he is absolutely a globalist, and he likes to speak from the perspective of seat 1A of the intercontinental jetliner."

Brûlé lives in London, where he works on each of *Monocle*'s issues for about two weeks. He spends the other 32 weeks of the year traveling. Brûlé has a winter flat in St. Moritz and a summer house on a tiny island he owns in the Stockholm Archipelago with his longtime partner, Mats Klingberg.

Further Reading:

Bloomberg BusinessWeek p64+ Jul. 5, 2010

(London) *Guardian* Feb. 12, 2007

(London) *Independent* Features p4+ Jan. 10, 2005

Marketing Magazine p10+ Jul. 30, 2007

New York Dec. 5, 2010

New York Times B p1+ Aug. 24, 200

New York Times E p1 Jan. 5, 2012

Observer Mar. 17, 2012

Ottawa Citizen B p1 Jul. 30, 1997

(Toronto, Canada) *Globe and Mail* C p1 Nov. 1, 1997

Burri, René

Photographer

Born: 1933, Zürich, Switzerland

René Burri believes that photographers must rely on their own emotional understanding of situations and timing as well as the subjects they are capturing in order to record socially significant images. "What counts is putting the intensity that you, yourself, have experienced into the picture. Otherwise it is just a document. But if you are truly successful in capturing the pulse of life, then you can speak of a good photograph," Burri remarked, as quoted by Joanna Symons for the London *Daily Telegraph* (September 9, 2006). Burri first received international acclaim for his photographic collection *Die Deutschen,* published in 1962, which documented the lives of Germans after World War II, but he is perhaps best known for his photographs of major political, historical, and cultural events, as well as for his iconic portraits of artists, political figures, and places. While Burri has been highly praised for his photojournalism, two of his most famous photos—"Men on a Rooftop, Sao Paulo," and "In the Ministry of Health, Rio de Janeiro"—are studies in geometry, modernity, and architecture that offer examples of the breadth of his oeuvre. In the opinion of many of his fellow photographers, critics, and admirers, his ability to capture larger-than-life events and personalities on film and his sympathetic and egalitarian eye for composition have made Burri one of the most important figures in the history of photography.

When Burri joined the photography collective Magnum Photo in the 1950s, he helped to forge the organization's reputation with his unwavering enthusiasm for extensive travel and his ability to put himself in the right place at the right time. Burri credits a combination of persistence and serendipity for his success. "Luck, you can't cultivate it," Burri told Robert Murphy, writing for *Women's Wear Daily* (May 4, 2004). "You have to work for it. I've always said that a good picture is like trying to catch a cab on Fifth Avenue around 5 o'clock. If you're not fast enough, the other guy will get it." According to Bruno Chalifour, who reviewed the retrospective collection *René Burri Photographs* (2004) for *Afterimage* (July 1, 2004), "Burri's style belongs to the Magnum school of photography, one that is known for the emphasis given to content and form. This esthetic works through precise composition and a total use of the frame implying two guidelines: firstly, a perfect organization of the content of the frame meant to synthesize the experience of the photographer and the events he or she witnessed; secondly, no cropping occurred during the printing process, and as a result what the viewer sees is exactly what the photographers saw in their viewfinders." Burri told Joanna Pitman for the London *Times* (March 2, 2004), "In a way, I was perfect for Magnum. I'm a stubborn, Swiss farmer-boy, a loner and a bit of a rebel. I fitted perfectly with this bunch of stubborn, independent, opinionated characters. We all had our different approaches. What linked us was not so much photography as an interest in Man and society." In an interview with Marcus Balogh for *Crédit Suisse* (October 18, 2004), Burri noted, "The ultimate photo—there's no such thing. But the camera is my third eye. I've even called it my mistress. It's become a part of me, just as a favorite and well-used tool becomes an extension of the craftsman's hand. … A photographer needs a good eye for composition and a sense of timing. The eye, heart, and brain have to come together behind the lens."

Education and Early Career

René Burri was born on April 9, 1933 in Zürich, Switzerland. Early in his childhood he developed an interest in the world outside of his landlocked country. His father, a chef, often brought home lobsters, clams, and oysters, provoking the young Burri to fantasize about their exotic places of origin. This curiosity about other lands manifested itself in other ways as well. "I still remember as a kid, being in the Boy Scouts, going to camps. The real interest wasn't the uniform, but traveling," Burri told Robert Murphy. "The excitement to see beyond the mountains was so incredible." During his youth Burri had developed an interest in documentary films. He hoped to become a director, but there were no film schools in Zürich at that time, so, in 1949, he enrolled at the Kunstgewerbeschule (School of Arts and Crafts) in Zürich to study photography composition, color, and design under Johannes Itten, Alfred Willimann, and Hans Finsler—the latter a leading proponent of the New Objectivity school, which emphasized a formalistic approach and still life in photography. In the decade after World War II, there was an increase in the desire for vibrancy and vitality in art, so much of Burri's training under Finsler proved obsolete. After he received his degree, in 1953, Burri embraced the more complicated methods of photography that he learned. "When I left school, where we photographed only coffee cups in light, I suddenly had to chase after my pictures. I took a while before I could move at the right pace," he recalled, as posted on Foto8.com.

In 1954 Burri undertook compulsory military service. With the permission of his supervising officers, he spent more of his time documenting events through photos and film than undergoing formal military training; he developed the photos in the barracks' bathtub, and some were used for promotional materials for the military training school. "I had just got my first Leica, and began by photographing everything—the railway station, mothers seeing their sons off, the barracks, manoeuvres, and so on," Burri explained to Michel Guerrin for the *Guardian Weekly* (August 12, 1984). "In the photos, you don't realise that the soldiers were using blank cartridges, or that our commanding officer was yelling things like 'You're dead!' at us. So I photographed death, while at the same time becoming aware of the power of the camera." Burri has described his time in the military as essential to his development as a photojournalist.

After completing his military commitment, Burri found work as a cameraman with the Walt Disney Film Company, working on a documentary film short, *Switzerland* (1955). "Films were my great interest," Burri told Robert Murphy. "Love stories. French films. Jean Gabin. … This kind of emotional stuff." Frustrated, however, by the lengthy and detailed production work involved in making a documentary, he realized he preferred the freedom of being an independent photographer. "I wanted just to get out there," he told Murphy. "Movies were too complicated. I learned very quickly that this third eye would allow me to be light and independent."

In 1955 Burri traveled to Paris to try to photograph his idol, the great Spanish artist Pablo Picasso, whose work he had seen and greatly admired at the Palazzo Peale in Milan, Italy, in 1953. Unable to gain an interview with Picasso after waiting outside his Parisian studio for a week, he went into the offices of Magnum Photos, a photographic cooperative started in 1947 that is owned and operated by its members and was located across the river from Picasso's home. Burri had shown his work to Werner Bischof, a Magnum photographer, shortly before Bischof's death in an accident in South America in 1954; Bischof had sent him an encouraging letter saying he had shown Burri's work to Robert Capa, Henri Cartier-Bresson, and other Magnum photographers and that they had liked it. Having recently finished a project on deaf-mute children in Switzerland, Burri showed the negatives to the Magnum receptionist. Although the woman seemed unenthused by Burri's work, she asked that he print several of the negatives and send them back to her. After submitting the requested photos, he returned to Switzerland, feeling disappointed. A short while later, he was surprised to receive a copy of *Life* from Magnum, with his photos printed inside. Shortly thereafter, Burri became an associate corresponding member of Magnum Photos; he became a full member in 1959.

Henri Cartier-Bresson became his mentor at the news photo service. "For years, at least in the beginning, if you have someone who shows you things or even gives you a hard time, that's how you learn most," Burri told Murphy, referring to Cartier-Bresson. "He was a great master of developing a scene and working to a climax—the decisive moment. For my character, I couldn't have done that. When I look at my contact sheets, there's no continuity. It's a little like I talk, in collages. Cartier-Bresson had this French way. Remember, Matisse was his idol. For me it was Picasso. Total anarchy." After joining Magnum Burri spent the rest of the 1950s traveling in around the world on various magazine assignments for the likes of *Bunte Illustrierte, Du, Jours de France, Life,* the *New York Times,* and *Paris-Match.* (The well-traveled Burri has kept every boarding card, press pass, and hotel receipt he has obtained on assignment; the entire collection weighs more than two kilograms.)

Initially Burri's goals were primarily journalistic. Having come of age during the Cold War, he had become skeptical about what he read or saw on television and wanted to contribute his version of truth to the discourse. He soon discovered, however, that photography was not the best method for documenting news because of the lag time between shooting a picture and getting it published. He told Michel Guerrin for the *Guardian Weekly* (August 12, 1984): "I remember an occasion in 1959 when I had just got back from Cyprus with pictures of Archbishop Makarios returning home. I was in a hotel room writing captions to my photos and half-watching television at the same time. What should I see but a report on events in Cyprus! It came as a shock. I got up and shouted at the television set: 'No, you can't do that, it's my story, and it's in my camera.' It was as though I were riding a horse and had just been overtaken by a train. I continued to go on photographic jobs, of course, but I realised I needed another way of saying what I wanted to say." Burri told Guerrin that in some ways he abandoned the job of being a reporter in order to "render something more permanent. I cast around for something to cover that was not a summit meeting, an election or a congress. The result was a book called *Les Allemands* ('The Germans'), which was not only a description of a particular nation in the '60s but my answer to the challenge of television." This book, Burri's first collection of photography, was first published as *Die Deutschen,* in 1962.

Later Career

During the 1960s Burri photographed artists such as Swiss surrealist Alberto Giacometti, Swiss-born architect and writer Le Corbusier, and Picasso. He also covered the funeral of the assassinated American president John F. Kennedy, one World Expo in Montreal and another in Osaka, the impact of apartheid in South Africa, and architecture in Brazil. These photos, as well as many others, were published in periodicals such as *Time, Life, Vogue, National Geographic,* and *Paris-Match.* In 1963 Burri traveled to Havana with Laura Bergquist, an American reporter on assignment for *Look* magazine, for an interview with the Marxist revolutionary Che Guevara, who was then the industry minister of Cuba. While Burri describes the encounter as primarily between Bergquist and Guevara, who sparred for hours on political and economic topics in a dark room, his photographs of the interview, which ran cropped underneath the text in the final publication, are now among his most famous portraits. In an interview with John Wilson of the BBC (April 23, 2013), Burri recounted that Guevara insisted on the blinds remaining drawn throughout their time together, and, while he shot eight rolls of film over two hours, in his view only one frame yielded a worthwhile shot.

Some critics have accused Burri of being obsessed with celebrity, but he has insisted that his interest has always been in the actions of well-known personalities rather than their fame. About filming personalities, Burri told Karolina Zupan-Rupp in an interview for the on-line *Vernissage-TV* (October 15, 2005): "It was primarily my interest in what those people did rather than whether I was able to take their picture or not. I wanted to get a closer look. It was real work; not just getting there, taking a quick picture and then leaving again. It took me ten years to get Corbusier's photo, for example; I had to earn his trust. They were outstanding personalities of the 20th century. It was about my interest in the people I had chosen. It wasn't just a celebrity obsession: that didn't exist back then. Today there are agencies and rules for everything, [making it] a lot harder to get access." In the 1960s Burri also revisited his interest in film and writing. In 1965 he created Magnum Films and directed four films for the company, on Israel, China, and the Swiss artist Jean Tinguely.

"The ultimate photo—there's no such thing. ... A photographer needs a good eye for composition and a sense of timing. The eye, heart, and brain have to come together behind the lens."

Burri is well known for his work covering conflicts around the world, including the Suez Crisis in 1956; the Six-Day War; war in Vietnam and Cambodia in the late 1960s and early 1970s; and violence in Beirut during the Lebanese civil war in the 1980s. His reportage from these conflicts was notable because his photographs rarely, if ever, depicted corpses, yet, in the eyes of reviewers, they conveyed fully a sense of the futility, waste, and meaningless of war. "It is virtually impossible to convey the horror of war in photographs," Burri told Balogh. "And I have too much respect for the dead to expose them to the voraciousness of newspapers and magazines. I remember a moment during the Six-Day War. I suddenly happened upon a black hand reaching out of the sand. I knew that it could have been a cover photo, but I didn't shoot it. I don't want to photograph death. I prefer to document the human story in another way. ... I'm interested in the before and after, the seemingly insignificant, which occurs alongside the shocking. Sometimes a look behind the scenes can show connections more clearly than a sensational photo." Asked by Guerrin if he ever was afraid of being killed while on assignment (as other Magnum photographers had been), Burri explained that often he was so absorbed in filming that he was unaware of the violence around him until after the fact. "I've never panicked under shellfire. ... Fear is not the real problem," he told Guerrin. "On the contrary, one is always trying to repress the urge to take yet another chance.

Look at those photographers who have lost their lives in war; a curious fascination always lured them back to the same battle zones—it was as though they felt they could never be hit by a bullet. ... When you're taking pictures and things are hotting up around you, you become aware of the danger too late. You suddenly get a flash of lucidity in all the haze around you. One day I was in a helicopter. As we took off, people started shooting at us from the ground. All of a sudden, I realised that the floor of the helicopter was made of aluminum, which meant that it might just as well have been made of cardboard: we were like sitting ducks." Peter Killer, a Swiss art and architecture critic, told Randy Kennedy for the *New York Times* (May 20, 2004): "Those who see his photographs from 30 years of reporting will never accuse Burri of masking the truth to make it more palatable. Nevertheless, even when they tell of war and death, Burri's photographs have something deeply human about them. There is not one image in Burri's oeuvre that denies the hope of a more civilized world."

During the 1970s Burri continued to travel the world on assignment; notably, he shot photo essays on the city of Chicago for *Du* and of Cuba for *Time.* He filmed President Richard M. Nixon's visit to Egypt in 1974 and went on the campaign trail in 1976 in Georgia with presidential candidate Jimmy Carter. Between 1979 and 1981, he worked on several assignments for NASA, producing portraits of the Apollo astronauts as well as photos pertaining to the space shuttle program. In the early 1980s, Burri was elected the European president of Magnum Photos. A retrospective survey of his work, captured in the volume *One World* (1984), was exhibited in Zürich, Paris, and Lausanne in 1984. In 1988 Burri was appointed art director of *Schweizer Illustrierte.* He also documented President Ronald Reagan's meeting with Soviet president Mikhail Gorbachev, in 1988; the student protest at Tiananmen Square in China, in June 1989; and the fall of the Berlin Wall, in November 1989.

As well as contributing to political journalism, Burri remained passionate about one of his earliest interests: architecture. During the 1990s he published photo essays and collections featuring the works of Mario Botta, Luis Barragán, and Le Corbusier. He also created *Utopia—Architecture et Architecte,* an exhibition focusing on international architecture that was displayed in Prague, Berlin, and Los Angeles. Burri has suggested that the themes of *Utopia* contrast with his reportage on conflicts and represent postwar optimism.

Over his career Burri has witnessed great advances in technology, which he believes have both improved and been detrimental to the photographer's art. Discussing these advances in photography with Zupan-Rupp, Burri explained: "Back then we had to send the film, there was censorship; and sometimes you would lose a film or you were late for a deadline. Today the picture is transmitted within seconds. I would say that's just the beginning. What's still important, however, is what's on the picture: you still need head, eyes, heart, and also feet. In that respect nothing has changed, whether it's paper, film, or digital. That's not the point, but rather what has become of it."

Nearly two dozen books of Burri's photography have been published, and he has been honored with numerous retrospective collections and exhibitions of his work. He held his first solo exhibition at the Art Institute of Chicago in 1963. Of his numerous exhibitions since, perhaps the most notable has been *Rétrospective 1950–2000,* in 2004–2005, curated by Hans-Michael Koetzle, originally at the Maison Européenne de la Photographie in Paris and then at museums in Lausanne, Milan, and Zürich. An accompanying volume, *René Burri Photographs,* edited by Koetzle, was published in 2004. *René Burri: Utopia—Architecture et Architecte,* focusing on the work of Oscar Niemeyer in Brasília and Le Corbusier's Cité Radieuse, was mounted at the Hermès Gallery in New York and the Leica Gallery in Prague in 2005 and the Galerie WestLicht in Vienna in 2006. Burri also gave the title *Utopia* to a later exhibition, one concerned with the work of five artists: Pablo Picasso, Le Corbusier, Jean Tinguely, Yves Klein, and Alberto Giacometti; this second *Utopia* was mounted at the Ausstellungsraum Klingental in Basel in 2010 and and Musée de Penthes in Geneva in 2013. Burri's exhibition *A Photographer, a World* was shown in Havana in 2007.

Over his long career Burri has been known for his black-and-white images, and although he also shot color photographs, these were largely unknown until Phaidon published *Impossibles Réminiscences* in 2013. Phaidon's promotional copy explained that the title came from an H. G. Wells short story and noted that, "The photographs are arranged according to a colour selection rather than date, place or topic." The book also offers childhood paintings by Burri revealing his early "understanding and appreciation of colour." The exhibition *René Burri: A Double Life,* at the Museum für Gestaltung Zürich, was timed to coincide with the book's publication. In 2013 Burri created the René Burri Foundation, entrusting his archives to the Musée de l'Elysée in Lausanne.

René Burri divides his time between Paris and Zürich. In 1963 he married Rosellina Bischof, the widow of Werner Bischof, with whom he had two children, Jasmin and Oliver. After her death in 1986, he married Clotilde Blanc; their son, Leon Ulysse, was born in 1994. Burri's hobbies include painting.

Further Reading:

(London) *Guardian* p28 Feb. 7, 2004

(London) *Times* II p15 Mar. 2, 2004

Guardian Weekly p13 Aug. 12, 1984

Newsweek p59 Feb. 16, 2004

New York Times E p1 May 20, 2004

Women's Wear Daily p12 May 4, 2004

Interviews with Burri:

BBC Radio Four, *Front Row*, with John Wilson, Apr. 23, 2013, www.bbc.co.uk; Vernissage TV, three-part interview with Karolina Zupan-Rupp (with transcripts available in English), May through Oct. 2005, vernissage.tv.blog/ 2005/10/16/rene-burri-museum-fur-gestaltung-zurich/

Selected Photography Collections:

Die Deutchen, 1962

Koh Samui, 1965

The Gaucho, 1968

Lost Pony, 1976

In Search of the Holy Land, 1979

One World, 1984

Ein Amerikanischer Traum: Fotografien aus der Welt der NASA und des Pentagon, 1986

Werner Bischof, 1990

Cuba y Cuba, 1994

Che Guevara, 1997

77 Strange Sensations, 1998

Photo Poche, 1998

Le Corbusier, 1999

Luis Barragán, 200

Berner Blitz, 2000

Che Guevara Cigar Box, 2004

René Burri Photographs, 2004

Impossibles Réminiscences, 2013

Burrows, James

Television director, producer

Born: 1940, Los Angeles, California, United States

"My mind is never a blank," the sitcom director James Burrows told Bill Carter for the *New York Times* (May 14, 1995). "If something isn't funny, I'll try nine ways to make it funny. I won't just quit on it. I'll change the straight line to get more ideas, or find a funny position for the actors." The "sorcerer behind the sitcoms," as the *Times* headlined Carter's article, Burrows has helped to create and served as resident director of several of the most popular series ever to air on American television (and, through syndication, in many countries overseas): *Taxi, Cheers, Frasier, Friends,* and *Will & Grace.* He has also directed the pilots for and, in many cases, episodes *of Night Court, Dharma & Greg, NewsRadio, Veronica's Closet, 3rd Rock from the Sun, Caroline in the City, Wings, Two and a Half Men, The Big Bang Theory,* and dozens of other television sitcoms, almost all of which went on to appear on primetime lineups. "Millions of TV viewers owe him trillions of laughs," Sid Smith wrote for the *Chicago Tribune* (April 26, 1998).

The shows Burrows has midwifed and nurtured are distinguished by their highly distinctive, quirky, flawed yet sympathetic characters, whose predicaments, yearnings, joys, and sorrows are portrayed with compassion and understanding as well as humor. Burrows explained to James Ulmer, of *DGA Quarterly* (Summer 2006), "I tell my writers, I'm here to protect your vision because I can dilute the homogenizing process of the network. Television, after all, is in the business of imitation, not innovation." Although many episodes of his shows have dealt with sensitive social issues, he has asserted that he and his collaborators refuse to proselytize and aim only to entertain and make people laugh. "He's not like anybody else," Harriet Harris, who had a recurring role on *Frasier* and whom Burrows directed in a theatrical production in 1998, told Sid Smith. "With Jim, the jokes always come out of character. I've worked with a lot of fancy theater directors in my time, and, the truth is, most people just can't do that." Burrows is also known for his ability to turn his casts into close-knit ensembles, giving viewers "the sense that these actors have been with each other for a long time," as he explained to Bill Carter. "And I do it by creating a lot of stuff that's not necessarily on the page."

A keen observer of human nature, Burrows studied direction at the Yale School of Drama, but his education in the dramatic arts began long before, at home: his father was Abe Burrows, a successful playwright, director, producer, and occasional performer whose friends included world-famous literary figures and people of renown in theater and film. "I look at it as if my father was a tailor, and I grew up in a tailor shop," James Burrows told Sid Smith. "The more I drifted into it, I realized I knew a lot more about making a suit than I thought." Burrows worked in theater for years before landing a job with MTM Enterprises, where he made his debut in television as the director of an episode of the *Mary Tyler Moore Show* in 1974. "When I was growing up I never thought I'd be as good as my father," he told Rick Marin for *Newsweek* (September 11, 1995). "I'm now coming to terms with the fact that maybe in my field I'm as successful as he was in his." According to Steve Johnson, writing for the *Chicago Tribune* (March 3, 2002), Burrows's achievements are a major reason why "the top shows have elevated the director from supporting player to co-star." A producer and executive producer as well as a director, Burrows has earned four awards for direction from the Directors Guild of America; ten Primetime Emmy Awards (five for direction and five for co-production);

an American Comedy Award for Lifetime Achievement, in 1996; and the Banff Television Festival Lifetime Achievement Award, in 2003. In 2006 he received a Career Tribute Award at the United States Comedy Arts Festival in Aspen, Colorado, sponsored by HBO, and 2013 he was nominated for the Television Critics Association Lifetime Achievement Award.

Education and Early Career

The second of two children, James Edward Burrows was born in Los Angeles, California, on December 30, 1940, to Abe Burrows and Ruth (Levinson) Burrows. He was raised in the New York City borough of Manhattan with his sister, Laurie, who married Peter Grad. Laurie Burrows Grad is a food writer who has hosted a television cooking show and currently edits the food and travel Web site Epicurus.com. Burrows's parents divorced in 1948; two years later his father married Carin Smith Kinzel. During Burrows's early years his father became celebrated among performers and writers for his extraordinary talents as a comic and satirist. Abe Burrows gained recognition among the public as a writer, from 1941 to 1945, for the radio show *Duffy's Tavern*; as the writer and star of his own radio programs, *The Abe Burrows Show* (1946–47) and *Breakfast with Burrows* (1949); and his appearances on *We Take Your Word* (broadcast on radio and TV in 1950), in which he displayed his erudition as well as his gift for extemporaneous comedy. His reputation grew exponentially with the success of the theatrical musical comedy *Guys and Dolls* (1950), which he co-authored. Abe Burrows's many credits as a writer and/or director for Broadway and Hollywood also include *How to Succeed in Business without Really Trying, Cactus Flower, Can-Can, Silk Stockings, Breakfast at Tiffany's,* and *The Solid Gold Cadillac.* His skill as a script doctor was legendary: the plea "Get me Abe Burrows!," according to various Web sites, remains a shorthand way of indicating that a script needs fixing.

As a youngster James Burrows was a member of the Metropolitan Opera Children's Chorus. He attended the High School of Music and Art (now known as the Fiorello H. LaGuardia High School of Music & Art and Performing Arts). After his graduation, in 1958, Burrows entered Oberlin College, in Oberlin, Ohio, where he majored in government and politics. "I had no desire to go into show business! New York was my father's town, and I was just Abe's kid," he told Caitlin Kelly for *Variety* (January 24, 2005). He earned a B.A. degree in 1962. Partly to avoid the military draft, he next enrolled at the Yale School of Drama, in New Haven, Connecticut. There, he learned directing from Nikos Psacharopoulos, who was a playwright as well as an instructor and whom Burrows described to Kelly as "inspirational." He earned an M.F.A. degree in 1965.

Later that year Burrows held a series of entry-level theater jobs. Then he worked for a short while as a dialogue coach for *O.K. Crackerby!,* a TV sitcom created by his father and Cleveland Amory that starred Burl Ives and ran for less than four months. In 1966 he served as the assistant stage manager for a musical adaptation of *Breakfast at Tiffany's,* starring Mary Tyler Moore, which his father directed and which closed after four preview performances. He next stage-managed another show directed by his father—a touring production of *Cactus Flower.* In 1968, again under his father's direction, he stage-managed *Forty Carats,* which starred Julie Harris and ran on Broadway for nearly two years. Watching and working closely with his father proved to be enormously valuable to Burrows. "In subsequent years, a lot of his gift and a lot of his skills seemed to come out of me at the strangest times," he told Terry Gross, who interviewed him for the National Public Radio program *Fresh Air* (March 9, 2006). "It's not that I learned them as much as ... they were like osmosis. I absorbed them." During rehearsals, like his father, Burrows pays more attention to dialogue than to actors' movements or facial expressions, and he often paces. He also laughs heartily at every joke, in part to encourage his cast.

In late 1970 Burrows directed an original play, *The Castro Complex,* starring Raúl Juliá. Mounted on Broadway, it closed after 14 performances. For several years after that, Burrows stage-managed or directed such shows as *The Odd Couple, Guys and Dolls,* and *The Last of the Red Hot Lovers* for dinner theaters and summer stock. One night, while he was watching *The Mary Tyler Moore Show* on TV, it occurred to him that his job and that of the director of that sitcom were similar, in that he had about eight days to prepare for each debut, while the director had a week in which to polish an episode that filled 20 minutes of air time. Burrows wrote a letter to Moore and her then-husband, Grant Tinker, and secured an internship at their company, MTM Enterprises. In addition to *The Mary Tyler Moore Show,* which had premiered in 1970, MTM had launched *The Bob Newhart Show,* in 1972, and *Rhoda,* in 1974. For about two months Burrows observed the management, direction, and production of those programs. He paid particular attention to the camera work, which at first seemed "daunting," as he recalled to Terry Gross. In the memoir *Tinker in Television* (1994), Tinker recalled that when Bob Newhart complained that Burrows's presence was making him nervous, Tinker had Jay Sandrich take Burrows under his wing. Sandrich, who directed 119 episodes of *The Mary Tyler Moore Show,* became his mentor and close friend. Sandrich told Kelly that he immediately recognized that Burrows "was a very talented young man with a great sense of humor. We'd talk about how and why I did things. He really got it." In 1974, in his maiden effort on TV, Burrows directed an episode of *The Mary Tyler Moore Show* called "Neighbors." During the next few years, he directed episodes of such MTM programs as *The Bob Crane Show, The Bob Newhart Show, Rhoda, Phyllis,* and *Paul Sand in Friends and Lovers,* and he directed the pilot of *Lou Grant.*

In 1977 James L. Brooks, a creator and executive producer of *The Mary Tyler Moore Show,* and three others left MTM to create their own sitcom, and they hired Burrows as principal director. Called *Taxi,* the show was set in the dispatcher's office of a New York City cab company. All the cabdrivers—except the one played by Judd Hirsch, who accepted his lot in life—worked part-time and dreamed of success in other areas (one character, for example, was an actor, another a boxer), but every attempt they made to improve their circumstances ended in failure. In addition to Hirsch, the cast included Danny DeVito, Tony Danza, Marilu Henner, Christopher Lloyd, Andy Kaufman, J. Alan Thomas, Jeff Conaway, and Carol Kane. Burrows directed 76 of the 114 episodes, all of which were shot with four cameras operating simultaneously. He told Terry Gross that *Taxi,* which ran from 1978 until 1983, was "probably the most difficult show I ever did because the cast was so divergent, the writing was so outrageous, the set was so gigantic, and it was the first really big show where I was in charge from the beginning." *Taxi* won 20 Emmy Awards, and Burrows himself won two, for direction, in 1980 and 1981.

In 1982 Burrows co-founded a production company with Glen Charles and Les Charles, brothers who had worked as writers and producers for both *The Mary Tyler Moore Show* and *Taxi.* "I never learned more about writing than I did from those two guys," Burrows told Sid Smith. The first project of Charles Bros./ Burrows Productions (later called Charles-Burrows-Charles) was *Cheers,* named for the fictional neighborhood bar in Boston, Massachusetts, that served as the setting for every show. (It resembled both the real Bull & Finch Pub in Boston and the fictional Duffy's Tavern from the radio show for which Abe Burrows wrote.) As at any bar, the main activity at Cheers (besides drinking) was conversation—indeed, as Burrows told Bill Carter, it seemed to him that that the Charleses' scripts "brought radio back to television"—with discussions among the characters about a great variety of mundane, frivolous, ridiculous, weighty, or sensitive subjects. The main characters were Sam Malone (played by Ted Danson), the libidinous, chauvinistic bartender and bar owner, a recovered alcoholic and onetime baseball player; Woody (Woody Harrelson), the childlike assistant bartender (a similar though much older character was played for three seasons, until his death, by Nicholas Colasanto); Carla (Rhea Perlman), a wisecracking waitress and harried mother of six; Diane (Shelley Long), a pretentiously intellectual graduate student who becomes a waitress—and, later, Sam's girlfriend—after being jilted by her fiance in the first episode; and such steady customers as Norm (George Wendt), a frequently unemployed accountant; Norm's best friend, Cliff (John Ratzenberger), a postman and know-it-all; and Frasier (Kelsey Grammer), a pompous psychiatrist. Shortly before the series's eleventh and last season, Bill Carter wrote in an assessment for the *New York Times* (May 9, 1993) entitled "Why Cheers Proved So Intoxicating," asserting that "The characters' very flaws are, in part, what makes them so irresistible."

For weeks after *Cheers* premiered, on September 30, 1982, it had very poor ratings; it avoided cancellation because of its fine critical reception and because NBC "had nothing to put on in its place," as Burrows told Kelly. Burrows nevertheless felt confident that the show was "something special," as he told Ed Will. *Cheers*'s viewership grew greatly during the 1984–85 season, when it aired after the already popular *The Cosby Show* and *Family Ties* and before *Night Court* and *Hill Street Blues.* In every season from its fourth, its Nielsen rankings placed it among the top-five TV shows; in its ninth season, 1990–91, it ranked first. Burrows directed about 235 of its 273 episodes and won Emmys as director in 1983 and 1991 and as co-producer in 1983, 1984, and 1990. The show itself won an Emmy as outstanding comedy series four times. When the last episode aired, on August 19, 1993, *Cheers* was being syndicated in three dozen countries, and revenues from syndication had topped half a billion dollars. In his 1993 *New York Times* appraisal, Carter reported that the *Cheers* cast described Burrows as "indispensable, the person most responsible for the show's longevity. … His leadership behind the scenes, they say, was equally essential to its success."

Burrows earned another Emmy, in 1994, for the direction of *Frasier,* a critically acclaimed and popular *Cheers* spin-off, in which Kelsey Grammer reprised his role as a psychiatrist, this time one who hosts a call-in radio show. *Frasier,* which debuted in September 1993 and ended its run in May 2004, also starred John Mahoney as Frasier's widowed father, Martin; Jane Leeves as Martin's health-care worker, Daphne; and David Hyde Pierce as Frasier's brother, Niles, also a psychiatrist. In *The 'Radio Times' Guide to Television Comedy* (2003), Mark Lewisohn described *Frasier* as a "comedy masterpiece," not least because it was "adult and sophisticated: the scripts were literate, the plots tight and the one-liners extremely funny and incisive." Burrows directed most of the first season's episodes and then, during the following three seasons, another 17.

Burrows's next project was *Friends,* the pilot for which aired in 1994. "I like to do shows with very strong writing," Burrows told Bill Carter in 1995. "When they sent me *Friends,* the writing just leaped off the page." The sitcom depicted six attractive 20-somethings (30-somethings by the end of the show's run) who relied on one another for emotional support. Roommates or neighbors living in the Greenwich Village section of New York, the three men and three women often hung out in a neighborhood coffee shop. In their conversations and approaches toward life, they displayed qualities associated with "Generation X": "dissatisfaction with middle-class jobs and values, sexual angst in the age of AIDS, the disintegration of the nuclear family, and—most tellingly—fear of commitment to either love or career," as Joe Chidley wrote for *Maclean's* (October 2, 1995). As Jess Cagle and Dan Snierson wrote for *Entertainment Weekly* (December 29, 1995–January 5, 1996), however, *Friends* was "the first successful Hollywood offering in which Generation Xers aren't depicted as nihilistic, self-doubting pop culturaholics, as they are in films like *Clerks, Reality Bites,* and *Slacker. …* Our Friends are working and learning and growing. … We get the feeling that these Friends are going to be okay." In its first season, *Friends* joined the ranks of the top ten shows on television then, and its stars—Jennifer Aniston, Courteney Cox, Lisa Kudrow, Matt LeBlanc, Matthew Perry, and David Schwimmer—became celebrities. Burrows, who directed 16 episodes during the show's 11 seasons, earned an Emmy award for his work in 1995.

To elicit good performances from actors, Burrows told Tom Walter for *the Chicago Tribune* (September 18, 1995), "you just try to make them feel they're part of the creative process." He and the actors "try to create things on the stage the writers haven't seen," he explained. He also said, "The best thing for an actor is to try it his way. The way they do it may not work but it may inspire me to try something else."

Later Career

Burrows directed the sitcom *Will & Grace,* which ran from September 1998 until May 2006. The show was about a lawyer who is gay (played by Eric McCormack) and an interior designer who is heterosexual (Debra Messing); best friends, the two live in Manhattan, usually as roommates. Will's friend Jack (Sean Hayes), who appeared regularly, is also homosexual, but unlike Will, he displays stereotypically gay mannerisms. "Jack can be incredibly outrageous because Will is not," Burrows told Terry Gross. "I think if Will wasn't on the show, we would get letters from the gay community about how Jack's portrayed … but because of Will, it allows us to do that." "By the simple trick of sophisticated writing and great acting, [*Will & Grace*] creates an idealized reality within which sexual identity is no more or less interesting than a person's natural hair color," Tom Maurstad wrote for the *Dallas Morning News* (February 22, 2000). "It's something that can be fun to talk about, but, really, what difference does it make?" From 2001 to 2005, *Will & Grace* ranked second in popularity, after *Friends,* among viewers 18 through 49 years of age. It earned more than 80 Emmy nominations and won 12. As executive producer, Burrows shared one of them, in 2000, in the category of outstanding comedy series.

Burrows was director and executive producer of the CBS comedy *The Class*, about members of a third-grade class who reunite 20 years later, establishing new connections and relationships. It ran for 19 episodes in the 2006–07 season, but it was not renewed despite having won the Favorite New TV Comedy People's Choice Award as well as garnering a nomination for an Art Director's Guild award (for excellence in production design for a multi-camera television series) and a Primetime Emmy nomination (for outstanding art direction for a multi-camera series). *Back to You,* with Kelsey Grammer and Patricia Heaton, was a series about a news anchor who departed his Pittsburgh TV station for the heady environs of Los Angeles television, only to lose his LA anchor job ten years later and return to the Pittsburgh station—sparring, as before, with his female co-anchor. Burrows directed 17 episodes that ran in 2007–08 on Fox; he was also executive producer. The Writers Guild of America strike forced the program off the air from mid-November 2007 until late February 2008. Burrows moved on to direct the 36 episodes of *Gary Unmarried,* about a recently divorced housepainter (Jay Mohr) sharing custody of his two teenaged children with his antagonistic ex-wife (Paula Marshall). The show aired on CBS for two seasons, from September 2008 until May 2010.

After directing five episodes of the shortlived ABC sitcom *Romantically Challenged,* with Alyssa Milano (April–May 2010), Burrows took on *Mike & Molly,* about an elementary-school teacher and a Chicago police officer who meet at an Overeaters Anonymous meeting and soon marry. *Mike & Molly* proved to be very successful; over 2010–2012, Burrows directed 48 episodes. Starring Gary Gardell and Melissa Mc-

Carthy, the show was nominated for a People's Choice Award for favorite new TV comedy in 2011 and in 2011–2013 garnered multiple Primetime Emmy nominations for McCarthy (she won in 2011) and for cinematography and art direction for a multi-camera series. *Partners* (September–November 2012), about law partners and their would-be life partners, reunited Burrows as director with creators and executive producers David Kohan and Max Mutchnick, of *Will & Grace.* Although it was the only new comedy CBS introduced in the 2012 fall season and was nominated for a People's Choice Award for favorite new TV comedy, the show had poor ratings by CBS standards and was swiftly canceled.

"I tell my writers, I'm here to protect your vision because I can dilute the homogenizing process of my network. Television, after all, is in the business of imitation, not innovation."

Burrows is the master of multiple-camera TV pilots, with an "unmatched track record," according to James Ulmer of *DGA Quarterly*, in this demanding specialty. At the start of 2013, for example, wrote Nellie Andreeva for Deadline Hollywood (January 30, 2013), he was slated to direct three, possibly four, pilots, and he had directed the pilots of four of the five comedy series then showing on CBS—*The Big Bang Theory, Two And A Half Men, 2 Broke Girls,* and *Mike & Molly.* He does not necessarily continue with pilot projects picked up by the networks, yet "Having Burrows helm the entire first season [of a new show] is probably the best insurance policy a nervous network can buy," wrote Scott Collins in the *Los Angeles Times* (September 27, 2010).

Burrows is committed to using multiple (typically four) cameras in his pilots and series, which are shot in a studio, usually before a live audience. Collins explained, "It's a theatrical style, a throwback to TV's earlier times à la 'I Love Lucy.' The trend runs counter to TV's current obsession with so-called single-camera (read: movie-like, no audience or laugh track, often shot on location) comedies." Burrows enjoys the immediate feedback of working before a live audience. He told Amy Dawes, in an interview for the Academy of Television Arts and Sciences (October 20, 2010), "I'm from theater. … If you don't keep it moving, you lose the audience." Speaking to Ulmer, Burrows commented, "The intricacies of single-camera producing don't interest me because in my shows, the camera isn't a character like it is in the movies. I'm not about pyrotechnics. My job in the pilot is to make sure that when people see these kids in the cast, they feel comfortable with them and want to tune into them next week." According to Collins, "what he's especially good at doing is fostering a warm sense of family among the actors and the viewers—a difficult quality to analyze and therefore to duplicate." Collins goes on to quote Billy Gardell of *Mike & Molly*: "That guy has forgotten more funny than most of us ever know." Burrows says his desire to keep the laughs coming is something that he treasures. He told Dawes, "I don't have to work anymore. I do it because I have so much fun doing it."

In 1982 Burrows directed the feature film *Partners,* written by Francis Veber (the scriptwriter for the 1978 motion picture *La Cage aux Folles*). The movie fared badly both critically and commercially. "I'm so sour on movies," Burrows told Bill Carter in 1995. "I don't like the two years you have to spend on them. I like the instant gratification, the eight-days-and-out of [a sitcom]. You know when you shoot in front of an audience if it's good." "If I found the right play," he added, "I would surely do theater." That opportunity came along in 1998, when Burrows directed a revival of the 1939 comedy *The Man Who Came to Dinner,* by George S. Kaufman and Moss Hart, presented at the Steppenwolf Theatre, in Chicago. "This is a joyous production," Richard Christiansen wrote for the *Chicago Tribune* (April 28, 1998). "Oh, what fun it is to see [the cast] all having such a good time—and giving us a wonderful night in the theater while they're at it." Christiansen also reported that "of the dozens of bits of business" that Burrows had "craftily invented," only three or four failed to produce laughs. Burrows also directed a number of TV movies, including *Strange Brew* (2010), written by David Kohan and Max Mutchnick; *Ab Fab*, also known as *Absolutely Fabulous* (2009); *The Mastersons of Manhattan,* with Natasha Richardson (2007); and *Dexter Prep* (2002).

"For a guru of the funnybone, Burrows is a serious fellow," Sid Smith wrote. From his first marriage, to Linda Solomon, which ended in divorce in 1993, Burrows has three daughters. (His production company is called Three Sisters Entertainment.) He has a stepdaughter from his second marriage, in 1997, to Debbie Easton. He lives in Beverly Hills, California, and owns a large collection of modern art.

Further Reading:

Chicago Tribune Tempo p5 Sep. 18, 1995

Arts & Entertainment p1+ Apr. 26, 1998

Tempo p2 Mar. 10, 2000

Entertainment Weekly p30+ Mar. 26, 2004

Fresh Air (transcript) Mar. 9, 2006

GQ p238+ May 1988

New York Times II p1+ May 14, 1995, E p1+ Sep. 29, 2005

Newsweek Sep. 11, 1995

Variety Jan. 24, 2005

Selected Television Shows:

as director

Fay, 1975

Phyllis, 1975

Mary Tyler Moore, 1974–76

Busting Loose, 1977

The Bob Newhart Show, 1975–77

Laverne and Shirley, 1976–77

Szysznyk, 1977

The Betty White Show, 1977

Lou Grant, 1977

Rhoda, 1977–78

Husbands, Wives & Lovers, 1978

Free Country, 1978

A New Kind of Family, 1979

The Associates, 1979

Good Time Harry, 1980

Best of the West, 1981

Taxi, 1978–82; *Night Court,* 1984

Valerie, 1986

All Is Forgiven, 1986

The Tortellis, 1987

Dear John, 1988

Disneyland, 1990

The Marshall Chronicles, 1990

Wings, 1990

The Fanelli Boys, 1990

Flying Blind, 1992

Cheers, 1982–93

Cafe Americain, 1993

The Boys Are Back, 1994

The Preston Episodes, 1995

Partners, 1995

Hudson Street, 1995

Caroline in the City, 1995

Newsradio, 1996

3rd Rock from the Sun, 1996

Pearl, 1996

Men Behaving Badly, 1996

Chicago Sons, 1997

Frasier, 1993–97

Fired Up, 1997

George & Leo, 1997

Dharma & Greg, 1997

Veronica's Closet, 1997

Union Square, 1997

Friends, 1994-98

Conrad Bloom, 1998

Jesse, 1998

The Secret Lives of Men, 1998

Ladies Man, 1998

Stark Raving Mad, 1999

Madigan Men, 2000

Cursed, 2000

Good Morning, Miami, 2002

Bram and Alice, 2002

Two and a Half Men, 2003

The Stones, 2004

Four Kings, 2006

Courting Alex, 2006

Teachers, 2006

Will & Grace, 1998–2006
The Class, 2006
The Big Bang Theory, 2007
Back to You, 2007–08
Hank, 2009
Gary Unmarried, 2008–2010
Better with You, 2010
 $#! My Dad Says,* 2010
Up All Night, 2011
Romantically Challenged, 2010–11
2 Broke Girls, 2011
Mike & Molly, 2010–2012
Partners, 2012–13
Friends with Better Lives, 2013
The Millers, 2013
Sean Saves the World, 2013

Selected Films:
Partners, 1982

Selected Plays:
The Castro Complex, 1970
The Man Who Came to Dinner, 1998

Chase, David

Television writer, director, producer

Born: 1950(?), Mount Vernon, New York, United States

David Chase—one of television's "few authentic auteurs," according to Peter Biskind, writing in *Vanity Fair* (April 2007)—wrote, produced, or directed several of the most highly regarded television series of the last 40 years, including *Almost Grown, Northern Exposure, I'll Fly Away,* and, most notably, *The Sopranos,* described by television critic Bill Carter in the *New York Times* as "by any standard, …a classic, career-defining achievement" (February 26, 2006). The extremely successful weekly HBO Mob drama, starring James Gandolfini and Edie Falco, won high acclaim for its realism in depicting the lives of a contemporary Mafia family. Much of that praise was for the show's clever juxtaposition of Mob activity and bourgeois suburban life. In one such episode, "College," the head of the Mob family, Tony Soprano, drives his teenage daughter to a college for an interview. After dropping her off, he tracks down a mob informant and strangles him to death; then he returns to the school and picks up his daughter. "It's the end of the millennium, and things are weird even for the Mob," Chase was quoted as saying in *TV Guide* (February 6, 1999). "It's what I love about them—these guys are surprisingly bourgeois." In February 2001 the Museum of Modern Art in New York City Kardish, showed the first two seasons of *The Sopranos*—the first time an American dramatic series for television had been shown at the museum. "The Sopranos is a cynical yet deeply felt look at this particular family man," remarked Laurence Kardish, senior curator of the Department of Film and Video, in the museum's press release. "David Chase and his team have created a series distinguished by its bone-dry humor and understated, quirky, and stinging perspective." In all the show earned 112 Primetime Emmy nominations and came away with 21 wins.

The Sopranos ended its long run on June 10, 2007, after six seasons and 86 episodes. The show had developed a cult following—including members of the Mafia, whom FBI wiretaps caught discussing the show. Its blackout finale evoked consternation, even anger, and admiration in nearly equal measure. Chase directed the episode—"Made in America"—as he had the show's pilot. On the controversy over the ending, Chase commented, "All I wanted to do was present the idea of how short life is and how precious it is. The only way I felt I could do that was to rip it away. … It's a cold universe, and I don't mean that metaphorically. If you go out into space, it's cold. It's really cold, and we don't know what's up there. We happen to be in this little pocket where there's a sun. What have we got except love and each other to guard against all that isolation and loneliness?" (London *Daily Mail,* December 17, 2012). The episode garnered a Directors Guild of America Award nomination, and it won an Emmy Award for writing and an American Cinema Editors Eddie Award for editing.

Chase made his debut as a film director with the semiautobiographical *Not Fade Away* (December 2012); he also wrote the script and co-produced the film. *Sopranos* alumni Steven Van Zandt (formerly of Bruce Springsteen's E Street Band) and James Gandofini joined in the project, Van Zandt as executive producer and musical supervisor and Gandolfini as an actor.

Education and Early Career

David Chase was born David DeCesare in Mount Vernon, New York, on August 22, 1945. His father worked in a hardware store. Chase grew up in the New Jersey suburbs of New York City. As a child he was a fan of old gangster movies starring such actors as Edward G. Robinson, who appeared in the classic *Little Caesar* in 1930, and James Cagney, the lead performer in the similarly standard-setting *Public Enemy* (1931). "*Public Enemy* was the movie that started my love affair with the gangster film," he told Bill Carter for the *New York Times* (February 28, 2001).

Chase was fascinated by the Mob, becoming excited when his father told him that the fathers of some of the children in his school were involved with Mafia activity. Chase received his B.A. from New York University and his M.A. in film from Stanford University, in Stanford, California.

"All I wanted to do was present the idea of how short life is and how precious it is. ... It's a cold universe, ... and we don't know what's up there. ... What have we got except love and each other to guard against all that isolation and loneliness?"

Chase co-wrote the low-budget horror film *Grave of the Vampire,* which was released in 1972. The film tells the story of a half-man, half-vampire who is conceived when a vampire rapes a human woman. Despising his vampire side as an adult, he sets out to find and confront his biological father. Chase was also credited with the story for the television film *Scream of the Wolf* (1974), in which a successful big-game hunter comes out of retirement to track down a killer animal. The hunter soon begins to suspect that the wolf in question might be supernatural. Chase also worked as story consultant and story editor for the television series *Kolchak: The Night Stalker,* which aired from 1974 to 1975. The horror/drama show starred Darren McGavin as Carl Kolchak, a Chicago newspaper reporter who, in the course of hunting down mysterious killers each week, found himself investigating paranormal and supernatural activities. Kolchak could never convince his editor (Tony Vincenzo) that what he had experienced was real. Chase also served as a story consultant on the television show *Switch* (1975–78), in which an ex-detective (Eddie Albert) and a man he had sent to prison (Robert Wagner) teamed up to form their own detective agency. From 1976 to 1980 Chase was a co-producer of the successful television crime drama *The Rockford Files,* starring James Garner, which won a 1980 Golden Globe Award for best television drama series.

Chase's screenplay for the 1980 television film *Off the Minnesota Strip* won him a Primetime Emmy award for outstanding writing in a limited series or a special. The film, which Chase also co-produced, tells the story of a Minnesota teenager (played by Mare Winningham) who runs away to New York City. Alone and without money, she is sheltered by a pimp and soon begins working as a prostitute. After her parents (Hal Holbrook and Michael Learned) take her home, she is forced to readjust to the Midwestern, middle-class lifestyle she once abhorred. In 1985 Chase was one of several directors who worked on the one-season renewal of the television program *Alfred Hitchcock Presents,* which retold some of the episodes from the original show while offering new tales of the bizarre. In 1988 he directed the acclaimed but short-lived CBS drama *Almost Grown,* about Norman and Susie Foley (portrayed by Timothy Daley and Eve Gordon), a couple on the brink of divorce. The show used pop songs to trigger flashbacks to earlier events in the couple's three-decade-long relationship. "Music has always been intrinsic to me with movies. … As a writer I've always been inspired by music," Chase said in an interview for HBO (at the HBO Web site). "I listen to music when I'm trying to think and I just like it." For his next television project, Chase served as an executive producer on the enormously successful television comedy/drama *Northern Exposure,* in which a New York doctor (Rob Morrow) just out of medical school sets up a practice in the tiny, remote Alaskan village of Cicely, whose residents include a group of eccentrics.

Chase was also involved in the production of another highly praised television series, *I'll Fly Away,* which aired from 1991 to 1993. That show, for which he shared a PGA (Producer's Guild of America) Golden Laurel Award for television producer of the year in 1993, was set in a small southern town in the 1950s and focused on a white lawyer (Sam Waterston) who gets involved in civil rights cases as the civil rights movement begins to gather steam. Meanwhile, the caretaker of his children (Regina Taylor), who is African American, becomes more aware of her own rights. In 1996 Chase *wrote The Rockford Files: Crime and Punishment,* a television movie in which James Garner reprised his role as Jim Rockford from the original series. For the movie, Chase also served as supervising producer and director. He shared writing credits for the low-budget film *Kounterfeit* (1996), in which an ex-criminal gets involved in a counterfeit money operation. When the counterfeiters are found out, a policeman is killed, and his sister tracks down the men responsible.

Later Career

Chase created the HBO series *The Sopranos,* on which he also served as executive producer and occasional director. All the major networks passed on *The Sopranos* before HBO picked up the show, which is about the day-to-day life of one Mafia family. "I want to tell the story about the reality of being a mobster—or what I perceive to be the reality of life in organized crime," Chase told Robin Dougherty for Salon (June 20, 1999). "They aren't shooting each other every day. They sit around eating baked ziti and betting and figuring out who owes who money. Occasionally, violence breaks out—more often than it does in the banking world, perhaps." The series gave Chase a chance to write on a subject that had always fascinated him and an opportunity to explore neglected elements of the gangster genre. "Those [old gangster] films were always about a guy and his father," he was quoted as saying in *TV Guide* (February 6, 1999), "and I thought it would be interesting to explore [Tony's] relationship with his mother." The head of the family, Tony Soprano (James Gandolfini), undergoes a midlife crisis; feeling anxious about his Mob life as well as about his relationship with his aging mother, Livia (Nancy Marchand, who died in June 2000), he seeks help from a psychiatrist (Lorraine Bracco). "Actually," Chase told Robin Dougherty, "it's based on my own family dynamic—a guy who is in therapy because his mother is driving him crazy." "Whatever came into my mother's mind, she said it," Chase told Steve Daly for *Entertainment Weekly* (January 7, 2000). "There was no censorship at all. And if you challenged her, she'd say, 'You're not going to change me. I know how to talk to people.'" Chase later told Daly that during the Vietnam War, his mother told him, "I'd rather see you dead than avoid the draft." In an effort to bring an additional level of realism to the show, he spoke to a former Mafia insider for details on Mob life. "When it comes time to be violent, the show is very violent," Chase told Josh Walk for *Entertainment Weekly* (January 15, 1999). "The hope is that you don't lose yourself thinking that these people are cuddly teddy bears. You see other parts of them that are very human and full of foibles and even sweetness, but they are very brutal men."

According to critic Bill Carter, writing in the *New York Times* (February 26, 2006), the cumulative achievement of *The Sopranos* "seems to have finally dispersed the ambivalence [Chase] always held about expressing himself on television, an art form, which, as he put it, "I was always trying to get out of." Still, after *The Sopranos* ended, he turned to film, as writer, director, and producer of *Not Fade Away* (2013). The film "offers an extremely knowledgeable and affectionate yet barbed survey of rock's explosive evolution," according to Stephen Holden, writing in the *New York Times* (December 20, 2012). Holden had earlier noted in the Times, in an article on the New York Film Festival (October 2, 2012), that *Not Fade Away* was the festival's official centerpiece, calling it "a vigorous rock-'n'-roll coming-of-age movie," adding, "In its scrappy fragmentary vision of 1960s America *Not Fade Away* shows accelerated cultural change leading to collective disorientation and bewilderment." Chase told Stephen Whitty, of the New Jersey *Star-Ledger,* "I don't know that I wanted to do a coming of age story. … But I wanted to do a story about the tension between security and freedom, the story of artistic dreams vs. the reality of creating something. Most of all I wanted to do a story about a period in music that changed the way a generation thought about a lot of things." Generally well received by critics, the film was not embraced by audiences. Blogger Matt Singer commented on-line on CriticWire: "Chase made *The Sopranos* on television and he was more than accepted; his ideas and intelligence practically revolutionized the entire medium. Then he moved to film, bringing the same level of sophistication and nuance, and what happened? Nobody cared. I still love film. But the fact that a genius can have so much success in one medium and so little in the other is deeply discouraging—and maybe very telling about the state of adult storytelling in both industries" (April 30, 2013).

After *The Sopranos,* HBO had signed David Chase to develop a miniseries beginning in the silent film era, a "Hollywood epic" to be called *Ribbon of Dreams.* The project has been in gestation since 2009.

Further Reading:

(London) *Daily Mail,* Dec. 17, 2012

Entertainment Weekly Jan. 15, 1999, Jan. 7, 2000, with photos; indiewire.com/criticwire, Apr. 30, 2013

New York Times E p1+ Jan. 11, 2000, with photos, E p1+ Feb. 28, 2001, with photo, C p1+ Jul. 16, 2001, with photo, AR p1 Dec. 5, 2012

Salon Jan. 20, 1999

(New Jersey) *Star-Ledger,* Entertainment, Apr. 30, 2013

TV Guide p42 Feb. 6, 1999, with photos

Peter Biskind, "An American Family," *Vanity Fair,* 2007, with photos by Annie Leibovitz

Vanity Fair, "The Family Hour: An Oral History of *The Sopranos*" (April 2012), with photo by Leibovitz

Books:

Thomas Fahy, ed., *Considering David Chase: Essays on the Rockford Files, Northern Exposure, and the Sopranos* (McFarland, 2008)

Brett Martin, *Difficult Men: Behind the Scenes of a Creative Revolution* (Penguin, 2013)

Brett Martin, *The Sopranos: The Complete Book* (Time Inc. Home Entertainment, 2007)

Selected Feature Films:

as writer

Scream of the Wolf, 1974

as co-writer

Grave of the Vampire, 1972; *Kounterfeit,* 1996

as writer, director, and co-producer

Not Fade Away, 2012

Selected Television Shows or Films

as story editor and consultant

Kolchak: The Night Stalker, 1974–75

as writer and co-producer

The Rockford Files, 1976–80

Off the Minnesota Strip, 1980

as director

Almost Grown, 1988

as co-director

Alfred Hitchcock Presents, 1985

as co-executive producer

Northern Exposure, 1990–95

as producer

I'll Fly Away, 1991–93

The Rockford Files: Crime and Punishment, 1996

as writer, executive producer, and co-director

The Sopranos, 1999–2007

Coddington, Grace

Fashion magazine director

Born: 1941, Wales, United Kingdom

Grace Coddington "is easily the world's most influential fashion editor, famous for transforming photographic spreads into narratives, a signature she pioneered in the 1970s at British *Vogue,*" Nadia Mustafa wrote for *Time* (September 8, 2003). For more than four decades, Coddington has worked all over the world with the fashion industry's top models and photographers to create memorable fashion images. After a successful career as a model in London, England, during the 1960s—she was known as "the Cod"—Coddington spent 19 years at the British edition of *Vogue,* a glossy fashion magazine based in London, where, in time, she became creative director. She left British *Vogue* in 1987 to become design director for Calvin Klein. Since 1988 she has held the title of fashion (or creative) director of the U.S. edition of *Vogue.* According to Mustafa, Coddington's signature aesthetic style is marked by a "witty, modern romanticism that makes readers feel they are flipping through a picture book instead of just looking at shots of models in pretty clothing." The designer Karl Lagerfeld told Sarah Mower for style.com, that Coddington "has the highest taste of modernity. She never, ever fell for a cheap trend." Speaking with Colin McDowell of the London *Sunday Times* (August 4, 2002), Anna Wintour, the editor of U.S. *Vogue,* said, "Grace has a body of work unmatched by any other fashion editor, because she has the best eye in the business. She can sense a trend before the designers have an inkling of what's going on." "I like fairy tales, and I like dreaming," Coddington told Nadia Mustafa. "I try to weave the reality into a dream. When readers pick up *Vogue,* I want them to smile. Everything should be a little tongue in cheek, a little dare-to-go-there." Coddington's honors include the 2002 Lifetime Achievement Award of the Council of Fashion Designers of America and the British Fashion Awards's 2009 Isabella Blow Award for Fashion Creator.

Very well known in fashion circles, Coddington was introduced to a wider public in *The September Issue,* a documentary film by R. J. Cutler (2009) that chronicled the production of the September 2007 issue of *Vogue,* which at 840 pages became the largest it had ever published and is still unsurpassed in advertising pages. The film gained much of its dramatic interest from the "forceful"—Coddington's word—creative tension between Wintour and Coddington, who had furiously resisted the filming but acceded when Wintour insisted, telling Coddington, "They really are coming to film your shoot. They are going to film your run-through, and this time you cannot get out of it." Coddington recounts this conversation in her *Grace: A Memoir* (2012), which she wrote with Michael Roberts (since 2006, fashion and style director at *Vanity Fair*), Coddington had earlier edited *Grace: Thirty Years of Fashion at Vogue* (2002) with Roberts, and, with her life partner Didier Malige and Roberts, *The Catwalk Cats* (2006), a charming book about her feline companions consisting largely of her whimsical sketches.

Education and Early Career

Pamela Rosalind Grace Coddington was born in Wales on April 20, 1941, and was raised on the remote Welsh island of Anglesey, where her parents ran a small hotel called Tre-Arddur Bay Hotel. She had an elder sister, Rosemary. As a youngster, one of her teachers wrote of her, as quoted by Colin McDowell, "Grace has a sweet way of getting her own will." During her early years she read British *Vogue,* which she would order from the local store in her hometown. "For me, the magazine represented an amazing fantasy world of sophistication and grown-ups," she recalled to Mark Holgate for the *New York* magazine Web site newyorkmetro.com. "I dreamt of getting away from the tiny place I was raised." When Coddington was 18, she moved to London, which, she told Holgate, she imagined "would be full of these amazing-looking women. ... I remember thinking that if I ever got to be one of those women, it would change everything. That was my dream—it was always my desire to be an incredibly elegant woman."

For a while Coddington supported herself as a waitress. She also took classes at a modeling school run by Cherry Marshall, a former model, where she was told that she had little chance of success in that field, because she did not have blond hair and was "not very pretty," as she recalled to Holgate. Nevertheless, in 1959 she won first prize in the category "Young Idea" in a modeling contest sponsored by British *Vogue*. The contest brought her to the attention of the photographer Norman Parkinson, who was, according to the Staley Wise Gallery (staleywise.com), the "preeminent fashion photographer in Great Britain from the late 30s until his death in 1990." Thanks to Parkinson, she soon found herself in demand as a model. Along with such icons of 1960s fashion as Jean Shrimpton and Twiggy, she became a fixture of the celebrity and fashion jet set of the time, whose members included the Beatles, the Rolling Stones, Vidal Sassoon, and Mary Quant. Coddington became a "Mary Quant girl," which she herself attributes (at Voguepedia) to having the famous Sassoon "five-point" haircut Quant herself sported. Anna Wintour recalled to Holgate that Coddington was a "huge celebrity in that world, an incredible beauty. I was in awe of her."

According to Coddington, although she was "never pretty," as she put it to Colin McDowell, she became popular because in those days, models had to supply their own shoes, belts, jewelry, and other accessories (as well as style their own hair and apply their own makeup), and she had "good accessories. I was always nosy about fashion and wanted to have the newest thing." Vidal Sassoon told Holgate that "with Coddington's bone structure, and that sense of herself, she had something beyond beauty." The late fashion editor Liz Tilberis, who worked with Coddington as a young *Vogue* intern, wrote in her memoir, *No Time to Die* (1998), "I can say without the prejudice of friendship that she was one of the greats, not in terms of mere beauty but because of the interpretive powers that enabled her to engage in the photographs on a level few models ever reach. Her face and posture could reflect haughty insolence, mischievous decadence, or serene come-hitherness, and her chameleon looks had expressed the myriad phases of fashion so successfully, you often had to look twice at a photo to check whether or not it was her." Coddington's looks were marred temporarily during the early 1960s, when she was involved in a car accident—her Cooper Mini was tossed on its side by football hooligans—that left her with a severed eyelid. Plastic surgery successfully repaired the damage.

In 1969 Coddington was hired by Beatrix Miller, editor of British *Vogue*, to join the staff as a junior fashion editor. In the conviction that she needed a change in her life, she abandoned modeling and quickly established herself as both capable and creative in the photographic side of print journalism. Norman Parkinson again served as her mentor. In 1976 she was named senior fashion editor, and in the early 1980s, fashion director. Among other tasks, a fashion director's job entails making many of a magazine's fashion and story decisions jointly with the publication's chief editor, selecting the photographer and models for specific layouts, and then, while acting as a kind of producer and inspirational guide during the actual photo shoots, ensuring that the photographer expresses in his or her photos the magazine's fashion ideas. Like film and theater, fashion photography is a collaborative effort, in this case between the fashion director, the photographer, the stylists, the models, and the hair and makeup artists, among others. While at British *Vogue*,

Coddington developed a fashion-spread style that was to become her trademark: the narrative epic, in which the photographs tell a story and are often set in vast open locales, such as cornfields, deserts, and bodies of water. Vicki Goldberg, in the *New York Times* (November 14, 1993), wrote that Coddington's work was informed by a "mild dose of poetic lyricism and so strong a devotion to good photographs that the picture occasionally upstages the clothes." "She is especially partial to gardens," Goldberg added. Glenn Belverio wrote for the on-line fashion magazine Hint (Summer 2002) that Coddington's style "veers from bucolic Puritanism (models schlepping hay in Amish fields) to pop posturing (a stripped-to-the-waist Puff Daddy leering at a couture-clad Kate Moss)." Regarding her job as creative director, Coddington told Holgate, "Of course, choosing the clothes to shoot is part of it, but it's also much more than that. It's playing with everyone's personalities and making sure that everything is jelling. When I'm on top of a mountain with a photographer who doesn't want to shoot something because it doesn't look sexy, and the magazine wants it in the issue—at that point, I'm the one who has to keep everyone motivated."

During her nearly two decades at British *Vogue,* Coddington helped to coordinate fashion shoots with such well-known photographers as David Bailey, Helmut Newton, Sarah Moon, Arthur Elgort, and Guy Bourdin. She was renowned for her perfectionism and her vision, to which she typically held fast. Her refusal to compromise, she told Holgate, is "the secret to my career: If you give in, you don't get perfection. I don't get close to perfection now, really," she continued, "but if you give in, then you'll never get anywhere near it." She also became famous for her ability to anticipate the next fashion trend. As Liz Tilberis wrote, "She could transform her personal style thoroughly and instantaneously—flowing robes would be replaced almost overnight by sculptural Yves Saint Laurent pantsuits, her long red hair suddenly chopped off and dyed punk blond—and it was guaranteed that any new look, no matter how radical and unimaginable, was a premonition of the next fashion wave, that a year down the road, everyone would be wearing it."

Later Career

The designer Calvin Klein told Holgate that Coddington was the "first European fashion editor to appreciate American design." In 1986 Klein asked Coddington to work with him. She accepted his offer, and in 1987 she moved to the United States, where she served as a design director for Calvin Klein Collection for a year. Coddington told Holgate, "He taught me so much about living in America. But I missed being all over the place"—that is, on location for photo shoots—"and seeing a lot of different people." "In the end," Klein told Holgate, "her passion was for working with photographers and doing her stories." In an article in the *New York Times* (August 20, 2009) about the making of *The September Issue,* R. J. Cutler seconded this view: "This woman's career is defined by extraordinary collaborations with photographers."

In 1988 Anna Wintour, the newly appointed editor of U.S. *Vogue,* hired Coddington as the magazine's creative director. The two had worked together at British *Vogue,* and while they sometimes clashed, they shared a deep respect for each other's talents. "I was over the moon when she came to the magazine," Wintour told Holgate. "Her vision was and is very close to mine." Before every photo shoot, Coddington told Holgate, "[we] have this game of pushing each other as far as we can. I would say, 'Why do we have to go through this every time?' But it's crucial to do it; it's that process which makes a story work really well." Tilberis summed up what she termed the "classic dilemma" between the two: "Grace was always going for the look, and Anna was always [going] for the reader." In an interview with Jay Fielden about the making of *The September Issue* (posted at the Voguepedia Web site), Coddington commented, "A lot of people say Anna's the business one and I'm the creative one. It's not true. She's the creative one. So many of the shoots

I do start with her ideas. She was the creative director of *Vogue* before I was, after all. I also believe that everyone needs an editor. What she does is edit and make my work stronger."

In 1993 a photographic retrospective of Coddington's work, entitled "Short Stories: 25 Years of Vogue Fashion by Grace Coddington," was held at the James Danziger Gallery in New York City. The exhibit included 375 pictures by 30 photographers. In a review for the *New York Times* (November 14, 1993), entitled "Fashion Imagery That Can Upstage the Clothes," Vicki Goldberg noted that the show, apparently the first of its kind, "[paid] tribute to a fashion director's influence not just on fashion but on photography." "Nothing could be better" for a "behind the scenes view of a fashion editor at work," Cathy Horyn wrote of the exhibit for the *Washington Post* (November 21, 1993).

"I try to weave the reality into a dream. When readers pick up *Vogue*, I want them to smile. Everything should be a little tongue in cheek, a little dare-to-go-there."

Coddington and her work are the subjects of *Grace: Thirty Years of Fashion at Vogue* (2002), which had a list price of $120 and sold out within months of its publication. Weighing more than 10 pounds and measuring 14.5 x 11.2 x 2.5 inches, the 408-page book was edited by Coddington and Michael Roberts (then *The New Yorker*'s fashion editor), both of whom served as art directors for the project, and offers forewords by Anna Wintour and Karl Lagerfeld. Included are pictures taken by many of the photographers with whom Coddington collaborated, among them David Bailey, Helmut Newton, Cecil Beaton, Sarah Moon, Sheila Metzner, Herb Ritts, Mario Testino, Annie Leibovitz, Ellen von Unwerth, and Bruce Weber. Sarah Mower wrote that the book is a "record of [Coddington's] working life" and tells "stories about the love affair between clothes, girls and the camera."

In 2007 the filmmaker R. J. Cutler persuaded Anna Wintour to allow him access to *Vogue*'s offices in order to make a documentary about the fashion industry. Originally, according to Coddington's memoir, Cutler intended to focus on the process of organizing the Metropolitan Museum of Art's Costume Institute gala. Instead the film became something larger as Cutler explored the intense creative pressures involved in putting together an important issue of a magazine that aspires to raise high fashion to the level of art. Coddington speculates that Wintour agreed to the filming in order to counter the portrayal of fashion as superficial and "utterly ridiculous," in, for example, *The Devil Wears Prada,* a film that particularly irritates her.

Critics found the narrative heart of the *The September Issue* in the creative dynamic between Coddington and Wintour. Of the film Coddington wrote in her memoir, "to my mind the point of it was to show the creative push and pull of the way Anna and I work together." The memoir was undertaken, as she wrote in its introduction, after the response to the film revealed to her that "maybe I had a larger story to tell."

Coddington is quiet and reserved," according to Michael Holgate, "her cool demeanor shot through with a dry wit and a self-deprecating sense of humor. …Yet she's also blessed with what her friend Michael Roberts … called 'the personality of a Bronte heroine; she has this absolute will, a quiet determination.'" In 1998 Liz Tilberis wrote, "To outsiders, Grace was and still is an enigma—elusive, severe, silent. If she rates you as someone who understands fashion, the beautiful statue becomes animated, and you are drowned in an eloquent runaway monologue about the color purple or a pinstripe. But if Grace dismisses you as unworthy of her commentary, you might as well be part of the wallpaper. This air of detachment and the impact of her presence as a fashion icon make her terrifying, even to this day." "With her mane of red hair, pallid complexion and pale eyes, there is something of the medieval penitent about Coddington," Colin McDowell wrote. After the release of *The September Issue,* Coddington seemed considerably more open to interviewers, yet some commentators thought that she remained reticent about certain aspects of her personal life and about her colleagues at *Vogue* and in the fashion industry generally.

Said to love "all things feline," in Holgate's words, Coddington has long been partial to Chartreux cats. Her marriages to the restaurateur Michael Chow and the photographer Willie Christie ended in divorce. For some years in the 1970s and early 1980s, she raised her nephew, Tristan, after the death in 1973 of his mother, her sister Rosemary. She lives with her partner, the hairstylist Didier Malige, and maintains homes in New York City and Wainscott, New York, on Long Island.

Further Reading:

Hint Summer 2002

Huffington Post Dec. 16, 2012

New York p126+ Aug. 26-Sep. 2, 2002, with photos

New York Times II p39+ Nov. 14, 1993, with photos, Aug. 20, 2009, with photos and a clip from *The September Issue*

the *New Yorker* Aug. 31, 2009

Time Sep. 9, 2003, with photo

Vogue p190+ Nov. 1993, with photo, p638+ Sep. 2002, with photo

Voguepedia, www.vogue.com

Books:

Vogue: The Editor's Eye, ed. by Eve MacSweeney, with an introduction by Hamish Bowles (Abrams, 2012)

Selected Books:

Coddington, Grace, Michael Roberts, and Jay Fielden, eds., *Grace: Thirty Years of Fashion at Vogue,* 2002

Coddington, Grace, Didier Malige, and Michael Roberts, *The Catwalk Cats,* 2006

Coddington, Grace, with Michael Roberts, *Grace: A Memoir,* 2012

Langhart Cohen, Janet

President and CEO of communications firm

Born: 1942, Indianapolis, Indiana, United States

Although Janet Langhart Cohen had previously had glamorous jobs in modeling, television, and media consulting, she readily acknowledges that one of the most important positions she has ever held was an unofficial one. In the late 1990s, as the wife of Secretary of Defense William S. Cohen, she became known as the "First Lady of the Pentagon." While the title didn't entail many clearly defined duties, Langhart Cohen took it upon herself to become an outspoken advocate for U.S. military personnel and their families, making it her mission to improve their living conditions and boost their morale. "[Military personnel] don't want very much," she told Lynn Norment of *Ebony* (November 2000). "They just want to know that people care, that they are interested in their lives and making sure they have what they need to survive." After the Clinton Administration left office, Langhart Cohen remained an influential voice in Washington, speaking out on hate crimes motivated by racial and gender discrimination. Calling for national reconciliation, she cited her own life experience as a black woman married to a white man whose background was very different from her own. She wrote two memoirs, including one with her husband, and she also embarked on a career as a playwright with *Anne and Emmett* (2009), which explores the tragic consequences of hatred.

Education and Early Career

Langhart Cohen was born Janet Leola Floyd on December 22, 1940, and was raised in a housing project in Indianapolis. (She retains the name Langhart from a short-lived first marriage that ended when she was in her 20s.) Her father, Sewell Bridges, left her mother, a hospital-ward secretary, when Langhart Cohen was young. She has an older sister who became a homemaker, and a younger brother who became a Xerox executive. The family's Indianapolis neighborhood was segregated, as were the schools Langhart Cohen attended until she went to college, at Butler University (1960–1962), on a scholarship. She credits her mother with teaching her to rise above discrimination. When Langhart Cohen was six years old, she and her mother were once denied service in a diner. In an interview with Eric Strauss for abcNEWS.com (April 28, 2000), Langhart Cohen recalled that in response to the incident, her mother told her, "There are people in this country who won't like you because you're colored. But you must never use color to measure them." As soon as Langhart Cohen was financially able, she purchased a home for her mother and convinced her to retire.

Langhart Cohen is an African American, but, she told Chuck Conconi of the *Washingtonian* (June 1994), "a lot of white gentlemen visited the slave quarters, [and] I also have connections to Native American blood." Almost always described as strikingly beautiful, she began her career competing in beauty pageants and modeling, most notably for the Ebony Fashion Fair, an annual production known for featuring extravagant designer clothing. (Its proceeds fund various scholarships and charitable organizations.) Her modeling poise soon landed her a position as a weekend weather girl at a Chicago television station, Channel 26 News, as well as a weekday position as host of her own program, *Indy People,* on WBBM-TV, the Indianapolis affiliate of CBS.

Langhart Cohen's television career encompassed stints as an anchorwoman, correspondent, and talk-show host. Eventually she appeared on several major networks, including ABC, CBS, NBC, and Black Entertainment Television, for the last of which she co-hosted the program *America's Black Forum* with civil rights leader Julian Bond. Thereafter she simultaneously took on two BET programs, *On Capitol Hill with Janet Langhart* and *Personal Diary,* which profiled notable African Americans. In 1975 she became the first African American to host a nationally syndicated show when ABC's "Good Morning," formerly a Boston regional offering, went national. She suffered

a slight setback in 1987, when she was fired from a Boston station "for refusing to pick lottery numbers," as Kevin Merida reported for the *Washington Post* (December 14, 1997). Referring to Vanna White, an assistant on the game show *Wheel of Fortune,* who was often derided for being decorative rather than talented, Langhart Cohen quipped that she refused to become "Vanna Black." Some observers have theorized that she would be as well known as Barbara Walters or Diane Sawyer were it not for the preconceived notions about black women held by white television executives. "She is … very forthright and very strong, and I think over the years that has presented problems to people who would expect her to be compliant or needy, subservient," her husband told Merida. "Obviously, there are many stories I could tell [about racism in the TV industry], and she could tell even more, but she is not complaining about it."

Langhart first met William Cohen, a Republican senator from Maine, in 1974, when she interviewed him about a book of poetry he had written. They kept in touch occasionally throughout the 1970s and 1980s. After Cohen's divorce from his first wife, in 1987, and the 1990 suicide of Langhart's second husband (Robert W. Kistner, a prominent gynecologist from whom she was estranged), the pair became close friends and eventually started dating, despite their many differences. Cohen was a white Republican, quiet and literary; Langhart was a black Democrat (she worked on Michael Dukakis's 1988 presidential campaign) who loved entertaining and going to gala affairs. After their wedding, on Valentine's Day 1996, they expected to retire from public life; Cohen had decided not to seek a fourth senate term. When he was offered the position of secretary of defense in President Bill Clinton's second-term cabinet, however, he couldn't refuse.

Later Career

Once Cohen moved his professional life into the Pentagon, Langhart Cohen soon followed, setting up an office down the hall from her husband. She accompanied him on many of his foreign trips and relished the opportunity to meet members of the American armed forces as well as various heads of state. "Janet is perhaps the most actively engaged first lady of the Pentagon, ever," Cohen explained to Norment. "She has committed herself with a passion I think is unrivaled by anyone. And she feels deeply about the men and women we are serving." During her tenure at the Pentagon, Langhart Cohen, whose style has been described as "part Eleanor Roosevelt and part Oprah Winfrey," tried to give American military personnel a greater voice in how the American government cares for them and their families. Her foremost achievement in this regard was organizing and hosting the Military Family Forum, which gathered enlisted personnel and some military spouses in Washington to talk about quality-of-life issues such as health care, salaries, and educational opportunities for their children. "I found that there were many things I heard that maybe Bill wouldn't hear," she told Linda D. Kozaryn of the American Forces Press Service (December 8, 1999). "I hear stories because I'm listening and asking questions like a journalist."

Hearkening back to her days as a broadcast journalist, she debuted the weekly television show *Special Assignment,* in 1998; the program, featuring Langhart Cohen's interviews with prominent Americans, was seen by troops around the world, and it spotlighted President Bill Clinton in the first installment. Together Cohen and Langhart Cohen created the annual Pentagon Pops, a musical salute to the military, at which

Medal of Honor recipients were recognized. In addition, they hosted the Secretary of Defense Annual Holiday Tour, which sent singers, comedians, and other entertainers on a whirlwind tour of overseas military installations just prior to the winter holidays. In a December 1999 DefenseLINK interview with Linda D. Kozaryn, Langhart Cohen explained her allegiance to those serving in the military: "I'm impressed with their dedication, their commitment—that they're willing to put their lives on the line for so little in terms of compensation, but for the values that we stand for. ... They're all heroes to me."

For a time Langhart Cohen had run her own consulting firm, teaching corporate executives how to improve their media images. In early 2000, anticipating her departure from the Pentagon at the end of the Clinton administration, she worked for a time as a senior marketing consultant with Rowan & Blewitt, Inc., a crisis- and issue-management firm (recusing herself, however, from any business having to do with the Defense Department). She was a member of the board of the nonprofit United Service Organizations (USO), which lends morale and welfare support to U.S. military personnel and their families, until November 2000.

Secretary Cohen served until George W. Bush was inaugurated as president in January 2001. After leaving office he founded the Cohen Group, an international business consulting firm. Langhart Cohen resumed her career as a communications consultant as founder and CEO of Langhart Communications, which offers "media training" and counsels clients, especially those in the public eye, on media relations and maintaining an effective public presence. The firm's clients include CEOs, politicians, and philanthropists, among others who must become adept at public speaking and making presentations.

"I found that there were many things I heard that maybe Bill wouldn't hear. ... I hear stories because I'm listening and asking questions like a journalist."

She continued to advocate for members of the military and their families and to take an active interest in public affairs, especially issues of racial and gender equality. On June 25, 2009, she offered brief testimony before the Senate Judiciary Committee in support of the Matthew Shepard Hate Crimes Prevention Act of 2009. In her testimony she revealed that before she was born, a cousin of hers had been lynched. She also noted that only two weeks earlier, a black police officer had been murdered by a white supremacist at the Holocaust Museum, where her play *Anne and Emmett* was to premiere that evening; her husband had been just 30 feet away from the shooting scene. Langhart Cohen characterized her play for the committee as an "imaginary conversation between two tragic victims of hate, Anne Frank and Emmett Till."

Langhart Cohen wrote poignantly on the subject of hate and its corrosive effects in her well-received memoir *From Rage to Reason: My Life in Two Americas,* written with Alexander Kopelman and published in 2004. In it she recounts her trajectory from the segregated Indianapolis projects to successful careers in modeling, television journalism, and business, and then to marriage to a white senator and the heights of the Clinton Administration. Early in her career she established friendships with Martin Luther King Jr. and other civil rights activists, such as Dick Gregory; King deemed her "too angry" to participate in the March on Washington. Gradually she learned to transcend her anger and channel her passion constructively. In *Love in Black and White: A Memoir of Race, Religion, and Romance*, William S. Cohen and Janet Langhart Cohen turned a similarly unsparing yet inspiring eye on their marriage, which, as Cohen noted in his preface, violated the social taboos with which they both had been raised. In July 2008 Cohen and Langhart Cohen convened a conference in Washington, DC, in order to "further a national conversation about the need for truth, tolerance, and reconciliation"; they edited the conference proceedings, which were published in 2009 as *Race and Reconciliation in America.*

Langhart Cohen regularly contributes commentary to the Huffington Post's political blog. In July 2013, in the wake of the acquittal on murder charges of George Zimmerman—the shooter of Trayvon Martin, an unarmed African American teenager—Langhart Cohen wrote a much-discussed op-ed article for the *Washington Post* urging President Barack Obama to step forward and articulate the pain and "quiet rage" in the African American community prompted by the verdict—"to talk boldly and truthfully about race and racism and why it still matters in the United States," as she put it. Three days later the president did just that, saying, "Trayvon Martin could have been me 35 years ago. And when you think about why … there's a lot of pain around what happened here, I think it's important to recognize that the African-American community is looking at this issue through a set of experiences and a history that—that doesn't go away." Some commentators expressed the view that Langhart Cohen's appeal had prompted the president's remarks. Langhart Cohen herself suggested to Vanessa Williams (*Washington Post,* July 20, 2013) that it may have been the "grace and grief" of Martin's parents that moved the president to speak, adding that, as Williams recounts, "by sharing his personal experiences with discrimination and calling on Americans to 'do some soul searching' about their own attitudes, Obama had 'elevated the conversation' about race."

Further Reading:

DefenseLINK Dec. 8, 1999

Ebony p154+ Nov. 2000 (with photos)

Washington Post F p1 Dec. 14, 1997 (with photos), Jul. 20, 2013

Washingtonian p58+ June 1994 (with photos)

Selected Books:

Langhart Cohen, Janet, with Alexander Kopelman, *From Rage to Reason: My Life in Two Americas,* 2004)

Langhart Cohen, Janet, with William S. Cohen, *Love in Black and White: A Memoir of Race, Religion, and Romance,* 2007

William S. Cohen and Janet Langhart Cohen, eds., *Race and Reconciliation in America,* 2009.

Selected Plays:

Anne and Emmett, 2009

Selected Articles:

"After Zimmerman Verdict, Obama Needs to Speak about Racism,"

Washington Post (July 16, 2013)

Dé, Shobhaa

Indian writer, television personality

Born: 1948, Maharashtra, India

Shobhaa Dé established herself as India's most commercially successful English-language author with a series of steamy novels that often drew comparisons to the work of the American writer Jackie Collins. She was widely denounced in her traditionally conservative country, where the graphic depictions of sex in her work earned her such nicknames as the "Maharani of Muck." Much of the criticism was aimed at the way women in her novels are portrayed. "Her women characters come out on top through sex or manipulation. It's just soft porn," Rita Dewan, a professor of gender economics at a university in Mumbai, told Miranda Kennedy for the *Nation* (May 27, 2004). Dé defended her female characters, describing them as strong and not just sexual. "The women in my books are definitely not doormats. They're not willing to be kicked around," she told Ajay Singh in an interview for *Asiaweek* (February 28, 1997).

Even Dé's harshest critics, however, could not disregard the impact she had on India's female population. "Writing about somebody dropping a sari and having an orgasm doesn't mean you're striking big notes for women," the film critic Shubra Gupta told Kennedy, "But she is India's first and only glamorous female brand name, and that means something." Ultimately, Dé was less concerned by reviewers' remarks than she was about her audience. "I think I know my readers better than the critics know them," she told Samita Bhatia for the Kolkata (Calcutta), India, *Telegraph* (February 26, 2005). Dé 's books have consistently appeared at the top of India's best-seller lists, and in 2003 she was named by Penguin India (now a division of Penguin Random House) as part of its 10,000 Club, for authors whose books have sold more than 10,000 copies each. In 2010 Dé was given her own imprint, Shobhaa Dé Books, at Penguin India. Dé's huge readership, not only for her novels but for her nonfiction books and her newspaper columns and blogs, has made her a force to be reckoned with in India.

Education and Early Career

Shobha Rajadhyaksha was born on January 7, 1948, in Maharashtra, India. The youngest of four children in a middle-class family, she was raised in Bombay (known as Mumbai after 1996) from the age of eight. Her father was a bureaucrat who was based in Delhi for many years. She attended Queen Mary School and St. Xavier's College, a Jesuit school Mumbai, from which she graduated with a degree in psychology. Upon graduation she decided to begin modeling. Although her conservative parents were opposed to her career choice, she succeeded in mollifying them with her promises that she would not dress in revealing outfits, pose with male models, or do anything to embarrass the family. By the time she was 21, she had risen to the top ranks of the modeling world. After a few years of modeling, however, she began working—at first as a copywriter—for Hira's Creative Unit, an advertising agency founded by the publishing tycoon Nari Hira. In 1970 Hira offered her the position of editor of *Stardust* magazine, despite her lack of editorial experience. Patterned after Hollywood gossip publications, *Stardust* reported on the rich and famous in Bollywood, as India's film industry is known. As an editor she popularized the use of "Hinglish," characterized in the *New York Times* (October 29, 2007) as a "heady, irreverent mix of Hindi (India's national language) and English (also recognized as one of the Indian language) that spoke to readers in an entirely new way." Following her ten-year stint at *Stardust,* she moved to another gossip magazine, *Society,* in the same capacity. In 1982 she launched *Celebrity,* an Indian version of the British magazine *Hello!,* which was itself an offshoot of the famous Spanish publication *Hola!*.

After a failed first marriage to Sudhir Kilachand, she married the widower Dilip Dé, a Bombay-based shipping mogul of Bengali origin, shortly after meeting him at a party in1984. "Dilip proposed to me in just ten minutes," she told Singh. "I made up my mind in four days." A year after their marriage, she sold *Celebrity.* Drawing on her knowledge of Bollywood and Mumbai's high society, she continued to write for such newspapers as the *Times of India,* the *Statesman,* and the *Sunday Observer* while raising her six children (four boys and two girls—two from her first marriage, two from Dilip Dé's previous marriage, and the remaining two from her marriage with De).

"Live fearlessly—whether you are a man or a woman. Realise your potential and enjoy the world."

In 1988 Shobha Dé 's life changed dramatically with a knock at the door of her $3 million penthouse overlooking the Arabian Sea. As she recounted to Singh, "There was this hunk of a man standing there. He asked me to write a nonfiction book about Bombay." The man turned out to be David Davidar, then the editor and publisher of the Penguin Group's Indian division. Dé reluctantly agreed to the project, and within three and a half months, she had completed not a nonfiction work but a novel, written in longhand at her kitchen table. "I was like a woman possessed. I just wrote and wrote until it was done," she told Singh. The work, her first novel, was called *Socialite Evenings* (1989). For the setting of its tale of a middle-class girl's rise into Bombay's high society, Dé drew on her own social circle. The book became an instant best-seller among the urban middle class in her native country, selling 40,000 copies, a considerable triumph by Indian standards. (At the time, in India, publishers of English-language novels broke even financially once 2,000 copies of a book were sold.) Dé was criticized, however, for writing graphically about sex and adultery. In an article in the *New York Times* (January 17, 1993), Edward A. Gargan quoted the freelance journalist Geeta Doctor (writing in *the Indian Review of Books*), as commenting that "Penguin India, who have published Ms. Dé 's books, should feel proud of themselves. Instead of merely aiming to produce good literature as we have been led to expect, they have decided to put themselves in the service of the country, masturbating the nation." The article also included comments by Dilip Roate of the *Economic Times* describing Dé's writing as "coarse, without class." He complained, "The two or three scenes of the kind that are described by mental juveniles as 'torrid' are narrated with the elegance of a bullying lout bragging about his conquests." Dé countered, telling Gargan, "It wasn't that explicit. It explored adultery, women walking out of marriages because they were bored. People found that shocking."

Some critics, including male members of Bombay's high society, were also less than enthusiastic about Dé 's second novel, *Starry Nights* (1991; reprinted in 2007 as *Bollywood Nights*). The reviewer S. Nihal Singh was quoted in the *Chicago Tribune* (February 7, 1993) as saying of the novel's protagonist, "We have a heroine, of the films and of the novel, who lives on a diet of men for breakfast, lunch and dinner, and sometimes in between." The book was groundbreaking for its unflinching look at India's film industry and its portrayal of a strong, sexual female protagonist. Miranda Kennedy wrote, "*Starry Nights* provided the first long-form, unflattering portrait of Bollywood. … The Hindi film industry, far more than Hollywood, has been reluctant to expose its dirty underbelly, because it relies heavily on family-oriented films and the pristine image of virgin stars. Dé has made it one of her life's missions to blow a hole in those perceptions." *Sisters* (1992), Dé's follow-up to *Starry Nights,* focused on the battle between two half-sisters for control of their father's industrial empire. In this novel Dé continued to explore strong, sexually liberated female characters, this time against the backdrop of big business.

Dé pushed the envelope even further with *Strange Obsession* (1994), broaching the subject of a love relationship between two female characters—a topic rarely encountered in South Asian literature and one considered taboo in Indian society. (Although rarely enforced, until July 2009 section 377 of the Indian penal code made any homosexual act illegal and punishable with life imprisonment; in August 2006 Dé joined many prominent Indians in petitioning the government of India to strike down the British-era law as a denial of fundamental human rights. In December 2013, however, India's Supreme Court ruled that the law had been improperly struck down, thereby restoring the ban.) Simran Bhargava wrote for the *New Delhi Pioneer* on January 9, 1993 (reprinted in the *New York Times,* January 17, 1993), "I couldn't ut down Shobha Dé's new book, *Strange Obsession.* And I didn't even like it."

Dé 's next two books prompted similarly mixed responses. In her fifth novel, *Sultry Days* (1995), set amid the world of journalism, Dé tackled the romance between a teenager and a man named God; *Second Thoughts* (1996) focused on a middle-class housewife trapped in an arranged marriage who enters into an adulterous relationship. Although many have characterized her books as second rate or nonliterary, Dé told Alexandre M. Barbosa for *Goa Today* magazine (January 1988), "I really don't care about labels and definitions. These are the books I have within me; they are the books I want to write and anybody is free to call it whatever they wish to. I don't like to categorise them. It is contemporary writing." The impact of her writing cannot be overlooked. A number of her books have been put on the syllabi of universities in the United Kingdom, the United States, and Australia as well as in India.

Dé ventured into the world of nonfiction with the release of her book *Surviving Men: The Smart Woman's Guide to Staying on Top* (1997), a radical departure from the sexual exploits depicted in her novels. The book, which explored the difficulties faced by women balancing careers and marriage in a male-dominated society, struck a chord with a large number of Indian women who were working outside the home. On a *Voice of America* program aired on January 23, 1997, Dé argued that the book was not an attempt to bash the opposite sex. "I believe Indian women have changed qualitatively, and are part of the modern world, and ready for the new millennium. But the Indian male is still in the 15th or 16th century, very medieval and refusing to be shaken out of this torpor." Dé next published *Speedpost: Letters to My Children about Living, Loving, Caring and Coping with the World* (1999), which touched on family values and adolescent anxieties, written in the form of a series of letters to her six children. "The letters were a literary device to raise certain issues. It was my way of marking [the new millenium]. And my kids loved it, too," she told Subha J. Rao for India's national newspaper the *Hindu* (February 10, 2003). The book found a large audience and was translated into Hindi; Marathi (spoken mainly in the Indian state of Maharashtra and in the central part of the country); Malayalam (spoken mainly in southwest India) and Gujarati (the official language of the Indian state of Gujarat on the country's west coast). Dé continued to distance herself from her pop-fiction work with her next effort, the autobiographical *Selective Memory: Stories from My Life* (1999), which Penguin India's David Davidar encouraged her to write. In it she openly discusses how she abandoned her first husband, a member of the wealthy Kilachand family, and her two eldest children, with whom she has since reconciled.

Later Career

In 2001 Dé chose to take a break from writing books. "At that time I felt the pressing need to slow down and to do different things," she told Samita Bhatia. She turned her attention to television and became a writer for the television serials *Swahbhimaan, Sukanya,* and *Lipstick.* She also conceptualized and wrote for the serial *Kittie Party,* which aired on Zee TV. Dé explained to Seema Pherwani, in an interview for *Indian Television* (October 20, 2004), "Television writing is an extremely stimulating experience for me. But it's all about being disciplined, as you have to write about eight to nine scenes for each episode." She also embraced her spiritual side in 2003, adding an extra *-a* to the end of her first name on the advice of a numerologist.

Dé's debut in front of the television cameras came in 2004 with the prime-time program *Power Trip,* which gave viewers an inside look into the lives of leading men and women in the corporate world. Besides her anchor duties, Dé was also responsible for the research, content, and look of the show, which was canceled after 28 episodes. She appeared in the documentary *Sunset Bollywood* (2005) and the five-part Italian television documentary series *Taccuino indiano* (2006, "Indian Notebook"), which introduced Italian viewers to the "constantly evolving reality" of India. Dé wrote the scripts for the television serial *Sarrkkar* (2005–2006), a political drama about a woman caught between family obligations and the power games thrust upon her by high-level politics. For some critics, the plot conception recalled the history of Prime Minister Indira Gandhi's family.

Dé returned from her self-imposed writing sabbatical with the release of the nonfiction work *Spouse: The Truth about Marriage* (2005), written in longhand on 11 lined notepads over the course of 8 months. "Other people watch birds, I watch marriages," she told Dilip Bobb for *India Today* (February 28, 2005). With this book Dé asserts that, despite the racy content of her novels, she considers herself a staunch traditionalist. "I am glad that I have cleared the confusion between real life and fiction. In real life, I have never been anything else but consistent," she said to Madhumita Bhattacharyya for the Kolkata, India, *Telegraph* (March 19, 2005). The book sold more than 10,000 copies in just three days and a record-breaking 22,000 copies in one month. Its success was attributed to the sharp increase in the number of divorces among young urban Indians—which was ultimately what spurred her to write the book. Unlike her earlier works, *Spouse: The Truth about Marriage* received favorable reviews from literary critics. As Bobb wrote, "There is the all-important issue of sex but again, she dissects this clinically, with intelligence and understanding. As someone who has performed a delicate balancing act between her career, husband, children, and friends, Dé is uniquely qualified to write on what makes a marriage work and what doesn't. She is quick to admit that this is not a how-to book and that there is no magic formula. Yet there is enough insight, examples and analyses, including self-analysis, that *Spouse* should be an essential wedding gift for all Indian couples."

Spouse was followed by a new work of fiction, *Snapshots* (2006), in De's familiar earlier vein. The novel deals with a reunion of six women who were school friends that descends into bitterness and shocking revelations.

Remarking that she herself was born in the year India became an independent nation, Dé reflected on modern India and its newfound prominence as an international power in *Superstar India* (2008). In *Sandhya's Secret* (2009) she embarked on a YA fiction series called Snappy Happy. *Shobhaa at Sixty: Secrets of Getting It Right at Any Age* (2010), intended, as she says in the book's preface, to show women how "to turn that dreaded number" (or any age at which they may have arrived) "into an advantage." "Longevity," she continued, "has no meaning if it is not coupled with wellness on all levels—physical, mental, emotional and spiritual." Dé returned to adult fiction (and steamy sex scenes) with *Sethji* (2012), a portrait of corrupt political culture.

Although Dé is not the first female novelist in India to write about sex, she is credited with taking sex out of the closet and making it an open topic of discussion among the women in her country. Despite the strong women's voices in her novels, Dé refuses to categorize the books as feminist works. "My books try to find ways that women can survive and cope in a world that's cruel to them," she told Kennedy. "But I tell stories in an entertaining format. I am not doing a Germaine Greer or Betty Friedan [noted feminists, Australian and American, respectively]. It's not just get up and fight for your rights; it is more sly and subversive." Dé advised women not to allow themselves to be confined by conventional social expectations. In an interview for Vaahini, a networking forum for professional women, she told Shilpi Madan: "Every human being should follow a dream—without dreams we become sheep. Live fearlessly—whether you are a man or a woman. Realise your potential and enjoy the world."

As a consulting editor for fiction at Penguin India, Dé worked with interesting new writers and manuscripts; her emphasis was on first-time authors and women's fiction. Commenting on having her own Penguin imprint, which she called a "huge honor and responsibility," Dé explained to Madan, "This new role is an extension of what I had been doing. … The thought behind the co-publishing venture is to bring two established 'brands' together—mine and Penguin's. It is also a way to inject freshness into an existing imprint."

Dé's columns and blogs for the Mumbai *Times,* the *Sunday Times,* the *Week,* and *Asian Age* have a readership in the tens of millions each month. Madan noted that, "As the country's most widely read columnist today, Dé wields the power to shape and mobilise public opinion through her musings." Dé also influences public discourse through her Twitter following. In July 2013 her tweet suggesting that Mumbai could separate from the state of Maharashtra ("Maharashtra and Mumbai??? Why not? Mumbai has always fancied itself as an independent entity, anyway. This game has countless possibilities") raised a public furor. The tweet prompted virulent attacks from the leaders of two of India's political parties, demonstrations at her home, and even what was viewed as a personal physical threat against her from a Congress Party MP. Dé dismissed the attacks as pre-election publicity ploys, saying that her tweet was purely satirical (in light of the announcement of the separation of Telangana from the state of Andhra Pradesh) and had been misconstrued, and that in fact she had not endorsed the idea of separation. "I suggest the political parties should concentrate on the potholes of Mumbai," she added.

Although Dé has generally enjoyed her celebrity status in India, one disturbing consequence was been the inordinate amount of attention paid to her by one specific fan—a woman who had been stalking her for 25 years before being arrested in May 2005.

Dé still prefers to write her columns and books in longhand form, from her home. "I love the feel of pen on paper. I have to see the work in my own writing to believe it is mine," she explained to Subha J. Rao. "Writing is a passion that I can never give up. The day things cease to excite, life is over. I don't want that to happen to me."

Further Reading:

Asiaweek Feb. 28, 1997

(Kolkata, India) *Telegraph* Feb. 26, 2005

Hindu Feb. 10, 2003

India Today p85 Feb. 28, 2005

MiD DAY Jul. 31, 2013

Nation June 14, 2004

New York Times IX p3 Jan. 17, 1993, Oct. 29, 2007

Penguin Books India Web site

Vaahini (undated; c. 2010): http://www.accenture.com/.

Selected Books:

Fiction

Socialite Evenings, 1989

Starry Nights, 1991

Sisters, 1992

Strange Obsession, 1994

Sultry Days, 1995

Second Thoughts, 1996

Snapshots, 2006

Sandhya's Secret, 2009

Sethji, 2012.

Nonfiction

Surviving Men: The Smart Woman's Guide to Staying on Top, 1997

Speedpost: Letters to My Children about Living, Loving, Caring and Coping with the World, 1999

Selective Memory: Stories from My Life, 1999

Spouse: The Truth about Marriage, 2005

Superstar India, 2008

Shobhaa at Sixty, 2010

Deutsch, Linda

Courtroom reporter

Born: 1943, Perth Amboy, New Jersey, United States

"I am the eyes and ears of the public," the courtroom reporter Linda Deutsch said to Nancy Mills for Mills's Spirited Woman newsletter (December 2003). "I'm there to say what happened, not to give any opinions on why it happened or who's responsible. I am an unbiased observer. TV cameras are not always there, and even when they are, people do not sit and watch every minute, they depend on the reporter to sum up what happened. … I fill two notebooks a day and bring it down to a manageable size where people can know what was said, what was important, what's happened, and if possible, how it felt to be in the courtroom when all this happened. There are such dramatic moments that you have to talk about what it felt like to be there."

Deutsch has been on the staff of the Associated Press (AP) for nearly 50 years, and for much of that time, she has been ranked among the foremost American courtroom journalists of modern times. When she joined the AP—at which speed, accuracy, objectivity, fairness, and the ability to cover varied subjects are highly valued—Deutsch welcomed the rush of adrenaline that deadline pressures stirred in her. Her articles have appeared in newspapers and on Web sites worldwide, and her work has occasionally taken her overseas—for example, to Guam, in 1975, when she wrote about the fall of Saigon, the event that marked the end of the Vietnam War. Among the wide array of events she has witnessed, she is best known for her detailed, objective reporting on some of the most sensational, newsworthy, and influential trials of recent decades, including those of Sirhan Sirhan, Charles Manson, Patty Hearst, Angela Davis, Daniel Ellsberg, Lynette ("Squeaky") Fromme, Joseph Hazelwood (the skipper of the *Exxon Valdez*), the four Los Angeles police officers who beat Rodney King, John Z. DeLorean, Michael Jackson, Phil Spector, Robert Blake, and O. J. Simpson. At the end of Simpson's criminal trial, in 1994, the AP awarded Deutsch its Oliver Gramling Reporter Award for her outstanding work. Two years earlier the AP had named her a special correspondent, a title she shares with only 18 past and present AP journalists.

Patt Morrison, the president of the Los Angeles Press Club, described Deutsch to the PR Newswire (March 24, 2005) as an "irreplaceable and irreproachable source of information to the millions who read her reportage, truly free from spin or slant" and as a "supremely and scrupulously thorough, accurate, fair and honest reporter who has the respect and regard of both sides in any trial she covers—before, during and after." "I can't think of anything I would rather do," Deutsch told Michele Norris, who interviewed her for National Public Radio (January 15, 2007). "It's like being in a theater every day. It's like being in the front row seat to history. … No other beat offers this kind of access to human emotion. You get at the heart of what people are about. And I think that the murder trial, whether it has any historical significance or not, is always of interest because people wonder: Could I do that? And I sit there and have to listen to both sides, put the pieces together, and present them to an audience. It's the most exciting thing I can think that any reporter could do."

Education and Early Career

Linda C. Deutsch was born in 1943 in Perth Amboy, New Jersey. Her mother was a writer. Deutsch began writing poetry and prose at an early age. On her ninth birthday, she received her first typewriter, from her father (who died before she reached her teens). Her first attempt at reporting sprang from her interest in the rock-and-roll star Elvis Presley. "I got the idea that I could start an Elvis fan club and I could put out a newspaper," she told Lesley Visser of CBS News (August 15, 2002). "And that's what I did. I published the *Elvis Times,* which went all over the world." In 1958, while Presley was serving in the U.S. Army, thousands of people signed a petition that Deutsch had organized, urging Dick Clark, the host of the popular TV show *American Bandstand,* to promote his music. As she recounts in the *Huffington Post* (April 19, 2012), Deutsch presented the 16-foot-long petition to Clark on camera on Presley's twenty-fourth birthday, January 8, 1959. At about the same time, Deutsch began working for a local newspaper, the *Asbury Park Press,* writing a weekly column about area high schools and, occasionally, other subjects and events. One of her uncles, a newspaper editor in Southern California, encouraged her to take up journalism as a career, telling her that it was exciting and would offer a stable income and opportunities to meet many people.

Deutsch attended Monmouth University (then called Monmouth College), in West Long Branch, New Jersey, where she majored in journalism. "I was interested in history and the way social trends evolve," she told Nancy Mills. Bank loans and earnings from part-time jobs enabled her to pay for her tuition and expenses. Deutsch wrote for the campus weekly and spent her summers interning at local newspapers. In the summer of 1963, she worked the night shift at the *Evening News* in Perth Amboy, reporting on municipal meetings and gathering information for obituaries. One day that summer, she learned that a major civil rights march was to take place in Washington, DC, on August 28. Although she was eager to attend, she "wouldn't dare have had the guts to say something [to the editor]," as she recalled to John Hughes for the *Orange County* (California) *Register* (November 14, 1995). "So I left him a note saying I thought the march was something the paper should cover. He called me the next day and said, 'OK, if it won't cost us anything, you can go.'" Deutsch hitched a ride to Washington with members of the Perth Amboy branch of the NAACP (National Association for the Advancement of Colored People), and, with an estimated 250,000 others, she witnessed Martin Luther King Jr. giving his historic "I Have a Dream" speech in front of the Lincoln Memorial. The next day her account of the march appeared on the front page of the *Evening News.* "After you do something like that, there's no turning back," Deutsch told Michelle Sahn for the East Brunswick, New Jersey, *Home News Tribune* (July 8, 2004). "I knew then that journalism was my life." In November of that year, when John F. Kennedy was assassinated, she volunteered to help workers at the *Asbury Park Press* prepare articles for the next day's edition, as a way of conquering the helpless feeling she experienced after hearing of the president's death. Her assignment—to make a list of all the local businesses and services that would be closed the day of Kennedy's funeral—made clear to her the public-service aspect of journalism. "It gave us a role in history," Deutsch told Hughes. "It was so amazing to realize that we could do something."

After she earned a bachelor's degree, in 1965, Deutsch covered entertainment news for several New Jersey newspapers. In 1967 she moved to Los Angeles, in order to be close to Hollywood, where many such stories originated. After a brief stint with the San Bernardino *Sun,* she got a job as a general-assignment reporter with the Associated Press. According to Joe Strupp of *Editor & Publisher* (July 12, 2007), she was the only woman in the Los Angeles bureau's 20-person office. Founded in 1846, the AP is the oldest news-gathering organization in the world. It is now a not-for-profit cooperative owned by its American newspaper and broadcast members. Worldwide the AP, which is headquartered in New York City, has more than 3,200 staffers, almost two-thirds of whom are journalists; they work in more than 280 locations, including every statehouse in the United States. The AP maintains a television news service and the AP Radio Network (APRN); offers AP Mobile, an award-winning news app; and has a strong social media presence.

Whenever she could, Deutsch wrote about the entertainment industry, with the thought of making it her area of expertise. Along with many other AP reporters, she covered the assassination of Senator Robert F. Kennedy of New York, in June 1968, during his bid for that year's Democratic presidential nomination. Her assignment as a "backup" reporter at the trial of the senator's killer, Sirhan Sirhan, was her "first huge, huge story in the L.A. bureau [of the AP]," and, in leading her to decide on court reporting as her specialty, "it changed my life," as she told Michele Norris. Her decision was reinforced in 1970, when she became the AP's principal reporter during the highly publicized, sensational trial of the cult leader Charles Manson and several of his followers, who had murdered the actress Sharon Tate (the pregnant wife of the filmmaker Roman Polanski), four of her friends, and two others in 1969. Deutsch has referred to her experiences during the nine-month trial (1970–71) as her own "trial by fire." "It was exhausting, and it was mind-bending," Deutsch explained to Norris. "You lived in a different reality, because you were suddenly in this world of this commune that [Manson] ran." She told Hughes, "At some point I realized that [a courtroom trial] was the greatest theater in the world. This was true theater, the morality play for our times. ... And it is the one story [in journalism] that has a beginning, a middle and an end." Deutsch attended many of the hearings at which Susan Atkins, Leslie Van Houten, and Patricia Krenwinkel (the women convicted of murder in the Charles Manson trial) applied, unsuccessfully, for parole. (The women's death sentences were commuted to sentences of life imprisonment after California abolished the death penalty, in 1972; Atkins died in prison in 2009.)

During the Sirhan and Manson trials, Deutsch had many conversations with the highly respected trial reporter Theo Wilson of the *New York Daily News.* Wilson became her "mentor, teacher, sister, and best friend," as Deutsch told Jeff Baker for the *Oregonian* (April 12, 1997), and before long their peers began referring to them as "Thinda" or "the Snoop Sisters." From Wilson, Deutsch learned that good trial reporters are always the last people to leave the courtroom, pay close attention only to what is said inside the courtroom (on the witness stand, by the judge, and by the lawyers), disregard anything lawyers or others say outside it (which is often "spin"), and never make up their minds about defendants' guilt or innocence until the trials end. "Theo believed in observation and description," Deutsch told Baker. "She always said, 'Keep writing, no matter what, and don't leave the courtroom unless you have to file.'" As an example of what one might miss by not following that rule, Deutsch mentioned that during the Manson trial, while some reporters were smoking outside the courtroom, Manson "leaped at the judge with a pencil in his hand"—a notorious incident bound to interest many newspaper readers. Theo Wilson died in 1997, a few days after she began a promotional tour for her book, *Headline Justice: Inside the Courtroom: The Country's Most Controversial Trials* (1996). Deutsch toured in her stead, between her AP assignments.

Later Career

In addition to the Manson trial, Deutsch covered numerous other highly publicized trials that riveted the public. Among these was the trial of Patty Hearst, a granddaughter of the newspaper magnate William Randolph Hearst; Patty Hearst was convicted in 1976 of taking part in a bank robbery along with members of the Symbionese Liberation Army, which had kidnapped her in 1974. (The AP had assigned Deutsch to spend a year looking for Hearst, by then a fugitive, which Deutsch did, to no avail.) Deutsch also covered the trials of Angela Davis (a one-time member of the Black Panther and Communist parties acquitted in 1972 of murder, kidnapping, and criminal-conspiracy charges in a case involving the killing of a judge during an escape attempt from a California courtroom); Daniel Ellsberg (whose 12 felony counts, stemming from his leaking a classified government report known as the Pentagon Papers to the *New York Times,* were dismissed in 1973); Lynette "Squeaky" Fromme (a follower of Charles Manson, who in 1975 was convicted of attempting to assassinate President Gerald R. Ford); Dan White (who assassinated San Francisco mayor George Moscone and Supervisor Harvey Milk and was convicted of voluntary manslaughter, but not murder, in 1979); the automobile executive and designer John Z. DeLorean (who in 1984 was acquitted, on grounds of entrapment, of charges of selling cocaine to undercover police and of conspiring in money laundering); Joseph J. Hazelwood (captain of the *Exxon Valdez,* who in 1990 was found guilty of misdemeanor negligence in connection with the spillage into Alaskan waters of more than 11 million gallons of oil from the ship); the criminal (1991) and civil (1993) trials of the four Los Angeles police officers whose videotaped beating of Rodney King, a black man, shocked the nation; singer Michael Jackson (who was charged with child molestation and was acquitted on all counts in June 2005); actor Robert Blake (who was tried and acquitted in March 2005 of the murder of his second wife, Bonny Lee Bakley, but in November 2005 was found liable in a California civil court for her wrongful death); record producer Phil Spector (convicted in 2009 of second-degree murder in the shooting death at his home of actress Lana Clarkson); and the concert promotion company AEG Live (which in October 2013 was acquitted in a negligence suit, brought by Michael Jackson's mother, Katherine, over the hiring of the doctor convicted in 2011 of involuntary manslaughter after giving Jackson an overdose of propofol, a powerful anaesthetic).

It was the televised criminal trial of the former football star O. J. Simpson—who was acquitted in 1994 of the murder of his ex-wife Nicole Brown Simpson and her friend Ronald Goldman but found liable for their deaths in a 1997 civil trial—that made Deutsch herself a widely recognized public figure, owing to her frequent appearances on camera in the course of doing her work. At the outset of Simpson's criminal trial, Deutsch's peers chose her to be the sole journalist in the courtroom during jury selection. Laurie L. Levenson, a former senior trial attorney and assistant chief of the Criminal Division of the Los Angeles district attorney's office, told Nerissa Young for the *Quill* (October 1, 1998) that Deutsch "can watch jury selection, which is like watching paint dry on the wall, and she makes it interesting." Simpson's defense attorney Johnnie Cochran told Young that he considered Deutsch "without peer." On one occasion another of Simpson's lawyers, Robert Shapiro, interrupted Deutsch's daily wrap-up of courtroom events to the media pool outside the courthouse to accuse her of being "too objective."

"It's like being in the front row seat to history. … No other beat offers this kind of access to human emotion. You get at the heart of what people are about."

"I try to put myself in the position of the juror," Deutsch told Hughes. "I've always believed that if you told the public what came out in a court, they could make their own decision." Deutsch's reporting of the Simpson trial earned her a Pulitzer Prize nomination—as well as a personal telephone call from Simpson at the conclusion of the trial, thanking her for remaining impartial. *Verdict: The Chronicle of the O.J. Simpson Trial,* co-authored by Deutsch, other AP reporters, and the true-crime writer Michael Fleeman, was published in 1995.

Deutsch told Michele Norris, "I always say that trials mirror history. That if you wanted to know what was going on in America at a specific time, you needed to walk into a courtroom and look around and listen to what was happening. And you would see, for instance in the Ellsberg trial, you saw the Vietnam War. In the Angela Davis trial, you saw the story of the Black Panthers. In the Patty Hearst trial, we had post-Vietnam alienation. ... You go on and on, and you come up to the more present time with the O. J. Simpson trial, which ... had all the elements of celebrity and racism and domestic violence—a lot of issues."

Deutsch is an advocate for greater media access to the courts. "It is a fight to cover the courts because a lot of people try to keep you out," Deutsch said, as reported by City News Service (May 7, 2001). "It is a daily First Amendment battle." She also battled what she views as a decline in journalists' objectivity, and she has argued that sensationalistic media coverage hurts journalists who seek to cover trials objectively. "The Simpson trial was a huge setback, not just for TV but for media in general," Deutsch told Michael Ollove of the *Baltimore Sun* (October 7, 1998). She commented to Joe Strupp of Editor & Publisher that the Simpson trial "had a real polarizing press corps—and I took a lot of heat for not taking a position." While she has no objection to having cameras in courtrooms, she felt that television coverage of the Simpson trial was often inaccurate, poorly researched, and inconsequential to the outcome of the trial, and that it often presented to the public a scene different from that experienced by the jurors.

Also contributing to the decline in media objectivity, Deutsch has said, is the desire of many television journalists to be celebrities. At a lecture she gave in 2005, as reported by Keith Brown for the *Asbury Park Press* (September 23, 2005), she complained that journalists sometimes forget that their primary concern should be reporting the facts. "That's what being a reporter is all about," she said. "[The public] should never know what you are thinking." At the same time, she said, "Journalists have always had soul. It's their business to have soul, to care." Coverage of the devastating effects of Hurricane Katrina, in her opinion, demonstrated that element of journalism powerfully.

Nancy Mills, of the blog Spirited Woman, asked Deutsch about the experience of covering murder trials. Deutsch responded that although it was similar to that of covering other news stories, "it's more intense. You have to be extremely focused. You can't miss a word or you might miss something crucial. You are in a courtroom were there are a lot of emotions. I'm covering things that are very sad, tragic. ... It also requires knowledge of the law, so it's very technical. If you don't understand what the legal terminology is—you're in big trouble. I never get involved with defendants. It's just not done. A lot of reporters do—some take a position against the defendant, as a lot of people did in the O. J. case. It's not my position. My job is to just watch and tell." Further addressing the pressures involved, she continued, "I have to tell you what I do is very exhausting. I think that any woman (anybody) who does this job is going to be working at a fever pitch. You're getting through every day, doing the job, writing about life and death issues."

Asked by Nancy Mills how she manages to get her stories written when her days are spent in courtrooms, Deutsch explained, "I dictate most of my stories. That was the thing that I learned at the AP from day one. I dictate them to a person who is writing them and putting them out on the wire as I speak. ... I am composing as I dictate with all the grammatical stuff, punctuation, paragraph marks and everything else. I call in and dictate all day. We're on the wire constantly."

Deutsch's awards include the Honor Medal for Distinguished Service in Journalism from the University of Missouri School of Journalism, the First Amendment Award from the Society of Professional Journalists, and the 11th American Judicature Society Toni House Journalism Award (for print journalism; reporter Angie Hendershot of WJRT ABC-12 in Flint, Michigan, also won, for outstanding reporting in the broadcast/electronic mediums).

According to Joe Strupp, Deutsch, who is single, "claims to be 'married to the AP.'" "I was a writer from the day I was born," she explained to Strupp in a phone interview. "I was very lucky because I knew what I wanted to do for a long time." Deutsch told Mills, "I think every day is a fight to maintain my integrity in the face of people who would like to compromise it. I have done that and I am proud of that."

Further Reading:

Baltimore Sun E p1+ Oct. 7, 1998

Editor & Publisher Jul. 2, 2007

(East Brunswick, New Jersey) *Home News Tribune* H p9 July 8, 2004

Los Angeles Times Magazine p5 June 6, 2004

Orange County (California) *Register* E p1+ Nov. 14, 1995

Quill p6 Oct. 1, 1998

Spirited Woman Newsletter Dec. 2003

Books:

Hayslett, Jerrianne, *Anatomy of a Trial; Public Loss, Lessons Learned from* The People vs. O. J. Simpson (University of Missouri Press, 2008)

Selected Books and Articles:

Deutsch, Linda, Michael Fleeman et al., *Verdict: The Chronicle of the O. J. Simpson Trial*, 1995)

Deutsch, Linda, and Richard Carelli, *Covering the Courts: An Associated Press Manual for Reporters,* 1999

Deutsch, Linda, "Flash and Trash," in *Covering the Courts: Free Press, Fair Trials, and Journalistic Performance,* ed. by Robert Giles and Robert W. Snyder, 1998 (originally published in *Media Studies Journal,* Winter 1998)

"Dick Clark: AP Writer Linda Deutsch Remembers Teenage Appearance on 'American Bandstand,'"Huffington Post, Apr. 19, 2012

Gopinath, Suhas

Internet entrepreneur

Born: 1985, Bangalore (Bengaluru), India

"I want to be like Bill Gates," Suhas Gopinath declared to Indrajit Basu of United Press International (November 28, 2003). When he was 16 years old, Gopinath was officially named the youngest CEO in the world: he is the founder, chairman, and CEO of Globals Inc., an information-technology (IT) firm that, according to its Web site, specializes in cost-effective Web- and software technology for small corporations and educational institutions, government, media and online services, financial services, and independent software vendors. Gopinath had already made a name for himself earlier, at 14; a product of the worldwide "dot-com" movement—which allowed almost anyone with computer savvy to start up an Internet-based company—he established the Web portal CoolHindustan. com, which provided up-to-date information on events in India for nonresident Indians. This innovation brought him recognition as the youngest Web developer in history. Despite having run into a series of legal obstacles as a result of his youth, Gopinath expanded Globals Inc. into a multinational corporation with offices in more than 11 countries, including the United States, the United Kingdom, Germany, Austria, Russia, Italy, Spain, Australia, India, and Bangladesh.

Gopinath's intensive focus on his growing company interfered with his school studies. As he told Mehru Jaffer of *Hardnews Media* (August 2009), "As a teenager, I lost many friends because their parents thought I was a bad influence [for neglecting his studies]. My mother, too, told me that everyone is not as fortunate as Bill Gates, the most famous school dropout to have made a success of his life. I am all for formal education but as long as it does not come in the way of a passion." He continued, "Entrepreneurs are not money-making machines. We add value to society. We give birth to new ideas. We provide jobs to unemployed young people. We don't just follow the beaten path. The uncertainty of an entrepreneur's life is what excites me. We make money but we also contribute to making the society a better place." In a later interview, with Shobha Warrier of Rediff.com (October 12, 2010), Gopinath said, "I have always believed that IT [Information Technology] is not just technology but a tool that can solve the problems of people."

Gopinath's youth and the rapid growth of his company attracted much attention. In 2005 he was invited by Robert B. Zoellick, the president of the World Bank, to join the World Bank's board. In order to "explore how ICT [Information and Communication Technology] can improve the quality of education in the emerging economies, by bringing in accountability and transparency," Gopinath explained to Shobha Warrier, Zoellick had "decided that they could not have only Americans on the board and needed people from across the world. … He preferred a young mind from an emerging country and that was how I got the invitation." Gopinath's area of interest was setting policies on ICT in university education "to reduce the number of unemployed eligible youth in the world." In 2006 Gopinath became the youngest person in the history of Karnataka to win the prestigious Rajyotsava Award, presented by the Indian government to individuals in a wide variety of fields. Later that year India's *Limca Book of Records* (comparable to the *Guinness Book of World Records*) listed him as the world's youngest executive. In 2007 the European Parliament and International Association for Human Values selected him for the Young Achiever Award. Gopinath was among 245 people from around the world—all under 40—selected in March 2008 as Young Global

Leaders by the Geneva, Switzerland-based World Economic Forum; he was the youngest-ever Young Global Leader. Gopinath's obligations as a Young Global Leader included attending meetings with prominent business leaders, politicians, and intellectuals from around the world to discuss global problems. He explained to *Current Biography* (2008) that the honor included participation in a global leadership program at Harvard University. Bruce Nussbaum wrote in his Businessweek blog, NussbaumOnDesign (March 17, 2008), "In a growing universe of private social networks, the YGL network has got to be one of—if not THE—most exclusive SN [social network] around. The YGL grouping is perhaps the paramount network in the globe."

Education and Early Career

The younger of two children, Suhas Gopinath was born on November 4, 1985, in Bangalore (known since 2006 as Bengaluru), India, the capital of the southern Indian state of Karnataka. Bengaluru has been called the Silicon Valley of India because of the concentration of technology companies and technology educational institutions in the city. Gopjnath grew up in a middle-class family that emphasized the importance of education. His father, M. R. Gopinath Rao, is an electronics engineer who worked for India's Ministry of Defense; his mother, Kala, is a homemaker. Commenting on his upbringing, Gopinath noted for *Current Biography,* "My parents always advised me from a very young age to lead a simple life, with humbleness and modesty irrespective of one's success, money or fame." When he was very young, he aspired to become a veterinarian; at age eight he started an animal-protection service with his friends called the Global Awareness Club. Each day Gopinath and the other members went around their neighborhood with sticks to protect stray dogs from harm by abusive children.

Gopinath's ambition to work with animals gave way to his fascination with the World Wide Web after he began accompanying his older brother, Shreyas, to a local Internet café. Suhas was then a student at the Air Force School in the Mathikere area of Bangalore. Shreyas, who later earned an M.B.A. degree from the Indian Institute of Management in Lucknow, was pursuing an undergraduate engineering degree at the time and was using the café to complete his school projects. A turning point in Gopinath's life came when his brother gave him a Hotmail.com e-mail account for his thirteenth birthday. Gopinath recalled for *Current Biography,* "I was overjoyed as my first Internet identity was created, and went to my school and distributed my e-mail address with its username and password to all my friends, because I had a misconception that my friends also [needed] to know my password when they [needed] to send me e-mail." His monthly allowance of just 25 rupees (approximately 50 cents in U.S. currency) was not enough for him to go to the Internet café every day, since the café charged 125 rupees per hour of Internet usage; but Gopinath eventually persuaded the café's owner, Shubha Dev, to let him open and manage the shop during lunch hours (1 p.m. to 4 p.m.) in return for free Internet use. It was during those three-hour spans that Gopinath began reading books on the Internet moguls Bill Gates, Michael Dell, and Sir Richard Branson, which helped fuel his entrepreneurial spirit. He was also greatly influenced by the Indian businessman R. Chenraj Jain, the founder and chairman of a premier group of schools and colleges across India, whom he has cited as his mentor. (Jain became a Globals Inc. nonexecutive director.)

Gopinath quickly learned the fundamentals of Internet use and then moved on to more complicated areas, such as figuring out source codes to Web sites. He explained to Shobha Warrier how he got started: "I got hooked [on] open source technology after I started looking for e-books on how to build websites. They were not available as they were created in proprietary sources. So I started using open source to build websites.

There is a freelance marketplace on the web where I could register and offer my services. … I registered myself there as a website builder. The first website I had to do was free of cost as I had no references. It was for a company in New York. My first income was $100 when I was 13 for building another website, but I didn't have a bank account."

Gopinath's preoccupation with the Web and his nascent business began to cause his grades to suffer. After he failed his Central Board of Secondary Education (CBSE) preparatory math exam, despite having previously been an excellent student, his school's headmistress warned his parents that he was in danger of failing his finals. At his mother's insistence, he took a four-month break from his Internet activities to study for and pass—with a first class—his final CBSE examinations. (His parents were not swayed by his argument that Bill Gates had dropped out of Harvard University before founding Microsoft.) Eventually he managed to balance his school requirements with his Web pursuits, continuing to teach himself at the Internet café. After passing his school boards, he pursued a bachelor's degree in information science for two years at the M. S. Ramaiah Institute of Technology in Bangalore, but he ended his formal education in 2005 when his responsibilities with the World Bank took him abroad so often that he could not fulfill the institute's attendance requirements. Gopinath told Shobha Warrier, "I come from a family where entrepreneurship is considered a sin. My mother was quite upset. She wanted me to do engineering, then an MBA and work in a good company. … I still feel that you cannot restrict yourself to bookish knowledge. I believe that practical knowledge is more important."

In 2000 Gopinath had launched the Web site CoolHindustan.com, an Internet portal that offered free e-mail and voicemail services. The site quickly became popular among Indians living in the United States and England, allowing them to send audio greetings to their families in India. Gopinath recalled to Hasnain Kazim of *Spiegel* (May 16, 2007), "I wanted to provide Indians all over the world with a forum to post public events, tips for eating out and everything else they're interested in." Just a week after he launched the portal, he was contacted by Network Solutions, a New York-based technology company owned by Verisign Inc., which expressed interest in hiring him. Unwilling to leave India and already envisioning himself as an entrepreneur, Gopinath did not accept. Not long afterward the company awarded him a certificate as a professional Web developer. With that designation, Gopinath, at 14, was officially recognized as the youngest Web developer in the world, as well as the youngest in history. A Fortune 1000 company (which he has not identified by name) then offered him a $2,000-a-week salary, chauffeur service, and an executive apartment to work as a full-time freelancer, but again he declined. He explained to Pratiksha Thanki for the *Times of India* January 12, 2007), "It was a tempting offer for a middle-class boy like me. But I never wanted to settle down in the United States and become an NRI [non-resident Indian]." (He has also said that he did not want to move away from his family.) In 2004, after a controversial news article on India-Pakistan relations appeared on the site (as a result of an open-source PHP script that Gopinath had developed that provided automated updates from popular Indian news feeds), CoolHindustan.com fell prey to a group of anti-Indian hackers who changed the logo on the Web site to "Cool Pakistan." Responding to mounting family pressure, Gopinath shut down the portal.

Concurrently with his work on CoolHindustan.com, Gopinath launched the firm Globals Inc., to offer Web-based services for small- and mid-sized companies. CoolHindustan.com operated as a means of drawing prospective customers to Globals Inc. Wanting to become a model for Indian youth, Gopinath attempted to register the company in India, but he was refused permission by the government because he was a minor. Still only 14, he decided to register the company in the United States, in San Jose, California, after proposing the idea to Clifford Leslie, a part-time student at a technical university. During that time Gopinath made a short visit to the United States to officially launch his company; Gopinath, Leslie, and Gopinath's friend Vinay M. Nellogi (also known as Vinay M.N.) are credited as the cofounders of Globals Inc. Not long after its launch, Gopinath's company was denied an outsourcing contract—worth half a million dollars—with the Singapore-based company Smith and Gale, also because of his age. "Many people didn't take me seriously," he recalled to Kazim. When he began to develop facial hair, he grew a moustache in order to appear older. He even met with India's then-president, Abdul Kalam, to try to have certain age-limit regulations for businesses lowered from 18 years to 16 years, but he was unsuccessful.

Later Career

In 2003—at Asia's largest IT event and trade fair, BangaloreIT.com, held in Bangalore—Gopinath brought Globals Inc. to the attention of the wider international business community. Calling the presentation a "memorable experience," Gopinath explained to *Current Biography,* "We were able to exhibit our competence and projects which we had already done. That impressed many visitors and media persons who visited our booth. Post event, we were able to market our services more easily because we had already proven our competence." That exposure helped to give Globals Inc. credibility in the eyes of many. In addition to its work with small companies, Globals began winning commissions to create Web sites for large corporations, advertisers, and educational institutions. "Most of the projects we undertake are small ones which do not require a memorandum of understanding or any legal pacts," he noted at the time, to Jay Shankar of Agence France Presse (November 6, 2003). While carving a profitable niche for the company, Gopinath assembled a team of employees who were 20- to 22 years old. Recalling his ambitious plans for Globals, he explained to Shankar, "I wanted to develop a platform for youngsters to develop their talents and to help them understand and get exposed to technology." As soon as he turned 18 and could legally do so, Gopinath registered his company in India, as Globals ITeS.

I still feel that you cannot restrict yourself to bookish knowledge. I believe that practical knowledge is more important."

In 2005 Gopinath was officially recognized by the Rotary Club as the youngest CEO in the world. Around that time CNBC and the organization e-Business Canada named him the youngest entrepreneur in the world; he was also recognized as the world's youngest CEO by many other media outlets, including the BBC, CBS News, the *Washington Times, Indian Express,* and the *Times of India.* By 2005, when Gopinath moved the company back to India, Globals Inc. had amassed more than two hundred customers around the world and set up offices in 11 countries. Roughly 65 percent of the company's revenues were coming from Europe. Gopinath later explained to Ashish Roy of the *Times of India* (July 26, 2012) that one of the reasons for Globals's success was that he had identified niche opportunities: "Most software companies in India concentrate on English-speaking companies. I realized that there were a lot of opportunities in non-English speaking companies of Europe. I approached Spanish companies but they turned me down as I did not know Spanish. I then contacted Spanish MBA colleges and provide me interns who knew both Spanish and English. I paid them a handsome stipend and bagged many contracts. I started my second office after US in Madrid." Globals continued to expand into non-English speaking markets, and the company came to focus on emerging markets, in India and also in Africa and Middle East.

Globals designed websites until 2007–08, when Gopinath decided to provide to software solutions to the education and healthcare sectors. He told Ashish Roy, "I have helped universities in automating their examination system. I have also worked for Indian government in Sarva Shiksha Abhiyan [the Education for All Movement, the goal of which is to universalize elementary education in India]. According to the Globals Web site, Gopinath himself co-created educube™ (formerly known as educationERP.net), one of the company's most widely used products. A software program that allows schoolteachers to record grades and attendance more accurately, educube™ initially was distributed to a thousand schools across India.

Commenting on his plans for the company, Gopinath told *Current Biography,* "Our goals for the future [are] to develop a world-class product in the field of education and to develop on-demand Web-based applications for various domains, by which we can create more employment." In October 2010, speaking with Shobha Warrier, Gopinath forecast his company's future along these lines: "We are now in the process of raising funds. Once we do it, we will separate the company into two—service and product development. I want to concentrate on products as I can't sail on two boats." Noting that there was "saturation in developed countries," he told Ashish Roy of the *Times of India* (July 26, 2012) that he planned to concentrate on Africa in addition to expanding in India. "I also have set a target to get my company listed in 2015. At present I am getting enough venture capital," he added.

At the Fortieth Annual St. Gallen Symposium in May 2010, as reported by Matthew Allen of Swissinfo. ch, Suhas Gopinath spoke about the challenges still confronting Indian entrepreneurs, especially younger ones: "Most companies in India are family owned so first-generational start-ups are looked upon with some suspicion. … Outside of the IT sector, there is very little start-up activity and it is hard to get access to bank credit until a company is four or five years old." Gopinath told the symposium audience that despite India's rapid development, as Allen put it, "bureaucracy and many ingrained social customs lag behind. [He] faced an uphill battle to be taken seriously at first and even had to conceal his business venture from his own family until it was well established."

Asked by M. K. Sireesha of Inspiration Unlimited (June 2013) about his management style, Gopinath commented, "I am a person who likes to lead from the back rather than leading from the front. I allow people to lead their teams and if they are falling somewhere, that is when I would want to intervene and help. Then, I take the back seat again. There was one point in my life when I had to lead from the front and I used to micro-manage everything. … Now, I entrust responsibilities to others and make every employee feel that he is the owner of the company. … As long as people make new mistakes, innovative mistakes and don't repeat them, I am all fine with it. … I keep meeting our employees to find out if they have any new ideas. New technologies keep coming up and the last thing I want to do is to be isolated from the IT world because that's been my passion and that's why I have reached this position."

In addition to his participation in the World Economic Forum's Young Global Leaders program, Gopinath serves on the Information and Communication Technology (ICT) Advisory Board of the World Bank Group and the National Expert Advisory Committee at the Ministry of Science and Technology of the Government of India. He is active in the Social Peace Foundation, and the Indian Institute of Technology (IIT Bombay) Entrepreneurship Cell, which is a incubator for young tech entrepreneurs. He won the 2009 SIP [Social Innovators Park] Fellow Award at the Global Social Innovators Forum and was named a 2010 Venture Fellow by the New York City Economic Development Corporation under New York City mayor Michael Bloomberg.

Gopinath lives with his family in Bangaluru. He has been designated as the Indian representative for the United Nations Youth Federation and Action Program and serves as a coordinator for Indo-Pak Youth programs. He is also a "brand ambassador" for the animal-rights organization PETA. Often working as many as 16 hours a day, he travels abroad extensively for his firm and frequently lectures on entrepreneurship at various institutions around the world.

Further Reading:

Current Biography 2008

www.globalsinc.com

Hardnews Aug.2009

India Express Nov. 6, 2003, Sep. 17, 2005

India Today p60 Oct. 22, 2007; Inspiration Unlimited Jun. 2013

SiliconIndia Jul. 14, 2011

Spiegel May 16, 2007

SwissInfo.com May 9, 2010

Times of India Jan. 12, 2007, Jul. 26, 2012

United Press International Nov. 28, 2003

XIMB Journal of Management September, 2007.

Gruber, Lilli

Italian politician, former broadcast journalist

Born: 1957, Bolzano, Italy

In 1987 Lilli Gruber became the first woman to anchor a prime-time television newscast in Italy. Thanks to her savvy grasp of current events and her telegenic manner, Gruber—who is widely known as "Lilli the Red" because of her striking hair color and left-leaning politics—was soon a celebrity in her native country. Although she was popular with viewers and respected by her peers, she was held in less esteem by Silvio Berlusconi, Italy's former prime minister, whom she severely criticized for his undue influence over the country's media. While head of the government, Berlusconi effectively controlled the state-owned media, and as one of Italy's wealthiest investors, he owned several private media companies as well. In 2004, in protest against Berlusconi's manipulation of the press, Gruber resigned her long-held position with state-owned Radiotelevisione Italiana (RAI). She then entered the political arena herself and, trouncing Berlusconi, won election to the European Parliament as a member of Romano Prodi's Uniti nell'Ulivo (Olive Tree Alliance) party.

Gruber served in the European Parliament until September 2008, when she resigned—shortly before the end of her term—to return to broadcasting. She joined a private TV channel, La7, anchoring *Otto e mezzi* ("Eight and a Half"), a daily political news and information program.

Education and Early Career

Dietlinde Gruber (nicknamed Lilli as a child) was born on April 19, 1957, in the South Tyrolese city of Bolzano (in German, Bozen), which is located near Italy's northeastern border with Austria. (Austria had surrendered Trentino-Alto Adige, the region that includes Bolzano, to Italy after World War I; many of the inhabitants are native German speakers and, like the Gruber family, have Germanic names.) In the 1960s the family moved to Verona, where Gruber's parents ran a successful construction business. Gruber has told journalists that both her grandmothers refused to speak Italian, steadfastly using German, but that her parents encouraged her to be open minded and cosmopolitan. "I remember when people asked me, do you feel Italian or German, and I would answer, European," she told Alan Cowell of the *New York Times* (July 3, 2004). "That was not a common answer back then [before the establishment of the European Union]." Gruber herself is fluent in four languages: Italian, German, French, and English.

Gruber, who has one brother and one sister, attended the Università Ca' Foscari di Venezia, where she studied modern foreign literature and languages. In 1981 she worked as an apprentice journalist with a local news station, Telebolzano, and the following year she began her professional career with RAI, as a radio and television news reporter and anchor. She spent two years with a German-language station and then moved to RAI Tre's Regionale del Trentino-Alto Adige. (In addition to its Internet portal RAI.TV World and the all-news satellite/Internet streaming RAI News24, RAI operates a number of digital terrestrial television stations, of which the three most prominent are RAI Uno, the leading Italian channel, aimed at a general family audience; RAI Due, which broadcasts a wide array of American sitcoms and dramas, children's shows, and newscasts; and RAI Tre, which is considered somewhat left wing and focuses on informative, educational programming.)

In 1987 Gruber reached a milestone in her journalism career when she became the first woman to anchor a prime-time newscast in Italy, on RAI Due's Tg2 (TeleGiornale 2). Therefore Gruber is sometimes compared with Barbara Walters, the first woman to anchor an American primetime newscast, on ABC. Gruber moved to RAI Uno as a prime-time anchor in 1990. As the anchor of *Ore 20* ("Eight o'clock"), she became a familiar and trusted face, reporting on a variety of international issues, including the fall of the Berlin Wall in 1989 and the reunification of East Germany and West Germany in 1990. In 1990 she co-authored (with Paolo Borella) a book about the momentous events, *Quei giorni a Berlin* ("Those Days in Berlin"; *Ritorno a Berlino* ["Return to Berlin"], a twentieth-anniversary edition, was published in 2009). During the early 1990s she continued to report on such major stories as the Gulf War, the collapse of the former Soviet Union, the conflicts between Israel and its Arab neighbors, and the election of Bill Clinton to the U.S. presidency, among other topics.

> **"We try to make information intellectually honest. It is hard to be objective, but I ask that of myself as a goal."**

In 1992 Gruber became the host and executive producer for a daily current-events program that aired on RAI Radio 1, and the following year she was awarded the prestigious William Benton Fellowship for Broadcasting Journalists from the University of Chicago. In 1994 she became the host and executive producer of another network program, the political talk show *Al voto, al voto* ("To the polls, to the polls"). That same year Berlusconi, who owned three major television networks—Canale Cinque (the direct competitor of RAI Uno), Rete Quattro and Italia Uno—as well as a variety of other media companies, was elected for his first term as prime minister, despite widespread allegations that he was guilty of bribery, tax fraud, and shady accounting practices. In the period before the election, he had appeared "on all three of his national networks from his study, announcing his decision to enter politics for the good of the country, as if he were a US President speaking to the public from the Oval Office," as Alexander Stille wrote for the *Nation* (November 11, 1999). Stille explained, "Politicians inimical to Berlusconi are almost invisible on his networks, while Berlusconi himself is the most visible figure on Italian TV—more so even than the elected prime minister [at that time, Massimo D'Alema] or the president of the republic. Because Italy's state TV has a longstanding policy against running political advertisements, Berlusconi's three national networks give him a virtual monopoly on election ads. Thus while Forza Italia [Berlusconi's party] can advertise essentially for free on Berlusconi's networks, his political rivals are in the no-win situation of paying him or doing without TV ads entirely." Berlusconi resigned after only seven months as prime minister, after being indicted for tax fraud and seeing his coalition government collapse. He ran again, in 1996 but lost to the center-left candidate, Romano Prodi. In 2001, however, he was once again elected and continued in office, through several changes of administration, until 2006; he subsequently won a third term (2008–2011).

Gruber, meanwhile, continued to report the news, winning exclusive interviews with celebrities and traveling to embattled regions to cover such history-making events as the ongoing war in the Balkans and the terrorist attacks of September 11, 2001. In the late 1990s she also became the host and executive producer of the German weekly newsmagazine *Focus TV*, aired on PRO7. Gruber returned to the Middle East in late 2002 to report on the buildup for the invasion of Iraq by the United States and its allies. She chose to remain in the war zone even after heavy fighting erupted and members of her television crew had fled. The long assignment became the subject of her next book, *I miei giorni a Baghdad* ("My Days in Baghdad"), which was published in 2003 and became a best-seller in Italy.

The situation at RAI, however, was becoming dire. As Berlusconi exerted a level of control that some characterized as censorship, several senior journalists were dismissed (or resigned in disgust), and shows were taken off the air for expressing anti-Berlusconi views. Stille explained the extent of Berlusconi's reach: "If you combined the political roles of ... George W. Bush and [then-] Senate majority leader Trent Lott, the media power of Ted Turner and Rupert Murdoch, the money of Ross Perot and Steve Forbes, and the real estate and the personal arrogance of Donald Trump, you would begin to get an idea of how long a shadow Silvio Berlusconi casts over Italian public life."

Gruber struggled to remain objective in her news coverage and resisted political pressure to inject into it a pro-government slant; she was once threatened for using the word "controversial" to describe a piece of legislation, and she was censured for using the term "occupation force" in a story about the war in Iraq. In late April 2004, a month after the resignation of RAI's chairperson, Lucia Annunziata, owing to similar pressures, Gruber quit her own post. "There is no other democratic country where one man can control six television channels, plus various radios, newspapers and magazines and at the same time be prime minister," she told Christopher P. Winner for the American, an independent online news magazine (June 1, 2004). "There is no democratic country where the same man controls directly or indirectly (RAI and [his private company] Mediaset together) over 90 percent of the advertising revenues of the television sector. We are not talking here about old-fashioned political mingling with the press business; we are talking about monopolistic control of electronic media by one man who represents one political side and reduces access to public television to his political enemies." Gruber was especially distressed that because of Berlusconi's actions, Freedom House, a New York-based think tank that monitors press freedom, had downgraded Italy's press freedom rating from "free" to "partly free"—on a par, as was noted by Irene Peroni of *La Repubblica* (June 15, 2004), only with the notoriously repressive Turkey. "I decided I was done with anchoring. I could not put my face on something so biased," Gruber told Alan Cowell.

Later Career

Shortly after her resignation, Gruber was contacted by Romano Prodi, by then the president of the European Commission. Prodi invited her to join the center-left Uniti nell'Ulivo ("Olive Tree Alliance"), Italy's main opposition coalition, for a run in the elections for the European Parliament. In June 2004 Gruber was elected, capturing, in Rome alone, 236,000 votes to Berlusconi's 116,000. Irene Peroni, reporting on the results for BBC News, wrote that Berlusconi had "received one of the most humiliating defeats of his political career at the hands of a disgruntled TV anchorwoman." In all Gruber captured more than 1,100,000 votes.

As a member of the European Parliament, Gruber caucused with the Socialist Group in the European Parliament. She served on the Committee on Civil Liberties, Justice and Home Affairs, the body responsible for protecting the rights of citizens of the European Union, and as an alternate on the Foreign Affairs Committee. She chaired the delegation that monitors relations with the Gulf States and co-chaired the Intergroup on Media, Freedom and Pluralism. In September 2008, however, before the conclusion of her term in office, Gruber announced in an open letter to her constituents that she was resigning from the European Parliament to resume her career in broadcasting—"with the same spirit of service and with similar goals"—as anchor of the well-established political news and analysis program *Otto e mezzi. Otto e mezzi* aired on the private station LA7, owned at that time by Telecom Italia Media and later by Cairo Communications, beyond the sphere of governmental influence. (Silvio Berlusconi had returned as prime minister in May 2008 and remained in office until November 2011, despite a welter of political and personal scandals.) Gruber explained her aspirations for *Otto e mezzi* to Silvia Fumarola of *La Reppubblica* (September 5, 2013): "We try to make information intellectually honest. It is hard to be objective, but I ask that of myself as a goal."

Gruber's books, all best-sellers, include *L'altro Islam* (2004; "The Other Islam"), about the rise of the Shia after the fall of Saddam Hussein, and *Chador* (2005; "Chador"), which explores the complexities of Iran, especially with regard to the place of women in Iranian society. In *America anno zero* (2006; "America Year Zero"), she examined the post-September 11, 2001, United States, including the nation's response to Hurricane Katrina and domestic political opposition to the policies of President George W. Bush. *Streghe: La riscossa delle donne d'Italia* (2008; "Witches: The Rescue of the Women of Italy") dealt with the contemporary struggles of Italian women to claim an equal place in society, looking to Spain and the Netherlands for positive examples with the goal of reviving a dialogue that until a few years ago, according to Gruber, was alive and fruitful. In *Eredità: Una storia della mia famiglia tra l'impero e il fascismo* (2012; "Legacy; A Story of My Family between the Empire and Fascism"), Gruber provides a gripping narrative of her German-speaking family's history in South Tyrol after the region was incorporated into Italy. Regarding this history as relevant to the wider history of Europe in the twentieth century, she told Luke Sticcotti of *Alto Adige* that she "decided to write about it when I came across a manuscript of my great-grandmother Rosa, a journal of extraordinary intensity that tells a great love story, a family saga and [the story of] a collective tragedy: the collapse of the Austro-Hungarian Empire, the arrival of Italian fascism and then the illusion that Nazi Germany could repair the wrongs they [had] suffered."

Gruber's journalism honors include, among others, the Carlo Schmid Preis (1995), the Premio Fregene (1998), and the Premio Spoleto (2001). For her coverage of the war in Iraq, she received widespread recognition, including the Sirmione Catullo Prize, the Ischia Prize and the Guidarello Prize; in November 2003 President Carlo Azeglio Ciampi conferred on her the honor of Cavaliere OMRI (Order of Merit of the Italian Republic). In 2002 she was in residence as a visiting scholar at the School of Advanced International Studies of Johns Hopkins University. She holds an honorary degree (2004) from the American University of Rome.

Gruber lives in Rome. She has written for numerous publications, including the newspapers *La Stampa* and *Corriere della sera*. She consistently tops lists of Italy's most glamorous women and is said to be responsible for a wave of interest in journalism careers among young Italian women, dubbed "Gruberines" by some observers. In July 2000 she married Jacques Charmelot, a French-born reporter for Agence France-Presse.

Further Reading:

Alto Adige Oct. 13, 2012

American Jun. 1, 2004

BBC News Jun. 15, 2004

European Parliament Web site

www.fembio.org, Jan. 2008 (by her sister, Micki Gruber)

La Repubblica, Jun. 15, 2004, Sept. 5, 2013

Nation Nov. 11, 1999

New York Times A p4 Jul. 3, 2004

Selected Books:

Gruber, Lilli, and Paolo Borella, *Quei giorni a Berlin* 1990 ("Those Days in Berlin"; twentieth anniversary edition: *Ritorno a Berlino*, 2009 ("Return to Berlin")

I miei giorni a Baghdad, 2003 ("My Days in Baghdad")

L'altro Islam, 2004 ("The Other Islam")

Chador, 2005 ("Chador")

Figlie dell'Islam, 2007 ("Daughters of Islam")

Streghe; La riscossa delle donne d'Italia, 2008 ("Witches: The Rescue of the Women of Italy")

Eredità: Una storia della mia famiglia tra l'impero e il fascismo, 2012 ("Legacy; A Story of My Family between the Empire and Fascism")

Haruka, Yōko

Author and television personality

Born: 1960s, Osaka, Japan

In the beginning of her book *Kekkon shimasen!* ("I Shall Not Marry!"), which was published in 2001, the Japanese writer and television personality Yōko Haruka recalls her father's funeral, at which her supposed inferiority to her male siblings was made painfully clear. As recounted by Ayako Doi, writing for *Foreign Policy* (November–December 2003) "[Haruka] was told to sit and walk behind her five brothers—younger as well as older—and made to understand that she wasn't wanted on the receiving line to greet relatives and family friends." This was only one of many consciousness-raising experiences that inspired Haruka to become one of the country's best-known feminist figures. The author of several books and essays that examine the institutionalized sexism of Japanese society, Haruka exhorts young women to first consider their own needs before bowing to the expectations of a rigid patriarchy. "Men, company, marriage, these are the things you can use to achieve your goals," she writes, as quoted by Doi. "But if they are no use, discard them."

Many women are taking Haruka's advice; in recent years, Japan has seen its fertility rate plunge dramatically, coinciding with trends that find younger women rejecting traditional roles in order to live on their own, pursue a career, and eschew marriage. If these trends continue, some experts note with alarm, Japan's population will be sliced in half over the twenty-first century. Haruka's words are thus seen by many as subversive, or even dangerous.

Education and Early Career

Yōko Haruka was born in Osaka, Japan, in the 1960s (WorldCat gives the date 1957), an era in which unmarried women past their youth were often referred to as "leftover Christmas cake," implying that they were undesirable or had outlived their usefulness. (Haruka does not disclose her exact age in interviews; according to critic Laura Dales in *Feminist Movements in Contemporary Japan* [2009], Haruka once commented in "Office Breeze," her newspaper column [1995–1996] for *Asahi Shinbun,* that the obsession with asking or revealing women's age reflects a desire to demean or neutralize women's individuality and value.) She was the youngest child and only daughter in a working-class family. During her childhood and adolescence, her needs were routinely ignored in favor of those of her five brothers. When she got her first bra, she has said, she kept it on around the clock, sleeping in it, because no family member had explained that she didn't have to. Only when she went on an overnight school trip did she discover her error. "It was a great relief to me," she said, as quoted by Ginko Kobayashi for the Tokyo *Daily Yomiuri* (June 24, 2000). As Haruka grew older, she chafed at her brothers' sense of entitlement. Her oldest brother, she claimed in *Kekkon shimasen!,* verbally abused his wife, who, in addition to bearing sole responsibility for all domestic chores, had to accommodate the wishes of her husband and also of his mother, who, as dictated by Japanese tradition, lives with them. Haruka's sister-in-law, according to Ayako Doi, "manages to smile self-effacingly even as she scurries to provide for their material needs, right down to putting a cold beer in her husband's hand as he steps out of his nightly bath." Haruka also recalls in the book her annoyance at an aunt's wish to find an "ordinary girl" to marry her son—by which she meant a complacent woman with no personal ambition besides keeping her husband fed and happy. Such family experiences were at the root of Haruka's early stirrings of feminist consciousness.

While in her early 20s, Haruka began a career in television, working as a *tarento,* a kind of hostess or side-kick on a variety show—a common role for pretty young women on Japanese TV. Describing these shows, which are quite popular in Japan, Stephen Lunn, writing for the *Australian* (July 27, 2000), explained that typically "a charismatic host [is] accompanied by an attractive 'flower.' No prizes for guessing the gender of the respective participants." The programs are a "microcosm of Japanese society," Lunn wrote, in that they "reduce the women to little more than a sounding board for the male host's ideas. If [the women] try to increase their profile or offer an unwanted opinion, trouble quickly follows." Male hosts, when feeling affronted by some instance of female audacity, frequently make disparaging comments about their female counterparts' age or marital status. Haruka often found the work demoralizing, but, at first, she did not fight back against the overt sexism. "Earlier in my career," she told Lunn, "I tried to hide the fact that I believed in feminism for fear I would lose my job."

Haruka worked on several such programs, acting as an emcee or a panelist; one of her more notable stints was on a popular quiz show called *Seikatsu shohyakka.* By the mid-1990s, she was an established presence on the Japanese television circuit. Despite her professional success, Haruka felt dissatisfied. "I had worked many years in television, but the longer I worked, the more hurdles were put in my path," she told Lunn. She had grown tired of the patronizing way in which she was treated by the men with whom she shared the camera. Her discontent extended to her personal life. Recently engaged, she feared that her fiancé would expect her to be a traditionally submissive wife, a role she was unprepared to adopt; she broke off the engagement. "I think we loved each other very much," she told Brendan Pearson of the *Australian Financial Review* (December 1, 2003). "But the best partner for him was someone who does not have a job, and stays home for him."

Haruka decided to attend classes taught by the feminist scholar Chizuko Ueno, at Tokyo University. Coming from a profession in which a heavy premium is placed on women's looks, Haruka found academia, with its focus on brains rather than beauty, to be liberating. Although she was initially intimidated by Ueno, soon Haruka was learning effective debate skills and reading seminal feminist essays. (She continued television hosting during her three years as a student.) At the end of her studies, Haruka wrote *Tōdai de Ueno Chizuko ni Kenka o Manabu* ("Learning How to Argue from Chizuko Ueno at Tokyo University"). It was published in early 2000; by summer it had sold 160,000 copies. The book summarized much of what Haruka learned under Ueno, including a list of ten tips for winning arguments; the first tip was "Be defiant when necessary." After the book's publication, Haruka took her own advice and started confronting men who made sexist comments on the air.

Later Career

The success of her first book prompted Haruka to continue writing, and she became a prolific author. *Hata-raku onna wa teki bakari* ("All a Working Woman Gets Is Enemies"), which became a best-seller, and *Kekkon shimasen!* were both published in 2001. Haruka's books were indicative of a major generational shift regarding marriage and family. Official statistics as of 2004 reported that half of all Japanese women in their late twenties were single. The number of unmarried women in their thirties, meanwhile, had tripled since the 1970s. Women who do marry are doing so later and having their children later as a consequence. "These trends have important economic implications for Japan, and are exacerbating an already ageing society,"

Pearson wrote. "Official figures [show] that the number of babies born [in 2002] was the lowest number since records began in 1899. In 2002, the national fertility rate stood at an all-time low of 1.32 children per woman." There is even a name in Japan for this crisis: *shoshika,* which means "decline in childbearing." The answer to why Japan is seeing such dramatic shifts can, in part, be found in the pages of *Kekkon shimasen!* In the book, Doi explains, Haruka compares being a working mother in Japan to playing "a cleverly designed computer game that one can never win. A woman who tries to follow tradition and do all the chores quickly runs out of energy. But if she leaves the laundry to the weekend or serves TV dinners, her husband will ask, 'What kind of woman are you?' On top of that, he wants her to peel his apple, get his cigarettes, make him coffee—and still have enough love and stamina for sex! Imagine how it would be if she had a baby or two?"

In Haruka's next book, *Haiburiddo ūman* (2003; "Hybrid Woman"), she moderates her position, advising women that they can achieve their goals without totally challenging patriarchal norms. The book recommends employing feminine wiles to influence men, rather than using more strident techniques. Though Haruka's softer stance in *Haiburiddo ūman* disappointed some feminists, she is not concerned about the criticism. Many of her opinions simultaneously straddle feminist ideals and the realities of daily life in male-dominated Japan. Laura Dales notes that "Haruka's particular brand of feminism informs and is informed by her experiences in the media. She is quick to point out that … her workplace is rife with sexism and gender inequality." On the rising trend of plastic surgery among women in television, for example, Haruka told Lunn, "I've heard a lot of women do that. But I don't think it's a bad thing if they can assure their job by making their breasts bigger or padding their bra." Indeed, Lunn writes, "Haruka has no desire to martyr herself to the cause of feminism on Japanese TV. She plans to work within the system, knowing that in Japan, unlike Australia, the U.S., or Europe, if she spoke out against a male colleague and was sacked, laws covering unfair dismissal are virtually non-existent."

"Young women now have economic power, and they are doubting things they never doubted before. … They are asking, 'What is happiness?'"

Laura Dales, however, voiced a different concern: that "the grandness of the Hybrid Woman model, its emotional detachment and its limited application outside certain social and financial circles" not only distinguish *Haiburiddo ūman* from Haruka's previous writings but exclude women who do not have the opportunity or choose not to relate to men on the terms Haruka outlines. Haruka's career, Dales notes, "has benefited from the notion of beauty as a commodity and no doubt reflects the expectations of femininity to which she herself has been subject. If women's beauty is commodified by society, the Hybrid Woman model does not attempt to dismantle the structures that keep its price high. … Women who actively challenge stereotypes of feminine beauty are excluded, as are women who strive but fail to employ physical beauty to attract [male] resources. More significantly, lesbian women and other women who are not interested in attracting men … are excluded" from the Hybrid Woman model.

Haruka continued her exploration of gender equality and women's roles in Japanese society with, among other books, *Kaigo to ren'ai* (2006; "Care of the Elderly and Romantic Love"); *Hataraku onna wa ude shidai* (2006; "For Working Women, It Depends on Skill"); *Iitokodori no onna* (2006; "Women Who Take Only the Best Parts"); *Onna no teki* (2007; "Women's Enemies"); *Onnatomodachi* (2008; "Girlfriends");

Kimuzukashii josei tono jōzu na sesshikata (2010; "Positive Attitude and Hard-to-Please Women") and *Shiniyuku mono no reigi* (2010; "Courtesy of Those Dying"). She also wrote fiction, including *Bijo no fukō* (2004; "The Unhappiness of Beautiful Women") and *Shufutachi no ōre!* (2008; "I of Housewives!"), as well as several "Little Clover Books" having to do with fortune telling and positive psychology.

Haruka lives in Osaka, where she continues to write. She is a sought-after speaker: in November 2012, for example, she was the featured lecturer at a workshop for gender equality sponsored by the Osaki-Kami-jima-cho Board of Education of the Hiroshima Prefecture. She enjoys baseball (she wrote about the Hanshin Tigers in *Yakyū wa Hanshin, Watashi wa dokushin* [2002; "For Baseball, Hanshin; For Me, Singlehood"]) and the all-female theater group Takarazuka Revue, which since 1914 has performed a mix of adaptations of Western musicals and adaptations of Japanese and other Asian folktales, literary works, operas, and manga. After the dissolution of her engagement, Haruka concluded that a man was not a necessary part of her life. "I need someone who understands me and who supports me, but I have come to the realization that someone does not have to be male," she told Pearson. "When I ticked off my must-have list in my ideal partner, there was only one thing that required [the] male sex."

Further Reading:

Australian M p8, July 27, 2000

Australian Financial Review p10 Dec. 1, 2003

(Tokyo) *Daily Yomiuri* p8 June 24, 2000

Foreign Policy Nov.–Dec. 2003

Books:

Bijo no fuko 2004

Dales, Laura, "Feminism and the Popular Media (Haruka Yōko's Feminism)," Chapter Five of *Feminist Movements in Contemporary Japan* (Routledge, 2009).

Shufutachi no ōre! (Chikuma Shobō, 2008)

Selected Books:

Tōdai de Ueno Chizuko ni Kenka o Manabu ("Learning How to Argue from Chizuko Ueno at Tokyo University," 2000)

Kekkon shimasen! ("I Shall Not Marry!," 2001)

Hataraku onna wa teki bakari ("All a Working Woman Gets Is Enemies," 2001)

Kaigo to ren'ai ("Care of the Elderly and Romantic Love," 2002)

Haiburiddo ūman ("Hybrid Woman," 2003)

Hataraku onna wa ude shidai ("For Working Women, It Depends on Skill," 2006)

Iitokodori no onna ("Women Who Take Only the Best Parts," 2006)

Onna no teki ("Women's Enemies," 2007)

Onnatomodachi ("Girlfriends," 2008)

Riguretto: Ima demo anata ga koishikute ("You Are Still Missed: Regret," 2009)

Kimuzukashii josei tono jōzu na sesshikata ("Positive Attitude and Hard-to-Please Women," 2010)

Shiniyuku mono no reigi ("Courtesy of Those Dying," 2010)

Shiawase no hōsoku ("Law of Happiness," 2010*)*

Honshin ga wakaranai toki ni yomu hon ("Book to Read when You Don't Know the True Feelings," 2013)

Jones, Scott

Inventor, technology entrepreneur, futurist

Born: 1960, Louisville, Kentucky, United States

Though relatively few people outside the high-tech industry know his name, Scott Jones has the potential to reinvent everyday life in the twenty-first century. He has already had a tremendous impact on people's daily interactions: billions of people worldwide use his patented voice-mail system every day. As the chairman of Gracenote Inc. and as the founder of Escient Technologies, he took steps toward merging Internet technology with ordinary electronic devices and appliances, reinventing our idea of entertainment and accessibility; many of the innovations of his companies are integral to such products as Apple's iPod, a portable device for storing and playing music that is currently in the hands of more than 350 million consumers, and iTunes, which allows users to purchase and download music on-line, among other functions.

"I have a strong desire to help change our world for the better," Jones remarked in a 2006 interview with *Current Biography.* The brave new world Jones envisions—in which people can contact anyone in the world, or enjoy any mode of entertainment they desire, at the touch of a button—frightens some, who believe that too great a reliance on technology can be harmful. Jones argues that technology is only what we make of it. "Technology can't make moral judgments; people can and do, sometimes not for the better," he said to *Current Biography.* "However, if correctly deployed, technology can help us further amplify what is most human about ourselves. Technology can save lives, significantly enhance the quality of life, and enrich the human experience. That is what motivates me."

Education and Early Life

Scott Alan Jones was born on October 5, 1960 in Louisville, Kentucky, to George and Barbara Jones. He was raised in Indiana, surrounded by a loving extended family. His interest in building and invention seems to have stemmed in part from the example of his father, an engineer who, among other projects, had overseen the construction for St. John's Medical Center in Anderson, Indiana. Jones's childhood was a happy one, in part because his relatives encouraged his inquisitiveness. "I had a wonderful childhood," Jones remarked in his interview with *Current Biography.* "I always had 'projects' where I was inventing and discovering things, and it helped to have access to my father's woodworking and metalworking shop. I conducted experiments with chemistry sets and electronics, that sort of stuff. At a fairly young age, my uncle taught me how to solder (he was a horse trainer at Churchill Downs who used some of the first PC's to help him manage his horses). I was very close to my grandparents, too."

Unlike the stereotypical inventor locked in a basement and isolated from the rest of the world, Jones was very outgoing and involved with people as a youth. As he told *Current Biography,* "Many times, I went on daylong 'adventures' that took me biking/hiking much further from home than my parents ever knew. I spent a lot of time reading 'classics' and I devoured *Popular Science* and *Scientific American* magazines. I loved math and science and had a particularly motivating set of science/math teachers in public junior high and high school. I also engaged in many entrepreneurial activities in my neighborhood: door-to-door sales of seeds [and] holiday gifts, [organizing and selling] tickets to carnivals and haunted houses, etc. I also played basketball in high school, which helped me acquire valuable team-building skills that have served me well in business."

One of Jones's childhood hobbies was to take apart electronic devices in order to see how they worked. His first contact with computers only deepened his desire to do so. "When I was 12 years old, I saw my first big computers at the local university while I was in Boy Scouts (my scoutmaster was a professor there) and I had the opportunity to program in BASIC during my teens," he recalled. "So, the interest was there at a very young age."

An excellent student, Jones acquired two years' worth of college credits during his time at North Central High School in Indianapolis. In the fall of 1978, he entered Indiana University (IU) with the intention of taking pre-med courses and ultimately becoming a doctor. Just one computer-science course, however, convinced him that his talents lay in engineering rather than medicine. Since Indiana University did not offer a degree in electrical engineering, he had to teach himself. The inventor told *Current Biography*: "I put an ad in *Byte* magazine for companies to send me their used electronics and computer 'leftovers' … and they did, but by the busload: I filled my basement with an electronics lab and taught myself a great deal about electronics and computers from the ground up. At IU, I was able to get a thorough grounding in chemistry, biology, math, physics, and computer science. This broad knowledge helped me to make various 'connections' in technologies in a Renaissance fashion."

While at IU, Jones worked at the university's speech-recognition laboratory, as a programmer, and at its neurochemistry laboratory, as a consultant. In the latter position he helped to develop cutting-edge technologies to monitor the electrochemical activities of the human brain. After graduating with honors in 1984, he served as a researcher for the Artificial Intelligence Laboratory at the Massachusetts Institute of Technology (MIT), in Cambridge. His position at the lab gave him access to advanced technology in robotics and the Internet—some years before those technologies were available to the general public.

In 1986 Jones left MIT to cofound his first company, Boston Technology Inc. (BT), with his friend Greg Carr. Jones's experience at the speech-recognition laboratory, as well as at MIT, convinced him that it was possible to build an electronic system that could record, store, edit, and play back human voices without the need for bulky answering machines and magnetic tape. "Starting in college, I developed an interest in having computers that were able to talk and hear—voice recognition stuff," he explained to *Current Biography*:

"While working at IU, I discovered a way to store human voice on the computer's tiny hard drive (these were the very first personal computers and were not very powerful at all). At MIT's Artificial Intelligence Lab, I discovered more about computerizing voice. I learned more about voice recognition but decided that one of the most important uses of the current technologies was the storage and distribution of digitally encoded voice. My patents relate to building massive storage networks that can handle the bandwidth requirements of voice. When we started the business [Boston Technology], I built a prototype of the first voice-mail system on a first-generation IBM-PC. It was used to demonstrate the technology to investors in order to raise financial capital for my company. We then sold relatively small voice-mail systems to small businesses. Meanwhile, I talked with patent attorneys about designs that I had to build very large, fully integrated voice-mail systems. These systems were not commercially viable until the federally mandated break-up of [the communications network] AT&T ("Ma Bell") created a situation where the resulting Baby Bell companies could sell "enhanced services" such as voice-mail."

While the Baby Bells—or the Regional Bell Operating Companies, as they were officially known—could offer voice-mail services to their customers, they were forbidden by law from manufacturing those systems themselves, as part of the effort to keep any telephone company from developing a monopoly. They therefore began looking for a company that had the technology to build an extensive, adaptable voice-mail system in a very short period of time. Jones, as it happened, had already developed a design for such a system; he needed only a team in place to make it work. "I pulled together a team of a half-dozen engineers in Cambridge, Massachusetts, to help build the first fully distributed, massively parallel computational platform for voice messaging," he recalled. "In order to build it, we had to merge technologies from separate industries: PCs from the computer industry and digital switching from the telecommunications industry. The really difficult parts of the project had more to do with making the system ultra-reliable and 'foolproof' rather than simply making it work."

Jones clinched the deal with the Regional Bells by telling them that he could deliver an inexpensive system 20 times bigger and more reliable than anything on the market—in just three months. The Bells jumped at the chance to get such a system so quickly; Jones's competitors had claimed that it would take 18- to 36 months to design and build something similar. At the time that the Bells entrusted Boston Technology with the project, BT's boss and principal architect was only 26 years old.

"It was intimidating, challenging and exciting all at the same time," Jones recalled for *Current Biography*. "We had good ideas and theories about how to build a massive voice-processing system, but nobody had ever done it before. We had to conduct many 'experiments' to determine what the various components were capable of doing. We had to merge together technologies that had not been combined before (PC's, local area networking, and switching technology). At times, we were not sure that we had all the 'right' pieces of technology to get the job done, but fortunately 'necessity was the mother of invention.' We found a way to meet our three-month deadline, but only by working around the clock—literally. For a month, I didn't even leave the office building. When I slept, it was under my desk using a sleeping bag that I kept in my office."

In 1988 Bell Atlantic became the first customer for Boston Technology's scalable voice-mail system (that is, a system that could be adjusted according to the size of the company), with Southwestern Bell and Bell-South quickly following suit. (Southwestern Bell later acquired its former parent company, in 2005, and became AT&T Inc.; in 2006 it acquired Bell South.) Now the standard for telephone companies worldwide, the voice-mail architecture Jones created remains the invention of which he is most proud. "It is very gratifying to know that this innovation has had a broad and pervasive impact on business and society," he remarked. "I believe that the 'time shifting' of voice communications has substantially changed our world at several levels. In addition to making life more manageable at a personal and business level in developed countries, it has had arguably even more impact in developing countries, where voice-mail provides a 'multiplier effect' for villages that have only one telephone among dozens of families and individuals, for example. And, for communities that have more cellular phone infrastructure than copper/fiber telecommunications infrastructure, voice messaging has allowed for a 'virtual answering machine' that further enhances and leverages newer communications technologies."

Later Career

The scalable voice-mail system made Jones a multimillionaire, which allowed him the freedom to do some things he had always wanted to do. Beginning in 1992 he left the daily operations of Boston Technology to pursue other interests, which included learning to pilot a variety of aircraft; he has since flown everything from gliders and hot-air balloons to helicopters and jets and has expressed an interest in developing technologies for the aviation field. In 1997 Boston Technology was sold to Comverse Technology Inc. for $843 million, forming a multibillion-dollar provider of products and services to telephone companies the world over.

Meanwhile, after a few years of traveling and pursuing other interests, Jones decided in 1995 to return to his roots in Indiana. There Jones began developing the ideas that led to the launch of Escient Technologies LLC, the high-tech company he co-founded in 1996 with Tom Doherty. Escient was established on the principle that as technology developed, the power of the Internet would be harnessed to electronic appliances used in the home and office. The company's motto was, "We make technology behave." During his 2006 interview with *Current Biography,* Jones elaborated on the company's work, explaining that Escient was devoted to "building entertainment solutions for homes and businesses that make it easier for people to enjoy and manage their music, movies, video content, home videos, personal photos, Web sites, etc. Today homes typically have central heating and air conditioning powered by a furnace that distributes the heated or cooled air to all parts of the house." Escient, he said, sought to build "the technologies to make an 'entertainment furnace' possible, only instead of distributing air, these technologies will distribute entertainment content."

In the years after its founding, Escient acquired more than a dozen businesses. In 1998, having already licensed compact-disc database (CDDB) technology to use in a 200-CD changer, Escient acquired CDDB and the CD-technology company ION, merging it and other companies into a firm christened Gracenote Inc., of which Jones became chairman. According to the account of the company at Jones's Web site, "Gracenote became the Web's first 'music browser' by allowing its licensees to recognize MP3s as well as CDs and to receive information about artists on the screen while users listen to music." Jones remarked to *Current Biography,* "I believe there are ways to significantly enhance the impact that music has on our lives by making it much more accessible. This applies to music that one currently owns, as well as music that is yet undiscovered for a particular individual. I have found that music can substantially alter attitudes, motivation, and mood. While intangible, I think this has [a] broad, pervasive impact on the world."

The CDDB acquisition proved controversial, since the CDDB project had begun as a freely available, open source database to which users contributed. Escient's TuneBase 100 product, however, depended on CDDB's database, and Jones had a large stake in ensuring that it remained available. By that time commercial pressures were forcing CDDB's hand. Steve Scherf, a cofounder of CDDB who remained with Gracenote, responded to criticisms in an interview with Eliot Van Buskirk of *Wired* (November 13, 2006): "The plain fact is, you can't close something that has been released under the GPL [General Public License]. The CDDB source-code genie was [already] out of the bottle. ... As for the data, I can only point out that all of the data ever submitted to CDDB before it became 'privatized' has been released to the public."

In 2003 the businesses of two Escient subsidiaries, Escient Convergence Corp. and OpenGlobe Inc., along with the Escient name, were sold to a Japanese corporation, D&M Holdings Inc. Five years later, in 2008, the media giant Sony purchased Gracenote for $260 million. Jones notes at his Web site that "Gracenote services are now utilized by the likes of Apple, Yahoo, and Sony, being accessed globally at the rate of 24 billion times per year through applications such as iTunes."

Since the beginning of his career, Jones has thrived on responding to challenges and confounding expectations, sometimes in unexpected ways. In an interview for Robert Jordan's book *How They Did It* (2010), Jones told Jordan, "When I did Voicemail, and then Gracenote, everybody said, 'You'll never get that done. You can't do that. That's not possible.' That's what fuels me to go bet big on an idea that can have significant impact on the world."

Inspired to participate in the 2005 DARPA (Defense Advanced Research Project Agency) Grand Challenge, a 175-mile race across the Mojave Desert by unmanned vehicles, Jones became the chairman and CEO of IndyRobotics, parent company of the Indy Robot Racing Team—which entered a vehicle in the race. Jones was co-team leader with Doug Traster, chief technology officer of IndyRobotics. The DARPA Grand Challenge is "the result of a mandate by Congress and the Department of Defense ... that by 2015, one-third of operational ground vehicles of the armed forces must be unmanned," according to the Indiana business television program *Inside INdiana with Gerry Dick* (August 15, 2005). In the finals the Indy Robotics vehicle crashed, owing to a software problem, but Jones adapted the technology that had been developed into a robotic lawn-mowing device for golf courses, ballparks, college campuses, and other large expanses of lawn, and in 2007 IndyRobotics became Precise Path Robotics Inc., of which Jones was chairman until July 2011.

"When I did Voicemail, and then Gracenote, everybody said, 'You'll never get that done. You can't do that. That's not possible.' That's what fuels me to go bet big on an idea that can have significant impact on the world."

In September 2006 Jones and Brad Bostic, the chairman of Bostech Corp., announced the debut of ChaCha, a "social search engine" that allows Internet as well as mobile device users to perform searches and interact with one of its 63,000 human research guides (paid on a per-question-answered basis). According to Julie Sloane, writing in *Fortune* magazine (October 16, 2007), "the idea of so-called social [human-aided] search isn't new—Yahoo started out that way—but that approach has long since been trumped by Google's algorithm-driven model." Sloane notes, however, that ChaCha, which does employ algorithms for the majority of its responses, aims to surpass Google and other competing services. With an estimated 32 million users per month, ChaCha's Web site claims that it is the "leading source for free, real-time Q&A and is one of the fastest-growing mobile and online publishers. ...Through its unique 'ask-a-smart-friend' platform, ChaCha has answered more than 2 billion questions since launch from 40 million-plus unique users per month" via online, iPhone, Android, mobile text, and voice inquiries. In June 2011 ChaCha added a computational dimension to its offerings by forming a partnership with WolframAlpha, by its own account the "world's largest curated data repository." A Butler University study (January 31, 2013) comparing the accuracy rates of the major Q&A mobile platforms found ChaCha—classed in the study's executive summary as human-assisted—to be the most reliable, surpassing Ask.com (crowdsourced), Bing (algorithm-only), Yahoo (crowdsourced), Iris.[2] ("virtual assistant"; an app for Android), and Google (algorithm-only), among others. In November 2011 ChaCha was named by *Forbes* magazine as one of "America's Most Promising Companies."

Throughout his career, Jones has consistently launched or collaborated on multiple businesses in additional to his major ventures. Jones chairs Gazelle TechVentures, a venture-capital firm established in 1999. In 2000 Jones and Gerry Dick co-founded Grow INdiana Media Ventures, a disseminator of business and technology news; Jones serves as its chairman. In 1998 he founded PowerFile Inc., at one time the "world leader in DVD storage libraries," according to its Web site, but shuttered in 2010. From January 2005 until

July 2011, Jones was also a director of MOG, a music subscription company founded by David Hyman, the former CEO of Gracenote.

Jones received an honorary doctorate in science from Indiana University and the Distinguished Entrepreneur Award from the Kelley School of Business at Indiana University, both in 2002. An honorary doctorate in engineering from Rose-Hulman Institute of Technology was conferred on him in 2005. The Indiana University School of Informatics and the Advisory council awarded Jones its career achievement award in April 2011.

The Scott A. Jones Foundation, founded by Jones in 1994, generously supports educational and cultural activities for children. At the Indianapolis Children's Museum, of which Jones is a trustee, the foundation was a major contributor to Dinosphere, an exhibition of dinosaur fossils presented in exciting settings reflecting life in the Cretaceous Period, more than 65 million years ago. The exhibition—also funded by the Lilly Endowment and other sources—includes a dinosaur dig, the Polly Horton Hix Paleo Prep Lab, a question lab, and an art gallery. To the Indianapolis Zoo, Jones donated a safari-themed Kômbo Family Coaster and the Splash Park, a water park for children opened in 2000. The foundation sponsored the zoo's 2013 black-tie Zoobilation event, an annual fundraiser that is also intended to raise awareness of wildlife conservation efforts. The foundation also supports educational organizations and research institutions devoted to information technology, communications, transportation, and the medical and life sciences. Jones has also served as chairman of the Indiana Technology Partnership (now TechPoint), the goal of which is to make Indiana the Midwest's high-tech center in the 21st century.

Jones's home in the Indianapolis suburb of Carmel, Indiana, has become something of a showplace for the technologies he has helped to develop. A 27,000-square-foot home on a 53-acre property, Jones's estate is at once old-fashioned and decidedly contemporary. Built in the 1930s, the house resembles a 19th-century English manor; after five years of renovation and extension, it became a monument to modernity, one with which Jones is in continual contact via the Internet. From almost anywhere in the world, he can control the heat, lights, and music playing in any part of the house, and through a vast array of cameras and heat sensors in every room and on the grounds, he can keep track of staff (including IT directors) or check in on his family. (The house also boasts a 20-seat movie theater, a 28-foot mahogany slide connecting floors, a library, and a 2,500-gallon saltwater aquarium.)

Jones believes that such connectivity allows him to be more productive. When asked by *Current Biography* if he ever felt himself to be a prisoner of his own technology, he replied, "I have the freedom to connect. And, being human, there are times when I want (and really need) to disconnect. I love having the power and freedom to be connected, to accomplish my goals from anywhere and at anytime. I love having access to my best tools without the constraints of location or time. However, it is important for me to understand that I control the technology—it doesn't control me. This can be difficult for some people who either become addicted to the technology or feel pressure from others to utilize the technology when it invades their personal boundaries. ... People must understand their priorities in life and be able to effect those priorities through their conscious use of these powerful technologies. ... Just as the Internet has dramatically changed people's ability to access and search broad amounts of information, this increased ability to do so with entertainment content will dramatically enhance the way people 'do' education, training, business presentations, business communications, and home entertainment."

Jones maintains a close relationship with his parents, who helped oversee the renovation of his estate, as well as with his sister, Susie. He has five sons. Twice divorced, in 1997 and 2004, he remarried in 2011.

Further Reading:

Business Wire May 8, 2000

Forbes Nov. 30, 2011

Fortune p140 Oct. 11, 1999, Oct. 16, 2007

Indiana University Web site

Indianapolis Monthly p108+ Oct. 2001, March 2012

Indianapolis Star C p1 Apr. 19, 2000

Scott A. Jones Web site; *Wired* Nov. 13, 2006

Books and Journals:

Jordan, Robert, "Scott Jones: Boston Technology, Indiana," in *How They Did It: Billion Dollar Insights from the Heart of America* (RedFlash Press, 2010).

Morris, Jeremy Wade. "Making Music Behave: Metadata and the Digital Music Commodity," *New Media & Society* 14, no. 5 (2012): 850–866

Kaspersky, Eugene

Cryptologist and business executive

Born: 1965, Novorossiysk, Krasnodar Krai, Russia

Kaspersky, Natalya

Business executive

Born: 1966, Moscow, Russia

Once a computer programmer working in the Soviet defense ministry, Eugene Kaspersky is now widely regarded as one of the world's most prominent experts on information security, protecting networks and computers from viruses and e-mail spam. With his wife, Natalya Kaspersky, and Alexey De Mont De Rique (also spelled De Monderik), who is now described at the company Web site as a corporate adviser, Eugene Kaspersky founded the information security firm Kaspersky Lab in 1997. Although Eugene and Natalya Kaspersky divorced in 1998, they continued to operate Kaspersky Lab Group together until May 2012. Thereafter Eugene Kaspersky remained as chairman and CEO of Kaspersky Lab, now "arguably the most important Internet security company in the world," according to Noah Shachtman, writing in *Wired* (July 23, 2012). Natalya Kaspersky, who sold her shares of Kaspersky Lab in February 2012, became owner as well as chief executive officer of InfoWatch, a former subsidiary of Kaspersky Lab founded in 2003 to specialize in the security of internal data and office communications. Eugene continues to work as the head analyst at Kaspersky Lab, of which he has also been chief executive officer since his ex-wife stepped down from the position in 2011. Kaspersky Lab is now the world's largest privately owned vendor of software security products. According to Bob Tarzey, writing for *Infosecurity* (October 4, 2013), it "is one of the few Russian software companies with a global footprint and has achieved a level of trust many Western business would envy; a jewel indeed."

While Eugene has received numerous accolades for his programming, Natalya has earned the respect of the international business community both for helping Kaspersky Lab emerge as a successful global company and for building her own company, InfoWatch. Unlike the notorious Russian "oligarchs" (well-connected individuals who made fortunes owing to the privatization of the Soviet economy), Eugene Kaspersky and Natalya Kaspersky did not gain a reputation for accumulating wealth based on past connections or dubious deals, but by hard work, talent, business acumen, and quality products.

Education and Early Careers

Eugene (in English his given name is also rendered as Yevgeny) was born on October 4, 1965, in Novorossiysk, a southern Russian city that is the country's largest port on the Black Sea. As a high school student, he attended advanced classes in math and physics sponsored by Moscow State University. After graduating from the Institute of

Cryptography, Telecommunications and Computer Science in 1987, he found a job as a programmer at a scientific-research institute within the Soviet defense ministry. In 1989 his computer became infected with the Cascade virus, which had appeared the year before and was one of the best-known computer viruses at that time. The virus piqued Eugene's curiosity. "I became interested in finding out how it worked, and in detection and disinfecting," he told a correspondent from *Network News* (February 9, 2000). "At first I used a local Russian AV program [*AV* is shorthand for "anti-virus"] but then I developed my own. It became a hobby, just like collecting butterflies, but I came to understand the business implications." Kaspersky's first anti-virus product was a program that could catch 40 computer viruses. He distributed it mostly to his friends, who told him they were very pleased with the product's effectiveness. Dedicating himself full-time to studying computer viruses, he left the defense ministry in 1991 to work at the Information Technologies Center of KAMI, a large Russian company that sold computers, among other products. There, he and several colleagues improved on his original AV program and developed a piece of software called AntiViral Toolkit Pro (AVP).

Natalya was born on February 5, 1966, in Moscow. Her father had a doctorate in mathematics and physics, and her mother was a design engineer. As recorded in an archived page of the Kaspersky Club Web site (January 26, 2007), Natalya has said that she was a "pampered child," and she was a staff member of the Young Pioneers, a Soviet-era mass youth organization for children ages 10 through 15. Despite her early desire to become a veterinarian, she began attending the Moscow Institute of Electronic Engineering in 1983 and graduated in 1989 with a degree in applied mathematics. (Later she was awarded a bachelor's degree in Business Administration from the Open University in the United Kingdom.) She met Eugene in January 1987, at the "KGB holiday centre called Severskoye," and they married before she finished her degree. Shortly after graduation, she found work as a research assistant at Moscow's Central Scientific Design Office. She began working at KAMI Information Technologies Center in 1994 and despite having, by her own account, little knowledge of computers and marketing and no managerial experience, she became general manager of the AVP project. "I could not help making mistakes," she has said, as recorded at the Kaspersky Club blog page. "For example, I tried to sell everything myself, and that was wrong." She claimed not to have "extraordinary qualities": "Patience and hard work can sometimes make up for the absence of some other qualities. … I just do my work, the same work every day. If you really want something and you do your best to get it, you are bound to succeed." Natalya wanted to open an independent company, but Eugene demurred. Her first effort to found her own company, based on data-recovery software, failed, but she gained valuable experience from this effort.

Although AVP won several prominent international awards in 1994, the watershed moment for Eugene's anti-virus products occurred in 1998, when the on-line computing world was plagued by a virus called CIH, written by a Taiwanese student named Chen Ing-hau. (The virus is also known as the Chernobyl virus, because some strains of the virus were programmed to become active on April 26, 1999, the thirteenth anniversary of the nuclear disaster in the Ukrainian city of Chernobyl, then part of the Soviet Union.) The CIH virus, according to reports, damaged hundreds of thousands of computers. "For three weeks, we were the only ones who had an antidote," Eugene told Irina Schedrowa for the *Financial Times* (May 10, 2000). Dealers in a range of foreign countries, including Italy, Germany, and the United States, sought Kaspersky's product. Exploiting the demand for their product, Natalya negotiated deals with software developers in Finland, Germany, and Japan to include AVP software in their own products.

The success of AVP earned Eugene Kaspersky and Natalya Kaspersky enough prestige and capital to enable them to establish their own business. At Natalya's urging, in 1997 she and Eugene left KAMI to co-found the independent Kaspersky Lab, together with Alexey De Mont De Rique. Natalya assumed the role of chief executive officer (CEO) and general director; Eugene continued as the head of anti-virus research. They managed a staff of 13 employees. Kaspersky Lab maintained the AVP product name, and several of company's early products, including AVP Silver, AVP Gold, and AVP Platinum, became quite popular, both in Russia and abroad. In the years after the company's founding, Eugene was often quoted as a computer-virus expert in technology publications. Kaspersky Lab's revenues and international presence swelled: from 1998 through 2000, annual revenue at Kaspersky Lab grew 280 percent. Almost 60 percent of its revenue came from non-Russian sales. By May 2000 Kaspersky Lab had a staff of 65 people and claimed 30 dealers operating in more than 40 foreign countries.

In November 2000 AVP was renamed Kaspersky Anti-Virus. Aside from its premier products, Kaspersky Lab also provided free on-line security-related Internet information services, including an exhaustive on-line virus encyclopedia (see www.securelist.com); according to Eugene's biography page at the Kaspersky Lab Web site, as of October 2013, the Kaspersky Lab virus database contained descriptions of nearly 100 million viruses. Kaspersky's signature product could detect all of these viruses, as well as an estimated 80 to 90 percent of unknown viruses. Regarding her company's successes in 2000 alone, Natalya Kaspersky announced in a company press release (November 14, 2000), "This year has become a milestone in the company's development. We have managed to change from a small company, operating within national borders, to a global data security developer having a strong position in many countries all around the world."

Kaspersky Lab company represented the emergence of a new set of skilled workers in Russia. As Natalya wrote in an article for *WorldLink* (January 1, 2001), in the 1990s "Russia was seen by institutional investors as a nation that possessed huge human resource talent but little ability to create and develop its own propriety technology and intellectual property." At that time many skilled programmers emigrated to Western Europe and the United States to pursue a wide range of well-paying information-technology jobs. For talented programmers Kaspersky Lab offered an alternative to departure. The success of Kaspersky Lab also earned Eugene and Natalya access to powerful avenues in government: in April 2001 Natalya and several other IT executives met with Russian president Vladimir Putin to advise him on the development of Russia's high-technology economy. They requested the simplification of several laws regarding expansion into foreign countries; two months later, Putin's administration obliged. By 2002 Kaspersky Lab had regional offices in Moscow, Cambridge (England), and California, and continued to sell products through licensed regional suppliers. In February 2002 Kaspersky Lab and the international consulting company Ernst & Young announced a joint venture for providing risk management with their information services. By December 2002 the company had a commercial presence in 50 countries.

Between 1997 and 2002, the Kaspersky Lab share of the Russian anti-virus market rose from 5 percent to 60 percent. By February 2002 Kaspersky Lab claimed to have about 800,000 private clients and a significant number of Russian corporate clients, comprising about 30 percent of the corporate market share. Kaspersky Lab was viewed as a competitor with such highly ranked international information-security companies as Symantec, TrendMicro, Panda Software, and Network Associates.

Kaspersky Lab had become so successful in warding off viruses that it, too, became the target of attacks by malicious programmers and hackers. In November 2002 hackers infiltrated the company's server, obtained a list of e-mail address belonging to the company's clients, and then sent those clients a worm (an invasive computer program). Later that month, however, Kaspersky Lab scored a coup when it unveiled the first Russian program to protect clients from spam e-mail. Eugene even suggested that if stricter regulations were not quickly introduced, the Internet could "die" because of the inundation of viruses. The increase in the number of virus threats boosted the size of the information-security market, the total revenues from which skyrocketed between 2001 and 2002.

"AV work is, for me, like investigating a crime is for a policeman," Eugene told the correspondent from *Network News* in 2000. In August 2000 Kaspersky detected a type of virus in several banks' computers that stole individuals' bank-account information, directing the information to a thief. Such a virus was the first of its kind and portended a significant change in the profile of the typical virus programmer. In December 2004 Eugene told a reporter for United Press International (December 10, 2004) that organized crime had become responsible for 90 percent of malicious code on the Internet, as mobsters attempted to steal money or attract people to Internet rackets. He also indicated that Internet banks were easy targets.

At least as far back as 2000, Kaspersky predicted the spread of viruses to the numerous electronic consumer products that are enhanced by connections to the Internet, including mobile cellular phones and Internet-enabled refrigerators. Eugene's warnings about viruses infecting mobile phones proved prophetic. In late 2004 three invasive programs, albeit minor ones, attacked cell-phone users connected to the Internet in a time span of fewer than 60 days.

Later Careers

In 2003, at Natalya's initiative, Kaspersky Lab had founded a new company, InfoWatch, to focus on securing companies' internal information and communications. Natalya stepped down as CEO of Kaspersky Lab in 2007, becoming its chairman while also becoming the CEO of InfoWatch. Natalya's global business and marketing expertise helped make InfoWatch a leader in the Russian data-loss prevention market, and it steadily expanded its global presence. In 2007 Natalya also became a shareholder in Nanosemantics, a company founded in 2005 by Igor Ashmanov and Alexander Klachin to develop innovative human-computer interfaces that make it easier for users to interact with Web sites. In 2010 InfoWatch and Ashmanov & Partners created JSC Kribrum, a company that develops cloud solutions for social-media monitoring analysis. (Igor Ashmanov is Natalya's second husband.) InfoWatch acquired the German company Cynapspro GmbH, a software security firm later called EgoSecure, in 2011, thereby becoming a group of companies. The Web site Software Russia noted that the "InfoWatch Group … also includes the Natalya Kaspersky Innovation Center, which creates and develops new technologies to be submitted to the Group to commercialize." InfoWatch further extended its corporate data loss prevention reach by first acquiring Appercut Security, a Russian developer of solutions to audit codes for vulnerability (from Rustem Khairetdinov, the deputy CEO of her own firm), and then a controlling stake in German antivirus security company G Data Software.

In February 2012, as reported by John E. Dunn for Techworld (February 6, 2012), Eugene Kaspersky drew back from plans to take Kaspersky Lab public, announcing that he would buy back the 20 percent stake sold to the private equity firm General Atlantic the previous year in a transaction said to have valued the company at $1 billion. According to the on-line Russian IT review CNews (May 17, 2012), General Atlantic had made a significant part of its purchase from Natalya. In 2011 she had announced that she had no plans to leave the board of Kaspersky Lab, but, she told CNews, she "changed her decision because Eugene Kaspersky, her former husband, refused to take the company public." Natalya left her position as chairperson of Kaspersky Lab in the summer of 2011. In May 2012 Natalya purchased InfoWatch outright, in an exchange of shares, and thereafter the two companies operated independently. Natalya told CNews, "The companies work in different segments; we work with large clients, the Kaspersky Lab, within the small and medium business segment and with ordinary customers. That is why there is no common concept and there is no synergy."

Driven by the ever-increasing volume and sophistication of "hacktivist" and other cyberattacks, Kaspersky Lab by this time approached its malware diagnostics and cybersecurity mission much more flexibly than it had initially, with highly integrated product suites. As Bob Tarzey of *Infosecurity* asserts (October 4, 2013), "traditional IT security is no longer good enough on its own to defend against the growing numbers of targeted attacks and other emerging threats." Kaspersky Lab has addressed these conditions with the global Kaspersky Security Network, which, according to Tarzey, "gathers data from over 60 million end-points from contributing Kaspersky customers, providing rapid protection by keeping all users' devices up to date with the latest information about malware and dangerous network links. … The latest release of Kaspersky End-point Security for Business (KESB) includes a set of features designed to counter zero-day [day of emergence] attacks. … The range of end-points protected has been extending to include tablets, smartphones and virtual devices. There is also an overall device management tool to manage patching, usage policy etc. … In addition, Kaspersky System Watcher introduces a context aware security capability."

There appears to be general agreement that the stakes are high. In 2010 a Belorussian analyst (who now works for Kaspersky) uncovered a U.S.-Israeli worm program, called Stuxnet, that destroyed nearly a thousand Iranian centrifuges. Stuxnet is regarded as the world's first acknowledged cyberweapon. In 2012 Kaspersky Lab, working at the behest of the UN's International Telecommunication Union, revealed another "weaponized computer program," called Flame. Eventually it was found to be another U.S.-Israeli cyberattack, aimed this time at Iran's oil ministry. As Noah Shachtman of *Wired* wrote (July 23, 2012), Kaspersky Lab's work on Flame proved that "Kaspersky Lab isn't just an antivirus company; it's also a leader in uncovering cyber-espionage." Inevitably Kaspersky Lab's concentration in this area has a political dimension, since Stuxnet and Flame (and other such cyberweapons—such as Duqu, a so-called Trojan program designed to collect intelligence) were created to advance the geopolitical goals of major world powers. Kaspersky has regularly been accused of having too close a relationship with the Kremlin. Shachtman points out, however, that in many ways, the relationship between Kaspersky Lab and the Russian government is not unlike that between the largest U.S. cybersecurity firms, such as Symantec and McAfee, and the U.S. government: "These security firms have all become key players in their home countries' network defenses and in cybersecurity investigations worldwide." Nevertheless, Symantec aggressively pursued its own government's Stuxnet worm, and Shachtman notes that, "It's hard to find a similar case of Kaspersky and the Kremlin working at cross-purposes."

"Kaspersky insists," Shachtman continues, "that malware like Stuxnet and Flame should be banned by international treaty, like sarin gas or weaponized anthrax. He argues that the Internet should be partitioned and certain regions of it made accessible only to users who present an 'Internet passport.' That way, anonymous hackers wouldn't be able to get at sensitive sites—like, say, nuclear plants. Sure, it might seem like we'd be sacrificing some privacy online. But with all the advertisers, search engines, and governments tracking us today, Kaspersky argues, we don't really have any privacy left anyway."

In a *New York Times* article (June 3, 2012) reporting Eugene Kaspersky's warnings about the enormous dangers posed by so-called cyberweapons, Andrew E. Kramer and Nicole Perlroth quoted Eugene as saying, "Antivirus companies are in a not easy situation. … We have to protect our customers everywhere in the world. On the other hand, we understand there are quite serious powers behind these viruses." Stuxnet demonstrated that such "powers" included governments. Kramer and Perlroth noted that "While the United States and Israel are using the [cyber]weapons to slow the nuclear bomb-making abilities of Iran, they could also be used to disrupt power grids and financial systems or even wreak havoc with military defenses." At the CeBIT technogy conference in Sydney, Australia, in May 2012, Eugene Kaspersky offered his own bald assessment, quoted by Kramer and Perlroth: "Cyberweapons are the most dangerous innovation of this century."

"My goal is not to earn money. Money is like oxygen: Good idea to have enough, but it's not the target. The target is to save the world." —Eugene Kaspersky

"Patience and hard work can sometimes make up for the absence of some other qualities...If you really want something and you do your best to get it, you are bound to succeed." —Natalya Kaspersky

---

Although Kaspersky Lab originated in Russia and many of its functions are still based there, its holding company has been registered in the United Kingdom since 2006. The company has new, high-tech headquarters in northern Moscow. The *Moscow Times* (December 20, 2011) reported that in 2011 the "second-largest tenant of office space in Moscow was Kaspersky Lab, which leased 29,840 square meters in the Olympia Park business center on Leningradskoye Shosse"; the company has since purchased the office park, retaining some tenants, including BMW. As of October 2013, according to analyst Alex Schenker, writing for the on-line security assessment site A Secure Life, Kaspersky Lab had 29 regional offices throughout the world and operated in 200 countries. Schenker summarized the company's reach: "Kaspersky Lab develops secure content and threat management systems that currently protect more than 300 million technology users around the world. Kaspersky ...also serve[s] more than 200,000 corporate clients around the globe." The Kaspersky Lab Web site states that the company now employs more than 2,800 specialists. Its anti-virus engine also powers a variety of anti-virus products and solutions offered by security vendors such as Sybari, F-Secure, Check Point, Juniper Networks, Bluecoat, and GFI Software, among some 150 other companies that are licensing Kaspersky Lab technology. The company also has a number of partnerships with internationally prominent technology companies, such as Samsung. Currently its four chief products are Kaspersky ONE Universal Security, for desktops, laptops, tablets, and smartphones; cloud-based Kaspersky PURE 2.0 Total Security, which adds to Kaspersky ONE secure storage of passwords and photographs; Kaspersky Internet Security Suite 2014; and its most basic product, Kaspersky Anti-Virus 2013.

InfoWatch describes itself in its LinkedIn profile as a "European software company." It is headquartered in western Moscow. Its Web site announces that it has "50% of the Russian and CIS market in the corporate information security sector."

Both Eugene and Natalya speak English, and Natalya also speaks German. Natalya participates regularly in business development seminars and conferences worldwide. Natalya's profile at the Software Russia Web site notes that she "is a member of several IT committees of Russian governmental organizations, a member of Board of Directors of the German-Russian Chamber of Commerce, and a member of the Russian-British

Chamber of Commerce advisory councils. Natalya holds multiple awards from top notch Russian and international IT and Business Associations. In December 2011 she was nominated as one of the Top-25 'Russians to Watch' by the *Financial Times*." Horasis named her Russian Business Leader of the Year 2012, and she was a "Top1000 Russian Managers of 2013" in IT, according to the Russian business daily *Kommersant* and the Association of Russian managers.

Eugene writes frequently regarding computer virology and often speaks at international seminars. His biography at the Kaspersky Web site notes that he "has earned a number of international awards for his technological, scientific and entrepreneurial achievements. He was voted the World's Most Powerful Security Exec by SYS-CON Media in 2011, awarded an Honorary Doctorate of Science from Plymouth University in 2012, and named one of Foreign Policy Magazine's 2012 Top Global Thinkers for his contribution to IT security awareness on a global scale." Eugene admits to having a "passion for fast driving" and he sponsors the Ferrari Formula One team. Nevertheless, he remains absorbed in his work. "My goal is not to earn money. Money is like oxygen: Good idea to have enough, but it's not the target," he told Noah Shachtman. "The target is to save the world."

The Kasperskys had two sons together. After their divorce, Natalya Kaspersky married businessman Igor Ashmanov and had three more children. Eugene and his girlfriend had a child together. In April 2011 Eugene and Natalya's 19-year-old son Ivan, going to his internship job at InfoWatch, was kidnapped and held for ransom. He was freed unharmed four days later after the Moscow police and the FSB (Federated Security Service; the national security agency, successor to the KGB) cooperated to trace the kidnappers and mount a rescue operation. Eugene asserted that social media had helped the kidnappers to follow his son's movements; Natalya contested this notion, however, saying that Ivan had not revealed sufficient information on-line to aid the kidnappers. Both Eugene and Natalya have supported restrictions on social media sites such as those that became law in July 2012 (along with a registry of banned sites and content and a means of enforcement that permits the government to censor any offending site). These restrictions are seen by many as intended not to protect children, as the Putin administration has claimed, but to stifle political dissent: Russian social-networking sites such as VK and LiveJournal have helped galvanize tens of thousands of protesters on behalf of opposition political figures such as Alexey Navalny. Natalya, however, told David Herszenhorn of the *New York Times* (July 10, 2012) that, in Herszenhorn's words, "some new restrictions were needed in Russia to protect children and that the fears of government censorship seemed overblown." She added, "Right now we have a tremendous freedom of speech in mass media, with no prohibited topics at all."

At his own blog page at the Kaspersky Lab Web site (July 25, 2012), Kaspersky countered any idea that he was interested in suppressing social media sites: "I have an active presence on Facebook, Twitter, Flickr, Google+, YouTube, LinkedIn and LiveJournal. I'm an active supporter of the possibilities social networking brings to open communication and dialogue. I constantly stress that social networks can be used for positive things, and would never wish this medium to be shut down or censored. Besides, I personally am open to all kinds of questions and dialogue. As is Kaspersky Lab as a whole."

John E. Dunn, writing for Techworld (July 25, 2012), recorded Kaspersky's insistence that the "very mission of our company is to fight cyber-crime all around the world—together with our colleagues in the industry. We don't do it just because it happens to be our business; we also do it because we believe that protecting the world from malware is critically important and will continue to allow us to live in a better, safer, more open and effective society. It's our underlying principle by which we stand firmly and always will."

Further Reading:

cNews Web site May 17, 2012

Computer Crime Research Center Web site Jan. 11, 2005

Financial Times p16 May 10, 2000, Sep. 25, 2012

Infosecurity magazine, Oct. 4, 2013

Kaspersky Lab Web site

Moscow Times Dec. 20, 2011

Nanosemantics Web site; *Network News* p50 Feb. 9, 2000

New York Times Jun. 3, 2012, Jul. 10, 2012

A Secure Life Web site Oct. 4, 2013

Software Russia Web site

Techworld Apr. 25, 2011, Feb. 6, 2012, Jul. 25, 2012

Wired Jul. 23, 2012, Nov. 1, 2012; WorldLink Jan. 1, 2001

MacFarlane, Seth

Animator, voice actor, writer, producer

Born: 1973, Kent, Connecticut, United States

"The real beauty of animation is that there are no boundaries to the types of stories you can tell or rules on how you can tell them," Seth MacFarlane told Bruce Newman for the *New York Times* (January 24, 1999). In the late 1990s, only three years after graduating from the Rhode Island School of Design with a degree in animation, MacFarlane created *Family Guy,* an enormously popular animated TV series with several characters voiced by MacFarlane himself. The show has been lauded by many for its cultural satire and mix of highbrow and lowbrow humor, and maligned by many others, who view it as tasteless. *Family Guy* aired on the Fox network for three seasons before being canceled owing to comparatively low ratings, but strong DVD sales, highly rated reruns, and the show's popularity among young males—an audience highly coveted by advertisers—persuaded Fox to bring the series back after a hiatus of three years. MacFarlane has won many honors for *Family Guy,* including Primetime Emmy awards in 2000 and 2002 and multiple Emmy nominations. In 2005 MacFarlane launched a second animated show, *American Dad!,* which follows the exploits of a family headed by a jingoistic CIA employee and features more political humor than *Family Guy.* MacFarlane's third animated series, *The Cleveland Show*—a *Family Guy* spinoff with African American main characters—debuted in the fall of 2009 and ran until 2013.

In one of the first deals of its kind, MacFarlane signed an agreement with Google in 2008 to create content directly for the Internet. He ventured into live-action sitcoms in 2007 with the short-lived *The Winner,* as a writer and producer; in 2013 he was co–executive producer of another live sitcom, *Dads,* which was panned by critics, even some generally appreciative of MacFarlane's brand of humor. MacFarlane's first feature film was *Ted* (2012; a sequel has been announced for 2015); he directed the film, was a co-writer, and not only voiced the eponymous stuffed teddy bear but acted the part as well, with motion-capture technology. (For this he was nominated for a 2013 MTV Movie Award for "Best Shirtless Performance.") In his second film, *A Million Ways to Die in the West*—slated for release in 2014; currently in postproduction—MacFarlane plays Albert, the lead character. MacFarlane is a frequent guest on television talk shows, including *The Tonight Show with Jay Leno, Conan, Jimmy Kimmel Live,* and *Larry King Now,* and in 2012 he was a guest host on *Saturday Night Live.* In February 2013 he proved to be a controversial host for the 85th Annual Academy Awards, at which he was also a nominee (with Walter Murphy, a frequent collaborator), for Best Original Song (*Ted*'s "Everybody Needs a Best Friend").

Education and Early Career

Seth Woodbury MacFarlane was born on October 26, 1973, in Kent, Connecticut. His younger sister, Rachael, is an actress (she voices a character on *American Dad!*). MacFarlane's father, Ronald, was a history teacher; his mother, Perry, was a guidance counselor and admissions adviser at the private Kent School, which MacFarlane attended. MacFarlane described his parents to Bruce Newman as former hippies who were "just coming out of it"; they raised him in a liberal household. "The style of humor that you'll see in the show is the same kind of tasteless humor that you'd find around my house when I was growing up," he told Newman. "Some of the foulest jokes that I ever heard came from my mother." MacFarlane showed a penchant for drawing at a very young age. At age eight he began publishing a comic strip, "Walter Crouton," in the *Kent Good Times Dispatch,* a local newspaper. The thought of animation, however, intimidated him, until he saw a television show about an animated film created by a college student. "I started experimenting with animation after that," MacFarlane told Newman. As a boy he also participated with his sister in local musical theater.

MacFarlane graduated from Kent in 1991 and then enrolled at the Rhode Island School of Design, in Providence, from which he graduated in 1995 with a B.A. degree in animation. MacFarlane initially wanted to work for the children's-animation giant Disney but later decided that he would rather make cartoons geared toward adults. (By then he had become a fan of the long-running animated prime-time show *The Simpsons,* created by Matt Groening.) While still a student, MacFarlane had created an animated short, *The Life of Larry.* One of his professors sent it to executives at Hanna-Barbera, the studio responsible for many of the animated programs that have appeared on American television since 1960. Impressed, the studio's executives invited MacFarlane to work for them, with the result that he moved to Los Angeles, California, shortly after graduating from college. Over the next few years, he worked on several Hanna-Barbera shows, including *Johnny Bravo* and *Dexter's Laboratory.* During that time the Fox network's program *MAD TV* showed an interest in airing *The Life of Larry,* but that deal ultimately fell through. Soon, though, executives at Fox invited MacFarlane to create and pitch an animated series. Over the course of six months, he singlehandedly wrote, animated, and did all the voices for an eight-minute presentation in 1998 that laid the groundwork for *Family Guy.* Fox was sold. "That the network ordered a series off of eight minutes of film is just testimony to how powerful those eight minutes were," Sandy Grushow, president of 20th Century Fox Television, told Newman. "There are very few people in their early 20s who have ever created a television series." At 24, MacFarlane was the youngest creator and executive producer in television.

Family Guy, which debuted in 1999, is set in Quahog, Rhode Island, and follows the adventures of the overweight, bumbling Peter Griffin, his considerably smarter and more attractive wife, and their two misfit teenage children. The family also includes Stewie, an evil toddler bent on matricide and world domination, and Brian, an Ivy League-educated, martini-swilling, talking dog. MacFarlane voiced most of the male characters, including Peter, Stewie, the lecherous neighbor Glenn Quagmire, and Brian, the last of whom, many journalists have reported, has the speaking voice closest to his creator's. MacFarlane told *People* (November 29, 2004) that of all the characters he voices, he has the most in common with Brian: "We're both liberal, enjoy a good Scotch and tend to get in awkward situations with women." He revealed to Gloria Goodale of the *Christian Science Monitor* (February 12, 1999) that his inspiration for the character Peter was the father of a friend, who fell asleep and began snoring in a theater during a showing of the film *Philadelphia* (about the political and social implications of AIDS)—behavior that "just appalled his family." As Goodale reported, that act of "innocent political incorrectness" appealed to MacFarlane.

Family Guy drew both praise and condemnation for its willingness to make jokes about any and all topics, often in the form of sudden asides unassociated with the plots. "MacFarlane's pell-mell wit recalls *The Simpsons*' fevered early-'90s creative peak," Michael Krantz wrote for *Time* (January 11, 1999). "Punch lines spill out furiously as the show spirals into multilayered flashbacks and inventive fantasies." The *Entertainment Weekly* (April 9, 1999) writer Ken Tucker, however, likened *Family Guy* to "*The Simpsons* as conceived by a singularly sophomoric mind that lacks any reference point beyond other TV shows." MacFarlane asserted his right to pull humor from any milieu, high or low. "Hopefully, people will think of us as a smart show," he told Jefferson Graham for the *Financial Post* (February 15, 1999). "If we do a penis joke, we'll back it up with a Norman Mailer joke. We want a wide variety of humor." MacFarlane also denied charges of being intentionally offensive. "We're not out to simply piss people off," he told Ray Richmond of the *Hollywood Reporter* (October 31, 2007). "It's not about being as offensive as we can be. It's about being funny."

MacFarlane took ribbing not only from some critics but from his peers in prime-time animation. In an episode of *The Simpsons* in which the Simpson family travels to Italy, a shot zooms in on a police blotter that says that Peter Griffin is wanted for the crime of "plagiarismo." Matt Stone and Trey Parker, the creators of the raunchy cartoon show *South Park,* devoted two full episodes to mocking MacFarlane's work, ending with the report that *Family Guy* is actually written by manatees. *South Park* also poked fun at the seemingly random content and timing of the humorous asides on *Family Guy.* "If something is funny enough, we do step out of the story," MacFarlane responded, as quoted by Alex Strachan for the Canwest News Service (November 1, 2007). "I mean, who the hell watches a sitcom for the story? You watch it because you want to laugh." He added that he had found the *South Park* episodes about *Family Guy* to be very funny.

Family Guy impressed most critics and struck a chord with young male viewers. It has won several honors, including Primetime Emmy awards for outstanding voice-over performance (2000) and outstanding music and lyrics (2002), for the lyrics written by MacFarlane. The show suffered, though, from several programming missteps on the part of the network, which rescheduled the show many times—a proven way to lose viewers—and put it opposite such formidable competition as World Wrestling Entertainment offerings, the hit sitcom *Friends,* and the popular reality-TV show *Survivor. Family Guy* came close to cancelation in 2000 but was revived at the last minute, only to be axed in 2002.

Following the show's cancelation, Fox responded to popular demand and released the three seasons of *Family Guy* on DVD. It also licensed reruns to appear on the Cartoon Network as part of the channel's late-night "Adult Swim" lineup. The DVD *Family Guy: Volume One* sold more than 2.2 million copies, and *Family Guy* was the highest-rated show on Adult Swim during that time. In 2005 executives at Fox approved new episodes of the series after three years—the longest hiatus of any network show ever to be brought back to life. *Family Guy* returned to the airwaves in January 2005.

Family Guy branched beyond its regular network slot and into other media. In 2006 High Voltage Games/2K Games (a subsidiary of Take-Two Interactive Software Inc.) released *Family Guy Video Game!,* voiced by the original Family Guy cast. A second video game, *Family Guy: Back to the Multiverse,* was developed by Heavy Iron Studios and published by Activision in 2012. MacFarlane has created several *Family Guy* specials, and his *Family Guy Presents: Stewie Griffin ... the Untold Story* (2005) was the first straight-to-DVD movie ever made from a television series. MacFarlane's well known affection for the *Star Trek* and *Star Wars* series and movies led to *Blue Harvest* (2007), the hour-long premiere episode of *Family Guy*'s sixth season, which recast *Star Wars* with the Griffin family and friends and used the premise of that famous science-fiction film series as a jumping-off point for numerous gags. An uncut version of *Blue Harvest* was released on DVD in 2008. In that year *Family Guy: Something, Something, Something, Dark Side*—a spoof of *The Empire Strikes Back,* the second film in the *Star Wars* series—was released on DVD. MacFarlane's parody of the *Star Wars* series continued in the video *Family Guy Presents: It's a Trap* (2010). Featuring MacFarlane and Alex Borstein, the actress who voices Lois Griffin, *Family Guy Presents: Seth & Alex's Almost Live Comedy Show,* aired in the fall of 2009, sandwiched between *Family Guy* episodes. The assemblage of skits and *Family Guy* clips was sponsored by Warner Bros. after being dropped by its original sponsor, Microsoft, because of its controversial content. *Entertainment Weekly* writer Ken Tucker characterized it (November 8, 2009) "nightclub set," with an orchestra and an audience. Tucker praised MacFarlane's singing voice and the dexterity with which he can switch in and out of character voices. The retrospective TV movie *Family Guy: 200 Episodes Later* was released in 2012.

The revived *Family Guy* arrived in May 2005 alongside *American Dad!*, a new show MacFarlane had created for the network during *Family Guy*'s hiatus. MacFarlane co-created *American Dad!* with Mike Barker and Matt Weitzman and did extensive voicing for the show, but he left much of its creative direction to Weitzman and Barker. Like *Family Guy, American Dad!* follows a nuclear family, headed this time by a bumbling CIA employee, Stan Smith. The more outlandish family members are a German-speaking goldfish and a junk-food-loving alien, both of whom Stan rescued from government experiments at Area 51 (the Nevada military base where some conspiracy theorists believe the U.S. government is hiding bodies of space aliens who crash-landed on Earth). The humor on *American Dad!* is more overtly political than that of *Family Guy,* satirizing current events, such as the George W. Bush–led "war on terror." MacFarlane told Bridget Byrne of the Associated Press (April 20, 2005) that the show's concept "sprang from the climate during the [2004 presidential] election … a very politically charged time." After a decade on Fox, *American Dad!* was slated to relocate to TBS in late 2014, following the show's 2013–14 season on Fox.

Although MacFarlane is liberal, he told Virginia Rohan for the Bergen County, New Jersey, *Record* (May 1, 2005), "We do try and satirize both sides—the knee-jerk flag-waving personality of Stan and the [daughter] Haley personality, the type who will burst into applause if [the liberal comedian and commentator] Bill Maher even sneezes." *American Dad!* received relatively good ratings but did not come close to the popularity of *Family Guy,* perhaps, some suggested, because it addressed issues about which the American public was not yet ready to laugh. "Stan's cluelessness approximates that of Peter Griffin's, only with the potential of a body count," David Kronke wrote for the *Los Angeles Daily News* (May 1, 2005).

Meanwhile, in 2008 MacFarlane had signed a deal with Google to create *Seth MacFarlane's Cavalcade of Cartoon Comedy,* an original series of animated shorts distributed by Google AdSense to various Web sites the users of which were thought to be *Family Guy* viewers. That project represented the first original content underwritten by Google for the purposes of on-line distribution. In early 2009 Priceline signed on as an additional partner, sponsoring MacFarlane's on-line animated short *Ted Nugent Is Visited by the Ghost of Christmas Past.*

Also in 2009 MacFarlane introduced *The Cleveland Show,* his third animated prime-time series. *The Cleveland Show* focused on Cleveland Brown, a character from *Family Guy*; the first episode of the new program found Cleveland and his son leaving Rhode Island for California. "Cleveland is African American, which needs to be mentioned here because the other characters in the show never stop mentioning it," Tom Shales wrote about the show for the *Washington Post* (September 29, 2009). "The humor doesn't necessarily promote racial stereotypes, but whenever a crude joke can be made out of it, Cleveland's race is mentioned—over and over, in scene after scene. The message that young viewers receive is that racial minorities are different, separate, apart from the norm." (The character Cleveland was voiced by a white actor, Mike Henry.) *The Cleveland Show* aired on Fox on Sunday nights, along with *The Simpsons, American Dad!,* and *Family Guy,* as part of Fox's "animation domination" programming block. *The Cleveland Show* was canceled by Fox in 2013, after four seasons and 88 episodes. MacFarlane announced that the Clevelands would be returning to Quahog.

MacFarlane's animated shows have been highly successful both despite and because of their edgy humor. As Ray Richmond noted, gags on *Family Guy* have included a character identified as a "loveable pedophile"; a Pez dispenser, modeled on the slain U.S. president John F. Kennedy, that disgorges candy from its head;

and an abandoned baby singing about having been left in a Dumpster. The humor has occasionally drawn complaints, as when Chris Griffin, a character on *Family Guy,* went on a date in a February 2010 episode with a woman with Down syndrome, who claimed to be the daughter of "the former governor of Alaska." The real-life former Alaska governor Sarah Palin, the 2008 Republican vice-presidential nominee, has a young son, Trig, with Down syndrome; Palin strongly criticized the airing of the episode. As quoted by the *Los Angeles Times* (February 17, 2010), MacFarlane responded in a statement, "From its inception, *Family Guy* has used biting satire as the foundation of its humor. The show is an equal-opportunity offender."

Later Career

The Winner, MacFarlane's first attempt at a live sitcom—he was executive producer of some episodes and evidently the writer of others—was created by Ricky Blitt, a *Family Guy* writer. Its protagonist, played by Rob Corddry, looked back on his life when he was in his thirties, a "late bloomer" still living at home with his parents. The show lasted just one season. MacFarlane's next foray into live sitcoms was *Dads,* written by Alec Sulkin and Wellesley Wild—MacFarlane's collaborators on *Family Guy*—for which MacFarlane, Sulkin, and Wild served as co–executive producers. Starring Seth Green and Giovanni Ribisi as successful video game developers whose fathers (played by Peter Riegert and Martin Mull) move in with them, wreaking havoc, *Dads* ran into critical resistance even before its premiere. Frasier Moore, writing in the Huffington Post TV blog (September 16, 2013), commented, "*Dads* is a display of parental abuse."

"It's not about being as offensive as we can be. It's about being funny.

MacFarlane's first feature film, *Ted* (2012), starring Mark Wahlberg, Mila Kunis, and MacFarlane himself as the stuffed teddy bear of the title, was notably successful with both audiences and critics, setting records for highest weekend gross of all time for an original R-rated comedy and then for highest-grossing R-rated comedy ever and taking in more than $500 million worldwide. MacFarlane directed the film, co-wrote the screenplay with Wild and Sulkin, and was co-producer in addition to starring as the foul-mouthed talking teddy bear who interferes with the relationship between John (played by Wahlberg), and his longtime girlfriend Lori (played by Kunis). There was immediately talk of a sequel, and Wahlberg signed on for a *Ted 2,* with a tentative release date in the spring of 2015. Meanwhile, Universal Studios had signed on for another film with the MacFarlane team, the comedy/Western *A Million Ways to Die in the West,* scheduled to be released in May 2014. MacFarlane co-produced and directed from a script he wrote with Wild and Sulkin. MacFarlane also stars in the film, as a timorous sheep farmer who backs away from a gunfight and consequently loses his girlfriend, played by Amanda Seyfried. The film co-stars Charlize Theron, Giovanni Ribisi, Liam Neeson, Neil Patrick Harris, and Sarah Silverman, among others.

MacFarlane's original song for *Ted,* "Everybody Needs a Best Friend," written with Walter Murphy, was nominated for an Oscar in 2013 in the category Best Achievement in Music Written for Motion Pictures, Original Song. This, however, was not his first award nomination as a composer. That came with his Grammy nomination in 1999 in the category Best Song Written Specifically for a Motion Picture or for Television, for *Family Guy*'s "Christmastime Is Killing Us," which MacFarlane wrote with Ron Jones and Danny Smith.

MacFarlane has established himself as a fine baritone, having appeared with the John Wilson Orchestra at the BBC Proms concerts in 2009 in the program "That's Entertainment: A Celebration of Classic MGM Film Musicals." MacFarlane again joined the John Wilson Orchestra in a 2012 Proms celebration of Broadway musicals, singing the music of Meredith Wilson (*The Music Man*), Richard Adler and Jerry Ross (*The Pajama Game*), and Frank Loesser (*Guys and Dolls, The Most Happy Fella*). MacFarlane's debut studio album, *Music Is Better Than Words*, a big band/standards album released in 2011, was nominated in the "Best Traditional Pop Vocal Album category" at the 54th Grammy Awards in February 2012. *Seth MacFarlane: Swingin' in Concert* ran on the Epix Channel in September 2011, with MacFarlane singing the pop standards included on *Music Is Better Than Words* with a 39-piece big band, conducted by Joel McNeely.

A resident of Los Angeles, MacFarlane in 2008 signed a four-year, $100-million deal with Fox, making him the highest-paid writer-producer working in television. "I get a lot of pleasure out of making shows," MacFarlane told Nellie Andreeva for the Reuters News Service (May 5, 2008). "It's a bonus to be getting paid well for it, and it's a double bonus to be getting paid exorbitantly for it."

Further Reading:

(Canada) *National Post* Arts & Life p9 Nov. 1, 2007

Christian Science Monitor Features p18 Feb. 12, 1999

New York Times II p38 Jan. 24, 1999, Sep. 3, 2000, Sep. 11, 2009, Sep. 29, 2011, June 19, 2012, Feb. 25, 2013

sethmacfarlane.net

Washington Post C p1 Sep. 29, 2009

Selected Television Shows:

as writer

Dexter's Laboratory, 1997–98

Johnny Bravo, 1997–2003

special material, *85th Annual Academy Awards,* 2013

as creator, writer, and producer

Family Guy, 1999–

American Dad!, 2005–

The Cleveland Show, 2009–2013

Seth MacFarlane's Cavalcade of Cartoon Comedy, 2009

Selected Films:

Family Guy Presents: Stewie Griffin ... The Untold Story, 2005

Family Guy Presents: Something, Something, Something, Dark Side, 2009

Family Guy Presents: It's a Trap (2010)

Family Guy: 200 Episodes Later, 2012

Feature Film:

Ted, 2012

Messier, Jean-Marie

Business executive, investment banking consultant

Born: 1956, Grenoble, France

"I am not realising a dream to become a media mogul. I am realising my dream of creating a truly global media company that is neither European or American-centric." According to the London *Sunday Times* (June 25, 2000), as quoted on Justpeople.com, those words were uttered by Jean-Marie Messier, then the chairman and CEO of the highly diversified French company Vivendi. Messier was speaking at a news conference at which he and Edgar Bronfman Jr., the head of the Canadian beverage and entertainment company Seagram's, announced the merger of their firms with the French concern Canal Plus to form a new conglomerate called Vivendi Universal. The deal brought under one umbrella Vivendi's operations, which ranged from waste management to the provision of utilities to publishing to television and phone service; Seagram's holdings, which included Universal Pictures and Polygram Records as well as distilleries; and Canal Plus, one of the biggest pay-TV businesses in Europe. A year later, according to Seth Schiesel in the *New York Times* (August 27, 2001), Vivendi Universal ranked as the fourth-largest media conglomerate on Earth, behind AOL Time Warner, Disney, and Viacom. In terms of total revenues, it was second only to AOL Time Warner.

Messier spent a dozen years in government service before entering the private sector, in 1989. He worked for the investment bank Lazard Frères before joining, in 1994, Compagnie Générale des Eaux (General Water Co.), one of France's oldest and most respected utility firms. Within two years he had become its head, and in 1998 he changed its name to Vivendi. As the chairman of Vivendi Universal—described by *New York Times* correspondent Mark Landler (July 7, 2002) as "France's first genuinely global communications company"—Messier directed an empire valued at about $55 billion, one that encompassed one of Europe's main cable companies as well as Universal Pictures and Universal Music Group. In contrast to the stereotypical corporate European modus operandi, which is characterized by caution and insularity, Messier conducted business at a fast pace and espoused a global vision.

Yet even more rapidly than Vivendi had been transformed into a leading player in the world media market, it collapsed, owing to massive debt, poor timing, and a series of missteps by Messier that alienated both Vivendi investors and a large segment of the French citizenry. People who had once regarded Messier as a hero came to view him as a traitor because of his all-but-stated objective of ending the French government's heavy subsidization of the nation's film industry, on one hand, and, on the other, spreading American-style pop culture. Throughout the first half of 2002, Messier tried to turn his company around, but on July 1, 2002, yielding to growing pressure from others within the firm, he announced his resignation. "In some respects, Mr. Messier set out to be an exception to the French exception," Mark Landler wrote. "In other respects, however, he was simply walking the treacherous path trod by other moguls who tried to straddle national and cultural divides."

Education and Early Career

The son of Pierre Messier and the former Janine Delapierre, Jean-Marie Raymond Pierre Messier was born into a middle-class family on December 13, 1956, in Grenoble, France. He attended the École Polytechnique, an elite business college in Paris, from 1976 to 1979. From 1980 to 1982, also in Paris, he studied at the École Nationale d'Administration, which trains French civil servants. On graduating he was hired by the French Ministry of Economy and Finance as inspector of finances, a position he held from 1982 until 1986. In 1986 he was selected to lead the Finance Ministry team that was preparing the first privatization of state companies in France. In this position he served as adviser to finance minister Édouard Balladur, who later (1993–1995) served as France's prime minister. With the resignation in 1988 of right-wing prime minister Jacques Chirac and his replacement by a Socialist, Michel Rocard, a new Finance Ministry staff was appointed, and Messier lost his job. In 1989 Messier joined the investment bank Lazard Frères & Co. as a general partner, thus becoming the youngest partner in the history of the century-old bank. During the five years he worked for Lazard Frères, he spent five months in New York City, where he learned American business practices.

In 1994 Messier was named chief executive of the executive committee at Compagnie Générale des Eaux, a Paris-based water, waste-management, public-transport, and construction company. (Essentially he was the company's second in command.) Générale supplied potable water to business, industry, municipalities, and residences; reaching about 70 million people, including 25 million in France, it was Europe's largest supplier of water. Messier assumed control of Générale in 1996, after his predecessor as chief executive officer, Guy Dejouany, stepped down. At the time of Messier's ascendancy, Dejouany and other Générale managers were being investigated for making illegal donations to political parties. In addition, in 1995, for the first time in its almost 150-year history, Générale had reported a loss—one amounting to $624 million. The company had also accumulated $9.6 billion in debt owing to unsound real-estate investments and the acquisition of a vast array of holdings, ranging from casinos to laundry services.

Recognizing that Générale had to divest itself of many of its holdings in order to stay afloat, Messier instituted radical changes. In his first few months at the helm, he trimmed the workforce by 10 percent (although, with 220,000 employees remaining, Générale was still the largest private employer in France). He also raised money by selling property across Europe worth $1.6 billion, the company's healthcare assets, and Générale 's majority stake in a private cable-television company. He then refocused the company by dividing it into two entities, one handling water service and waste management and the other dealing with communications. "We had to reform strongly and abruptly," Messier told John Tagliabue for the *New York Times* (October 14, 1997). "Now we are in a position to be more aggressive."

Armed with the money earned from divesting Générale of many of its assets and from financing through eurobonds (bonds issued by an international syndicate and offered to investors in a number of countries simultaneously), Messier reinvested in water and waste-management facilities. In 1997 he bought out Leigh Interest, a British waste-management company, for $187.4 million; in 1998, for $6.2 billion, he bought the US Filter Corp., the largest private American water company as well as the largest global supplier of industrial water-treatment equipment and services. By 1998 Générale had become active in more than 80 countries. It ranked as the top energy supplier and the leading waste-management company in Europe, operating 187 municipal heating works (which provide heat to homes and businesses) and collecting more than 15 million tons of household and nonhazardous industrial waste annually. In addition, Générale had become Europe's leading private transport operator, with a fleet of 8,000 local and intercity buses and 2,400 train cars transporting more than 600 million passengers a year.

With regard to communications and the media, Générale 's goal, Seth Schiesel quoted Messier as saying, was "to be the world market leader in the five fields of content that we consider as key for this digital age: music, movies, games, education and sport." Through a stock swap, in early 1997 Messier increased Générale's share in the French multimedia group Havas to 30 percent. Among other products, Havas published the Larousse encyclopedias and the weekly French magazine *L'Express*. Of greater importance to Messier was Havas's controlling interest in Canal Plus, Europe's largest cable- and pay-TV company. In 1998 Messier became the leading shareholder in Havas, thus giving Générale control of Havas's stock in Canal Plus. Earlier, in 1997, Générale had completed a deal in which British Telecom, Mannesmann, and SBC Communications acquired minority stakes in Générale 's telecommunications subsidiary, Cegetel, the owner of SFR, a French wireless operator. In Messier's first year and a half as Générale 's head, the company reported net profits of $320 million on revenues of $28.5 billion. "The changes at Générale have been significant during the last eighteen months," Messier told an interviewer for *Director* magazine, as quoted on the Web site of Jeremy Josephs, a journalist whose specialty is France. "Not just by French, but also by international standards. If you look at our divestitures during this period, they are close to 10 billion dollars—and I don't think that there are many groups in the world that have gone through such a revamping in such a short period of time. I have made some new choices and tried to recover some of the flexibility of the group. I feel that we are well-placed too, because in so far as utilities and communications are concerned, there is much to be done in the years ahead."

In mid-1998 Messier changed the company's name to Vivendi, which is a form of the French word for "living." The following year he acquired Pathe S.A. for Vivendi for $2 billion in stock. The largest film production and distribution company in France, Pathe S.A. also held stock in Canal Plus, which helped Vivendi tighten its grip on the satellite television network. In addition, the deal gave to Messier Pathe's 17 percent stake in British Sky Broadcasting, a Canal Plus rival that was controlled by Rupert Murdoch's News Corp. With the aim of trying to merge Canal Plus and British Sky Broadcasting, Vivendi increased its stake in Canal Plus to 24.5 percent. Negotiations toward a merger failed, however, because the question of who would run the blended company could not be resolved. Messier later sold his stake in British Sky Broadcasting to satisfy the European Competition Commission.

Later Career

Vivendi made additional strides toward becoming a major global multimedia power when, in June 2000, it acquired the Canadian-owned firm Seagram's for $34 billion. (At the same time, Vivendi and Canal Plus merged.) The merger was approved by the European Commission in October 2000 after the companies promised concessions to dilute the power of their combined business. Seagram's holdings included Universal Pictures, a major Hollywood studio that owned a library of more than 24,000 television episodes and 3,000 feature films, and the Polygram music group, which, with its many labels (among them Motown, Mojo, Island, and Def Jam Records), was the largest record company in the United States in terms of sales. Vivendi also acquired Seagram's beverage business, which it later sold for $8.15 billion. Edgar Bronfman Jr., the head of Seagram's before its merger with Vivendi, served as executive vice chairman of the new company until his resignation, on December 6, 2001.

When the Vivendi-Seagram's deal was announced, Vivendi stocks dropped, reflecting stockholders' doubts about the wisdom of such a massive expansion. (By September 2001 stocks of Vivendi Universal, as its name had become in December 2000, were still 31 percent lower in value than Vivendi's had been before the purchase.) Other large corporations had passed up the opportunity to buy Seagram's, and many in the business world thought that Vivendi had paid too much for the company. (According to Carol Matlack in *Business Week* [July 3, 2000], Vivendi paid "a 46 [percent] premium on Seagram's pre-bid price.") Moreover, many observers warned that Vivendi had greatly overestimated its ability to manage Universal.

Expressing a widely held view, one analyst told Reuters, as quoted by David Ignatius in the *Washington Post,* that "The chance of the French succeeding in running a U.S. music and film business properly is about zero." "Most of the reactions were skeptical," Messier acknowledged to Peter S. Goodman of the *Washington Post* (June 23, 2000). "Basically, the classic French, European reaction: 'OK, that's the concept, but if it could exist, a U.S. company would have done it already.'"

Despite the merger, more than half of Vivendi's roughly $40 billion in revenue continued to come from water distribution, waste management, and construction. Determined to increase the size and scope of Vivendi Universal, in 2001 Messier made a series of additional purchases: he spent $2 billion for 35 percent of a Moroccan telephone company, $2.2 billion for the Boston-based educational publisher Houghton Mifflin, and $372 million for the Internet site MP3.com. In partnership with the United Kingdom-based Vodafone AirTouch, the world's largest wireless telephone provider, Messier also prepared to launch a new European Internet portal to be known as Vizzavi. As Messier envisioned it, Vizzavi would be accessible by mobile telephones, desktop computers, and hand-held devices and would generate a whole new market for a subscription service to Universal's music catalog. "Can you tell me how to reach 100 million people across Europe?" Messier said to Peter S. Goodman. "That's what Vizzavi is." The launch of Vizzavi was delayed, however, because Web-enhanced, rapid-action cell phones were not yet available to consumers.

In 2001, after several failed attempts due to insufficient demand from institutional investors, Messier siphoned off Vivendi's water and construction business into Vivendi Environment, a separate stock offering. Also in 2001 Vivendi and the Sony Corp., headquartered in Tokyo, Japan, announced their joint formation of a new company to rival Napster's on-line music-sharing service. Pressplay, as it was called, covered Vivendi's and Sony's music catalogs through an exclusive licensing agreement and is offered as a paid subscription service. "No one can imagine launching online music without the world's number one and number two companies," Messier declared, as quoted on BBC News (February 23, 2001). He added, "We hope to licence 50 [percent] of the world's music." The subscription service was one of Messier's favorite tools for furthering business. "It's through a subscription relationship that you can identify what the customer is really doing and not doing, loving and not loving," he told Seth Schiesel. In late summer 2001, Cegetel announced the creation of Universal Music Mobile, a new service available through its SFR mobile-phone operation in France. The service included such benefits as personal voice-mail greetings recorded by pop stars. With the goal of expanding Vivendi's horizons in another direction, Messier (in collaboration with four other major Hollywood studios) announced plans for a system that would allow consumers to download movies over the Internet.

In early 2002 Vivendi's Universal Music Group was the world's largest music operation, with annual sales totaling around $6 billion. As of August 2001, Universal Pictures had the largest share of the box-office market for that year. By that time Vivendi had also become the second-largest publisher of computer games; its Blizzard games, which included the "Diablo" series, among others, were highly lauded. Canal Plus, which aimed to expand throughout Europe, began to take losses. Meanwhile, Cegetel had enrolled more than 12 million customers in France. Eager to keep his company's image up to date, Messier moved the Paris headquarters of Vivendi to modern offices near the Arc de Triomphe; the new site featured an Internet café on the ground floor. Messier also shifted his personal base of operations to New York City, proclaiming a love for the city and becoming heavily involved in its social and philanthropic scene.

In December 2001 Vivendi Universal purchased, for $1.5 billion, 10 percent of EchoStar, a satellite television company that had made inroads into the suburban American cable-television markets and had more than five million subscribers in the United States. At the time Messier and his colleagues believed that Vivendi could fortify EchoStar with new technology and Universal movies and television programs. Shortly afterward Messier announced a $10.3 billion deal to set up a new company called Vivendi Universal Entertainment, which would run the conglomerate's American movie, television, and theme-park business. To head this company, Messier hired the former ABC, Paramount, and Fox mogul Barry Diller, who also retained control of the USA Networks. With hopes high for the success of this venture, American depository receipts for Vivendi Universal rose 6.43 percent on the New York Stock Exchange after the deal. In the spring of 2002, Vivendi gained control of the entertainment assets of USA Networks; with the acquisition of USA Interactive, as it was renamed, Vivendi secured majority control of the Home Shopping Network, Ticketmaster, Hotel Reservations Network, and the Web site Expedia, among other businesses.

All was not well with Vivendi Universal, however. In 2001 Canal Plus, which aimed to expand throughout Europe, had suffered large losses for the fifth straight year, as a result of rising programming costs. In March 2002 Vivendi reported an astounding $12 billion loss, attributed to Canal Plus's troubles, Vizzavi's faltering business, and reduced values of other Vivendi acquisitions. With investor pressure mounting, on April 16, 2002, Messier fired the head of Canal Plus, Pierre Lescure. The reason, Messier told a news conference, as reported by John Tagliabue in the *New York Times* (April 17, 2002), was the need to "change the team, to give it a fresh start. Canal Plus used to have a soul and profit. The impression is that it has lost a little bit of both." But an angry Lescure charged, according to Tagliabue, that his removal showed that Messier's intention was really "to reduce the channel to a simple editor, with distribution passing into the hands of foreigners responsible for audiovisual material." Although Vivendi's share price revived somewhat following the shakeup at Canal Plus (which included the resignation of Lescure's second-in-command), it remained at about 50 percent below what it had been when the Seagram trade had been completed. Many French people resented Messier's actions, not least because Canal Plus acted as a funnel through which the French government financed 80 percent of all French films. Moreover, many still felt angry about a December 2001 interview in which Messier said, as quoted by Alan Riding in the *New York Times* (December 24, 2001), "The Franco-French cultural exception is dead"—a reference to the French system of promoting films made in France through subsidies and mandatory investment, and by requiring 40 percent of movies broadcast on French television to be French productions. Messier insisted in vain that he had been misquoted; even the president of France, Jacques Chirac, and members of the nation's cabinet criticized him.

In mid-April 2002, Vivendi announced that it would sell one of its publishing units, so as to reduce the company's overall $33 billion debt by about $1 billion (in euros). At a Vivendi Universal shareholders' meeting later that month, the attendees—angered about a fall of 35 percent in the value of Vivendi stock since the beginning of the year—heckled Messier and urged him to resign. Messier, however, announced that Vivendi Universal had had a better-than-expected first quarter, thanks to a rise of 16.5 percent in revenues over the previous year's first quarter from its telecommunications and media units. Displaying an unusual level of humility, Messier confessed to the shareholders, as quoted by Alan Cowell in the *New York Times* (April 25, 2002), "I was clumsy and involuntarily contributed to a certain measure of misunderstanding by communicating too much. I got the message, and I'm fixing it." Messier also announced that he would invest his previous year's bonus in Vivendi stock.

Whatever Messier gained in good will at that meeting evaporated a week later, when Vivendi announced that it intended to ask a Paris court to annul the results of two shareholder votes. (The shareholders had rejected two of Messier's proposals: to set aside 5 percent of the company's shares for stock options for senior managers, and to raise some $2.7 billion by issuing new shares of stock.) Messier claimed that the balloting system had been tampered with. While his board of directors continued to support him, members of the Bronfman family, who held seats on Vivendi Universal's board of directors, led a growing chorus calling for his resignation.

Nevertheless, Messier pressed on. He announced that, to lower Vivendi Universal's debt, he had reduced his company's stake in Vivendi Environment by 15.5 percent, through sales of stock. With Vivendi Universal's share in Vivendi Environment reduced to less than 50 percent, Vivendi Universal would no longer be required to consolidate Vivendi Environment's debt on its books. Nonetheless Messier's indecision over how to rid Vivendi of the shares gave investors the impression that the company was desperate to raise cash; panicky investors sold large amounts of stock, thus lowering the value of Vivendi Universal's shares by 25 percent. With prices down 67 percent since the start of the year, Vivendi's stock offering was now lower than it had been in 13 years. The value of Vivendi Environment stock also dropped. As a result Messier's prediction that he would raise about 1.7 billion euros fell short by about 200 million euros. Further weakening Messier's position was the decision of Bernard Arnault, the head of the luxury-goods conglomerate LVMH and one of Messier's closest allies, to step down from the board, on June 25.

"The least trace of bitterness will stop you moving on. See those who betrayed you, so that you can work with them. Because to work is to live."

On July 1, 2002, faced with an increasing lack of confidence in him and bad news from Moody's Investors Service (Moody's downgraded Vivendi's debt to junk-bond status and lowered the rating on the firm's long-term debt to below investment grade), Messier resigned as chief executive and chairman of Vivendi Universal. "I am leaving so that Vivendi Universal stays," Messier declared in an announcement, according to Suzanne Kapner and Laura M. Holson in the *New York Times* (July 2, 2002). "You cannot lead a company if the board is divided." Messier was replaced by Jean-René Fourtou, the vice chairman of the French-German pharmaceuticals company Aventis. Nevertheless, as Andrew Ross Sorkin noted in the *New York Times* (July 1, 2003), in 2002, "Mr. Messier was the second-highest-paid executive in France … with a package valued at 5.6 million euros ($6.4 million). Seth Schiesel and John Tagliabue, analyzing Messier's ouster for the *New York Times* (July 2, 2002), wrote that the "accumulated results of Mr. Messier's penchant for speaking his mind, acting precipitously and alienating the French business establishment proved insurmountable," despite Vivendi's respectable revenues.

In his 2002 memoir *Mon Vrai Journal* ("My True Diary"), as reported by John Tagliabue in the *New York Times* (November 15, 2002), Messier ascribed his fall to what Tagliabue paraphrased as "an old-fashioned boardroom plot against him orchestrated by members of the Bronfman family," also singling out "above all" the machinations of the "French insurance magnate Claude Bébéar, whom Mr. Messier depicts as one of the grand puppet masters of French capitalism."

The day after Messier's resignation, disclosures about Vivendi Universal's shady accounting practices regarding British Sky Broadcasting sent its stock price plummeting, as investors feared that new revelations might send the company into bankruptcy (as happened to such American companies as Enron and World-com). Under Mr. Fourtou, Vivendi moved to divest itself of assets, and it eventually returned to profitability.

Following his resignation Messier faced legal proceedings that stretched out for more than a decade. According to Nicola Clark, writing for the *International Herald Tribune* (June 28, 2004), Messier "paid a $1 million fine to the Securities and Exchange Commission, agreed to forgo a $25 million severance package and [was] barred from serving on the board of any United States-listed company for ten years." She added that Messier and Vivendi remained "the focus of more than a dozen shareholder lawsuits in the United States and Europe." The BBC News (January 21, 2011) reported that in 2004, the French stock market regulator fined Messier 1 million euros (later reduced to 500,000 euros). Clark added that French prosecutors were "pursuing several elements in their investigation, including a series of stock repurchases in September and October 2001 that may have violated French market rules and allowed the company to manipulate its share price. They are also looking into accusations of insider trading and misuse of company money by Vivendi executives as well as examining the accuracy of financial statements published by the company in 2001 and 2002."

In January 2010 a federal jury in Manhattan held that Vivendi Universal had committed securities fraud but found no individual liability on the part of Messier or of Guillaume Hannezo, Vivendi Universal's former chief financial officer. Vivendi Universal immediately moved for a motion of judgment as a matter of law or, alternatively, for a new trial. The court's opinion, as recounted in *Securities Litigation Report* (April 2011), was issued more than a year later, in February 2011. Taking into account a U.S. Supreme Court decision (*Morrison v. National Australia Bank* (2010), it dismissed the claims of a class of shareholders who had purchased Vivendi shares on foreign exchanges. It also denied Vivendi's motions for either a summary judgment or a new trial; Vivendi planned to file an appeal. In October 2013, as reported by Leila Abboud of Reuters (October 31, 2013), a civil case commenced in the Paris Commercial Court, brought by pension funds and financial institutions from outside France who were excluded from the 2010 U.S. class action suit. (Messier was not party to this action.)

Meanwhile, Messier's trial in France, in which Hannezo, Edgar Bronfman Jr., and others were also defendants, opened on June 1, 2010. The plaintiffs were small investors and Vivendi itself. Although the French state prosecutor had announced in June 2010 that it would not pursue its case against Messier, the case did go to trial. As explained by Matthew Saltmarsh and Eric Pfanner in the *New York Times* (January 21, 2011), "In France, an investigating judge often takes the lead in complex investigations. The judge is not bound by the prosecutor's opinion when deciding whether to send people to trial, though it is unusual for the two to arrive at radically different conclusions," as happened in this case. On January 21, 2011, Messier was found guilty in Paris Criminal Court of misleading shareholders and worsening the company's precarious financial position by soliciting funds. He was given a three-year suspended sentence and fined 150,000 euros. (Edgar Bronfman Jr. was found guilty of separate charges.) Messier appealed the verdict, and that appeals trial commenced on October 28, 2013.

In *Mon Vrai Journal,* Messier speculated about his own future: "I don't yet know very well the country (both sides of the Atlantic, no doubt), nor the business, nor the partners, nor the opportunities toward which I will turn," he wrote, as Tagliabue (November 15, 2002) reported, "But it's the dimension of entrepreneur and builder that inspires me most." In 2003 Messier founded a "boutique" merger advisory firm, Messier Partners, based in London and New York. Many of the firm's clients were his longtime friends and business associates. Messier's *Le jour où le ciel nous est tombé sur la tête* ("The Day the Sky Fell on Our Heads"), an analysis of the recession of the early 2000s, was published in 2009. Following its publication, correspondent Jo Johnson of the London *Financial Times* (February 6, 2009) noted that Messier had retreated from the public eye for a time but had begun to assume a more public role during the banking crisis as an adviser of French president Nicolas Sarkozy, his longtime friend. Writing in *Mon Vrai Journal,* Messier had excoriated Johnson and *Le Monde* correspondent Martine Orange for what he called their "tabloid" methods in writing their book about his downfall. But when Messier and Johnson met in Paris in early 2009, Messier told Johnson that "Forgiving people is what you need to do to rebuild yourself. The least trace of bitterness will stop you moving on. See those who betrayed you, so that you can work with them. Because to work is to live."

In his media mogul days, pundits called Messier J6M, an abbreviation of his long nickname—Jean-Marie Messier, *moi-même, maître du monde* ("Jean-Marie, myself, master of the world"), bestowed on him by a popular French puppet show that satirizes celebrities. His autobiography, *j6m.com* (2001), was a best-seller in France. He married Antoinette Fleisch in 1983; the couple have three sons and two daughters, but they separated in 2005. Messier is known for his easy-going manner, strong grasp of figures, and—before his departure from Vivendi, at least—brilliant salesmanship. At one time he served on the boards of directors of Alcatel; BNP-Paribas; Cegetel; Compagnie de Saint-Gobain; LVMH-Moët Hennessy-Louis Vuitton; UGC (a European chain of movie theaters); USA Networks; the Whitney Museum of American Art; and the New York Stock Exchange (he was only the second non-American to sit on that board). At the height of his success, in recognition of his achievements, the French government in 2001 named him a chevalier of the French Legion of Honor. Fluent in English, Messier maintains homes in both Paris and New York City.

Further Reading:

BBC News Feb. 23, 2000, Jan. 21, 2011

Business Week p57+ May 20, 2002, p64+ July 1, 2002, with photo, p48+ July 8, 2002

Fortune p136+ Sep. 3, 2001, with photo, p51 May 13, 2002, p32+ June 10, 2002, with photo

JeremyJosephs.com

New York magazine p24+ May 13, 2002

New York Times D p1 Oct. 14, 1997, C p1+ Apr. 17, 2001, Aug. 27, 2001, with photos, A p1+ Dec. 24, 2001, Apr. 17, 2002, Apr. 25, 2002, Jul. 2, 2002, Jul. 5, 2002, Jul. 7, 2002, Nov. 11, 2002, Mar. 7, 2003, Apr. 7, 2003, Jul. 1, 2003, Jun. 28, 2004, Oct. 23, 2009, Jun. 2, 2010, Jan. 21, 2011

New Yorker p31 July 15, 2002

Reuters Oct. 31, 2013

Time Sep. 13, 1999

Securities Litigation Report April 2011

Vanity Fair p194+ Oct. 2002, with photo

Washington Post A p23 June 21, 2000, E p1 June 23, 2000

International Who's Who 2001

Books:

Briançon, Pierre, *Messier Story* (Grasset, 2002)

Johnson, Jo, and Martine Orange, *The Man Who Tried to Buy the World: Jean-Marie Messier and Vivendi Universal* (Portfolio, 2003.)

Selected Books:

Messier, Jean-Marie, *j6m.com:* Faut-il avoir peur de la nouvelle économie?, 2001 (*"j6m.com: Is It Necessary to Fear the New Economy?"*)

Messier, Jean-Marie, and Yves Messarovitch, *Mon Vrai Journal,* 2002 ("My True Diary")

Messier, Jean-Marie, *Le jour où le ciel nous est tombé sur la tête,* 2009 ("The Day the Sky Fell on Our Heads").

Omidyar, Pierre

Internet entrepreneur, philanthropist

Born: 1967, Paris, France

Pierre M. Omidyar is the founder of the popular Internet auction site eBay, which had almost 120 million active users as of the second quarter of 2013. E-bay users bought and sold more than $175 billion in goods during 2012. On any given day, millions of items—ranging from cars, jewelry, and sporting goods to antiques, toys, and celebrity memorabilia—are listed on the site, which draws users from virtually every country in the world. In 1998—the year Omidyar took his company public with an IPO (initial public offering) and instantly became a billionaire—he hired Meg Whitman to oversee eBay's day-to-day operations. Thereafter he remained eBay's chairman and its largest shareholder, holding 10 percent of its stock, but he focused increasingly on philanthropic activities. In September 2013 Omidyar's net worth was reported by *Forbes* as $8.5 billion.

Together with his wife, Pam, Omidyar has formed the Omidyar Group to manage his wide-ranging philanthropic efforts. Forbes reports that the Omidyars "have been perhaps the biggest private donors to the fight against human trafficking over the last half decade," working through their Humanity United foundation. In 2005 the Omidyars created Omidyar-Tufts Microfinance Fund at Tufts University (from which both Omidyars graduated and where they met). Their $100 million gift to Tufts, the largest in the university's history, was intended to "accelerate the growth of the microfinance industry, while generating income to support university programs." They also provided initial funding for the Tisch College of Citizenship and Public Service at Tufts.

Omidyar has taken a particular interest in promoting both civic engagement and government transparency and accountability. In 2011 he founded the Democracy Fund, a "catalyst for change" that, according to the Omidyar Group Web site, "supports risk-taking innovation and strategies that shift the incentives driving political behavior." The Omidyar Group invests in or donates to nonprofits and for-profit organizations alike, and (unlike many philanthropic organizations) it seeks to help these organizations become effective and self-sustaining by providing not only funding but managerial training and support. "Charity is inherently not self-sustaining, but there are problems in the world, such as natural disasters, that require charity," Omidyar has written (*Harvard Business Review,* October 6, 2011). "Philanthropy is much more. ... If we want to make sustainable change, we have to put all the tools at our disposal to their best possible use." Omidyar seeks out "impact investing" opportunities that "[align] incentives between the private and public sectors to create enormous social benefit" (Huffington Post, June 6, 2013). According to Jon Swartz of *USA Today* (February 14, 2012), "The Omidyars' brand of philanthropy, based loosely on a venture-capital firm's approach, has been a powerful agent for social change."

Omidyar is drawn especially to journalism, believing that a functioning democracy requires an informed citizenry. In 2010, with Randy Ching, he founded Honolulu Civil Beat, a respected on-line investigative reporting news service covering Hawaii. In September 2013 Civil Beat partnered with the Huffington Post to form Huffpost Hawaii, a regionally oriented news and opinion site. (The Omidyars live in Honolulu.) In October 2013 Omidyar generated enormous public interest when he announced that he would launch a wholly new independent mass media organization in cooperation with journalist Glenn Greenwald, the controversial reporter for Britain's *The Guardian* newspaper who orchestrated the publication of Edward J. Snowden's revelations about the international surveillance operations of the U.S. National Security Administration. "We'll be working with [Greenwald and his colleagues Laura Poitras and Jeremy Scahill] and others," Omidyar wrote at the Omidyar Group Web site, "but we have a long way to go in terms of what the organization looks like, people's roles and responsibilities—all of those things still need to be worked out."

Education and Early Career

Pierre Morad Omidyar (pronounced oh-MID-ee-are) was born June 21, 1967, in Paris, France. As a child, he moved with his parents to Maryland, where his father, an Iranian-born surgeon, worked at the Johns Hopkins University Medical Center. His mother, Elahé Mir-Djalali Omidyar, a linguist, taught at Georgetown University and the University of California at Berkeley. (In 2000, with her son, she founded the Roshan Cultural Heritage Institute, a non-profit organization dedicated to supporting Persian culture.) When he was in eighth and ninth grade, Pierre Omidyar attended Punahou School in Honolulu. He became interested in computer programming at the Potomac School in McLean, Virginia. In 1984 he graduated from St. Andrew's Episcopal School, a college preparatory school in Potomac, Maryland. Omidyar's first paying job (at age 14) was to devise a program to print catalogue cards for the school library, for which he made $6 an hour. After earning a degree in computer science from Tufts University, in Medford, Massachusetts, in 1988, he moved to California, where from 1989 to 1990 he worked for Claris Software, an Apple Computer subsidiary. In 1991 he co-founded Ink Development, later renamed eShop, which developed a platform for Internet commerce and was eventually purchased by Microsoft. Later that year, he joined General Magic, a developer of mobile computing devices, as a software engineer. In his spare time he designed pages for the newly expanding World Wide Web.

In 1995 Omidyar designed a Web page that allowed people to list items for sale and take bids. (The persistent story that he was inspired to start eBay by his fiancée's desire for an online site through which to build her collection of Pez candy dispensers was concocted in 1997 by a publicist.) At first, the service was free, but by early 1996, Omidyar had begun charging a fee for listings and taking a small commission on sales. Within a few months, he was able to quit his job at General Magic and concentrate on running his service full-time.

"Mr. Omidyar had drilled into one of the richest veins of the on-line world," wrote Saul Hansell in a profile for *the New York Times* (November 15, 1998), "the desire of people to connect with others who share their interests." By 1997 Omidyar had acquired a business partner, Jeff Skoll, and moved eBay from his living room to its current headquarters, in San Jose, California. Omidyar took the company public in September 1998. Within two months, the price of the stock had climbed from $18 to more than $120 per share. In 2002 eBay acquired PayPal, an online payment processing firm now used to process the majority of eBay's online transactions.

"I didn't set out to create a huge business on eBay," Omidyar told Hansell. "When it happened, I just took advantage of it."

Later Career

After eBay became a public company, Omidyar and his wife, Pam, devoted much of their time to philanthropic causes. They began in June 1998 by establishing the Omidyar Foundation, which focused on nonprofits and funded grassroots projects to combat hunger, poverty, and illiteracy all over the world. The Omidyars' initiatives currently are organized within the Omidyar Group as four divisions: HopeLab, a collection of youth-targeted efforts "harnessing the power of technology and play to improve health" (as described at the Omidyar Group Web site), founded in 2001; the Omidyar Network, a "philanthropic investment firm" specializing in "market-based efforts" to "catalyze economic and social change," founded in 2004; Humanity United, a foundation devoted to advancing peace and human freedom, founded in 2005; and the Ulupono Initiative, a Hawaii-focused "impact investing firm that uses for-profit and non-profit investments to improve the quality of life for island residents," founded in 2009. Each of these core divisions pursues multiple avenues and investment opportunities.

Of the four components of the Omidyar Group, the Omidyar Network has the most prominent public profile. Writing in the *New York Times* (July 30, 2011), Stephanie Strom singled out the Omidyar Network for its efforts to provide not only financial support but executive coaching and management training for the organizations it funds—especially in the area of human resources, which generally is especially difficult for nonprofits. The Omidyar Network became especially well known for its commitment to journalism. David Carr, writing in the *New York Times* (October 21, 2013) about the influx of Silicon Valley entrepreneurs into the journalism sector, noted of Pierre Omidyar that: "Since founding the Omidyar Network in 2004 with his wife, Pam, ... he has backed more than two dozen organizations that work in news and transparency, including the Poynter Institute, the Sunlight Foundation, and the Transparency and Accountability Initiative. 'Technologists have a view, perhaps inflated, that they can make the world better,' Mr. Omidyar said. ... 'There may be limits to doing it only through technology, or perhaps you get tired of doing it only through technology. So getting into content and broad communication is appealing.'"

Omidyar made his own foray into such "broad communication" in May 2010, launching the Honolulu Civil Beat, of which he is chief executive officer and publisher. At the time Civil Beat began publication, Honolulu was about to lose one of its two daily newspapers (leaving only the Honolulu *Star-Advertiser*). Omidyar told Janis L. Magin of the *Pacific Business News* (May 13, 2011) that he saw the "need to have an independent voice focused on public affairs," noting that the "number of journalists reporting on government has declined during the past 10 to 15 years, especially in local markets, including Hawaii." The site is financed by subscriptions and donations—ultimately backed up by Pierre Omidyar's fortune, yet Omidyar has said that at some point, the news outlet must be community-supported and self-sustaining. It does not accept advertising. "I don't think you can support public affairs journalism solely with advertising," Omidyar told Magin. While Civil Beat eventually partnered with the ad-driven Huffington Post in an effort to secure what Sarah Darville of Nieman Journalism Lab (June 20, 2013) called "greater revenue diversity," the Civil Beat and HuffPost Hawaii sites remained separate, and only the latter carried advertising. Civil Beat kept its subscription model, although the subscription cost was halved and a "metered" system was introduced whereby nonsubscribers could access a certain amount of content before paying for full access.

Jay Rosen of PressThink (October 16, 2013, post) is among those who think that Omidyar has gained valuable insights from Civil Beat's twin efforts to secure financial sustainability and pursue its public-interest journalistic goals. On the latter Rosen cites Adrienne LaFrance, who spent two years as a city hall reporter at Civil Beat, writing for Reuters (October 17, 2013): "Civil Beat represented a return to fundamentals: shoe-leather reporting, an emphasis on filing Freedom of Information Act requests and examining public records, close coverage of government spending and campaign finance. ... Omidyar's goal for us was simple and neutral: Ask tough questions on behalf of the public to make this community a better place." Frequently such questions were not answered by public officials promptly or forthrightly. In August 2013 Civil Beat editor Patti Epler announced the creation of the Civil Beat Law Center for the Public Interest:

"The law center's primary mission is to help the media and the public get access to government information. … The center will advise the press—print, TV, radio, online, bloggers—and the public on government access at no cost." Epler emphasized that the "new law center is an independent organization that shares Civil Beat's name, but beyond that it has no affiliation with our news site. It does share our mission of encouraging government transparency."

In the spring and summer of 2013, after receiving an overture from the Washington Post Company, Omidyar explored the idea of purchasing the *Washington Post* (now owned by Jeff Bezos of Amazon). Omidyar had been thinking for some time about the apparent collapse of journalism's business model. Asked by Renee Montagne of National Public Radio (October 24, 2013) why he had decided not to pursue that opportunity, Omidyar responded, "As an entrepreneur, you know, we do tend to like to build things from the ground up and build them, you know, the way we would want to build them, instead of going into an existing institution."

"Technologists have a view, perhaps inflated, that they can make the world better. … There may be limits to doing it only through technology, or perhaps you get tired of doing it only through technology. So getting into content and broad communication is appealing."

Still, "That process," he wrote in an Omidyar Group post (October 16, 2013), "got me thinking about what kind of social impact could be created if a similar investment was made in something entirely new, built from the ground up. I developed an interest in supporting independent journalists in a way that leverages their work to the greatest extent possible, all in support of the public interest. And, I want to find ways to convert mainstream readers into engaged citizens." He had arrived at a plan that galvanized the media establishment and captured public attention worldwide: "Right now, I'm in the very early stages of creating a new mass media organization. …What I can tell you is that the endeavor will be independent of my other organizations, and that it will cover general interest news, with a core mission around supporting and empowering independent journalists across many sectors and beats. The team will build a media platform that elevates and supports these journalists and allows them to pursue the truth in their fields. This doesn't just mean investigative reporting, but all news."

Omidyar wrote that he had contacted journalist Glenn Greenwald, then working for Britain's *The Guardian* and the main journalistic conduit for the information about U.S. National Security Administration's surveillance program revealed by Edward Snowden. He wanted, according to his post, "to find out what journalists like [Greenwald] need to do their jobs well." Omidyar learned that Greenwald and his colleagues Laura Poitras (the documentary filmmaker who first connected Snowden and Greenwald) and Jeremy Scahill (national security reporter for *The Nation*) "were already on a path to create an online space to support independent journalists." They had decided "to join forces," Omidyar wrote.

According to Jay Rosen at PressThink, based on his own conversations with Omidyar, "Omidyar believes that if independent, ferocious, investigative journalism isn't brought to the attention of general audiences it can never have the effect that actually creates a check on power. Therefore the new entity … will have to serve the interest of all kinds of news consumers. It cannot be a niche product. It will have to cover sports, business, entertainment, technology: everything that users demand." "As the founder of eBay," Rosen remarked, "[Omidyar] clearly has ideas about how a next generation news company can be built from the ground up." Like Civil Beat, the new news organization will be entirely digital. In his conversations with Omidyar, Rosen gleaned some insight into the latter's motivations: "When the freedom to practice hard-hitting investigative journalism comes under threat here, [Omidyar] said, that's not only a problem for our democracy but for the chances that democracy can work anywhere." The new organization "will be designed to withstand that threat." Omidyar told Renee Montagne, "Technology evolves, and it always disrupts. And so I think we're today, rather than looking backwards at old business models that we wished still existed, we're looking forward to this incredible opportunity."

Some observers see the large-scale entry of tech entrepreneurs into journalism as potentially transformative. "The involvement of smart technologists such as Bezos and Omidyar," wrote Emily Bell in the London *Guardian* (November 3, 2013), "is creating a less predictable world for market-driven journalism; costs are no longer tied to the ebb and flow of market revenue. There is nothing new in government, venture capital or rich donors funding news, but for a US industry that has always seen profitability as the root of good journalism, it is an important moment."

In 1999 Pierre Omidyar married Hawaii-born Pamela Kerr, a fellow Tufts graduate (B.S., Biology), who also studied molecular genetics at the University of California, Santa Cruz. Pam Omidyar chairs HopeLab and Humanity United, and she is a director of the Ulupono Initiative as well as an advisory council member of The Elders, described at the Omidyar Group Web site as an "independent group of eminent global leaders, brought together by Nelson Mandela, who offer their influence and experience to support peace building and alleviate human suffering." In April 2011 Pam Omidyar donated $1 million to the University of Hawai'i's Mānoa's Confocal Microscopy Laboratory at Moku O Lo'e for a new microscope intended particularly to study physiological activities in coral reef ecosystems.

Pierre serves as chair of eBay and of the Omidyar Group; trustee of the Omidyar-Tufts Microfinance Fund, the Santa Fe Institute, and Honolulu's Punahou School (from which President Barack Obama graduated the year before Pierre arrived there as an eighth-grader); commissioner for the President's Commission on White House Fellowships; and director of the Hawaii Leadership Forum/Omidyar Fellows program and of the Ulupono Initiative. Among other honors, he has been elected to the American Academy of Arts & Sciences (2009).

Together with Pam Omidyar, Pierre was awarded the Carnegie Medal of Philanthropy in 2011. Pierre and Pam each received an honorary degree (Doctor of Public Service, honoris causa) from Tufts University in 2011. In the same year they were on the Forbes list of the "World's 7 Most Powerful Philanthropists."

The couple has three children. In 2006 the Omidyar family moved from a 45,000-square-foot mansion in the suburbs of Las Vegas to a far less lavish home in the well-heeled Kahala district of Honolulu. In August 2010 Pierre and Pam Omidyar committed to the Giving Pledge, organized by Bill and Melinda Gates and Warren Buffett, publicly promising to give away a majority of their wealth to philanthropy.

Further Reading:

Civil Beat Web site

Forbes Web site, *Forbes* May 1, 2000, Nov. 8, 2012

(London) *Guardian* Apr. 21, 2010, Nov. 3, 2013

Harvard Business Review Oct. 6, 2011

Honolulu Magazine Aug. 2012

Huffington Post Oct. 20, 2011, Jun. 6, 2013

New York Times 3 p9 Nov. 15, 1998, with photo; Nov. 4, 2005, B2 Jul. 30, 2011, B1 Oct. 17, 2013, B1 Oct. 21, 2013

Nieman Journalism Lab (Jun. 20, 2013)

(London) *Observer,* Oct. 19, 2013

Pacific Business News May 13, 2011

PressThink Web site (Jay Rosen), Oct. 16, 2013

Reuters Oct. 17, 2013

USA Today E8 Nov. 16, 1998, with photo, Feb. 6, 2012

Books:

Adam Cohen, *The Perfect Store: Inside eBay* (Little, Brown, 2002)

Solomon, Lewis D., *Tech Billionaire$: Reshaping Philanthropy in a Quest for a Better World* (Transaction Publishers, 2009).

Rice, Linda Johnson

Publishing executive

Born: 1958

Linda Johnson Rice is the chairman of Johnson Publishing Co., the largest African-American-owned-and-operated publishing firm in the United States. Founded by her father, John H. Johnson, in 1942, Johnson Publishing Co. is headquartered in Chicago, Illinois. The company is synonymous in the public mind with its publications *Ebony,* a general-interest magazine, and *Jet,* a weekly newsmagazine; it also owns and manages Fashion Fair, a cosmetics line, and ran the *Ebony* Fashion Fair, a touring fashion show that raised millions of dollars for United Negro College Fund scholarships and other charities, until 2009. The Johnson Publishing Co. brands cater to African-American consumers. "I think of what a terrific entrepreneur and pioneer my father was," Rice said in an interview with Ed Gordon for the National Public Radio program *News & Notes* (July 4, 2005), "and how he realized 60 years ago that there was no real voice for African-Americans to really see themselves in a very positive and successful light, in a light of achievement." In the *Chicago Tribune* (February 15, 2009), Joshua Boak wrote: "Linda Johnson Rice is proud to have inherited her father's mission of chronicling the African-American experience in *Ebony* and *Jet* magazines," quoting Rice as saying, "It's my job to move that legacy forward."

As a child Rice often accompanied her parents to the Johnson offices. "They sort of developed her for the business," William Berry, a journalism professor and former editor at *Ebony,* told Shashank Bengali for the University of Southern California (USC) publication *Trojan Family Magazine* (Winter 2002). "Early on she got exposure to all aspects of the business. I've watched her career over the years, and she's retained the availability of an ordinary person who has extraordinary access to power and capital." After graduating from college, in 1980, Rice began to work full-time for Johnson Publishing Co. She later attended night classes and earned a master's degree in business administration. In 2002 Rice was named chief executive officer (CEO), a title she held until 2010. That title "wasn't something that was handed to me on a silver platter," she told Adrienne Murrill for Northwestern University's alumni magazine, *Kellogg World* (Summer 2007), adding, "I worked for it throughout my whole adult life."

Education and Early Career

Linda Johnson Rice was born on March 22, 1958, in Chicago. She was adopted by John H. Johnson and Eunice W. Johnson, the latter of whom served as the Johnson Publishing Co.'s secretary and treasurer. The couple also had an adopted son, John Jr. (He suffered from sickle-cell anemia and died at the age of 21, in 1981.)

After taking out a $500 loan with his mother's help, John H. Johnson, the grandson of slaves, created a magazine for African-Americans, *Negro Digest,* in the early 1940s. The publication's circulation reached 50,000 within a year. In 1945 Johnson began publication of a monthly magazine entitled, at the suggestion of his wife, *Ebony.* He created *Jet* in 1951. Over the following decades, those publications became staples in African-American homes. Johnson established Fashion Fair Cosmetics in 1973. *Negro Digest* was discontinued in 1976. John Johnson died in 2005, and Eunice died five years later.

Before the age of 10, Rice had begun spending time at Johnson Publishing Co.'s headquarters. "It was a giant babysitter," she said in the interview with Bengali. William Berry told Bengali, "She was always asking you questions, trying to figure out what you were doing. She had that great innocence and candor of a younger person." Rice would sometimes attend editorial meetings at the *Ebony* offices, where she would occasionally give advice about which image to use on the cover of the magazine. "We'd struggle over different pictures, and then Linda would say something like, 'Well, so-and-so's not frowning in that picture. I like that one better,'" Berry recalled to Bengali. "And sometimes you thought, 'You know, she's right.'" As a child she would also travel with her mother to Paris, France, and to Italy, where they would shop for the Ebony Fashion Fair. In her youth Rice also enjoyed horseback riding; she has won a number of equestrian awards.

Rice wanted to attend college in Southern California, having taken a liking to that region after her parents purchased a vacation home there when she was 14 years old. After visiting the University of Southern California (USC) campus, she decided that the school was a good fit for her. "It just felt so comfortable," she recalled to Bengali. "I liked the atmosphere. And I could tell there was a fascinating mix of people." In 1980 Rice received a B.A. degree in journalism from USC's Annenberg School for Communication. "There was nothing pretentious about Linda at all," Tanya Turner, a former USC student who knew Rice, said to Bengali. "Everybody knew who she was, she was very popular, but she was a regular student, just there to get an education like we all were." During the summers of her college years, Rice filled low-level jobs at the family's company; after receiving her undergraduate degree, she served as the vice president and fashion coordinator of *Ebony* magazine until 1985, when she became her father's executive assistant. "I had her sit in on all the meetings," John H. Johnson recalled to Bengali. "She was copied on all the important correspondence that came to me, plus she got my answers. She was right there with me at all times."

While working as vice president and executive assistant to the publisher, Rice attended classes at the J. L. Kellogg Graduate School of Management at Northwestern University, in Evanston, Illinois. During that time she also traveled to Europe to help choose models for the Ebony Fashion Fair. "Going to school part-time and working is never easy," she said in an interview with *Ebony* (November 1992). "But going to Northwestern was very interesting. I went part-time at night, and it was interesting to get the perspective of other people going to school at night. You learn a lot from them, especially from study groups." Rice has said that her graduate education helped prepare her for her role as head of Johnson Publishing Co. "We did a lot of case study work [at Northwestern], which is really the Harvard Business School method also," she explained in the *Ebony* interview. "And it really taught you how to think through a problem. How to recognize what the problem is. How to come up with different strategies to solve the problem. How to look at the competition and the barriers to entry, as they call it. And then how to come up with a conclusion for it. And I think that was very important."

Later Career

In 1987 Rice received an M.B.A. degree. Two days after her graduation, she became Johnson Publishing Co.'s president and chief operating officer (COO), positions she held until 2002, when her father appointed her the company's CEO. Prior to the announcement of her promotion, John H. Johnson had been away from the company for nearly a year owing to health problems, and Rice had taken on his responsibilities. "The way it happened was so poignant," she told Caroline V. Clarke for *Black Enterprise* (June 30, 2002). "We had just finished our regular editorial meeting for *Ebony,* and after every meeting I [would] stay and talk to my dad about the issues of the day. Once everyone left, he hands me this formal letter on his stationery and the first paragraph says, 'Thanks for all you've done while I was out. You've done a wonderful job.'" She continued, "So, I just thought this was a congratulations letter, and I said, 'Dad, this is so sweet.' Then

I kept reading, and the second paragraph says, 'In light of all that you've done, I want you to have the title of CEO.' At first I was totally speechless, then I looked at him and said, 'I've been working toward this my whole life.' He was silent for a moment, then he said, 'Well, you'd better leave before both of us start crying.'"

As CEO Rice was responsible for overseeing the company's domestic and international business operations. She created new packaging, advertising, and product launches for Fashion Fair Cosmetics. She also launched the Web site EbonyJet.com and helped to redesign the print magazines, making them more trendy and sleek. In addition, she approved an agreement with the Associated Press to digitize and sell photos from the company's archives. In 2005 Rice announced plans to license merchandise that would advertise the *Ebony* brand on products such as clothing, personal technology, and home goods. The company signed a deal with TurnerPatterson, a marketing and licensing company that targets minority consumers. "We have built up the brand name of *Ebony* over the last 60 years, and it's a name that's very well recognized," Rice told Eric Herman for the *Chicago Sun-Times* (June 20, 2005). "I thought this would be a growth opportunity for the company, and a great way to brand the name in other areas." She told Herman that her father approved of her decision: "He thought it was a great idea. He told me, 'You're the CEO. You're in charge.'"

"It's my job to move that legacy forward."

In addition to her post as CEO, Rice became chairman (the title she prefers) of the Johnson Publishing Co. in 2008—three years after her father died. Also in 2008 she authorized a revenue-sharing agreement with Google, which made past issues of the magazines available on-line. In early 2010 Earvin "Magic" Johnson, a famous retired National Basketball Association player, expressed interest in purchasing *Ebony* and *Jet* magazines, but he was unable to negotiate a deal with the company. Later that year, after the death of her mother, Rice stepped down from her position as CEO. She was replaced by her longtime friend Desirée Rogers, a former White House social secretary, who had recently become a corporate strategy consultant for Johnson Publishing Co. Although she no longer controls the day-to-day operations of the company, Rice continues to hold the title of chairman.

Like so many other mainstream publishers, Johnson Publishing Co. has struggled with the economics of publishing in an Internet- and mobile device era, suffering declining circulation, advertising volume, and revenues. In July 2011 Rogers announced that J. P. Morgan would take a minority stake in the company. In a post at the Web site Madame Noire (July 12, 2011), Charing Bell commented on the "end of an almost 70-year legacy" as the "last bastion of black-owned media space known as the Johnson Publishing Company …will now only be partly black-owned." Bell added that "perhaps this investment will give Johnson Publishing the financial boost needed to navigate through the ever-changing and evolving black aesthetic," even while expressing misgivings about what she saw as the magazines' focus on a "faux sense of 'race pride' where conspicuous consumption is framed as the symbol of success for today's modern black family." Desirée Rogers set about rebranding the company's signature publications and hired an outside circulation management consultant. These and other strategic moves stemmed the company's short-term losses; the base rate quoted for advertisers stabilized and by the fall of 2011 circulation had markedly improved.

Still, Johnson Publishing Co. faces significant challenges. As David Mendell wrote in *Crain's Chicago Business* (November 25, 2013), the company has seen its market change. Mendell quoted Andrea Zopp, president and CEO of the nonprofit Urban League, as saying, "Johnson Publishing and Johnson (Products)—those companies grew and thrived when there was real segregation in the market. Today, that segregation is waning. The business model that John Johnson and Ed Gardner pursued—dominating the black market because the larger white consumer market was closed to them—no longer exists." In September 2013, Rice announced that the company had secured a credit arrangement with Gibraltar Business Capital to "help us to continue building on the Johnson Publishing Company legacy." In January 2012 the company announced that it had sold its imposing headquarters building at 820 South Michigan Avenue and would move within 18 months to smaller, albeit still impressive, quarters several blocks to the north.

Rice has served on the boards of the United Negro College Fund, Kimberly-Clark Corp., Omnicom Group Inc., Magazine Publishers Association, and Northwestern Memorial Corp., among other organizations. Her honors include the Women of Power Award from the National Urban League, the Trumpet Award from Turner Broadcasting, and the Alumni Merit Award from the University of Southern California, of which she served as a trustee. She has been named one of Chicago's 100 Most Powerful Women by the *Chicago Sun-Times* and has been included on *Crain's Chicago Business*'s lists of 40 Under 40 and the 100 Most Influential Women.

In 2011 Rice sold her four-bedroom, 5,393-square-foot condominium at the Carlyle, a lakefront building in Chicago, which she had purchased in 1987. According to an April 12, 2010 article on the Chicago Real Estate Forum Web site, Rice, who also owns a home in Palm Springs, California, was going to move into her parents' condo, which is also located at the Carlyle.

From 1984 to 1994 Rice was married to Andre Rice, a stockbroker who later founded two private investment companies. She and her former husband are the parents of a daughter, Alexa Christina. In 2004 Rice married Mel Farr Sr., a former National Football League player who currently owns automobile dealerships in Michigan.

Further Reading:

Advertising Age p40 Aug. 10, 1987

Black Enterprise p136 Jun. 30, 2002, July 11, 2011

Chicago Tribune p7 July 28, 1999, Feb. 15, 2009

Crain's Chicago Business Nov. 25, 2013

Ebony p208+ Nov. 1992

Madame Noire Jul. 12, 2011

(National Public Radio) *News & Notes* Jul. 4, 2005 (Northwestern University)

Kellogg World Summer 2007 (University of Southern California)

Trojan Family Magazine Winter 2002

Roberts, Robin

Television anchor, producer, journalist, sportscaster, writer

Born: 1960, Tuskegee, Alabama, United States

After Hurricane Katrina slammed into the U.S. Gulf Coast, in 2005, the ABC-TV newscaster Robin Roberts reported on the disaster at the site of the devastated Mississippi town where she had spent much of her youth. Katrina struck only a few months after Roberts was named a co-anchor of the long-running ABC News program *Good Morning America* and three and a half years after she left her "dream job," as an anchor for the sports network ESPN. Referring to her repeated visits to her hometown, both as a journalist and as a volunteer in rebuilding efforts, she told Gary Pettus for the Jackson, Mississippi, *Clarion-Ledger* (April 4, 2006), "Personally and professionally, this has been the defining moment for me. I had struggled, I had wondered if I should move from sports to news. When Katrina hit, I looked to the heavens and said, 'Now I get it.'" "Once you've done sports, you can do anything," she told Mike Lacy for the Biloxi, Mississippi, *Sun Herald* (April 25, 2002). "The subject matter has changed, but I have the same journalistic approach whether I'm talking about the Yankees or Osama bin Laden."

Roberts is the most prominent African American female anchor on morning network television. She began her career in broadcasting during her years as a student at Southeastern Louisiana University, with jobs at local radio stations. For seven years after her college graduation, having resolved to gain experience and hone her skills "in the minors," as she explained to Hal Karp for *Black Enterprise* (April 1997), she worked for a series of television stations in Mississippi, Tennessee, and Georgia. In 1990—two years after she had rejected a job offer from the network because she felt that she was not yet sufficiently prepared—she joined ESPN as a host and reporter. During the next dozen years, she appeared on programs including *NFL Prime Time, SportsCenter,* and *In the SportsLight* and concurrently, for four years, hosted *Wide World of Sports* on ABC. (The Walt Disney Co. owns ABC; Disney is the majority owner of ESPN, which it operates in a joint venture with the Hearst Corporation.)

For *Good Morning America,* broadcast from Times Square in New York City since 1999, Roberts has reported from war-torn or otherwise troubled places in the Persian Gulf region and Africa. In March 2007 she hosted a town-hall-style meeting with U.S. senator and Democratic presidential hopeful Hillary Rodham Clinton. She was chosen for a coveted one-on-one interview with the University of Tennessee's fabled women's basketball head coach Pat Summitt in November 2011 after Summitt announced she had been diagnosed with early-onset dementia. Roberts was contacted by the White House in May 2012 to conduct an interview with President Barack Obama in which he declared his support for same-sex marriage. She handled numerous other assignments for ABC in addition to her anchor work. In February 2009 she hosted the Academy Awards preshow for ABC, and she did so again in 2011, 2012, and 2013. She hosted her fifth annual "In the Spotlight with Robin Roberts: Countdown to the CMA Awards" program in November 2013; she also presented the Entertainer of the Year award at the CMA (Country Music Awards) ceremony. Roberts has interviewed not only Hollywood and sports celebrities but many prominent political leaders and other influential people, among them Michelle Obama.

In July 2007 Roberts disclosed on-air that she had been diagnosed with an early stage of breast cancer. She underwent surgery and treatment. Having returned to *Good Morning America* just ten days after her surgery, she included in many of her broadcasts updates about her chemotherapy and her physical and emotional reactions to it. Roberts and *Good Morning America* took a similar approach five years later when Roberts again found herself battling a life-threatening illness. In April 2012 she learned that she had myelodysplastic syndromes (MDS), a rare blood- and bone-marrow disorder, possibly traceable to her breast cancer treatments. She underwent a bone-marrow transplant in September, having fortunately found a bone-marrow "match" in her sister Sally-Ann. After a five-month recovery—during which *Good Morning America* again regularly kept audiences informed about her progress and she sometimes even participated in the program—Roberts returned to the air, anchoring *Good Morning America* on a limited basis beginning in late February 2013 and then, in September, with the approval of her doctors, on a full schedule.

Roberts is the author of the memoir-cum-inspirational/advice book *From the Heart: Seven Rules to Live By* (2007), first published not long before she received her breast cancer diagnosis. The paperback edition published in 2008 incorporated a new chapter on her response to her breast cancer diagnosis and treatment: "Make Your Mess Your Message." She credits this advice to her mother, with whom she wrote *My Story, My Song: Mother-Daughter Reflections on Life and Faith,* as told to Missy Buchanan (2012). In May 2013, as Julie Bosman reported in the *New York Times* (May 22, 2013), Grand Central Publishing announced that Roberts would pen a memoir to be published in April 2014 dealing with her experiences with serious illness as well as "'the life lessons she continues to learn, and her inspiring return to the *G.M.A.* anchor desk.'"

Education and Early Career

The youngest of four children, Robin René Roberts was born to Lawrence Roberts Sr. and Lucimarian (Tolliver) Roberts on November 23, 1960. Her brother, Lawrence Jr., is a teacher; her sister Sally-Ann is a TV anchor in New Orleans, and her sister Dorothy is a social worker. Her mother was the first African American to serve as chairwoman of the Mississippi State Board of Education. Her father, a career U.S. Air Force officer, served during World War II with the Tuskegee Airmen, a now-celebrated all-black fighter-pilot squadron in the U.S. Army Air Corps. The Roberts family lived on a series of Air Force bases until Robin was eight, when they settled in the small town of Pass Christian, Mississippi, on the Gulf of Mexico near the Keesler Air Force Base in Biloxi. "My father taught me that anything is possible," Roberts told Kimberly C. Roberts for the *Philadelphia Tribune* (June 15, 2007). "In the 1930s he had the nerve to ... dream about flying when Blacks in this country had very little, if any rights. ... And ... not only dream it, but make it a reality. ...We would say, 'I want to do this. I want to do ... that.' ... He never looked at us and said, 'You can't do that!' or 'That's impossible!' He was like, 'If that's what you want to do, you have my full support.'" In *From the Heart: Seven Rules to Live By,* Roberts wrote that her parents, who came of age in the 1930s, had experienced racism firsthand but refused to let it hold them back. "My parents never let us use race as an excuse."

Roberts's interest in sports began at an early age. "No matter what sport it was I loved it, loved it, loved it. Loved every aspect of it, seeing how fast I could run, competing against someone else," she told Beth Usewicz for the Women's Sports Foundation Web site. At 10 (12 or 13, according to some sources), she won a Mississippi state bowling competition. She later became proficient at tennis, and in the eighth grade, already 5' 10" in height, showed unusual skill at basketball. She was the star player on her high-school women's basketball team and drew the attention of college scouts. She won a scholarship from Southeastern Louisiana University, in Hammond, where she played on the Lady Lions basketball team. By that time, as she told Usewicz, she had concluded that her abilities on the court would never reach professional level. Retaining her desire to be involved with sports, she took the advice of her sister Sally-Ann and decided to make a career as a sportscaster. She appeared on a campus sports show between classes and basketball practice, and, concurrently, got a job as a disk jockey at a small Hammond radio station that specialized in country-and-western music. She worked at the station every day for an hour or so beginning at 6:00 a.m. and then returned there at noon to write copy. "I scratched a lot of good ole Merle Haggard records before the station let me host a sports show," she told Ylonda Gault Caviness for *Essence* (May 2007). In her junior and senior years, she was named the basketball team's Most Valuable Player, finishing her collegiate career as Southeastern Louisiana's all-time leading scorer (1,446 points) and rebounder (1,034). She graduated with a B.A. in communications, cum laude, in 1983.

In the same year Roberts landed a position as a $5.50-per-hour weekend sports anchor at WDAM-TV in Hattiesburg, Mississippi, where her sister had once worked. In taking that job, she had declined an offer to report news for the local ABC affiliate, because she wanted to gain experience in a less high-profile setting. The next year she turned down the chance to serve as a news anchor for WLOX-TV, in Biloxi, Mississippi, in favor of hosting—for a smaller salary—that station's sports segment of the news. In 1986 she became a sports anchor and reporter for WSMV-TV, in Nashville, Tennessee. Roberts told Beth Usewicz that some men expressed skepticism about any woman's ability to cover sports. Among them was a viewer who called the station before her on-air debut. "I told him to let me do a couple of reports and call me back in six months," she said to Usewicz. "In less than half of that time, he called back and said, 'Nah, you are all right.'"

In 1988 Roberts turned down a chance to rise in the sportscasting world, when ESPN asked her to host a show. Although her ambition, when she was a college student, had been to work for ESPN by 1990, she felt that she did not yet have enough experience to make the most of the opportunity and gain "staying power," as she put it to Hal Karp. Instead, in 1988 she moved to Atlanta, Georgia, to work at WAGA-TV as a sports reporter, covering major-league games. With her co-host, Mike Roberts (not a relative of hers), she also contributed to Atlanta's highest-rated morning radio show, on WVEE-FM. Her popularity with listeners grew after she beat the National Basketball Association star player Dominique Wilkins in a free-throw shoot-out.

When ESPN again offered her a job, Roberts signed on as an anchorwoman. On January 29, 1990, she became the first African American female anchor on that network, as the host of the night edition of *SportsCenter.* Within a month she became the first female host of an NFL pregame show, filling in during that broadcast in the absence of the regular host. Soon afterward she received primetime slots on *Sunday SportsDay* and *NFL PrimeTime,* hosting both for the next five years. In addition, she had her own series, *In the SportsLight,* which premiered in 1995. On that show she conducted interviews and discussed the effects of athletics on the lives of public figures. Also in 1995 Roberts signed a joint $3.9 million contract with ESPN and ABC. She served as a host for ESPN's coverage of the Olympics, for Women's National Basketball Association games from 1997 to 2000, and, in 1999, for *Vintage NBA,* a weekly ESPN program that focused on one sports figure per episode. Her job also included coverage of professional football and basketball drafts, Ladies Pro Golfing Association competitions, and world tennis events, and she was the first female play-by-play announcer for men's college-basketball games. From 1995 until 2001, she hosted *Wide World of Sports,* which airs on ABC. She also appeared on segments of *Prime Time, Good Morning America,* and *Good Morning America Sunday.* Roberts earned three Emmy Awards for her ESPN sportscasting. She worked with Millbrook Press and writer Bill Gutman on a six-book series about sports for children, especially girls, called *Get in the Game! With Robin Roberts* (2000–2001).

In April 2002 Roberts was elevated from contributor to news reader on *Good Morning America,* where she had been serving as a fill-in anchor for several months. Her reservations about making the move from

ESPN to *Good Morning America* evaporated after she had a conversation with the retired tennis champion Billie Jean King. "She said, 'What, are you an idiot? … Go, go. It is a bigger platform for you,'" as Roberts recalled to Usewicz. Concurrently, for three years, she also served as an ABC News correspondent and contributed to Sunday-morning shows on ESPN. In March 2003 she traveled to Kuwait to report on preparations for the impending U.S.-led war in Iraq. "I had no qualms about doing my job and needing to be there [in Kuwait] for it," she told Donna Petrozzello for the *New York Daily News* (March 11, 2003). "If you're a journalist, this is the biggest story there is. To see it for yourself and relay that information back to viewers is what the job is meant to be." Other news stories Roberts reported concerned the effectiveness of sky marshals on airplanes; a controversial custody battle involving an adolescent's biological father and the youngster's longtime male caregiver; the effects of the September 11, 2001, terrorist attacks on New York City's World Trade Center on Rockville Center, the Long Island town that was the home of more than 20 victims of the attacks); debates concerning stem-cell research; and gentrification in the Harlem section of New York City.

Later Career

In May 2005 Roberts was promoted to third anchor of *Good Morning America,* alongside Diane Sawyer and Charles Gibson. On accepting that position, she officially left ESPN, ending her 15-year association with the network. The following August Hurricane Katrina destroyed most of Pass Christian, along with large parts of many other cities and towns in the Gulf Coast states. In the aftermath of the storm, Roberts traveled to Pass Christian with an ABC crew to report on the disaster. On her arrival she attempted to find her family before a live broadcast scheduled for 6:00 a.m. that morning. With the help of local police, and with only 15 minutes to spare before she was to face the cameras, she found members of her family alive and unhurt in their home. When she appeared on the air, a question from Gibson about the well-being of her family brought her to tears. "I had just heard of a man who lost his wife in the storm," Roberts recalled for Pettus. "I was grateful my family was safe, but I knew there were countless people waking up that morning not knowing if their family was. That's when everything caught up with me. I believe when people saw me crying, they knew it was bad." Viewer sympathy led ABC to "adopt" Pass Christian, in collaboration with the Salvation Army and the Corporation for National and Community Service. With Roberts reporting, the rebuilding of the town by residents and volunteers was chronicled on *Good Morning America.* In August 2007 Roberts announced on the program that while progress had been made, much restoration work remained.

Earlier, in 2006, Gibson had left *Good Morning America* to host ABC's "flagship" evening news program, *ABC World News.* With his departure, Roberts and Sawyer became the only all-female team to anchor a morning network show. Former broadcast journalist Carol Jenkins (then president of the Women's Media Center, a non-profit progressive women's media organization) told Felicia R. Lee for the *New York Times* (November 16, 2006), "For all the talk about competition between women, Diane and Robin clearly like each other and work well together." Victor Neufeld, the senior executive producer of *Paula Zahn Now,* on CNN, told Lee that Roberts and Sawyer "are just so relaxed and likeable together," and said, "Robin has this tremendous force of personality as well as being someone you feel you want to hang out with."

On July 31, 2007, Roberts revealed on *Good Morning America* that she had received a diagnosis of an aggressive form of breast cancer—"triple negative," which is resistant to some forms of treatment and to which African American women are more prone than the female population in general. Roberts had first discovered the lump during a self-examination, a factor that she was to emphasize later in an effort to encourage *Good Morning America* viewers to take an active role in protecting their own health. The next month she underwent surgery and then a course of chemotherapy that extended until January 2008. In November 2007, after her hair began to fall out—a common side effect of chemotherapy—she had her head shaved, a process that was filmed and then shown on *Good Morning America.* She began to wear a wig during broadcasts so as not to distract viewers from the news she was reporting. On a broadcast of *Good Morning America* in April 2008, Roberts removed her wig. "I've taken my cue from people here and from viewers, especially [cancer] survivors … who said, 'When it's time to literally flip your wig, you'll know,'" Roberts explained, as quoted by Michael Starr in the *New York Post* (April 22, 2008). By October 2008 no sign of Roberts's cancer could be detected. That month she earned the 2008 Roswell Park Cancer Institute's Gilda Radner Courage Award. Soon afterward Roberts auctioned off her wig, with the proceeds going to the Bridge Breast Network, an organization that provides services to low-income and uninsured breast-cancer patients.

Diane Sawyer left *Good Morning America* in December 2009 to become anchor of *ABC World News,* following Charles Gibson (who had retired) in that position. Roberts was then joined as *Good Morning America*'s co-anchor by George Stephanopoulos, former communications director and policy adviser in the Clinton White House. According to Brian Stelter, as recounted by Jethro Nededog of Reuters (April 24, 2013), network executives were uncertain at first of how successful the pairing of Roberts and Stephanopoulos was proving to be. There was speculation that Roberts might be replaced, but she had built considerable viewer loyalty. Rather than replacing either co-anchor, ABC producers in 2010 added Josh Elliott and Lara Stephens to the *Good Morning America* roster, a highly successful move to more of an ensemble model for television morning shows. By April 2012, together with Elliott and Stephens, the Roberts-Stephanopoulos team (also including weatherman Sam Champion) had led *Good Morning America* back to the top of the morning show ratings. As noted by Stelter, the "ABC morning show first broke *Today*'s 16-year weekly winning streak among total viewers in April 2012, and then its streak among the key news audience, 25- to 54-year-olds, in July. … The big win came in November [2012] when *GMA* won its first sweeps month both in average total viewers and in the key demo." ("Sweeps week" ratings—actually ratings over a four-week period four times a year—are used to determine local TV advertising rates.)

After covering the Academy Awards in February 2012, Roberts had realized that she was "abnormally tired," as reported by Brian Stelter in the *New York Times* (August 30, 2012). She consulted her doctor, and on April 19—the same day, Stelter noted, that Nielsen announced that *Good Morning America*'s audience ratings had surpassed NBC's *Today*'s for the first time in 852 weeks—she was told that she had myelodysplastic syndromes (MDS), a rare blood- and bone-marrow disorder, possibly traceable to her breast cancer treatments. Shortly afterward, in May 2012, Roberts learned (while undergoing a procedure to extract bone marrow for testing) that she would interview President Obama the next day. When she announced her diagnosis publicly in June 2012, in a note to her colleagues read shortly afterward on the air, she recounted that, "The combination of landing the biggest interview of my career and having a drill in my back reminds me that God only gives us what we can handle and that it helps to have a good sense of humor when we run smack into the absurdity of life." Ben Sherwood, president of ABC News, prefaced his release of her announcement with his own statement: "We love Robin, the heart and soul of ABC News, and we'll stand arm in arm with her as she fights this new battle. She is the captain of our GMA team; she has been the keystone of our recent victories; and she will lead the program for many years to come."

Roberts again shared her treatment and recovery with *Good Morning America*'s audience, publicizing the work of the Be the Match Registry, a nonprofit organization run by the National Marrow Donor Program.

She went on leave from *Good Morning America* a day earlier than planned in order to go to the bedside of her critically ill mother, who died on August 30. Three weeks later Roberts underwent a bone-marrow transplant, the bone-marrow donor for which was her elder sister Sally-Ann, herself a co-anchor, at WWL-TV in New Orleans. (In 1998 Sally-Ann's reporting team won an Edward R. Murrow Award for late-breaking news).

After a five-month recovery—during which *Good Morning America* again regularly kept audiences informed about her progress; she participated in the program through videos from the hospital and diary entries and even via Skype—Roberts returned to *Good Morning America,* at first on a limited basis, beginning in late February 2013. To mark her return, ABC broadcast a special edition of *20/20* presenting her story. Roberts was briefly hospitalized in mid-April owing to an infection, but she returned to the show days later. Speaking with Jordan Zakarin of the *Hollywood Reporter* (April 10, 2013), Roberts reflected on her decision to allow the public to share so much of her life during her illness, surgery, and convalescence. "It was difficult," she said, "to show my low points. It was difficult to admit that I had moments of feeling defeated, and really being honest with feeling that I was slipping away, because I'm always seen as an upbeat person, and I am, I'm optimistic, but it was difficult. I don't know of anyone who has done that, in the position I'm in, you're very vulnerable when you show yourself like that. But in the end I thought it was best to do that, to be honest about it." "I am a bit more serious in my outlook on life," she continued, "but it's still striking that balance. But my enthusiasm when that alarm clock goes off at 3:45 and going into the studio, that has remained the same, and my approach." In May 2013, at an awards ceremony in Manhattan, Roberts and ABC News accepted a George Foster Peabody Award recognizing the public service campaign the show created around Roberts's treatment. In September, with her recovery finally complete, she again took on a full schedule.

"It helps to have a good sense of humor when we run smack into the absurdity of life."

Roberts received the Excellence in Journalism Award, Broadcast Media, from the Center for the Study of Sport in Society, at Northeastern University in 1993. In 1994 she was inducted in the Women's Institute on Sport and the Education Foundation's Hall of Fame. She was honored with the President's Award from the Women's Sports Foundation in 2001, and in 2002 she was named Journalist of the Year by *Ebony.* In 2012 Roberts was inducted into the Women's Basketball Hall of Fame for her impact on the game of women's basketball through both her playing and her broadcasting. ESPN awarded her its Arthur Ashe Courage Award in 2013. The CoachArt Champions of Courage and Hope Award was conferred on Robin and Sally-Ann Roberts in October 2013. In addition to the 2012 Peabody Award, Roberts and her *Good Morning America* colleagues won three consecutive Emmy awards for outstanding morning program, in 2007 (shared with the *Today Show*), 2008, and 2009.

Variety (October 18, 2013) reported that after accepting the CoachArt Champions of Courage and Hope Award, speaking of her sister Sally-Ann, Robin said, "I literally have her DNA. … I have her blood type now. I have her allergies. I have her sweet tooth. Though more importantly, I have her zest for life and her desire to be of service to others." Diane Sawyer, speaking of Roberts, told Felicia R. Lee, "I think there's nothing more exciting than someone who has a truly good heart and a completely wicked sense of humor." Every day Roberts reads selections from *Streams in the Desert,* by L. B. Cowman, a 1920s book of devotionals (passages that aim to enable readers to get closer to God) that once belonged to her maternal grandmother. Every morning, she told Scott Ross and Renell Richardson during an interview for the Christian Broadcasting Network (June 19, 2007), she repeats what she called the "prayer of protection," the key words of which—light, love, power, presence—now appear on a wristband devised by Roberts's friends that is sold to raise funds for the Be the Match Registry. Roberts lives on the Upper West Side of Manhattan, in New York City.

Kelli Bozeman, in a review of *From the Heart: Seven Rules to Live By* for *Mississippi Magazine* (May 1, 2007), wrote, "Roberts' 'rules,' sprinkled throughout *From the Heart,* inspire readers to ready themselves for opportunities, focus on small goals, take chances, be persistent, and keep faith and family close to the heart. But she offers encouragement for breaking the rules as well. 'There is no playbook for your own unique, wonderful life,' she writes. 'Ultimately, you've got to live it for yourself.'"

Further Reading:

ABC News Web site

Black Enterprise p56 Apr. 1997

(Jackson, Mississippi) *Clarion-Ledger* D p1 Apr. 4, 2006

Ebony p118+ Mar. 2006, p192+ May 2007

Essence p192 May 2007

(London) *Guardian* May 10, 2012

Hollywood Reporter Apr. 10, 2013

Knoxville News Sentinel June 6, 2012

Mississippi Magazine p120+ May 1, 2007

New York Times E p3 Nov. 16, 2006, MM24 Apr. 21, 2013, April 22, 2013, C3 Aug. 30, 2013

Philadelphia Tribune E p6 Jun. 15, 2007

Reuters April 25, 2013

shemadeit.org

Women's Sports & Fitness p467 Nov./Dec. 1991

Women's Sports Foundation Web site

Books:

Stelter, Brian*, Top of the Morning: Inside the Cutthroat World of Morning TV* (Grand Central Publishing, 2013)

Selected Books:

Lieberman-Cline, Nancy, and Robin Roberts, with Kevin Warneke, *Basketball for Women: Becoming a Complete Player,* 1996)

From the Heart: Seven Rules to Live By, 2007

Roberts, Lucimarian, with Robin Roberts, *My Story, My Song: Mother-Daughter Reflections on Life and Faith,* as told to Missy Buchanan, 2012)

Rogers, Desirée

Publishing executive

Born: 1959, New Orleans, Louisiana, United States

Desirée Rogers, who in June 2010 was named CEO of the Johnson Publishing Co.—the home of *Ebony* and *Jet* magazines—is no stranger to positions of power. The former White House social secretary has also served as the executive director of the Illinois Lottery and as an executive with Peoples Energy Corp. of Chicago, Illinois. Rogers was included on *Crain's Chicago Business*'s lists of the Top 25 Women to Watch and 40 under 40 Business Leaders, and she has been recognized by *Black Enterprise* as one of the Top 50 Most Powerful African American Business Women and the Top 75 Most Powerful Blacks in Corporate America.

While Rogers carried out her duties at the White House with both style and businesslike precision (she was the first social-secretary appointee to have an M.B.A. degree), her longtime devotion to fashion and well-publicized, expensive lifestyle did not sit well with a public in the throes of economic hardship; she was also criticized for referring to the president of the United States as a "brand"—a term that she intended to point to her efforts to have the White House reflect the tastes and priorities of President Barack Obama. A security breach at an otherwise successful state dinner in late 2009 led to Rogers's resignation. In 2010 Rogers began her tenure at Johnson Publishing Co. by overseeing what Richard Prince described for the Root (March 5, 2011) as a "top-to-bottom redesign" of *Ebony*. From a new Web design and new content to an update of the 65-year-old logo, Rogers is seeking to deliver *Ebony* to "a new generation of readers," Prince wrote.

Education and Early Career

Rogers was born Desirée Glapion on June 16, 1959 in New Orleans, Louisiana. According to Amy Chozick, writing for the *Wall Street Journal*'s *WSJ.Magazine* (April 30, 2009), she is a descendant of a Creole vodou priestess, Marie Laveau Glapion. Her father, Roy Glapion Jr., was a public-school teacher and sports coach who later became athletic director of New Orleans schools; finance chairman of the Zulu Social Aid and Pleasure Club, a Mardi Gras krewe; and a member of the city council. Chozick reported that Roy Glapion "used to ask little Desirée to serve drinks or gumbo and help entertain when company arrived." Her mother, Joyce, founded three day-care centers with Desirée 's maternal grandmother, Marie. Desirée and her younger brother, Roy, were raised in a privileged home, but she was determined to succeed in her own right. "I never had to say, 'Go do your homework,'" her mother recalled to DeNeen L. Brown for the Richmond (Virginia) *Times Dispatch* (February 22, 2009). Growing up in New Orleans's Seventh Ward, Desirée attended high school at the Catholic, all-girl Academy of the Sacred Heart, from which she graduated in 1977. She then enrolled at Wellesley College, in Wellesley, Massachusetts, and she earned a B.A. degree in political science in 1981. While in college Desirée participated in an exchange program, traveling to Switzerland to study international politics and business. During her time abroad, she was inspired to obtain a graduate degree in business administration. "Since I was a child I wanted to run a business," she told Barbara Rose for the *Chicago Tribune* (September 12, 2004). "I love to see people achieve excellence, their own excellence."

Desirée Glapion spent two years in the workforce before attending business school. She worked in sales for the Xerox Corp. and as a supervisor for AT&T. "It was part of my game plan," she told Genevieve Buck for the *Chicago*

Tribune (July 3, 1991). "I knew I never wanted to be a salesperson, but I wanted to understand the skill. And I wanted an introduction to managing people as a way to influence their work." She earned an M.B.A. degree from Harvard University, in Cambridge, Massachusetts, in 1985 and then moved to Chicago to work again for AT&T, this time in operations. In 1987 she moved briefly to AT&T headquarters in New Jersey. Three weeks later her boyfriend, John Rogers Jr., the founder of the investment firm Ariel Capital Management, proposed to her. She accepted and moved back to Chicago, where she took a job with the Levy Organization, which oversees real-estate and food businesses. The couple married in 1988 and had a daughter, Victoria, two years later.

John Rogers, a Chicago native, was well-connected and introduced his wife to the city's leaders in business and politics. Young and highly successful, the couple quickly became socially prominent. Outside of their work, they became philanthropists, and Desirée Rogers served on the boards of Children's Memorial Hospital and the Chicago Children's Museum and on the women's board of the Museum of Contemporary Art, among other positions. Larry Levy, head of the Levy Organization, told Buck, "She was a star, but … she wanted to run her own company." After leaving the Levy Organization, Rogers founded Museum Operations Consulting Associates. The firm specialized in "operating and providing consulting services to museum retail stores," Buck wrote.

When the Republican Jim Edgar was elected governor of Illinois, in 1990, members of his transition team suggested that Rogers apply for a state job. (A Republican during those years, Desirée Rogers was a delegate at the 1992 GOP national convention.) "John and I had discussed such a possibility—that one of us, probably me, would at some point become involved with a not-for-profit organization or with the city or state government," Rogers told Buck. She submitted her application and was appointed soon afterward to run the Illinois Lottery, where she headed a staff of 330. Her job primarily involved managing costs and increasing sales, tasks she approached with enthusiasm. She made changes to the managerial structure and evaluated the advertising firm affiliated with the agency, which had not been done since the lottery's inception, in 1974. Rogers impressed her employers from the start; Governor Edgar's executive assistant for economic and policy concerns, Mike Belletire, told Buck that Rogers was a "breath of fresh air." Rogers and her team reversed the decline of the lottery with innovative marketing techniques. They came up with a new slogan, "Somebody's gonna Lotto … it might as well be you," and implemented a 1-800 number and credit-card payment options. By 1995 the lottery had increased its revenue by 7 percent. Rogers gained celebrity in Chicago by appearing on the lottery's television segment. Later, in a conversation with William Norwich for *Vogue* (February 2009), she compared her experience with the Illinois Lottery to her job as White House social secretary, saying that she "met a true cross-section of people" while heading the lottery. "The common thread among them never was just getting rich, but being able to do something wonderful—like adding a room to the house for an elderly mother, or paying for the grandkids' tuition. If I can re-create that kind of enthusiasm at the White House, then I'm doing my job."

Rogers left the lottery in 1997 and was hired at Peoples Energy gas company as vice president of corporate communications, ushering her, as Genma Stringer Holmes wrote for the *Tennessee Tribune* (March 11, 2010), into the "gentleman's club of regulated utilities." In an interview with Jeff Share for Pipeline & Gas Journal (November 1, 2005), when asked how her background had helped prepare her for working in the energy industry, she responded: "In 1997, the utility industry was starting to change as residential deregulation began in Illinois. I thought my skill set might be helpful, given I was coming from the outside and might have a different point of view. It has been very exciting to combine the disciplines of marketing and operations." Rogers oversaw customer operations, marketing, sales, media relations, and community and government affairs. She led the company in what she referred to as a "branding campaign," she told Marcia Froelke Coburn for *Chicago* magazine (August 2000), to improve Peoples Energy's public image. "We are a 150-year-old company," she said. "But, really, energy is not something you think about. You expect it to work; you get your bill, you pay it." She added, "It's a matter of thinking about how my product touches people's lives and how can I make people aware of that." In 2000 Rogers was named chief marketing officer, and in 2004 she was elected president of Peoples Energy's subsidiaries, Peoples Gas and North Shore Gas.

In 2008 Rogers was appointed president of social networking for the Allstate Financial insurance company. She was charged with the task of developing an on-line network through which customers could connect with one another regarding retirement and financial services. "The idea of the [social network] would be to have a forum where people can talk about these things among themselves and, at the same time, [Allstate would] provide them with factual information about financial products and retirement," she told Nathan Conz for *Insurance & Technology* (August 11, 2008).

Meanwhile, after getting married, Rogers had become close friends with Valerie Jarrett, then deputy chief of staff under Chicago mayor Richard M. Daley, and Linda Johnson Rice, chairwoman of the Johnson Publishing Co. Jarrett, currently a top presidential adviser, reportedly took the young Obamas under her wing after she hired Michelle Obama for a job in the mayor's office in the early 1990s. In addition, John Rogers had played basketball at Princeton University with Michelle Obama's brother, Craig M. Robinson. Thus, Rogers's relationship with the future president and first lady began even before Barack Obama's political career. Published sources are not clear as to when or whether Rogers changed her party affiliation, but she was a major fund-raiser during the 2008 presidential campaign of Barack Obama, a Democrat.

Later Career

In November 2008, when Rogers had been with Allstate for only a few months, Obama was elected president. Shortly afterward he appointed Rogers as White House social secretary, making her the first African American to hold the post. With encouragement from the Obamas, Rogers was determined to redefine the position, in which she would be responsible for coordinating all events at the White House, from state dinners to the annual Easter egg rolls on the White House lawn. She saw her mission as both making the White House more open to the public and making it reflect the "Obama brand." Rogers began by ruffling a few feathers. "It is a tradition among former White House social secretaries that whenever a new person is named to that position, her immediate predecessor hosts a lunch to welcome her into what they call their sisterhood," Bob Colacell wrote for *Vanity Fair* (June 2010); Rogers's welcome lunch was hosted by Amy Zantzinger, a social secretary during the George W. Bush administration. It was attended by other women who had held the position in the past, including the group's doyenne, Letitia "Tish" Baldrige, who served during the John F. Kennedy administration. Colacell was told by a "Washington insider": "Tish gave [Rogers] some advice, and Desirée said she didn't care about tablecloths and china and flowers—that was not what she was there to do. For her, a woman like Tish is a dinosaur. She's not interested in what she has to say." According to Chozick, writing in the Wall Street Journal, "previous administrations [had] kept the East and West Wings separate," but "Rogers and her five-person staff [were] a vital part of its political operation, according to a White House aide." Nevertheless, Rogers fought back against early critics of Michelle Obama as first lady who were dismayed that she did not immediately seize a policy role in the administration, instead projecting a more traditional image. Chozick recounts that Rogers countered, "All these rules we've put in place for ourselves, we're saying, 'Ladies, smash them, be who you want to be.'"

"Above all," Chozick wrote, "Rogers is a world-class networker—the ultimate social engineer, not just planning White House dinner parties as well as her own intimate soirees but also connecting powerful people in her orbit." Rogers said to Brown, "Partly for me as a businessperson, it was important this not be a job that I would be picking flowers all day—even though I think that is fun. That is not what I want to do for my job. I don't think that is where I would add the most value."

Rogers and First Lady Michelle Obama endeavored to make the White House more accessible, or, as Chozick wrote, to make it the "people's house." In an effort to celebrate American culture, Rogers scheduled nightly events, including poetry jams, music concerts, and dance and theater performances, involving such celebrities as filmmaker Spike Lee, jazz musician Esperanza Spalding, Irish-American poet Paul Muldoon, and the popular group Earth, Wind and Fire. "Our goal really is to bring the house alive," Rogers told Rachel L. Swarns for the *New York Times* (May 12, 2009) about that diverse assemblage. "We're all American, but all of us come from different backgrounds. We want to expose Americans to other Americans that are doing brilliant work." Rogers was also credited with revamping traditional White House events, such as the Easter egg roll, which, for the first time, families across the country could attend via an on-line ticket lottery.

> **"I think it's fair to say I feel much more comfortable in business than in politics."**

A force in both business and high society, Rogers became the most highly publicized social secretary in recent memory, if not ever. Although by all accounts she performed her job with impressive efficiency (and often to sparkling praise), her glamorous lifestyle away from the job became the subject of public scrutiny. During a time of high unemployment and economic turmoil, some observers found her appearances at fashion shows and in expensive clothing on magazine covers to be insensitive. Her undoing as social secretary, however, was a security gaffe during the Obamas' first state dinner, in honor of visiting Indian prime minister Manmohan Singh, in November 2009.

During an otherwise "elegant evening, a logistically complicated affair for 300-plus guests," Jocelyn Noveck wrote for the Associated Press (December 4, 2009), a couple—Tareq and Michaele Salahi—entered uninvited. The next day the "crashers," as they became known, posted on-line photos of themselves mingling with the president and other high-ranking officials. Although it was acknowledged that the Secret Service should have checked for the Salahis' names on its list of invited guests, lawmakers and noted journalists, including Maureen Dowd of the *New York Times*, blamed Rogers for not checking each guest in herself. Adding fuel to the fire, Rogers had seated herself among the guests. Noveck wrote that some accused Rogers of "putting her own aggrandizement over her job." Tish Baldrige came to Rogers's defense, telling Noveck, "I have sat at state dinners and so have many other social secretaries. Of course, you're constantly getting up. But I don't begrudge her at all for seating herself at the dinner." John Rogers—who had divorced Desirée Rogers amicably in 2000 and who had attended the state dinner—said to Noveck, "It's extraordinary to see someone's life's work mischaracterized in this way. I just don't understand it. She's working 12–15 hours a day, just trying to do a great job. Desirée has brought excellence to everything she's done in her life."

Rogers and members of the Secret Service were asked to appear before Congress for hearings, on the grounds that the security breach had endangered the lives of the first family. The director of the Secret Service testified, but Rogers did not. In February 2010 she resigned. In retrospect, she told Jeremy W. Peters of the *New York Times* (October 1, 2010), "I think it's fair to say I feel much more comfortable in business than in politics. ...I'm much more comfortable in a meritocracy and in reward for good work as opposed to a political environment, where I feel like all of that can be confused."

Four months later Rogers accepted a position as the new CEO of Johnson Publishing Co., which owns both *Ebony* and *Jet* magazines. Those publications, aimed at an African American readership, were established in 1945 (*Ebony*) and 1951 (*Jet*). Rogers set out to draw new advertisers and improve Web content for the iconic magazines. According to a reporter for the Jacksonville (Florida) *Free Press* (October 14, 2010), the average monthly circulation for *Ebony* had fallen 14 percent from 2009 to 2010; that of *Jet,* a weekly magazine, had declined by 12 percent. "I'm not trying to be a hero here," Rogers told the *Free Press* of her efforts to boost revenue. "I'm trying to take my time and really make certain that we do what we need to do to be solid." Rogers spearheaded a major redesign of *Ebony* that debuted in April 2011. She told Phil Rosenthal for the *Chicago Tribune* (March 6, 2011) that she referred to the new look as "*Vanity Fair* plus *O* (the Oprah Winfrey magazine) plus soul," and that with it she hoped to attract "the next generation of *Ebony* readers." Her new management team reorganized the sales force and revamped editorial strategy, seeking to appeal to younger readers while still meeting the expectations of the magazine's loyal older readership. By the end of 2011, *Ebony*'s advertising and rate base had dramatically improved. In January 2012 Johnson Publishing Co. unveiled a redesigned Web site calculated to appeal to a younger demographic.

Rogers was named one of the seven co-chairs in charge of organizing Chicago mayor-elect Rahm Emanuel's inauguration, held on May 16, 2011. In May 2013 Mayor Emanuel choose Rogers to chair the board of Choose Chicago, the city's non-profit tourism marketing organization, asserting that "her unique talents and experience are a perfect fit for this important role."

Chozick wrote about the 5-foot ,10-inch, photogenic Rogers, "Her voice is a smooth unaccented soprano with a hint of a playful Louisiana drawl that she uses to add an extra kick to a story every now and then." Linda Johnson Rice said to Coburn, "I think people often find Desirée cold, even to the point of frosty at first. But that's an initial reaction. Underneath, she is a warm and funny person." In 2003 Rogers was diagnosed with early-stage breast cancer; she is now cancer-free and has become an advocate for women's health. Rogers is single and lives in Chicago.

Further Reading:

Associated Press Dec. 4, 2009

Chicago magazine Aug. 2000

Chicago Sun-Times p1 Dec. 12, 1993, May 20, 2013

Chicago Tribune p5 July 3, 1991, C p1 Sep. 12, 2004, Mar. 6, 2011

Insurance & Technology Aug. 11, 2008

(Jacksonville, Florida) *Free Press* p7 Oct. 14, 2010

New York Times May 12, 2009, Oct. 1, 2010

Pipeline & Gas Journal p12 Nov. 1, 2005

(Richmond, Virginia) *Times Dispatch* J p8 Feb. 22, 2009

Tennessee Tribune A p4 Mar. 11, 2010

Vanity Fair p162 June 2010

Vogue p180 Feb. 2009

Wall Street Journal WSJ Apr. 30, 2009.

Romenesko, Jim

Journalist

Born: 1953, Walworth, Wisconsin, United States

The journalist Jim Romenesko was among the Internet users who introduced blogs, or Web logs, Web pages to which the creator regularly posts personal opinions and experiences, news about topics of interest to the creator, and links to other sites. Blogs sprang up in the 1990s, rapidly disseminating information and links to the blogging community. In 1989 Romenesko had begun publishing a print "fanzine" (a small, highly specialized niche magazine by and for enthusiasts) called *Obscure Publications.* "Its mission," he recalled in a September 4, 2011 blog post, "was to review fanzines and profile their editors." In 1998 Romenesko set up a Web site called the Obscure Store and Reading Room in order to sell fanzines online. "My challenge," he continued, "was to get 'customers' to my website. I decided to do that by linking to stories that I found interesting." Drawn to bizarre news stories since his days as a police reporter for the *Milwaukee Journal,* Romenesko posted brief summaries of strange or shocking stories that he found daily in on-line newspapers and magazines, together with a link to the source page. That project led to his establishment of another Web site, mediagossip.com, at which he posted links to gossip and news concerning newspaper and magazine publishing, television, and other media-related fields.

Mediagossip.com quickly became a "must-read" for media professionals nationwide. Romenesko later ran a slightly altered version of the blog, under the name MediaNews.org, under the auspices of the Poynter Institute, a nonprofit journalism school located in St. Petersburg, Florida. "My No. 1 reason for doing this is enjoyment and entertainment," he told Kimberly Marselas of *American Journalism Review* (September 1999). With MediaNews.org, Greg Mitchell wrote for *Editor & Publisher* (November 25, 2002), "Romenesko gained no small measure of fame (at least in [the publishing] world), and a familiar cry was heard across the land: 'Have you seen Romenesko today?' Here at [*Editor & Publisher*] we are proud of our Web site, … but getting a link on Romenesko always guarantees additional (though sometimes hysterical) feedback." In 2000 Romenesko was included on *Forbes* magazine's list of the "Power 100," the 100 most-powerful people working in the media.

After 12 years with Poynter (during which he was, as he acknowledged, well paid), Romenesko announced his "semi-retirement." He planned to continue to post "casually" to his Poynter blog, which would be taken up by other journalists and renamed Romenesko+, but he would launch a new venture devoted to reporting on the media as well as other topics. Before his scheduled date of departure arrived, however, a puzzling contretemps arose over supposedly unacknowledged quotations in his link summaries. He abruptly left Poynter, focusing thereafter on his own new blog, JimRomenesko.com.

At first Romenesko ran the Obscure Store and Reading Room from his small apartment in Evanston, Illinois, while working for *Milwaukee Magazine* and later the St. Paul, Minnesota, *Pioneer Press.* Once a Starbucks coffeeshop in his area began offering Wi-Fi, he worked much of the time from Starbucks and occasionally other coffeeshops. In 2004 he started the blog Starbucks Gossip, which covered the Starbucks Coffee company. The blog acquired a large following of company employees and customers. In a tweet posted at Starbucksgossip.com, dated October 11, 2013, Romenesko announced that after nearly a decade, he would no longer post to the site. Nevertheless, he continued to run tweets there.

Education and Early Career

One of ten children, James P. Romenesko was born on September 16, 1953, in Walworth, Wisconsin, a town close to the northern border of Illinois. His father, Merlin, was the town's school superintendent, and his mother was a homemaker. When Simon Dumenco, writing for *New York* magazine (May 8, 2000), asked him about the occupations of his siblings, Romenesko replied, "Well, let's see, one brother is a CFO for a company in Chicago. Um, most of 'em are accountants, actually. And one owns a hardware store." Four of his five sisters became schoolteachers; the fifth went into marketing. From early on Romenesko had an interest in news and journalism. He recalled to Dumenco that each week the Walworth Public Library received the Sunday *New York Times* on the following Wednesday, and he was "always the only person who touched it or read it."

Romenesko graduated in about 1975 from Marquette University, in Milwaukee, Wisconsin, where he had studied journalism. He then began working for the *Milwaukee Journal.* "Graduating and getting hired was like the greatest thing in the world," Romenesko recalled to Dumenco. "I mean, I just remember springing out of bed in the morning, anxious to go to work." Romenesko served as the *Journal*'s suburban reporter during the day and its police reporter at night. His night job showed him a "side of life that I never saw when I grew up," as he told Dumenco. "In Walworth, … probably the most riveting thing was a truck went the wrong way around the village square—and this is the truth. The picture [of the truck] was in the paper. … Then you're thrown into a situation where, you know, people are stabbed 55 times and you get to go to the morgue and look at the Polaroid snapshots." In a conversation with Jacquelyn Mitchard for the Madison, Wisconsin, *Capital Times* (June 30, 1981), Romenesko said that the first morgue report he ever saw nauseated him: he vomited after reading its first half. He gradually lost his squeamishness, and in his final months with the *Milwaukee Journal,* in 1982, he self-published dozens of coroner's reports (with the names of the dead deleted) in a 150-page book called *Death Log.* The book contains sections on such causes of death as "autoerotic mishaps" and misadventures involving pork chops, and it offers "uncensored logs … of some of the most grisly and sorry finales as ever were," as Mitchard wrote. "They're the details that never make the newspaper reports, the grim facts masked by the word 'unexpectedly' in obituaries. … The cackle of police-beat humor … runs throughout the book."

After he left the *Milwaukee Journal,* Romenesko worked from 1982 to 1995 as an editor at *Milwaukee Magazine.* There he wrote a column called "Pressroom Confidential," which offered his insider's take on Milwaukee newsroom- and television-station politics. Romenesko described "Pressroom Confidential" to James Poniewozik for Salon.com (June 10, 1999) as the "best-read column" in the magazine, according to reader surveys; it won national awards in three consecutive years. From 1996 to 1999 Romenesko served as a new-media- and Internet reporter for the St. Paul *Pioneer Press.*

Earlier, from 1989 to 1999, Romenesko published a print fanzine called *Obscure Publications,* which covered the world of fan magazines. *Obscure Publications* often discussed legal issues facing small underground publishing ventures and featured strange news reports that appeared either in print or on the Web. In early 1998, as an offshoot of *Obscure Publications,* Romenesko set up the Web site Obscure Store and Reading Room (obscurestore.com), which every day contained brief summaries of and links to weird, ludicrous, or sordid news stories. Romenesko rose at around 5:00 a.m. daily to search for such accounts in scores of newspapers and periodicals found on the Web; he then posted links to the original source of his selections on his site, along with short summaries indicating the nature of the selection. On July 18, 2003, for example, Romenesko's own headlines for the links listed on obscurestore.com included "[Department of

Motor Vehicles] refuses to give driver's license to man with upside-down signature," a story from the news section of delawareonline.com; "Boy, 6, drives car 30 miles in search of his mother," from the Austin, Texas, *American-Statesman* Web site; and "Judge green-lights inmate's goal to become a woman—on taxpayers' dime," from the *Newsday* Web site. In the "store" part of the site, Romenesko offered for sale copies of old and obscure magazines—for example, *Angry Thoreauan, Jersey Beat,* and *Temp Slave.*

In May 1999, having come across and featured many stories related to the media—such as accounts of celebrities in the publishing world, editors, television broadcasters, media tycoons, and gossip columnists, for example—Romenesko set up a Web site dedicated exclusively to news stories about the media. On mediagossip.com, as he called it, he posted a roundup of what he considered each day's top media news stories, in addition to links to a variety of publications and commentaries about the media. Mediagossip.com was an immediate hit. Almost from its inception, the site had several thousand daily readers. "The not-so-secret reason for Romenesko's success is the media's incredible self-absorption," Dan Kennedy wrote in an article posted on bostonphoenix.com (September 9–16, 1999). "I confess to having been immediately hooked after I saw that he'd included me in his list of media columnists."

Later Career

Mediagossip.com caught the eye of Bill Mitchell, director of Poynter Online, the Web site of the Florida-based nonprofit journalism school. In 1999 Mitchell hired Romenesko to maintain a media news site for Poynter. Romenesko's new Web page, called MediaNews, appeared at poynter.org. It averaged more than 14,000 page views per day in 2000, according to Lori Robertson in *American Journalism Review* (September 2000). Robertson, who described Romenesko as a "computer maven and journalism junkie," commented that "Romenesko's page … has changed the way news about the media is disseminated, creating an instant forum for the self-referential world of journalism. Suddenly articles in a regional daily or local alternative paper or city magazine have an immediate national audience." Robertson identified another source of Romenesko's appeal: "He updates the page as news happens throughout the day. As a result of his efforts, MediaNews has emerged as the Web stop for the immediate industry scoop, including much about small markets and alternative publications."

According to Simon Dumenco, Romenesko often received e-mail messages from "journalists plugging their own stories, journalists passing along industry gossip, journalists complaining about other journalists." Dumenco wrote, "Romenesko's site has become the place for journalists to see and be seen—sort of like a virtual Michael's or Elaine's" (referring to two New York City restaurants then popular with media professionals; Elaine's has since closed). The influence of Romenesko's site can be measured by the number of powerful and well-known people in media who have relied on it as a source of news or a forum in which to publicize their views. Peggy Noonan, a former speechwriter for President Ronald Reagan, told Dumenco, "A friend of mine at *Entertainment Weekly* told me [that Romenesko's is] the first site she goes to in the morning, and that's true of most of the people she works with. So now I visit regularly. I like it that [Romenesko] worries about journalistic standards. The way I see it, the site is a public service." "Getting picked up by [Romenesko] is the new bragging right among gossips," Tom Prince, the executive editor of *Allure,* told Dumenco.

The word *empowering* has been used to characterize Romenesko's blog, at which lively and rapid-fire exchanges often took place. Howard Kurtz—a longtime *Washington Post* columnist who later covered politics and media for The Daily Beast and hosted the CNN media criticism program *Reliable Sources* before moving to Fox News—told Dumenco, "I think the clever and sometimes sardonic way that Romenesko packages and presents his daily media download has a lot to do with the site's charm," noting that Romenesko's blog enabled "two-way communication." One way Romenesko encouraged that communication and also ensured that the media establishment would regularly visit his site was to invite anyone with legitimate media news to share to submit it. Sometimes to the chagrin of media executives, lower-level employees did. By the time Romenesko became established at Poynter, according to Michael Calderone, writing at the Huffington Post (August 24, 2011), "some of the country's top editors complained that he was publishing internal memos and [alternative-weekly] stories detailing their newsroom spats." But in the years that followed, Romenesko told Calderone, "It got to the point where editors sent me their own memos and admitted they were crafting their memos for publication on Romenesko." Robertson retailed a telling remark by Doyle McManus, then chief of the *Los Angeles Times*'s Washington bureau (and now an editorial page columnist for the paper): "If it's there, you know that most of your colleagues in the profession have either looked at it or printed it out and handed it to someone in the newsroom."

In his profile of Romenesko for *Portfolio* magazine (June 16, 2008), Howell Raines, former executive editor (2001–2003) of the *New York Times,* noted that the "verb form of Romenesko's name quickly established itself as journalistic shorthand for getting zapped, often fatally, by unflattering publicity"—as Raines himself had experienced with Romenesko's coverage of the Jayson Blair plagiarism scandal that afflicted the *Times* in 2003. (The scandal eventually cost Raines his position.) "I never really blamed the messenger," Raines wrote in *Portfolio,* but in Romenesko's blog he discerned threats far more consequential than the discomfiture of media editors and executives. "Since then, however, hard times have hit the newspaper business, and today, many editors are … grousing that Romenesko's blog … feeds gloom and doom in the nation's newsrooms with its instantaneous reporting of layoffs, declining ad revenues, and fire-sale prices being paid for metropolitan dailies." Worse, "Newspaper publishers assumed that even if the printing press disappeared, the internet would still have an insatiable need for their basic product—verified facts, hierarchically arranged by importance. But Romenesko's rapid growth showed that even newsrooms are part of the emerging market for an unprocessed sprawl of information, delivered immediately and with as few filters as possible. … In short, it's not technology per se that's killing newspapers; it's plummeting demand for quality information." "That's the big picture for journalism and Romenesko," Raines concluded. "They are both being done in by large impersonal forces like the commoditization of news, accelerated obsolescence, mutating news values, and what happens when newspapers try to wring 21st-century profits from the 18th-century technique of transporting … individualized packages of words on paper." Raines further observed that, "Traditionalist critics view Romenesko as the guy who opened the first and biggest hole in the sacred wall between news and gossip in reporting about the media. The newer media blogs, however, see him as being confined by passé, self-imposed rules, such as his steady refusal to make his own website into a political soapbox." Raines took note of Jim Romanesko's instinct for fairness. Indeed, although Romenesko (as he reflected in his September 4, 2011, announcement of his "semi-retirement") at first allowed comments at his media blog, he stopped running them when he felt that "discussions got out of hand." In about 2005 he "reinstated them, realizing that I couldn't (and shouldn't) control every word and thought on my site."

Romenesko, however, continued to adapt and thrive. Bill Mitchell, who directed Poynter.org for ten years, observed (August 24, 2011) at the Poynter Web site that, "Especially after the September 11 attacks, Poynter faculty embraced [Romenesko's] site as an essential way to reach working journalists with resources they needed in increasingly challenging times. … Romenesko has sustained the most reliable—and readable—daily chronicle of one of journalism's most important eras. He also helped transform aggregation and curation … to a craft with significant consequence for journalism. Jim's blog brought transparency to newsrooms, equipping readers and staffers alike to hold those organizations accountable in the way that they scrutinize the operations of others."

In his September 4, 2011, post, Romenesko announced not only that he was "semi-retiring" from blogging at Poynter Online but that he would soon close the Obscure Store and Reading Room. He had tired of news aggregation and wished to return to a more reportorial role—while not, however, abandoning his media-watch efforts. "After aggregating for a dozen years, I decided to shift gears a bit and do some reporting too," he said. "It's a good change of pace."

"The first time I really sampled the internet, in 1989, I knew this would be a culture-changing force, and I wanted to be part of it."

Both Romenesko and Poynter must have anticipated a smooth transition. Romenesko's blog would remain at Poynter with irregular posts from Romenesko and contributions from several Poynter faculty. Romenesko himself would launch JimRomenesko.com, a new blog at which he would cover "media and other things I'm interested in." Moreover, during Romenesko's tenure at Poynter, the media landscape had undergone enormous changes. "Mary," who commented on Romenesko's announcement of his more limited relationship with Poynter, astutely pointed out that, "This site preceded social media and made anonymity both a strategy and an asset." Julie Moos, director of Poynter Online and Poynter Publications, noted in her own announcement of their changed relationship (August 24, 2011) that, "Twitter has become an increasingly important tool for Jim and for Poynter. … Jim will continue to tweet frequently about media and tech from the @romenesko account and from the @poynter account." Then, however, in what David Carr of the *New York Times* (November 11, 2011) called a "bizarre spat" with Moos and Poynter over the use or absence of quotation marks in his link content summaries, Romenesko left Poynter early, pointedly resigning—via Twitter—seven weeks before the planned date, in what Carr called "typically understated style." Carr continued, speaking of Poynter, "To those of us who read and followed him, it seemed like an ill-advised way to end a run that was remarkable in all aspects. He was a proto-blogger, helping to define the form; an arbiter and observer of the great unwinding of journalism; and an eerily fair aggregator of other people's work. … When you buy into an blogging autodidact—especially one as subtly funny and dark as Mr. Romenesko—you take the bitter with the sweet."

In remarks made to Jeremy W. Peters, writing for the *New York Times* (August 24, 2011), Romenesko spoke about his future direction, saying that he was going back to reporting, his original interest.

At JimRomenesko.com, he would continue to cover media but would also pursue other topics that interested him, including, Peters wrote, food, finance and real estate. Romenesko told Peters,"My role kind of vanished. I was a town crier but just one of many." Peters added that Romenesko acknowledged "that the social media revolution had left him somewhat disoriented but determined to find something more rewarding." In this he succeeded, in his own opinion and those of other observers. Dan Reimold wrote at MediaShift (February 2, 2012), "He is blogging with a renewed vibrancy and candor." Reimold reposted a tweet on Romenesko from Carl Lavin: "One person can=change," adding that Lavin saw improvements in Romenesko's work: "'In his post-Poynter product, Jim has expanded his sourcing and list of topics and seems to pay even more attention to packaging,' he said. 'If anything, there is now a broader range of topics — all related to newsrooms, the people, processes and products that make them hum.'" (Food, finance, and real estate have not been much in evidence.) Andrew Beaujon, Romenesko's successor at Poynter Online's MediaNews blog, now known as MediaWire, commented that Romenesko was "doing a lot more reporting and it seems really energetic and engaged. He was a model for media reporters before and he's even more so now." Reimold concluded that "Romenesko also now seems to finally get social media. He tweets, posts and interacts on Facebook, bases blog posts on Twitter and Facebook feedback, and has activated Facebook comments to appear below all posts along with regular site comments."

Romenesko told Mark Lisheron of the *American Journalism Review* (February 23, 2012), "It's not work. It doesn't feel like work, it feels like a hobby." Lisheron commented, "However unpleasantly [his resignation from Poynter] occurred, Romenesko believes both parties have benefited from his departure. Romenesko is roaming further than he has in years, picking and choosing stories that interest him and adding his own reporting to his customary felicitous aggregating." Jack Shafer of Reuters told Lisheron, "He is so much more competitive now. It's like hearing the old voice in those news feeds. We're happy to have Jim back."

In his profile of Romenesko for *Portfolio*, Howell Raines called Romenesko a "cloistered digital monk." Raines wrote that Romenesko's "way of life"—his early rising, long and mostly solitary working hours, and continual preoccupation with the world of media—"grew from his hunch about the future of social interaction." In a virtual interview Romenesko told Raines, "The first time I really sampled the internet, in 1989, … 'I knew this would be a culture-changing force, and I wanted to be part of it.'" More recently Romenesko has tended his blog while circulating among a wider constellation of local coffeeshops. Romenesko has taught courses in fanzine publishing and history at the Milwaukee Institute of Art and Design and in feature writing for newspapers at the University of Wisconsin, in Milwaukee.

Further Reading:

American Journalism Review p15 Sep. 1999, p28+ Sep. 2000, Jun./Jul., 2011, Feb. 23, 2012

Editor & Publisher Nov. 25, 2002, with photo

Huffington Post Aug. 24, 2011

JimRomenesko.com

MediaShift Feb. 2, 2012

New York p32+ May 8, 2000, with photo

New York Times Aug. 24, 2011, Nov. 10, 2011, Nov. 11, 2011

obscurestore.com

Portfolio magazine June 16, 2008

poynter.org

Selected Books:

Romenesko, James, comp., *Death Log,* 1982

Ruiz Guiñazú, Magdalena

Newspaper and broadcast journalist

Born: 1935, Buenos Aires, Argentina

The long career of the Argentine journalist Magdalena Ruiz Guiñazú has spanned one of the most sordid eras in her country's political history. Like so many Latin American journalists whose chosen vocations have been practiced against a backdrop of repression and political violence, Ruiz Guiñazú has been the target of repeated death threats and other forms of intimidation because of her ongoing investigations into human rights abuses during the 1970s and 1980s, when Argentina was ruled by a military junta that tortured and killed thousands of people branded political dissidents. Of the years of the "dirty war," she told Victoria Molnar of *El País* (Uruguay; September 5, 2013), "They were very terrible times. … I felt terribly responsible because [my children] lived with me and suffered threats. …it was: "We will kill, we will kill you all." … I was afraid at the time, of course, but … basically [I] was determined not to loosen and … I felt very supported." Amidst such tumult, Ruiz Guiñazú's bravery and journalistic integrity made her one of the country's most popular and trusted journalists and broadcasters.

After the return of democratic rule to Argentina in 1984, Ruiz Guiñazú was appointed by President Raúl Alfonsín to the Comisión Nacional sobre la Desaparición de Personas, known as CONADEP ("National Commission on the Disappearance of Persons"), established to investigate and make public the record of the military junta's horrific human rights abuses. The commission was headed by novelist Ernesto Sábato, and he wrote a foreword to its report, which was entitled *Nunca más* ("Never Again"). The following year the report was used in the prosecution of high-ranking military personnel. Fearful of a military coup during this unstable period—during which there were several armed rebellions— President Alfonsín declared an amnesty, leaving many lower-level officers and others complicit in the military's crimes both unpunished and discontented. Some of those convicted were eventually freed. Thereafter, tension over the dirty war years remained endemic in Argentine society. In 1997 a naval officer who had come forward in 1995 to confess his part in the dirty war (he had, among other actions, participated in pushing live victims from airplanes into the open ocean) was attacked by unknown assailants who carved into his forehead the initials of three journalists to whom he had made these admissions. One of them was Magdalena Ruiz Guiñazú.

In recent years Ruiz Guiñazú has continued to speak out vociferously in support of freedom of the press. Asked to comment on the relationship of press freedom and freedom of expression, Ruiz Guiñazú told Victoria Molnar, "They are sisters, are very close to each other. … You have to be responsible for what you express, of course. But a country without freedom of the press is a country that gives no guarantees for democracy." Under the government of neo-Perónist Cristina Fernández de Kirchner, she (among other independent Argentine journalists) has been subject to subtle (and less subtle) forms of harassment, including a tax audit following her presentation of her press freedom concerns to the Organization of American States's Inter-American Commission on Human Rights (IACHR). Still, as she told Victoria Molnar, "I am a free person … [and] I've said what I believe needs to be said."

In addition to her print journalism and television work, Ruiz Guiñazú has hosted her own early morning radio program, *Magdalena tempranísimo* ("Magdalena Unearthly") for nearly three decades, two with Radio Mitre (owned by the Argentine media conglomerate Grupo Clarín) and seven with Radio Continental (owned by the Spanish company Prisa). In October 2013 Continental announced that Ruiz Guiñazú's contract would not be renewed when it expired at the end of the year. According to Josef Crettaz of *La Nación* (October 4, 2013), Ruiz Guiñazú responded that she had no intention of retiring, but she would not divulge her plans. The previous May, Ruiz Guiñazú had launched a weekly television magazine program, *Magdalena y el país* ("Magdalena in the Country"), on the Grupo Clarín's Metro station.

Education and Early Career

Magdalena Ruiz Guiñazú was born on February 15, 1935, in Buenos Aires, one of four children born to Enrique Ruiz Guiñazú, soon to become foreign affairs minister for Argentina, and his wife, María Celina Cantilo Ortiz Basualdo. Enrique Ruiz Guiñazú was a controversial foreign minister; persisting in keeping Argentina neutral during World War II, he was suspected of having fascist sympathies. Magdalena Ruiz Guiñazú began her career in the 1960s, writing fiction for a women's magazine. While it was a stultifying place to work—Ruiz Guiñazú told Daniel Drosdoff, a reporter for United Press International (July 26, 1987), "personally, I think the idea of women's programs and women's magazines constitutes discrimination"—she was fortunate to start her career prior to the devastating economic downturn caused by the military dictatorship that followed in the next decade. In the mid-1970s she worked as a journalist in television news, notably the *Videoshow* news program under the direction of Jorge "Cacho" Fontana.

Ruiz Guiñazú's career took a more serious turn in the late 1970s, at a time of intense political upheaval that would usher in a dark period in Argentina's 20th-century history. A military junta led by General Jorge Rafael Videla took over the country on March 24, 1976, toppling the government of President Isabel Martínez de Perón, who, as vice president, had assumed the presidency after the death of her husband, Juan Perón, on July 1, 1974. (Juan Perón's previous wife, Evita, wildly popular with average Argentineans, had died in 1952.)

Videla unleashed an insidious reign of terror over the next several years, kidnapping and murdering thousands of political dissidents and suspected critics of the government, including union leaders, student activists, and anyone who dared to speak out against the regime. A reporter for the Associated Press (July 28, 1985) wrote, "A year before it seized power in 1976, the army had received orders to 'annihilate subversion.' And it gave the word *annihilate* its ultimate meaning." The period between 1976 and 1983 is often referred to as Argentina's "dirty war," and the thousands kidnapped, tortured, and killed by the military are referred to as the "disappeared."

This was an atmosphere in which it was unlikely that a journalist could report on corruption and survive. More than a hundred journalists were reportedly "disappeared," and Ruiz Guiñazú's success in carving out a career in the media during this time was an exceptional feat. As she recounted to Beatriz V. Goyoaga for *Variety* (November 30, 1998), "I was lucky to start in one of the two private radio stations that existed during the dictatorship. The management supported me and allowed me to report things others couldn't." During the dirty war, Ruiz Guiñazú was a regular radio presence and also wrote for the newspaper *La Nación,* one of the most respected and widely read newspapers in South America.

Besides covering the atrocities being committed under the ruling junta, Ruiz Guiñazú kept abreast of important incidents taking place in the Falkland Islands (known to Argentineans as the Islas de la Malvinas), 300 miles east of the Argentine coast, in 1982. The islands had been occupied and administered by Britain for more than a century, but Argentineans believed that the land was rightfully theirs. On May 10, 1982, on the orders of General Leopoldo Galtieri, a Videla successor whose short but catastrophic reign saw the country's economy spiral downward, Argentine troops invaded the islands in what many contend was a brazen attempt to stir up Argentineans' sense of nationalism to divert attention from the dismal domestic situation. The conflict, known in Argentina as the Guerra de las Malvinas, lasted 72 days. In the end the Falkland Islands remained under British control. Argentina's military government was thoroughly discredited by this quick defeat, and it soon collapsed.

After the return of civilian rule, Raúl Alfonsín won a landslide election victory to become the first democratically elected president of Argentina in more than two decades. Among his first actions in office was assembling a historic commission, the National Commission on the Disappearance of Persons, to investigate the abuses committed by the country's military leaders during the preceding years. The commission comprised 16 members, of whom six were chosen by the Argentine congress and ten appointed by the president himself, who selected them for their "zeal in the defense of human rights and public prestige," according to an official decree quoted by Edward Schumacher in the *New York Times* (December 17, 1983). Ruiz Guiñazú was among the ten chosen by the president. Other members, in addition to Ernesto Sábato, included two jurists, a heart surgeon, academics, and religious leaders.

By spring 1984 Ruiz Guiñazú and her fellow commission members were immersed in their investigations. In March the commission made headlines with its investigation of the Navy Mechanics School, located in a suburb of Buenos Aires; the school had functioned during the dirty war as a prison camp, and it had been the site of the grisly torture and murder of scores of prisoners. (Some 280 similar sites would eventually be discovered.) Ruiz Guiñazú was among the members of the commission who went to the grounds of the Clandestine Detention Center at the Navy Mechanics School, along with a handful of former prisoners who had somehow survived. She was appalled by what she saw. As she told an Associated Press reporter (March 16, 1984), "I have been to Europe and done stories [on the Dachau and Auschwitz concentration camps]. But I never expected to see such a thing in my own country."

Nunca más, the commission's report, was issued in 1984. It was instrumental in bringing to courts martial several former military figures involved in the killings and kidnappings. The 1985 proceedings—at which, among other testimony, one teenager testified that his toenails had been ripped out and electrodes attached to his genitals, and a farmer told of his dog frequently returning from jaunts bearing human remains—were branded "Argentina's Nuremberg Trial" by the press.

Later Career

In 1987 Ruiz Guiñazú moderated Argentina's first televised political debate, which took place on August 17 between Juan Manuel Casella of the Radical Civic Union (the party of President Alfonsín) and Antonio Cafiero of the Justicialist Party (more commonly referred to as the Peronists), both of whom were running for the governorship of Buenos Aires. The debate was riveting, and the race was virtually deadlocked in the days before the September 6 election. (Cafiero was the victor.) Also in 1987, Ruiz Guiñazú was hired by the Clarín media company to appear on a recently acquired AM radio station, Radio Mitre. Her current-affairs show, *Magdalena tempranísimo* ("Magdalena Unearthly") aired early in the morning and attracted a wide, diverse audience. Ruiz Guiñazú's contract with Clarín called for total freedom of speech. "I needed to have this in writing," she explained to Beatriz V. Goyoaga, "because it is an essential part of my life and work. I've also kept total independence from the commercial earnings of my program, which is not the case with all journalists in this country." Ruiz Guiñazú's reports often dealt with such inflammatory subject matter as government corruption. Consequently, she became the subject of numerous death threats—especially as the atrocities committed by former military men were being brought further to light. Ruiz Guiñazú was forced to have a police escort accompany her on her way to and from work for months at a time.

In 1995 Ruiz Guiñazú reported the story of the former naval officer who broke a military code of silence by confessing to participating in the kidnappings and murders of political prisoners during the dirty war. In 1997, two years after the story had broken, he was attacked by a group of men who carved into his face the initials of the three journalists who had interviewed him. Ruiz Guiñazú was one of the three—an "M" had been carved into the man's forehead to represent her first name. On June 24, 1997, Ruiz Guiñazú received four menacing phone messages, including one that stated, "The next one is going to be [you]." No arrests were made in the case. "I consider this part of a threatening campaign against independent journalism," she said, as quoted in a press release posted on the Web site of the International Freedom of Expression Exchange.

Ruiz Guiñazú, in an interview on Radio Continental, had been the first journalist to bring to public notice the Mothers of Plaza de Mayo, who posed the first organized resistance to the military regime. The Mothers of Plaza de Mayo regularly met in the plaza in front of the presidential palace (the Casa Rosado) and held nonviolent demonstrations demanding justice for their children, presumed to be among the "disappeared" (as the victims of the dirty war were called by its chief perpetrator, General Jorge Rafael Videla). The Mothers (several founding members of which themselves were later "disappeared") attracted domestic and international support and became a major political movement. In 1986 the Mothers split into two organizations. One, the "Founding Line," continued to focus on recovering and identifying remains and bringing perpetrators to justice. The other, called the Mothers of Plaza de Mayo Association, pursued wider and more militant political goals, and it supports the neo-Peronist Justicialist Party of Cristina Fernández de Kirchner. In April 2010 Hebe de Bonafini, the longtime leader of the Association, accused Ruiz Guiñazú, among others, of having collaborated with the military junta. Magdalena Ruiz Guiñazú indignantly rejected these charges and produced a record of a February 1984 interview with De Bonafini in which the latter acknowledged Ruiz Guiñazú's role in giving the Mothers media exposure at a time when no one else dared to and praised her journalistic work under the dictatorship. "We remember with much affection you were the first to speak of the Mothers on the radio," De Bonafini said then. "You do not ever forget." On April 29, 2010, the president of the Mothers of Plaza de Mayo Association led a public "ethical and political trial" in front of the Casa Rosada, "convicting" certain journalists, including Ruiz Guiñazú, of being accomplices of the dictatorship. Posters were displayed of photographs of the "accused." The president of the Federal Council of Audiovisual Communication, appointed by President Fernández de Kirchner, was one of the "witnesses." The "trial," as reported by the Clarín Web site (November 7, 2013), was broadcast on the state-owned television Channel 7. Ruiz Guiñazú lost the defamation case, however, on the basis of a 2009 law that negated the crimes of libel and slander in matters considered to be of public interest.

The matter did not end there. On November 1, 2013, Ruiz Guiñazú and fellow journalists Joaquín Morales Solá, Nelson Castro, Luis Makhoul, Alfredo Leuco, Mariano Obarrio and Jose "Pepe" Eliaschev appeared before the Organization of American States' Inter-American Commission on Human Rights (IACHR) in Washington, District of Columbia, to express their concerns about threats to press freedom in Argentina. Together they addressed three principal areas (according *to La Nación,* November 14, 2013). First, they noted instances of public demonization of journalists and independent media, acts of intimidation intended to pressure journalists into self-censorship. Second, the delegation spoke of the use of discretionary public funds intended for government advertising to support partisan political propaganda in outlets friendly toward the government rather than legimate government interests. Finally, they spoke of the serious problems that persist in Argentina regarding restricted access to public information. (According to Nina Agrawal, writing in the Summer 2012 *Americas Quarterly,* "Argentina is one of the few countries in the Western Hemisphere without a freedom of access to information law.") Ruiz Guiñazú cited the De Bonafini-led "trial" as well as other attacks, verbal and physical, on independent Argentine journalists. The delegation also charged that the government had pressured private advertisers not to place ads in *La Nación, Clarín,* and *Perfil,* all major independent newspapers regarded as being critical of the government that are supported by advertising.

Returning to Buenos Aires after presenting her testimony, Ruiz Guiñazú was promptly visited by two agents of the Argentine tax authority demanding her financial records for the preceding two years. As recounted in *La Nación* (November 7, 2013), the government alleged that the audit was a routine procedure triggered by her request to have her taxes reduced. Ruiz Guiñazú denied having made any such request. In any case commentators expressed doubt that the seven thousand-plus taxpayers who had asked for a tax reduction had each received a similar personal visit from government agents. As reported in *Perfil* (November 6, 2013), the political opposition denounced the action; one center-right party member of the Chamber of Deputies, Laura Alonso, called it a "form of retaliation, subtle and indirect censorship, to intimidate" those who disagreed with the government. Another center-right politician, Federico Pinedo, likened the action to that of a police state, citing previous instances in which the government had launched tax audits to punish journalists for speaking out. A day after the tax inspectors went to Ruiz Guiñazú's home, Leuco was assaulted on the Avenida de Mayo by a group of men who beat him and stole his backpack, which contained his irreplaceable notes but nothing of appreciable material value.

"But a country without freedom of the press is a country that gives no guarantees for democracy."

Shortly before Ruiz Guiñazú and her colleagues appeared before the IACHR, Argentina's Supreme Court affirmed the country's new media law, which, as Hannah Strange explained in the London *Telegraph* (October 29, 2013), will "force private media to surrender broadcasting licenses if they exceed strict ownership and audience limits, paving the way for the dismantling of the Clarin empire with which [President Cristina Fernández de Kirchner] has long sparred. The verdict was hailed as victory for free expression by Kirchner supporters but decried as the death knell for independent journalism by her opponents. Grupo Clarin, the largest media group in Argentina, claims the law is a thinly-veiled attempt to silence a leading voice against her government. With a nationwide television network, cable operations and multiple regional TV and radio stations as well as newspaper interests, Clarin is the only company big enough to affected by the law, which it argues is squarely aimed at its destruction."

A profile of Ruiz Guiñazú at the Fundación Konex Web site notes that she produced a number of television documentaries, including *El día del juicio* (1999, "The Day of Judgment," about the trials of officers of the dictatorship), *El día después* (2000, "The Day After," marking 15 years after the fall of the junta), *Estela* (2009, "Estela," the story of Estela Carlotto and the Grandmothers of Plaza de Mayo), *Secretos de familia* (2008–2010, "Family Secrets"), and Héroes de un país del Sur (2012, "Heroes of a Southern Country," biographies of important twentieth-century Argentineans). Her anchor stints included *Dos en la noticia* (1996–1997, "Two in the News," with Joaquín Morales Solá) and *National Geographic* (2000–2001).

In addition to her radio, newspaper, and television journalism, Ruiz Guiñazú is the author of a number of books, including novels (*Huésped de un verano,* 1994, "Summer Guest"; *La Casa de los secretos,* 2011, "The House of Secrets"); short-story collections (*Historias de hombres, mujeres y jazmines,* 2002, "Stories of Men, Women and Jasmine"; *Había una vez ... la vida,* 1995, "Once upon a Time ... Life"); and biographical volumes based on her television programs (*Secretos de Familia,* 2012, "Family Secrets"; *Héroes de un país del Sur,* 2011, "Heroes of a Southern Country"). Ruiz Guiñazú is a founder (1959) of the Asociación de Periodistas de la Televisión y Radiofonía Argentina, an organization that works for freedom of the press. Widely considered an influential champion of human rights and one of the Argentine media's most vociferous critics of government corruption, she has won (as of 2013) 14 Martín Fierro Awards (one of Argentina's top journalism prizes, named after a famous Argentine writer) over the course of her career; in 1994 she was given the Martín Fierro de Oro, a lifetime-achievement honor. In August 2013 the Inter American Press Association (IAPA), and organization founded to promote excellence in journalism and the defense of freedom of expression across the continent, awarded its Grand Prize for Press Freedom journalists to Ruiz Guiñazú and to Menacho Diego Cornejo, of Ecuador. She was named a fellow of the National Academy of Journalism in September 2005.In 2003 Ruiz Guiñazú was presented with a Lifetime Achievement Award at the International Women's Media Foundation's Courage in Journalism Awards. Her other awards include France's Légion d'honneur (Legion of Honor, 1994) and Italy's Ordine al merito della Repubblica Italiana (Order of Merit, 1984), in recognition of her human rights work.

Noting that she is of Basque descent, Ruiz Guiñazú told Victoria Molnar of *El País,* "the downside is that I am stubborn and the positive side is that I am firm in my concepts." She was married for 15 years to César Doretti and is the mother of five children, three daughters and two sons. The couple separated in 1967. Eventually Ruiz Guiñazú met Sergio Dellachá, who was her partner for twenty-seven years, until his death in 2006. She has eight grandchildren. Molnar called Ruiz Guiñazú "a woman of character, restless and relentless." "But the truth is," Ruiz Guiñazú told Molnar, "that I love what I do, my job is part of my life and the most important is the strong relationship and endearing affinities that I have with my audience. As a journalist I feel a lot of responsibility. I realize that … I'm not a private citizen. I give you information and [try] as little as possible to filter my own ideas."

Further Reading:

Americas Quarterly Summer 2012

Clarín Web site Nov. 7, 2013

Fundación Konex Web site

International Women's Media Foundation Web site

La Nación Oct. 29, 2012, Oct. 30, 2012, Dec. 1, 2012; Oct. 4, 2013, Nov. 7, 2013, Nov. 14, 2012

El Nuevo Herald Nov. 14, 2013

(Uruguay) *El País* Sep. 5, 2013

Perfil Nov. 6, 2013

Radio Mitre Web site

(London) *Telegraph* (October 29, 2013)

Variety p58 Nov. 30, 1998

Selected Books:

Fiction

Huésped de un verano, 1994 ("Summer Guest")

Había una vez ... la vida, 1995 ("Once upon a Time ... Life")

Historias de hombres, mujeres y jazmines, 2002 ("Stories of Men, Women and Jasmine")

La Casa de los secretos, 2011 ("House of Secrets").

Nonfiction

Ruiz Guiñazú, Magdalena, with Father Rafael Braun, *¡Qué mundo nos ha tocado!,* 2001 ("What a World We Have Had! Conversations between Two Performers of Our Time)

Héroes de un país del Sur, 2011 ("Heroes of a Southern Country")

Secretos de familia, 2012 ("Family Secrets")

Saatchi, Charles

Art collector, advertising executive

Born: 1943, Baghdad, Iraq

On December 8, 1998, when Christie's London auctioned off 130 pieces of modern art from the collection of Charles Saatchi, the reaction was mixed. Part of the proceeds from the auction went to establish scholarships at four art schools in England, yet few journalists were convinced that Saatchi's motives for selling the works had been purely altruistic. Some pointed out that any new talents emerging from the schools would feel beholden to Saatchi, who has a reputation for voraciously snapping up the work of young artists while they still command modest prices. Others noted that Saatchi had intended to keep a portion of the profits himself and stood to reap a financial windfall. In the past the collector had almost monopolized the works of certain artists, such as Sean Scully and Julian Schnabel, causing a shortage of available pieces and driving up their prices. He had then divested himself of much of the art, and their market value had later collapsed. "He's really a commodities broker who's been let loose on the art world," Scully declared to the *New York Times Magazine* (September 26, 1999). "He claims to love art, but his is the love that the wolf has for the lamb.

The owner of one of the largest private collections of contemporary art in the world, Saatchi started his career as a copywriter for an advertising agency. With his brother Maurice, he founded Saatchi & Saatchi, which was the largest advertising firm in the world in the 1980s. Because of his long connection to the business of persuasion, many of his critics wonder whether he has used advertising techniques to generate hype about his private collection of art. Saatchi favors controversial and iconoclastic pieces, such as Damien Hirst's preserved animal parts and Chris Ofili's dung-strewn canvases. The shock value of Saatchi-owned works has attracted enormous media attention, leading to speculation that the hype has helped inflate the value of his collection. Others, however, maintain that Saatchi has acted no differently than any other art collector, and that his devotion to contemporary art has helped bring attention and money to talented young British artists.

The questions surrounding Saatchi will not likely dissipate, because he rarely gives interviews, does not like to be photographed, and is almost never seen at the usual art-related functions. That Saatchi tried to remain reclusive even though he championed some of the most controversial art of the 1980s and 1990s is just one of the paradoxes in his life. A nonreligious man who built a synagogue in honor of his parents, a host who throws lavish parties and often does not even make an appearance at them, Saatchi is a person around whom an aura of mystery developed. When, in 2010, he announced that he would donate his Saatchi Gallery in Chelsea, with 200 works of art, to the nation, his offer was met with as much suspicion as gratitude. To date, the government has not accepted the gift.

Education and Early Career

Charles Saatchi was born on June 9, 1943 in Baghdad, Iraq, to Nathan and Daisy Saatchi, both Iraqi Jews. The second of four sons, he was particularly close to his younger brother Maurice, born three years after him. In 1947, after purchasing two textile mills in northern London, Nathan Saatchi had the foresight to move the family to England. After World War II conditions became difficult for Jews in Iraq. Among other restrictions, they were excluded from government-run schools, prohibited from buying land, and denied jobs in the civil service. Shortly after the Saatchis left, about 120,000 of the 135,000 Jews in Iraq also fled the country.

Using contacts he had established in the Middle East, Nathan Saatchi turned the textile mills into thriving businesses, and the family eventually moved into an eight-bedroom home in Highgate, an expensive and exclusive section of London. Saatchi was sent to Christ College, a secondary school in the Finchley section of London, but he was an indifferent student and dropped out at the age of 17. Afterward he reportedly spent most of his time riding his motorcycle around London and partying. A dark-haired, handsome youth, he was enamored with American popular culture. "I grew up on Chuck Berry and Elvis Presley," he told Deborah Solomon for the *New York Times Magazine*. "I grew up in the cinema. I was completely in love with anything American." Saatchi spent a year in the United States when he was 19. During a visit to the Museum of Modern Art, in New York City, he saw a Jackson Pollock painting for the first time. He has described the encounter as a "life changing" experience.

When Saatchi returned to England, he was no closer to deciding on a career. He returned to school to study design and was, by all accounts, a mediocre student. Eventually he decided to enter the advertising business. During his year in the United States, he had developed a taste for television, and he was often amused by the humor and boldness of American advertising. In 1965 he was hired as a junior copywriter in the London office of Benton & Bowles, a large advertising agency based in the United States. He met Ross Cramer, an art director at the agency, and the two discovered that they worked well together. Benton & Bowles was a relatively conservative agency, and the pair soon felt that their creativity was being stifled. They defected to Collett Dickenson Pearce, a new company that had already garnered a reputation for nurturing talent. They flourished there, creating a series of highly successful ads for Selfridge's department store, one of which brazenly proclaimed, "The most valuable thing shoplifters get off with in Selfridge's are the girls at the cosmetic counter." Openly defying the British Institute of Practitioners of Advertising, which frowned on showing a competitor's product in an ad, the pair produced a campaign that favorably compared a Ford car to a Jaguar, a Rover, and a Mercedes.

Despite their success, Saatchi and Cramer were not content to work for others, so in 1967 they decided to open CramerSaatchi, a consulting firm with cutting-edge creativity that could be hired by more established agencies on a single-project basis. They were joined by Jeremy Sinclair, a recent graduate who agreed to write copy for £10 a week. The trio was responsible for several ads so memorable that they are still cited, decades later. One particularly famous piece was done for the Health Education Council (HEC), which wanted to promote birth control. The ad showed a visibly pregnant man with the caption, "Would you be more careful if it was you that got pregnant?" Another ad for the HEC showed a saucer full of thick, unsightly tar and was captioned, "No wonder smokers cough." The consultancy gradually evolved into a full-fledged advertising agency, thanks in part to the success of the HEC ads.

In 1970 Cramer announced that he was leaving the firm to pursue a long-deferred dream of directing films. In search of another partner, Saatchi thought of his brother Maurice, with whom he had remained close since childhood. Maurice had been working as an assistant at Haymarket Publishing, a publisher of trade journals, among them one that covered the advertising industry. Although he had no direct experience in advertising, Maurice had a good grasp of finance, and the two reasoned that they could benefit from each other's skills. They called their new enterprise Saatchi & Saatchi and announced the partnership with a full-page ad in the London *Sunday Times,* trumpeting the agency's creativity, efficiency, and economy.

Saatchi has credited the ad, which cost almost one quarter of their start-up capital, with bringing the brothers national attention.

The partnership was allegedly tumultuous. One oft-cited, possibly apocryphal story involves Charles beating Maurice to the ground with an office chair during a dispute. But the brother's collaboration was unquestionably a success. Maurice, charming and gregarious, was the ideal front man. Charles, increasingly more reclusive as time passed, oversaw the creative aspects of the agency and avoided clients. (In one instance when Maurice brought a client into the agency, Charles posed as a janitor to avoid having to be introduced.) One of their highest-profile accounts came in 1978, when the agency was asked to create an advertising campaign for Margaret Thatcher, then the Conservative Party's candidate for prime minister in the upcoming election against the Labour Party. This marked the first time that an advertising agency had been hired by a political candidate in England. The brothers produced a now-legendary poster that showed an endless unemployment line under the slogan, "Labour Isn't Working." Although the poster was placed in only about 20 sites around the country, Thatcher partially credited it with her electoral victory on May 3, 1979. The brothers were even invited to the victory party at 10 Downing Street, the British prime minister's official residence.

Known as "the brothers" in advertising circles, the pair rapidly expanded their company, buying up so many smaller advertising agencies that the press began calling them Snatchi & Snatchi. The brothers also bought consulting agencies, hoping one day to form a company that could offer, in addition to advertising expertise, services in public relations, research, and finance. Commentators have theorized that the brothers' status as immigrants in the class-conscious atmosphere of Britain was responsible for their incredible drive. Whatever the reason, by 1986 Saatchi & Saatchi was the biggest ad agency in the world.

Having reached the top, however, the Saatchis found that the agency's gigantic size had begun to create headaches. Upset that Saatchi & Saatchi was handling the accounts of some their competitors, some clients defected to other agencies. RJR Nabisco, a large manufacturer of tobacco and food products, stopped consulting the brothers when Saatchi & Saatchi produced an antismoking campaign for an airline. Moreover, some stock analysts questioned the amount that the brothers had paid to buy out other agencies and became even more skeptical when they attempted to purchase Midland Bank. Combined with the lackluster performance of the brothers' consulting businesses, these doubts caused the share price of the company to tumble. By the time the 1990 recession hit and dried up the money companies were willing to spend on ads, Saatchi & Saatchi reported losses of almost $100 million and verged on bankruptcy.

The brothers stepped down as co-chief executives and were replaced by Robert Louis-Dreyfus. Maurice was eventually ousted as chairman, in 1994, and the siblings sold their share in Saatchi & Saatchi, which was later renamed Cordiant. In 1995 they moved a few blocks away to start, with Sinclair, the ad firm M & C Saatchi. With the combined experience of the brothers and Sinclair, the enterprise has provided stiff competition for their old firm. It managed to steal, for instance, one of Cordiant's most lucrative accounts, British Airways. Although Charles maintained an office at M & C Saatchi, most observers feel that he stayed involved in advertising for his brother's sake. He worked with a few select accounts that caught his interest, but for the most part, his energy was focused on his art collection. Charles Saatchi sold his remaining stake in M&C Saatchi in October 2006, having ended his active involvement with the agency two years earlier.

Later Career

Saatchi's interest in art was sparked by his first wife, Doris Lockhart Dibley, whom he had met while working at Benton & Bowles. Then a senior employee of the firm, Dibley was a tall, sophisticated blond who was described by one journalist as looking like a heroine in an Alfred Hitchcock thriller. She was married to a race-car driver, and after their divorce, she agreed to move in with Saatchi. They lived together for six years before marrying, in 1973. A Sorbonne graduate, Doris encouraged Saatchi to collect contemporary art. His first acquisition, in 1969, was a canvas by Sol LeWitt, of the Minimalist school. The couple flew regularly to New York to frequent galleries and make purchases. At one point estimated to be worth more than $250 million, their collection included 21 paintings by LeWitt, 17 by Andy Warhol, 27 by Julian Schnabel, and the work of scores of others. Saatchi was given a £100 million credit line from Citibank with which to buy art, and he tended to buy it in bulk, several pieces at a time. In 1985 the couple's holdings had become so extensive that they opened the Saatchi Gallery in St. John's Wood, a residential neighborhood in London.

In 1987 Saatchi and his wife divorced. Saatchi began to sell off much of the artwork they had purchased together. "I loved Minimalism very passionately," he told Deborah Solomon, "but when you realize there are other things in life besides Carl Andre and Robert Ryman, it's difficult to look at them and have the same love affair." Journalists sympathetic to him reported that Saatchi was merely trying to shed some of his past, as any man painfully ending a marriage might. Others leveled what would become a familiar charge over the years: that Saatchi was clearly trying to make a profit and was more an avaricious dealer than a real collector.

Gary Hume, a young artist known for unusual paintings of wooden doors, didn't dispute that Saatchi had made a profit when selling his work, but still came to his defense. "I think Charles Saatchi is really great," he told Kevin Goldman, the author of *Conflicting Accounts: The Creation and Crash of the Saatchi & Saatchi Advertising Empire* (1997). "Without him, the young contemporary art world here wouldn't happen. And, although he takes your work and makes money out of it, although he is the biggest dealer in Britain, Saatchi is the saving grace. His purchases early on enabled me to live for six months. He bulk-buys when he buys. It's good for the people because they make more money."

As he divested himself of the art that he and Doris had jointly chosen, Charles replaced the pieces with the works of a group of artists in their early 20s who had attended Goldsmiths, a progressive London college that focused on the humanities and arts. In 1990 he acquired his first piece by Damien Hirst—a work called *A Thousand Years,* which features a glass case containing a decomposing cow head, complete with flies and maggots. "I thought of it as punked-over Minimalism," he explained to Solomon. Saatchi enthusiastically began collecting and displaying pieces by Hirst and his fellow Goldsmiths graduates. He attended one- or two shows a day, often before they opened to the public, and frequented artist-run exhibits in unfashionable areas as well as slick, established galleries. Sometimes he would buy an entire show, as he did in 1993 when he stumbled upon an exhibit of five paintings by then-unknown Simon Callery.

The popularity of the artists he was supporting spread, and Saatchi began lending his pieces to other institutions to exhibit. The response of the press to this practice was mixed. Saatchi's critics saw the loans as blatant self-promotion and a chance to boost the profiles of his chosen artists. The debate came to a head in 1997, when the staid Royal Academy of the Arts, which had been established in 1768, mounted a show called *Sensation: Young British Artists from the Saatchi Collection.* It featured several works by Hirst, including *Physical Impossibility of Death in the Mind of Someone Living,* a piece consisting of a dead shark suspended in formaldehyde. Mark Quinn's *Self,* a bust of the artist made out of eight pints of his own frozen blood, was shown in a special refrigerated case. Ron Mueck's contribution was a 3-foot-long sculpture of his dead father, and the Chapman brothers were represented by a tableau of deformed, childlike mannequins seemingly engaged in erotic activity. The work that caused perhaps the biggest furor was Marcus Harvey's portrait of Myra Hindley, a convicted murderer of children. Composed of children's hand prints, the portrait shocked even the imprisoned Hindley. One newspaper called the museum the "Royal Academy of Porn," and some critics charged the museum administrators with promoting sensationalism for the sake of revenue. Although the academy denied a financial motive for mounting the show and declared that its only intention was to display a wide range of art, the exhibit was a resounding financial success, decreasing the museum's operating deficit by almost $2 million.

A similar furor erupted when the show traveled to the Brooklyn Museum of Art, in New York City, in the fall of 1999. Even before he saw any of the artwork, Rudolph Giuliani, the New York City mayor, criticized the exhibit and threatened to pull city funding from the museum. The painting that most raised the mayor's ire was a depiction of the Virgin Mary by black artist Chris Ofili. Ofili is known for using elephant dung, which in Africa represents power and fertility, to embellish his canvases. The mayor found the juxtaposition of a beloved religious figure with animal excrement and cutouts of pornographic images to be highly offensive, and many Catholic groups agreed with him. The museum attempted to appease Giuliani by promising to remove Ofili's painting and accepting a reduction in the city's subsidy for the duration of the show. But museum officials became upset when details of the negotiations were leaked to the media prematurely. They decided to mount the exhibit as planned and initiated a lawsuit in federal court against the mayor, accusing him of violating the First Amendment. The City of New York filed a lawsuit of its own, in an attempt to evict the museum from its city-owned building. Despite all the legal wrangling, the show opened on October 2, and on opening day alone more than 9,000 tickets were sold, a record number for the museum.

The exhibit sparked additional debate on both continents about the ethics of a museum exhibiting a one-owner collection. It was feared that the prestige of a museum's name could later inflate the monetary value of the artworks and thus provide an ulterior motive for the collector to loan his pieces. Although Saatchi asserted that he had no immediate plans to sell any of the featured works, more doubts were raised when it was revealed that the show was sponsored, in part, by Christie's auction house. The Royal Academy and the Brooklyn Museum have both taken the position that individual collectors throughout history have often acted as arbiters of popular taste, and that it is therefore valid to exhibit a private collection.

The exhibit traveled next to the National Gallery of Australia in Canberra, and the controversy in the United States abated. Meanwhile, in England, Saatchi continued to be subjected to skeptical treatment from some members of the press. Of a 100-painting gift he made to the Arts Council of England, *Art Monthly* (March 1999) wrote, "They say you shouldn't look a gift horse in the mouth, but when the gift horse comes from Charles Saatchi, it is worth taking a long, hard look at those teeth." Saatchi's seemingly generous gesture was said to be an attempt to save on storage charges by having the Arts Council warehouse 100 of his lesser pieces. Attention next turned to an exhibit at Saatchi's gallery entitled *New Neurotic Realism.* The 1999 exhibit featured the works of a group of British artists even younger than the YBAs, some of whom had even studied under the original YBAs at Goldsmiths. Far from causing the kind of stir that *Sensations* did, this show was seen by some journalists as simply a weak attempt to make Saatchi's new stable of artists seem trendy and relevant.

In April 2003 the Saatchi Gallery moved to a larger space, in County Hall (the former Greater London Council building) on the South Bank in London near Westminster Bridge. Saatchi was pleased with gallery attendance, but the two Triumph of Painting shows he mounted there suffered what Stuart Jeffries of the *Guardian* (September 6, 2006) called a "critical mauling," and Saatchi continually clashed with the landlord, the Shirayama Shokusan company of Japan, and the building's manager, Cadogan Leisure Investments. In October 2005 landlord and manager succeeded in getting the gallery evicted on grounds of having violated its lease, an. By this time, however, Saatchi had already announced that he would move to a new gallery in Chelsea.

Nealy a year and a half earlier, in May 2004, a catastrophic fire in a London warehouse rented by the art packing and handling company Momart had destroyed a number of the signature pieces in Saatchi's so-called BritArt collection, including Tracey Emin's *Everyone I Have Ever Slept With 1963–1995* and the Chapman brothers's *Hell.* According to James Meek of the *Guardian,* who wrote a two-part investigative story on the fire (Sept. 22, 2004), the "media focused almost exclusively on the loss of works in the collection of the former advertising mogul Charles Saatchi, and on three artists in particular: Tracey Emin, Damien Hirst and the Chapman brothers, Dinos and Jake. This was partly because Saatchi released the news of the damage to his collection early … and partly because Emin, Hirst and the Chapmans were lead characters in Britain's great popular narrative of celebrity, money, talent and scandal." Meeks wrote of the "hostility and skepticism" toward contemporary art exhibited in reactions to the fire—"always focusing on Emin, Hirst and the Chapmans and on how easy modern art was to make" while neglecting the destruction of significant amounts of work by a number of important but lesser known artists, such as Gillian Ayres (18 paintings lost), Patrick Heron (50 paintings lost), and Adrian Heath (40 paintings lost).

"I don't know how much of the art I like is significant; I hope some of it is. Who knows what will last?"

In October 2008 Saatchi opened his new Saatchi Gallery on King's Road in Chelsea, in the former military complex known as the Duke of York's Headquarters near Sloane Square. The gallery was to have opened with *USA Today,* showing Saatchi's recent purchases of American art, but because of construction delays at the new gallery spcae, *USA Today* opened instead at the Royal Academy. "America has been in the doldrums for 15 years," Saatchi remarked at the time, "and for me is now as exciting as Britain was in the early '90s." The Chelsea gallery opened instead with *The Revolution Continues: New Art from China,* which attracted more than four thousand visitors daily. The new gallery was praised by critics: "With its airy galleries, glass stairwells and walkways, its long views through rooms of all sizes, it's one of the most beautiful art spaces in London," wrote Laura Cumming in the *Observer* (11 October 2008). Of the opening show itself, Cumming commented, "What Saatchi is offering is a rapid glimpse of the kind of international art that circulates around the world's biennales and auction houses, plus some finds of his own, before he sends it back out for sale again."

To near-universal astonishment, Saatchi announced in July 2010 that he planned to donate the 70,000-square-foot gallery and more than 200 works of art to the British public in 2012. The art works offered, the value of which was estimated space at more than $37.5 million, included the Richard Wilson "Oil Room" installation, *20:50* (the only permanent installation at the Saatchi Gallery); Emin's *My Bed*; and works by the Chapmans and Grayson Perry. The gallery was to become the Museum of Contemporary

Art, London. The gallery entered into discussions with various government departments that might own the works on behalf of the public. "The gift would," wrote Carol Vogel in the *New York Times* (August 20, 2012), "also include artworks that could be sold to acquire other art so that the museum could remain a showcase for the latest works. … The gallery said in a statement that [Saatchi] felt it was 'vital for the museum to always be able to display a living and evolving collection of work, rather than an archive of art history.'"

By August 2012, however, Saatchi's offer had had no takers. Discussions with Arts Council England (to which Saatchi had previously made gifts) evidently came to nothing, and the Tate did not step forward. As Carol Vogel had reported, there were complications in that the gallery building "does not belong to Mr. Saatchi. He rents it from Cadogan Estates, a London developer. (Cadogan Estates said in a statement that it hoped the government would keep the gallery there.)" Jonathan Jones wrote at the *Guardian*'s Art blog (August 20, 2012), "Two years on, Saatchi's gift is without a home. The collector now plans to establish a foundation for the art works, and to appoint a board of trustees to manage it." Jones went on to comment, "Perhaps there have been arguments behind the scenes about curatorial influence (Saatchi loves to curate: does he want a say in how galleries show his collection?) Perhaps there have been quibbles about obligations to show the work continuously, rather than keeping it in storage. This is speculation. … But [the] Tate prides itself on a very different aesthetic take on contemporary art from that identified with Saatchi. His art collecting in the 1980s and 1990s, a period when he was central to new British art, was strong on shocks and thrills, low on the sort of cultural theory that loves such forms as live art. By contrast, Tate has tended to champion what it sees as the "real" international avant garde, artists who are big on theory, and weaker when it comes to image-making power." Jones concluded, "Tate did not light the fire of modern British art; Saatchi did. … The Tate made no such bold commitment, and now appears to want to write his achievement out of history." In October 2013, Saatchi auctioned off 50 large sculptures and installations, including Emin's *To Meet My Past* (2002) and the Chapmans' *Tragic Anatomies* (1996; shown in the Sensations exhibit), in order to raise funds to support free public access to the Saatchi Gallery and its education programs.

In 2006 Saatchi launched Your Gallery (later Saatchi Online), a digital gallery for new art. As Carol Vogel explained, "Besides showing off his collection, it allows artists who register to post their work and sell it without having to pay a fee to a gallery or dealer." She noted that it "also has a social-networking component, allowing art students to talk to one another and post their work." School of Saatchi, a BBC program aired in November–December 2009, showcased the work of aspiring artists.

A July 3, 2010, editorial in the *Observer* addressed Saatchi's achievement: "If Saatchi's collection represents anything, it is the restless immediacy and attention-deficit search for sensation that has characterised his times. This one-man Medici understands as well as anyone the ways in which visual art has been forced to fight for space in mixed media lives."

Chronically self-deprecating—before meeting Deborah Solomon of the *New York Times* in London, he told her, "You can't possibly be serious about this interview. It's just ridiculous that you would cross the Atlantic to meet a man who speaks in monosyllables and has nothing of interest to say"—Saatchi seldom gives interviews and rarely answers the criticisms leveled against him. Yet regarding charges that he sought to manipulate the art market, he defended himself to Solomon: "If I were interested in art as an investment, I would just show Picasso and Matisse. But that's not what I do. I buy new art, and 90 percent of the art I buy will probably be worthless in 10 years time to anyone except me. I don't know how much of the art I like is significant; I hope some of it is. Who knows what will last?" In his interview with Saatchi for the *Guardian*,

Stuart Jeffries—calling Saatchi the "most voracious of contemporary art collectors"—quoted him as saying, 'Before, I was always mouthing off about how there aren't enough collectors. Now there are just too many. They're all very young and very rich, and they all like to collect art the way they buy their funds.'" Saatchi was increasingly repelled by the glitzy world of "uber art dealers" and their super-rich, status-obsessed clients; he carefully distinguished the "mega-art blowouts" from the majority of gallery shows. Writing in the *Guardian* (December 2, 2011), Saatchi commented, "Not so long ago, I believed that anything that helped broaden interest in current art was to be welcomed; that only an elitist snob would want art to be confined to a worthy group of aficionados. But even a self-serving narcissistic showoff like me finds this new art world too toe-curling for comfort. … I am regularly asked if I would buy art if there was no money in it for me. There is no money in it for me. Any profit I make selling art goes back into buying more art. Nice for me, because I can go on finding lots of new work to show off. Nice for those in the art world who view this approach as testimony to my venality, shallowness, malevolence. Everybody wins."

In 1990 Charles Saatchi married Kay Hartenstein, a former ad representative, and their daughter Phoebe was born in 1995. The couple divorced in 2001, however, and two years later Saatchi married Food Network star and cookbook author Nigella Lawson. They were divorced in 2013. Saatchi, who simply claimed that they had become estranged, had been photographed seven weeks earlier "clutching the TV cook by the throat" during an argument on the terrace of a London restaurant, as reported by Sam Jones ("and agency") in the London *Guardian* (July 31, 2013). Jones continued, "Saatchi later told the Mail on Sunday the pictures gave a 'wholly different and incorrect implication. … I am disappointed that [Lawson] was advised to make no public comment to explain that I abhor violence of any kind against women, and have never abused her physically in any way.'"

Further Reading:

Art and Auction p46+ Dec.13, 1998, with photos

Art Monthly p1+ Nov. 1997, with photos

BBC News Oct. 21, 2005

Forbes p42+ Jan. 13, 1997, with photos

(London) *Guardian,* Jan. 15, 1999, May 28, 2004, Sep. 22, 2004, Dec. 2, 2011, Aug. 20, 2012, Jul. 31, 2013

New York Times C9 Jul. 2, 2010

New York Times Magazine, Sep. 26, 1999, with photo

(London) *Observer* Oct. 11, 2008, Jul. 3, 2010

OM p38+ Oct. 1988, with photos

Vanity Fair p116+ June 1995, with photos

Books:

Goldman, Kevin, *Conflicting Accounts: The Creation and Crash of the Saatchi & Saatchi Advertising Empire* (Simon & Schuster, 1997)

Hatton, Rita, and John A. Walker, *Supercollector: A Critique of Charles Saatchi,* 4th ed. (Institute of Artology, 2010)

Kent, Sarah Richard Cork, and Dick Price, *Young British Art: The Saatchi Decade* (Booth-Clibborn Editions, dist. in North America by Harry N. Abrams, 1999)

100: The Work that Changed British Art, text by Patricia Ellis (Jonathan Cape in association with the Saatchi Gallery, 2003)

Selected Books:

My name is Charles Saatchi and I Am an Artoholic: Everything You Need to Know about Art, Ads, Life, God and Other Mysteries, and Weren't Afraid to Ask—, 2009)

Be the Worst You Can Be: Life's Too Long for Patience & Virtue, 2012;

Babble, 2013; The Naked Eye, 2013

Schwartz, Gil

Communications executive, humor columnist, writer

Born: 1951, Illinois

"I think that Schwartz is necessary to Bing and Bing is necessary to Schwartz. We feed off each other," Gil Schwartz, chief communications officer and executive vice president for CBS Corp., told David Bauder for the Associated Press (July 12, 2006). Schwartz, CBS's chief spokesperson, is also known as Stanley Bing, the pseudonym he assumed when he began writing a column for *Esquire,* in 1985. Four years earlier he had taken a job as a public-affairs associate for the TelePrompter Corp.; he became a communications executive at CBS in 1996, after a series of promotions that took place following TelePrompter's acquisition by Westinghouse Broadcasting (Group W) and the latter's merger with CBS. Since 1989, when his first book appeared, Schwartz—as Bing—has published two novels, *Lloyd: What Happened* and *You Look Nice Today,* and ten volumes that, with tools ranging from acerbic wit to gentle satire, poke fun at the corporate world and its denizens. Among these books are *Biz Words: Power Talk for Fun and Profit*; *Crazy Bosses: Spotting Them, Serving Them, Surviving Them*; *What Would Machiavelli Do? The Ends Justify the Meanness*; *Rome, Inc.: The Rise and Fall of the First Multinational Corporation*; and *Executricks: How to Retire While You're Still Working.*

"I don't know if I'd have gone this route if I hadn't started out as a mole within the corporate government, but once Bing popped out, he sort of had a life of his own that was a nice addition to my own," Schwartz explained to Dorian Benkoil for mediabistro.com (March 22, 2006). "They say you're supposed to write about what you know. … I write about organizations and how they work on people. I write about festering, bleeding, suffering humanity, put to work in stultifying social structures that attempt to squeeze the life out of them and almost never succeed. I write about madness and struggle and triumph in a constricted, formalistic environment that brings both the best and worst out of people." Schwartz told Melissa Thomas for the *New York Sun* (July 8, 2004) that he would last "about a month if I was a full-time writer. I like being on the inside, being part of something." From 1995, when he left *Esquire,* Schwartz, as Bing, wrote two dozen columns a year for *Fortune*; many of them are currently posted on his blog, stanleybing.com, which he launched in 2007. Under his real name, he wrote a column for *Seventeen* (in the guise of a 17-year-old boy) from 1984 to 1990, and since 1993 he has produced a column for *Men's Health* (signed Gil Schwartz). He has also written articles for other publications, including *Mademoiselle, Working Woman, New York,* and *PC Computing.*

Education and Early Career

Gil D. Schwartz was born on May 12, 1951, in Illinois. His father was a social worker who studied group dynamics—a subject in which Schwartz, too, has become a specialist of sorts, at least regarding groups in the world of business. Schwartz's family moved from Highland Park, Illinois, to New Rochelle, a suburb of New York City, when he was 11. He attended Brandeis University, in Waltham, Massachusetts, where he earned a B.A. degree in theater arts and English. In the half-dozen years following his graduation, he worked as a humor writer for the *Boston Phoenix* (a weekly alternative newspaper that focused on the arts and entertainment; it closed in March 2013) and as a theater-company manager, among other jobs. At age 28 Schwartz moved to New York City, with the expectation, as he told Jack Myers for mediavillage.com (March 15, 2004), that with his "rugged good looks and on-screen charisma," he would be cast in leading-man roles on the stage or in TV shows filmed in the city. Instead, he said, he found himself playing such parts as the "slow witted henchman, criminal, and bad guy." Schwartz told Bauder that he earned a part on the soap opera *As the World Turns* because "they were looking for someone who looked like he would take a bribe." Writing in *PR Week* (June 24, 2002), Claire Atkinson pointed out that "his character was shot in the trunk of a car, ensuring no comebacks."

Schwartz next turned to writing plays. Two of them—*Ferocious Kisses* (1982) and *Love As We Know It* (1985)—were mounted Off-Broadway and directed by Josh Mostel (a son of the comic actor Zero Mostel). In a review of *Ferocious Kisses* for the *New York Daily News* (February 3, 1982), Don Nelson described it as a "parody that burlesques show-biz sleaze to make its point." "Schwartz' ear is acute," Nelson continued. "He skillfully reproduces the jargon and kissy-poo bogus affection that passes for communication within the scurrying maze of devious managers, pettifogging press agents and scheming hangers-on that populate the theatrical world." Stanley Bing was a character in *Love As We Know It,* described in a *New York Times* review by Walter Goodman (November 4, 1985) as a series of thematically related skits in which the humor eventually "becomes strained; its synthetic quality shows through." Edith Oliver wrote in the *New Yorker* (November 11, 1985), that, "As is true with many humorists of limited experience, Mr. Schwartz's effort to be funny occasionally shows, thereby, of course, killing his joke. More often than not, though, the effect is carefree, sly, and original; there are many more hits than misses." Schwartz's third play, *Taking Care of Business,* was premiered by the Pennsylvania Stage Company in Allentown, Pennsylvania, in 1988. In the Allentown *Morning Call* (March 18, 1988), Geoff Gehman labeled the play a "Punch-and-Judy show for adults" attacking "decadent capitalism." Gehman recounted that when Schwartz "expanded 'Taking Care of Business' from one to two acts, a 'pedal-to-the-metal, full-bore farce' became a roller coaster of comic exaggerations with a fatalistic engine." According to Gehman, Schwartz "now … admits that 'you can't do good within the system—once you take part in its evils. This is a play about a man who receives his just rewards. … People under pressure are comic; they also make wrong decisions, which hurt them.'"

Years before, in 1981, to support his writing, Schwartz had found work as an associate in the public-relations department of the TelePrompter Corp., which was then among the largest cable-systems operators in the United States. His responsibilities included speechwriting. Through what Bauder labeled a "Byzantine series of corporate acquisitions," Schwartz's job led directly to his current position: shortly after his arrival the Westinghouse Broadcasting Co., also known as Group W, acquired TelePrompter, and Schwartz became the company's manager of public relations. He was named director of communications for Group W Cable in 1984, and he retained that title after the company abandoned the cable format two years later. When Group W merged with CBS, in 1996, Schwartz was made CBS Television's senior vice president for communications.

Meanwhile, in February 1985, *Esquire* published the first of Schwartz's essays on corporate strategies for men in their 30s, "How to Draw the Line," in which he offered advice about preserving one's personal life while progressing professionally. He conceived of the column, called "Executive Summary," and the Bing character in collaboration with David Blum, an *Esquire* editor. "I wanted to express what it's like to work for a living," he said to Thomas. He told Dorian Benkoil, "Inside every suit, there's a human being. When I was a kid, I always loved stuff about guys with secret identities. Zorro in particular. Big nerd by day. Guy in a silky black cape at night, flying through windows, saving people, being sort of dangerous and legendary. This was as close as I could get to that." The column changed over the years in ways that reflected

Schwartz's corporate ascent. He told Benkoil facetiously that when he began writing it, "I was younger, and didn't understand at the time how splendid senior management generally is."

Bing's first book was *Biz Words: Power Talk for Fun and Profit* (1989), an amalgam of humor and advice for those aspiring to climb the corporate ladder. It contains a glossary of terms commonly used in business circles, along with their "true" definitions according to Bing. "It will come as no surprise to anyone who has read Bing's monthly … column … that each Biz Words definition is at once hilarious but dead-serious," J. Michael Kelly wrote for the Syracuse, New York, *Post-Standard* (June 4, 1989*). Crazy Bosses: Spotting Them, Serving Them, Surviving Them* (1992), Bing's next book, catalogues the types of neuroses that supposedly afflict employers and suggests ways for workers to deal with them. Types of crazy bosses, as Bing pigeonholed them, include the bully, the narcissist, the paranoid boss, the "bureaucrazy" boss (a mixture of wimp and fascist), and the disaster hunter—"the shared terminal stage of all four types," as Alan Farnham wrote in a review of *Crazy Bosses* for *Fortune* (May 4, 1992), as posted on CNNmoney.com. "Since craziness has become pandemic (and thus inescapable)," Farnham continued, "Bing recommends sane employees give up all hope of escaping crazy bosses and concentrate instead on learning how to manage them. With a little cleverness, he says, and a great deal of care, the rational underling can topple his crazy boss without himself getting crushed in the process. To that end, Bing provides advice specific for each type of boss. … This book's tips on office politics ring true. Where crazy bosses are concerned, Bing is bang-on." An updated edition of *Crazy Bosses* appeared in 2007.

Later Career

Bing's last column for *Esquire* appeared in that magazine's July 1995 issue; his first for *Fortune* was published in its August 7, 1995, edition. Five months later Bing's identity was revealed in the *New York Times* (January 8, 1996) by Mark Landler, in a piece about a feature article entitled "The Smartest and Dumbest Moves of 1995," in *Fortune.* In his introduction to that article, Bing had poked fun at the Walt Disney Co. for what he described as its "colonization" of ABC, CBS's chief rival. Bing's words were generally seen as a "backhanded salute" to the competition, Landler wrote. "Now that he is chief spokesman for CBS, Mr. Schwartz might find it harder to keep the opinionated Mr. Bing in the shadows," he continued, noting that in 1992, while promoting *Crazy Bosses,* Schwartz had appeared on ABC's *Good Morning America* "without a disguise, but as Mr. Bing." At that time, however, "despite appearing on national television, Mr. Schwartz was able to maintain a low profile as Stanley Bing, in part because of Group W's rather nondescript image in the broadcast industry." Schwartz told Benkoil, "I'd been outed internally a while before, so very few insiders were shocked, maybe that made things easier." Since being exposed as Bing, Schwartz has often said that his dual identity is the worst-kept secret in publishing. David Blum, who was then a *New York Times Magazine* contributing editor, told Landler that the distinctly different contributions to society of Bing and Schwartz "could be one of the great synergies of modern times. It's pretty much unheard of for the top P.R. guy at a major American corporation to write a humor column." Discussing the potential for a conflict of interest to compromise the work of Schwartz, or Schwartz as Bing, Howard Stringer, the former president of the CBS Broadcast Group, told Landler, "Given that Andy Rooney has a column in which he routinely ridicules the network, and that David Letterman does it on his show, I think it's in the grandest tradition of CBS."

Bing's first novel, *Lloyd: What Happened: A Novel of Business,* appeared in 1998. It follows an ambitious executive and the changes he undergoes while carrying out layoffs deemed necessary for an anticipated merger. Schwartz told Jennifer Nix for *Daily Variety* (March 16, 1998) that Lloyd is "a decent enough guy, who doesn't have the greatest hairline, who's a little chunky and who makes well into the mid-six figures, but who sees through the corporate crap when he isn't closing his eyes." The book contains 80 satirical pie charts and graphs, with such titles as "Percent of Lloyd's Bosses Displaying Insane Behavior" and "The Battle for Lloyd's Soul." The inclusion of a 5,000-word excerpt of the novel in *Fortune* (May 11, 1998) was the first appearance of fiction in that magazine since 1947. In an undated review for mindjack.com, J. M. Frank wrote, "Stanley Bing's main goal here is social satire. You will not be moved to tears by this book, nor discover deep insights into the nature of our modern world. But you will be entertained, and you will laugh. … The author … has a keen eye for the small hypocrisies in human behavior. The sense of realism and believable characters makes this satire work." In a less enthusiastic review for the *New York Times* (May 28, 1998), Joe Queenan complained that the book was much too long and that there were not enough funny scenes. "In the end," he wrote, "Lloyd: What Happened may try to do in prose what Dilbert does in pictures. Unfortunately, as is often the case, a picture is worth a thousand words. Especially a thousand of these words."

In *You Look Nice Today* (2003), Bing's second novel, a secretary brings a sexual harassment lawsuit against her boss, a corporate executive, after he attempts to have her transferred out of his department. A large portion of the book is dedicated to footnoted transcripts from the harassment trial. David Exum, in a critique posted on bookreporter.com, wrote, "Although You Look Nice Today is purely fictional, it does a triumphant job in detailing the conclusion of corporate excess in America at the end of the 1990s," and he expressed the opinion that "the trial itself is possibly Bing at his best." An anonymous reviewer for the *New Yorker* (September 8, 2003), by contrast, wrote, "Unfortunately, the courtroom animates Bing's comic gift less effectively than the daily grind of the office and the soul-smothering masquerade of being a company man." Ron Charles, the reviewer for the *Christian Science Monitor* (September 4, 2003), noted that *You Look Nice Today* "does nothing to disturb those pernicious stereotypes" according to which women who file complaints about "boorish advances, off-color jokes, and crude bargains for promotion" are "bad team players, humorless shrews, or fragile hysterics who misinterpret the most harmless remarks. … But it's very funny."

In addition to his magazine columns, Bing wrote a series of satirical "self-help" books skewering corporate capitalism, often slyly parodying trendy business books that seized on historical figures as abundantly successful exemplars of the capitalist vision. His *What Would Machiavelli Do? The Ends Justify the Meanness* (2000) is a satirical manual supposedly invoking the Renaissance writer, philosopher, and diplomat Niccolò Machiavelli, whose *The Prince* is often taken as a paean to political expedience, as a guide for getting to the top of the business food chain. *Throwing the Elephant: Zen and the Art of Managing Up* (2002) offers advice on how to do well with "elephant" bosses. Schwartz told Peter Johnson for *USA Today* (March 19, 2002) that *Throwing the Elephant* advises workers to view themselves as having "incredible minimal importance. You are tiny. You have no significance. If you just do your job and abandon hope, you have much more power and much more access to happiness. It's people who try to be as big and as important as the elephant who suffer miserably." *The Big Bing: Black Holes of Time Management, Gaseous Executive Bodies, Exploding Careers, and Other Theories on the Origins of the Business Universe* (2003) collects Bing's *Esquire* and *Fortune* columns. In *Sun Tzu Was a Sissy: Conquer Your Enemies, Promote Your Friends, and Wage the Real Art of War* (2004), Bing "assails the ancient Chinese war philosopher, a favorite of vicious bosses, and offers what he calls a handy guide to making war in the workplace," as Melissa Thomas wrote.

In *100 Bullshit Jobs ... and How to Get Them* (2006), Bing offers his mathematical formula for finding the "BS Quotient" of a variety of jobs, including wine-industry professional, pet psychic, life coach, consultant, executive vice president—new media, and "writer of this book."

Rome, Inc.: The Rise and Fall of the First Multinational Corporation (2006), as William Grimes wrote for the *New York Times* (March 18, 2006), "simply reverses a common metaphor, the business as an empire, and looks at the Roman empire as a multinational corporation, with a business model, a coherent management structure and greedy executives." "Mr. Bing, on occasion, plays fast and loose with facts. ... But on the main questions, Mr. Bing proves to be a keen analyst," and "the funny parts ... are very funny." *Executricks: How to Retire While You're Still Working* (2008) was soon rewritten for recessionary times and published in paperback as *How to Relax Without Getting the Axe* (2009). Bing explains in his new "Author's Note" in *How to Relax* that although two years earlier, when the first edition appeared, "the world was a different place," "practitioners of the executive arts are, of course, all around us still. Some are sitting in executive country clubs that have bars on the windows. ... Personally I am more interested in the guys who engineered the downfall of our economy, made millions—in some cases hundreds of millions of dollars—and then, when the time bombs they had planted blew up, took huge bonuses and moved on to new and bigger jobs. These are the masters ... to whom we all must kneel, if only to tie their shoelaces together. ... The ultimate trick is to play your game no matter what condition the field is in." *Board Room Babies*, a 30-page Kindle Single, was published in 2011; it counts the ways in which corporate executives, the "aspirational icons of our infantile, narcissistic age," are, in fact, like babies. A month before the publication of *Board Room Babies*, Schwartz's *Bingsop's Fables: Little Morals for Big Business* (2011) appeared. Its "Translator's Note" succinctly states the perspective that animates Bing's oeuvre: "For many a truth is spoken in jest"; the fable genre—mordant, pithy, and obviously if not overtly moralistic—may be Bing's ideal literary form.

"They say you're supposed to write about what you know. ... I write about organizations and how they work on people. I write about festering, bleeding, suffering humanity, put to work in stultifying social structures that attempt to squeeze the life out of them and almost never succeed."

In 2004 Schwartz was named executive vice president of the newly created CBS Communications Group, responsible for public relations, media relations, and corporate and internal communications for all the divisions directed by Leslie Moonves, the president and chief executive officer of the CBS Corp. On December 31, 2005, Schwartz became chief communications officer and executive vice president of CBS Corp. "Gil is clearly a great consigliere," Moonves said, as quoted by Pamela McClintock in *Daily Variety* (November 5, 2004). "He's a great adviser, not only on press issues, but on issues that go across the company." When Benkoil, in March 2006, asked Schwartz how he succeeds in balancing the seemingly contradictory pursuits of business humorist and corporate spokesman, Schwartz said, "I really see no reason to comment on that at this time."

In the same month, at CBS's annual affiliates meeting—held that year in Las Vegas, Nevada— Schwartz, in the guise of the late singer Johnny Cash, sang songs about CBS and the television industry, written by himself. Anybody who has attended those meetings in recent years, Michele Greppi wrote for *Television*

Week (June 5, 2006), knows that "Schwartz's portion of the program is a must-see laff riot, an annual look at the network business as only he could see it or say it." In one song, "Wholesome Prison Blues" (set to the tune of Cash's "Folsom Prison Blues"), Schwartz lamented, "When I was just a baby, my mama told me, 'Tex / You can program violence, just never program sex.' / So we stuck to rotting corpses, on shows like CSI / But when I think of nipple jewelry / I hang my head and cry." "It's almost impossible to direct conversation with the highly entertaining Schwartz," Claire Atkinson wrote in *PR Week*. "He is, after all, a master of manipulation."

Schwartz lived in New Rochelle, New York, while his children, Nina and Will, were growing up. He currently maintains homes in Manhattan and Mill Valley, California, where he lives with his second wife, Laura Svienty, a writer. Svienty founded the Web site PhilanthroFlash.

Further Reading:

Associated Press July 12, 2006

CBS Corp. Web site

mediabistro.com Mar. 22, 2006

New York Sun p13 July 8, 2004

New York Times p33 Jan. 8, 1996

PR Week p17 June 24, 2002, Aug. 30, 2011

Selected Books:

Fiction

Lloyd—What Happened, 1998

You Look Nice Today, 2003.

Nonfiction

Biz Words, 1989

Crazy Bosses, 1992

What Would Machiavelli Do?, 2000

Throwing the Elephant, 2002

The Big Bing, 2003

Sun Tzu Was a Sissy, 2004

100 Bullshit Jobs … and How to Get Them, 2006

Rome, Inc., 2006

How to Retire While You're Still Working, 2008 (revised and published in paperback as How to Relax without Getting the Axe, 2009)

Bingsop's Fables: Little Morals for Big Business, 2011

Board Room Babies (a Kindle Single), 2011

Appendixes

Historical Biographies

Julio Arce

Mexican-born American journalist

As a columnist for his own highly successful newspaper, which served the Hispanic community of San Francisco, Arce became the most influential Latino journalist of his day. His satiric pieces on the everyday culture of the city's teeming Mexican neighborhoods are considered an invaluable record of the era.

Areas of Achievement: Journalism

Born: January 9, 1870; Guadalajara, Jalisco, Mexico

Died: November 15, 1926; San Francisco, California, United States

Early Life

Julio G. Arce (AHR-say) was born in Guadalajara along the Pacific coast of west-central Mexico, into a privileged family. His father, a respected surgeon, wanted him to study medicine, but Arce lacked a commitment to the sciences and opted to study pharmacy. His first love, however, was journalism; journalism was committed to depicting the real-life world, and it could effect real social and political change. Such power intrigued Arce. While completing his pharmacy studies, Arce started his own student newspaper, *El amigo del pueblo* ("Friend of the People").

After finishing his degree, Arce went north to Mazatlán in the state of Sinaloa, where he, along with a friend, opened a pharmacy. He remained a frequent contributor to local newspapers and even started his own limited-circulation paper, in which he published original fiction and poetry as well as literary reviews. Now in his mid-twenties, Arce decided he needed the challenge of a large city and moved to Culiacán, where he established *Mefistófeles* ("Mephistopheles"), the city's first daily newspaper and the first to be printed on a mechanical printing press. His writings caught the eye of the local newspaper, *El occidental ("The Western"),* run by long-entrenched political powers. Seen as their friend, Arce enjoyed the respect such government support brought, and his career as a journalist and university professor was secure.

Life's Work

Arce, however, soon grew restless. His observations of life in the city, particularly in the impoverished neighborhoods of the working class, led him to increasingly more strident objections to the political status quo. In 1909, as the editor of the newspaper *El diario del pacifico ("The Pacific Diary"),* Arce began to attack the revolution of

Francisco Madero, and he came under fire from the governments with increasing frequency. When Maderist forces arrived in Culiacán, Arce hurriedly returned to his hometown, where he immediately began another antigovernment newspaper, *El diario de occident* ("The Western *Diary*"). He also agitated publicly on behalf of journalists who had been jailed. In late 1915, after being jailed himself for two months by forces loyal to Venustiano Carranza, Arce and his family went into exile to the United States, determined (unlike many other political refugees) never to return to Mexico.

Arce headed to San Francisco, which had a large Mexican American community, including many exiles sympathetic to Arce's politics. He became director of *La Crónica* ("The Chronicle"), a short-run neighborhood newspaper; after his efforts had made it a success, its owners sold it, whereupon Arce began a newspaper of his own, reviving the name *Mefistófeles.* To help support the paper Arce requested and received a small stipend from the Carranza government. Nevertheless he decided to close down his newspaper and return to *La Crónica*, which he built into *Hispano-América*. He became the newspaper's owner and publisher in 1919. *Hispano-América,* which Arce resolutely kept nonpolitical, quickly became the most influential and respected newspaper covering San Francisco's Hispanic population. In 1916, in addition to his work as managing editor of the newspaper, Arce had begun writing a short weekly column (a genre known as a *crónica*) recording the everyday life of the Mexican working-class community in the Bay Area, specifically the struggle of Mexican Americans to adjust to the cultural, social, religious, and economic life of their adopted country. To distance himself from the often caustic observations offered in the columns, which were written in the first person, Arce used the pseudonym Jorge Ulica, which he had first employed in his writings when he was a pharmacy student. (In Mexico he had also used the pseudonym Krichoff for his *crónicas.)*

Over the next decade, Arce's *Crónicas diabólicas* ("*Diabolical Chronicles*") became a staple of the Mexican community in San Francisco; within five years, it was syndicated throughout the Southwest. In each column (typically fewer than a thousand words long), Arce told a story drawn from his observations of the Latino community. The stories were intended to teach, often with little subtlety, how immigrants should deal with the challenges of adjusting to their adopted country. With often biting (if ferociously funny) satire, the columns encouraged immigrants not to be too quickly mesmerized by the American way of life (broadly seen as amoral and mercenary; American culture had long been one of Arce's targets for satire) and not to lose too quickly their cultural, religious, and familial ties to the homeland. Arce was particularly harsh toward immigrants who sought to adopt the English language, mocking their fractured "Spanglish," and toward those who would abandon the Catholicism of their homeland for American Protestantism. He also criticized Mexican American women, whom he felt were far more susceptible than men to the fetching glitter of American influences and in turn pushed Mexican men to become more Americanized—that is, effeminate and domesticated. The columns made Jorge Ulica the most widely read Hispanic writer in the American Southwest of his time.

Arce's untimely death in his mid-fifties robbed the community of one of its most vital and engaged observers. His work lapsed into neglect until, as part of the Chicano studies movement, a collection of his best pieces was published in 1982.

Significance

Like Samuel Clemens (better known as Mark Twain), Arce was both an elitist and a satirist who used a persona to deliver his most acerbic pieces. That makes placing Arce within a broad Chicano literary tradition problematic as he (or his persona) appears to be looking down with disdain on the very culture he is seeking to define and maintain, although the satire is so blunt and so heavy-handed that it may be ironic. Nevertheless, Arce's success as a newspaper publisher and his unswerving and passionate defense of working-class Mexican culture, its lifestyle, and its customs in the face of the pressures of immigration mark his journalistic pieces as critical, even seminal, texts in the study of assimilation in the United States.

Joseph Dewey

Desi Arnaz

Cuban-born musician, actor, and business executive

Immortalized as "Ricky Ricardo" in the 1950s television sitcom I Love Lucy, Arnaz began his entertainment career as a musician and film actor before becoming America's first major Latino television star. Yet he made his most significant contributions to the entertainment industry as an innovative producer.

Areas of Achievement: Music, television, entertainment business

Born: March 2, 1917; Santiago de Cuba, Cuba

Died: December 2, 1986; Del Mar, California, United States

Early Life

Desiderio Alberto Arnaz y Acha III, better known as Desi Arnaz (ahr-NAZ), was born in 1917 in Santiago de Cuba, near the eastern end of Cuba. His father, Desiderio Alberto Arnaz, was a popular local politician who was then the mayor of the town of Santiago and who also served in the Cuban legislature. Desi Arnaz's mother, Dolores de Acha, was the daughter of a founder of the Bacardi rum company. Arnaz, an only child, grew up sharing in the privileges of a wealthy, elite family, but this protected existence ended abruptly in 1933, when Fulgencio Batista y Zaldívar overthrew the government of Gerardo Machado y Morales. In the tumultuous revolution following Batista's coup, the Arnaz family lost all of its property, and Arnaz's father was imprisoned. Desiderio Arnaz was released from prison six months later, and the family fled to Miami, Florida. Meanwhile Batista built a dictatorial regime in Cuba that would last nearly three decades. Although Arnaz's father eventually reached an accommodation with the Batista regime, Desi Arnaz seems never to have considered returning to Cuba permanently.

Arnaz had begun studying English at his Cuban high school, but mastery of that language came slowly to him, impeding his employment opportunities in the United States. His speech retained a distinctive Cuban inflection. He wanted to go to college, but his formal education ended in 1936, when he graduated from a Roman Catholic school in Miami (where the son of the gangster Al Capone was his best friend). Meanwhile he struggled to find remunerative work, taking on such odd jobs as cleaning birdcages in stores. During the winter of 1936, Arnaz began playing guitar and singing in a small rumba band. While performing in Miami, Arnaz caught the attention of the famed Latin bandleader Xavier Cugat, who invited Arnaz to join his traveling band in New York after he finished school a few months later.

Life's Work

Through working with Cugat, Arnaz learned how to run a band and launched his professional career. By the following winter, he was leading his own Cuban band in Miami. Becoming known for popularizing Cuban conga-line dancing, Arnaz got another major break in 1939 when he was cast in the Broadway production of Lorenz Hart's and

Richard Rodgers's new musical *Too Many Girls* as a Latin American boy who comes to an American college to play football. Afterward, he reprised that role in a film version of *Too Many Girls* (1940) that starred Lucille Ball. He and Ball quickly struck up a relationship, and they eloped to Connecticut in November 1940. By the accounts of both partners and other observers, the 20-year marriage that ensued was both passionate and stormy, and it was weakened by Arnaz's persistent womanizing and penchant for high-stakes gambling. Only a few years later, Ball filed for divorce, but the couple quickly reconciled. They lived on a small ranch in Los Angeles's San Fernando Valley, not far from the Hollywood film industry and Los Angeles music clubs. Ball continued to work in films, but Arnaz's film roles were limited because of his Cuban "accent." He therefore concentrated on working with his Cuban band.

After the United States and Cuba entered World War II at the end of 1941, Arnaz was given a commission in the Cuban navy, but he decided instead to enlist in the U.S. Navy. Because he was not a citizen, however, he was not allowed to volunteer. Nevertheless, in May 1943, he was drafted into the U.S. Army. A recent knee injury kept him from combat duty, so he served out of a military hospital near his home, directing United Services Organization (USO) programs for wounded soldiers.

After the war Arnaz organized another Latin orchestra. In 1948 Lucille Ball was cast as a dizzy housewife on the CBS radio series *My Favorite Husband*. A few years later, CBS invited Ball to adapt the series for television. Ball agreed—on the condition that she could play opposite her real-life husband, Arnaz. The network was reluctant to air a television series featuring a Latino married to a woman of European extraction but eventually relented, allowing Arnaz and Ball's new Desilu Productions to produce the show. This development transformed Arnaz's life. It allowed him not only to work regularly with his wife for the first time since their marriage but to develop what may have been his greatest talent—that of television producer.

The original concept for the new television show was to pair Arnaz and Ball as show-business stars whose busy careers left them little time together, as had been the couple's real-life experience. Eventually, however, it was decided to make Arnaz a moderately successful Cuban bandleader named Ricky Ricardo and Ball a zany housewife who ceaselessly connives to get into show business. This formula worked perfectly. The resulting *I Love Lucy* program topped television ratings throughout its long run (1951–1960) and continued in syndication into the twenty-first century.

More importantly, however, the show helped revolutionize television. Arnaz and Ball were nominally coproducers, but Arnaz made most of the business decisions. He began by persuading CBS to let Desilu produce the show in Los Angeles instead of New York. At the time most shows were broadcast live in the East, and viewers in the West later watched low-quality kinescope pictures filmed from studio television monitors. To make West Coast production acceptable, Arnaz had *I Love Lucy* shot directly on film, ensuring that all regions would see high-quality pictures. Using film also ensured that every episode would be permanently preserved for future reruns. Desilu was not the first to use the three-camera film technique—it had been pioneered as early as 1947 by Jerry Fairbanks at NBC—but it did innovate by filming before a live audience and using an overhead lighting system devised by cinematographer Karl Freund.

At the same time, Arnaz persuaded CBS to grant Desilu full ownership of all *I Love Lucy* episodes. Because kinescoped programs had never been used for reruns, CBS appeared to be giving up nothing of value. The filmed episodes later proved to be enormously valuable, however, and Desilu's ownership of all the television programs it would go on to produce enabled the company to expand its studio space as it grew under Arnaz's guidance. Eventually, Desilu took over the studios of RKO Pictures.

Despite Arnaz and Ball's busy producing and performing schedules, they made several feature films together during the 1950s. They also had two children, Lucie Arnaz (born in 1951) and Desi Arnaz, Jr. (born in 1953), both of whom would later go into show business. Arnaz oversaw the production of other Desilu television programs. Eventually the strains in Arnaz and Ball's marriage became intolerable to both of them, and the couple divorced in 1960. By this time their show business careers were going in different directions. In November 1962, Arnaz sold his interest in Desilu Productions to Ball, who thereby became the first woman to head a major television studio, even while she continued to star in television situation comedies. (Ball sold the studio to Gulf+Western in 1967, and it became Paramount Television, now called CBS Television Studios.) Meanwhile Arnaz formed his own production company, Desi Arnaz Productions; he produced *The Mothers in Law* (1967–1968) for United Artists/NBC and later gradually withdrew from producing. In 1963 Arnaz married Edith Mack Hirsch, remaining with her until she died in 1985. Ball also remarried. Nevertheless she and Arnaz remained friends through the remainder of Arnaz's life.

Throughout the 1970s Arnaz appeared frequently on daytime television shows and made occasional guest appearances on primetime shows. In 1976, he published his autobiography, *A Book,* a candid and lively account of his life up to 1960. He and his second wife spent their remaining years in semiretirement in Del Mar, California. Arnaz was planning a second volume of his autobiography when he succumbed to lung cancer on December 2, 1986.

Significance

The public will long remember Arnaz as "Ricky Ricardo," but to people in the entertainment industry he will be remembered chiefly as a producer who pioneered modern production techniques, helped shift television production from New York to California, and set a precedent for rich syndication deals. He will also be remembered as the first Latino to star in an American television series. Indeed, during the 1950s, he was probably the best-known Cuban in America until the rise of the revolutionary leader Fidel Castro.

R. Kent Rasmussen

Gus Arriola

American cartoonist and animator

Arriola was a largely self-taught cartoonist and animator. His highly acclaimed comic strip *Gordo* ran for more than 40 years in dozens of newspapers, humorously and artistically introducing American readers to the rich Latino culture and its diverse traditions.

Areas of Achievement: Cartooning, animation

Born: July 17, 1917; Florence, Arizona, United States

Died: February 2, 2008; Carmel, California, United States

Early Life

Gustavo Montaño Arriola (mon-TAHN-yoh ar-ee-OH-lah), the son of Mexican-born Aquiles Arriola, was the youngest of nine children. His mother died when he was an infant, and an older sister brought him up. As a child, Arriola spoke only Spanish. He learned to read English and gained an early interest in sequential art from colorful Sunday comic strips, such as *The Katzenjammer Kids*, *Krazy Kat*, and *Little Orphan Annie*. The Arriola family moved from Arizona to Los Angeles, California, in 1925. Gustavo, known as Gus, attended Manual Arts High School, where he first took classes in art, design, and life drawing. He graduated from high school in 1935. Because of the Depression, he was unable to afford further education.

In 1936 Arriola was hired at Mintz Columbia–Screen Gems studios, where he worked on in-between animation for *Krazy Kat*, *Scrappy*, and other cartoons. The following year, he moved to Metro-Goldwyn-Mayer (MGM) studios, where he did in-between work before joining the Screen Cartoonists Guild, after which he became an assistant animator and eventually contributed original stories to animated short subjects. At MGM Arriola worked on *Tom and Jerry* cartoons and was part of the team that produced such other titles as *The First Swallow* and *The Dance of the Weed*.

At MGM Arriola met his future wife, Mary Frances Servier, who worked as an inker and painter. They married in 1942 and later became parents of a son, Carlin.

Life's Work

It was while designing Mexican characters for the MGM film short *The Lonesome Stranger* (1940) that Arriola first conceived of an idea for his own comic strip, *Gordo* ("Fatso"). The strip concerns the cartoon exploits of the unflatteringly nicknamed central character, Perfecto Salazar Lopez, a chubby Mexican bean farmer who later becomes a tour guide. Gordo, modeled on comic actor Leo Carrillo, interacts with a human cast that includes his nephew, Pepito; his best friend, Paris Keats Garcia ("The Poet"); a romantic widow, Artemesia Gonzalez; and his housekeeper, Tehuana Mama. The strip also features a group of animals that make incisive comments to one another but whom humans cannot understand. These include Senior Dog, a Chihuahua; cats, such as Poosy Gato; a six-legged hipster spider, Bug Rogers; and miscellaneous talking owls, worms, pigs, and chickens. A major theme of the well-drawn, beautifully designed strip was the universality of experience: although humans throughout the world may look and sound different from one another, they have the same hopes and fears and the identical range of emotions. Humor, too, is a common bond.

Especially in his more experimental Sunday strips, Arriola wove ancient Mexican designs into the comic's headers and borders, emphasizing the artistry of his ancestors. Throughout *Gordo*'s run, Arriola incorporated threads from folktales, showcased native culture, and illustrated examples from local traditions that collectively encouraged readers to discover and explore the uniqueness of Mexico for themselves.

In 1941 Arriola sold the concept of *Gordo* to United Features, a New York City syndicate. He left MGM to produce the strip just before the United States entered World War II. Subject to the draft, Arriola enlisted in the U.S. Army Air Force. Thanks to the Hollywood grapevine, he learned that a new group was being formed to produce military training materials, and he secured an assignment with the First Motion Picture Unit. Stationed in Culver City, California, Arriola spent the war working with a cadre of writers, directors, artists, and cartoonists who made animated films about how to use top-secret equipment, such as the Norden bombsight, and created three-dimensional models and realistic landscapes for practice bombing runs. While in military service, Arriola received special dispensation to continue his fledgling comic strip. For more than 40 consecutive months, he did a series of single gags on Sundays, which was enough to keep *Gordo* going through the war years.

After the war Arriola and his wife moved to La Jolla, California. To get into the flow of producing six daily strips and a Sunday page for *Gordo*, Arriola for 18 months hired a former Warner Brothers animator to handle lettering and background inking—the only time in the strip's 44-year run that he used an assistant. (In the mid-1950s, *Playboy* cartoonist Eldon Dedini and *Dennis the Menace* creator Hank Ketcham completed the strip for a few weeks while Arriola was ill.) At its peak, *Gordo* ran in more than 250 newspapers across the country and was featured in the comic pages of English-language dailies in Mexico and Finland.

Popular with fans and Arriola's peers alike, *Gordo* was nominated four times as the National Cartoonists Society's best humor strip, winning the awards in 1957 and 1965. Arriola also won an award in 1957 from the San Francisco Artist's Club for his use of color and design and received an Inkpot Award in 1981 for his work.

Arriola lived for a time in Phoenix, Arizona, before moving permanently to Carmel, California, where for two years in the early 1960s he operated a Mexican crafts shop. Arriola ended *Gordo* in 1985, partly because his son, the inspiration for one of the characters in the strip, died. Another reason was that he had developed a slight tremor, the precursor of Parkinson's disease, complications from which eventually took his life.

Arriola and his wife remained on the Monterey Peninsula, where they lived off the proceeds from sales of the original artwork from *Gordo* strips, which were sold through the Carmel Art Association gallery. Arriola also contributed artwork to benefit more than a dozen community causes, including the Alliance on Aging, Carmel Public Library Foundation, Guide Dogs for the Blind, Hospice of the Central Coast, Monterey Jazz Festival, Pacific Grove Museum of National History, Salvation Army, Red Cross, and Society for the Prevention of Cruelty to Animals. The Arts Council of Monterey bestowed on Arriola a lifetime achievement award shortly before his death in 2008, aged 90.

Significance

Gus Arriola's *Gordo* (1941– 1985) was the first syndicated, widely circulated comic strip to focus on Latino culture and traditions, and one of the few ethnically based cartoons of its era. The only other comparable effort was William de la Torre's *Pedrito* ("Little Pedro"), a minimalist strip that appeared in *The New Yorker* magazine between 1948 and 1953 and was distributed in the United States and Canada by the small Mirror Enterprise Syndicate. Though in its early years *Gordo* perpetuated stereotypes of Mexicans, complete with fractured dialogue, for most of its lengthy run the strip showcased Arriola's pride in Latino culture. In 1948 Arriola included a recipe for refried beans and cheese, anticipating by many years the popularity in the United States of Mexican food. He also inserted many Spanish words and phrases (*amigo, compadre, hasta la vista*) that have since become commonplace in American speech. Beginning in the 1960s, when Arriola frequently traveled to Mexico to gather material, he incorporated aspects of Mexican history and folklore into the strip.

Arriola was also one of the first cartoonists to address environmental concerns; his tribute to author Rachel Carson won recognition from the Smithsonian Institution. He received a Citizen of the Year award from Parade of Nations for promoting education and positive attitudes, and California honored him by designating a Gus Arriola Day. Perhaps his most lasting contribution, however, was in paving the way for later Hispanic-themed cartoons, such as *Baldo* and *La Cucaracha,* that celebrated the Latino experience.

Jack Ewing

Sir William Maxwell Aitken, Baron Beaverbrook

Canadian and British newspaper publisher, investor, and politician

Beaverbrook gained a fortune in Canada and later in England by selling bonds and investing in businesses with economic potential, notably in British newspapers. He created the Beaverbrook Foundation to continue his charitable interests after his death.

Areas of Achievement: Publishing, business, politics

Born: May 25, 1879; Maple, Ontario, Canada

Died: June 9, 1964; Cherkley, Surrey, United Kingdom

Early Life

William Maxwell Aitken, later first Baron Beaverbrook, was born in Maple, Ontario, Canada, on May 25, 1879. His family soon moved to Newcastle, New Brunswick, Canada, where his father, a Presbyterian minister, had accepted a new position. Aitken always identified Newcastle as his hometown. He was described as a mischievous boy, and his "puckish" character remained with him his entire life. Uninspired by school, he made pocket money by devising numerous stratagems, such as selling soap to obtain a bicycle. At age 13 he founded a newspaper, a career he would pursue with greater success later in life. After failing the Latin examination for university entrance, he accepted a position as a law clerk, but he spent time selling life insurance and as a correspondent for a local newspaper. He bought a bowling alley, which he resold at a profit, and he lost money investing in frozen meat, which was ruined in a thaw.

In 1900 Aitken abandoned selling insurance policies in favor of selling bonds. The Canadian economy was booming, but the stock exchange was limited in scope and most businessmen purchased bonds. Aitken was an excellent salesman, and his integrity was beyond dispute. With his commissions he bought stagnant companies, made them profitable, and sold the now-more-valuable stock. He then moved on to invest in other companies. His Royal Securities Corporation was the first company to sell bonds in eastern Canada.

By 1907 Aitken had become a millionaire in Canadian dollars. He was involved, however, in disputes with his fellow investors in the Royal Securities Corporation; his partners wanted higher dividends, but Aitken preferred to retain profits for future investments. His success was owing in part to his appreciation of the value of personal publicity, and in the early twentieth century publicity meant coverage in newspapers. The apex of Aitken's financial accomplishments occurred in 1909 and 1910, when he organized a number of successful mergers in such businesses as cast-iron manufacturing, railroad freight-car construction, and the cement- and steel industries. His appreciation of a unified Canadian market was in part a reaction to the growing economic power of the United States. Aitken saw the British Empire as a potential economic unit, and for the rest of his life he championed the cause of "imperial preference," which would knit the empire into a single economic whole by encouraging free trade within the empire and establishing tariffs against nonempire nations.

Life's Work

In 1908 Aitken made his first trip to London, where he acquired several new businesses, including London's Colonial Bank. He was introduced to Andrew Bonar Law, a Conservative Party politician and a fellow Canadian who shortly became Aitken's greatest hero. Aitken returned to England in 1910, and although he frequently said he would eventually make his permanent residence in Canada, he never did. Through his business connections in London—he briefly became a major shareholder in Rolls-Royce—he became involved in politics as a member of the Conservative Party. His tie with Law strengthened, and he developed connections with several of England's major publishers and journalists, notably Lord Northcliffe of the *Daily Mail*, an icon of "popular" journalism, and R. D. Blumenfeld, editor of the *Daily Express*. With Law's support, in 1910 Aitken was elected a member of Parliament from Ashton-under-Lyne, a textile center near Manchester. Aitken only rarely attended Parliament, preferring then and later to be a go-between among the major politicians of the day, working out compromises and obtaining solutions. After World War I began, in 1914, he published a newspaper for Canadian troops in Great Britain and France, as well as creating the Canadian War Records Office.

In Britain Aitken's most lasting economic endeavor was in the newspaper business. In 1911 he invested in the *Daily Express*, which had been failing financially. He acquired a controlling interest in the newspaper in 1916. At the same time, he was deeply involved in the machinations that brought down Prime Minister H. H. Asquith, bringing to power David Lloyd George. Lloyd George requested that King George V grant Aitken a peerage, in part because of the support the government was receiving from Aitken's newspapers. In February 1917 Aitken took his seat in the House of Lords as Lord Beaverbrook, the name taken from a stream where he had fished as a boy. In the new government, Beaverbrook became the chancellor of the duchy of Lancaster and was placed in charge of war propaganda. He resigned his position at the end of the war in 1918, vowing never to hold office again unless there was another war. Beaverbrook enjoyed politics, however, and although he remained a Conservative, he was never a reliable party politician. After World War I he disposed of Royal Securities Corporation and the Colonial Bank; newspapers became his central interest.

Beaverbrook used his newspapers to publicize himself and to advocate his long-standing commitment to imperial preference, but he was also sincerely interested in publishing the best possible newspapers. He invested heavily in the *Daily Express*, and he increased the newspaper's profits by expanding its advertising, an innovative practice that eventually was adopted by most other newspapers. He also was a strong believer in providing "news," and his publications had more foreign correspondents than any of the other British newspapers. In 1918 Beaverbrook started publishing a second newspaper, the *Sunday Express*, and in time this newspaper held an important position among elite newspapers, such as the *Sunday Times* and the *Observer*—and popular but at times salacious publications, such as *News of the World*. Although London was the center of English newspaper publishing, Beaverbrook also founded the *Scottish Daily Express*. In 1923 he acquired the *Evening Standard*. Beaverbrook allowed the editors of his newspapers to have considerable leeway in both content and policies, although he exerted his control in his advocacy of empire and in his opposition to socialism and any British involvement in European or continental affairs.

Beaverbrook remained a wealthy man during the Great Depression. In early 1929 he sold his stocks and put the money in bonds, thus insulating himself from the worldwide stock market crash. As a solution to the economic crisis, Beaverbrook, through his newspapers, launched an "Empire Crusade," which was a continuation of his long campaign for imperial preference. This campaign fared no better than his earlier attempts, because there was widespread fear among voters that imperial preference would result in increased food prices. As the shadow of fascism spread across Europe, Beaverbrook favored a policy of "No More War" through British isolation from continental affairs. He opposed the League of Nations, believing the organization was more likely to lead to war than to peace. Through his newspapers, he continually predicted that there would be no war in Europe, or no war that would involve Great Britain. Britain nevertheless declared war on September 3, 1939, after Nazi Germany invaded Poland. In May 1940, after the crushing German campaign in Western Europe, Winston Churchill became Britain's prime minister. Shortly afterward, after the fall of France in June, the Nazis began their assault on Britain. One of Churchill's earliest acts was to appoint Beaverbrook minister of aircraft production. In this position Beaverbrook's energy and unorthodox methods enabled Britain to win the Battle of Britain, and this victory was perhaps "his finest hour."

After World War II, Beaverbrook withdrew from politics. He opposed the socialism of the Labour Party and deplored the developing Cold War between the former Allies. In addition to his English residences, he acquired a home in southern France and two in the West Indies, and throughout the year he journeyed from one to another, always keeping in close contact with his newspapers by telephone. He wrote several well-regarded works on the events and people of the World War I years.

It is impossible to know the extent of Beaverbrook's fortune because he gave much of it away during his lifetime, but one biographer estimates that it was in the range of $40 million. His benefactions were often in the form of investments that he made in the name of the recipient. His gifts were distributed to members of his family, friends from childhood, political friends and foes, educational institutions, and the Presbyterian Church. In 1947 Beaverbrook became chancellor of New Brunswick University at Fredericton, New Brunswick, Canada. He already had a long connection to the university, and through the years he had provided many scholarships for the university, as well as funding its gymnasium and a residence for men.

In 1959 Beaverbrook donated his personal art collection to the people of New Brunswick, establishing the Beaverbrook Art Gallery in Fredericton. The gallery's original permanent holdings included English landscapes, such as those of J. M. W. Turner and John Constable; portraits by Sir Joshua Reynolds and Thomas Gainsborough; works by the French painters François Boucher and Jean-Honoré Fragonard; and works by Canadian artists, including members of the Group of Seven. Also donated to the gallery were several works by Salvador Dalí belonging to Christofor Dunn, who became Beaverbrook's last wife. Evidently believing that his own collection was sufficient, Beaverbrook made little provision for additional purchases or further expansion of the gallery's facilities. The gallery, which was designated as New Brunswick's Provincial Art Gallery in 1994, nevertheless continued to add to its collections, focusing on paintings by Canadian artists.

In 1906 Aitken married Gladys Drury, who was from one of Canada's most distinguished families. It proved to be a satisfactory marriage, and the couple had three children. Beaverbrook had other female relationships, but he was devastated when Gladys died in 1927. For many years, until her death in 1945, his closest female companion was Mrs. Jean Norton. In 1963, the year before his death, he married Christofor Dunn, the widow of an old Canadian friend.

Significance

Beaverbrook's major economic legacy consisted of his profitable British newspapers, particularly the *Daily Express* and *Sunday Express*, which provided England's middle classes with publications that were readable and interesting and presented accurate coverage of the major news stories of the day. In addition to creation of the Beaverbrook Art Gallery, his most enduring philanthrophic achievement was the establishment in

1954 of the Beaverbrook Foundation, a grant-making institution that supports numerous charitable causes in Canada and the United Kingdom.

Eugene Larson

Priscilla L. Buckley

Editor, journalist

For decades Priscilla L. Buckley was seen by many as the guiding light of, and organizing strength behind, the conservative magazine National Review, for which she worked for more than 40 years. Although her brother William F. Buckley Jr., as editor in chief, received more attention, Priscilla Buckley's work with the magazine was applauded by many on the right of the American political spectrum.

Areas of Achievement: Journalism

Born: Oct. 17, 1921; New York City, New York, United States

Died: March 25, 2012; Sharon, Connecticut, United States

Early Life

Priscilla Langford Buckley was born in New York City on October 17, 1921, the daughter of William Frank Buckley Sr. and Aloïse Steiner Buckley. Investments in Latin American oil companies turned her father into a multimillionaire; when he died, in 1958, he was worth an estimated $110 million. Buckley grew up on an estate, Great Elm, in Sharon, Connecticut, with her ten siblings. They included William F. Buckley Jr.—the founder and editor in chief of *National Review,* host of the public television series *Firing Line,* and best-selling columnist and novelist—who is considered one of the founders of the modern American conservative movement. Another brother, James L. Buckley, served as a Republican U.S. senator from New York from 1971 to 1977.

Priscilla Buckley spent much of her childhood at exclusive schools abroad. She went to primary school at Cours Fenelon in Paris, France, before being sent to St. Mary's Convent in South Ascot, England. Returning to the United States, she attended high school at the Nightingale-Bamford School, in New York City. After graduating from Nightingale-Bamford, she enrolled at Smith College, in Northampton, Massachusetts, where she was managing editor of the school's newspaper. She received her bachelor's degree in 1943. World War II had created unprecedented job opportunities for women as men departed for military assignments, and in 1944 she turned down a $35-a-week job at *The Book of Knowledge* to work for $18.50 a week as a copy girl at the United Press (UP) office in New York City. She was one of just six women among United Press's two hundred employees at its New York City office. To save money Buckley shared a small apartment in the city and walked the more than 30 blocks to work and back.

Buckley worked diligently and was soon promoted to a position at UP's Radio Sports Desk and then the UP Radio Desk, where incoming news stories from around the globe were rewritten in 15-minute segments for radio stations across the country and sent out by teletype. On V-J Day, news of the Japanese surrender arrived on her shift, and she wrote up the UP news story reporting the effective end of the war. In later years Buckley credited her time at the radio news desk with having shaped her own writing style; she kept her sentences short and always had to be conscious of how her writing sounded. In 1949 Buckley left New York to become news editor of radio station WACA in Camden, South Carolina, a position she held until the following year.

In 1951 Buckley began what became a short stint working for the Central Intelligence Agency (CIA) in Washington, D.C., as a reports officer, a job she referred to as "paperpushing." She enjoyed what she called "spy school." Multilingual, she was assigned to the agency's Eastern European headquarters. She left the CIA in 1953 to become a correspondent for United Press International in Paris. There, she worked at the American desk, where she and her co-workers gathered all the incoming news from France and then translated and rewrote it for the international English-language wire. Buckley became known for covering all types of stories and lending a personal touch to them. All her articles were signed "P. L. Buckley" in order to disguise her gender.

Life's Work

In 1956 Buckley—then in her early thirties— was persuaded by her younger brother William F. Buckley to leave Paris and UPI for a job as assistant editor at his two-year old conservative magazine *National Review.* She accepted in part because her elderly father was poor health; based in New York, she would be closer to home. She began at *National Review* as a writer, publishing her work anonymously, as she had in her early days at United Press. When *National Review*'s original managing editor, Suzanne La Follette, retired, Priscilla Buckley was recommended for the post by Whittaker Chambers, a Communist-turned-conservative who was a member of the magazine's editorial board. In 1959 she became managing editor.

Buckley remained managing editor of *National Review* until 1985, when she was made senior editor of the magazine. During a number of her years with *National Review,* she shared an office with editor James Burnham in the magazine's cramped quarters on East 35th Street in Manhattan. Between them, Buckley and Burnham managed to keep the peace among their opinionated, sometimes fractious, colleagues, or at least ensure that the magazine ran relatively smoothly. Priscilla Buckley edited the work of numerous highly regarded conservatives, among them George Will, Gary Wills, Paul Gigot, David Brooks, Joan Didion, and Mona Charen. Charen wrote that Buckley was a "brilliant editor, but also a terrific prose stylist herself." In 1999 Buckley retired from her position as senior editor, but she continued to work for *National Review* as a contributing editor.

Buckley's first book, *String of Pearls: On the News Beat in New York and Paris,* was published in 2001, when she was 78 years old. The book recounts her experiences as a reporter for the United Press in New York and Paris in the 1940s and 1950s. Unwilling to present her longtime friends and colleagues in anything other than a flattering light, she declined to write a history of *National Review.* She chose instead to write a memoir, *Living it Up with the National Review* (2005), which deals with her life at the magazine but also chronicles her travels and tells family anecdotes. From 1976 to 1980, she wrote a column, *One Woman's Voice,* for Princeton Features. Her articles, book reviews, and travel pieces appeared in the *New York Times Book Review, Harper's Bazaar, Chronicles, Cosmopolitan,* the *American Spectator,* and the *National Review,* among other publications.

Priscilla Buckley never married. She served as a trustee of Sharon Hospital in Sharon, Connecticut; Big Bothers of New York; Church Homes; the Hotchkiss Library in Sharon; and the Maplebrook School in Amenia, New York. Buckley was also governor of the Sharon Country Club and twice served as president of the club (she was the first woman to fill that position). In addition, from 1984 to 1991 she was a member of the U.S. Advisory Commission on Public Diplomacy.

Significance

Priscilla Buckley helped shape the editorial profile of the *National Review,* and thereby she had an important role in shaping the modern conservative movement. For all of the think-tank denizens and professors William F. Buckley attracted to the magazine, as Priscilla Buckley herself said, her brother understood that an experienced "working journalist" would be essential to the magazine's success. Priscilla Buckley filled this critical role, and she managed the magazine with a steady and singularly even-tempered hand. Over her long tenure as editor, she helped many prominent conservative writers hone their skills.

Geoff Orens

Edith Maude Eaton

British-born Chinese American writer and journalist

With the publication of her selection of short stories, Mrs. Spring Fragrance, in 1912, Edith Maude Eaton became one of the first authors of Asian and European descent to be published in the United States. Drawing from her own experience as a woman of Chinese and English descent, Eaton wrote about the lives of Chinese immigrants in North America and provided a glimpse into the experiences of Chinese women and interracial couples, who had been neglected by the major literary works of the period.

Areas of Achievement: Literature

Born: March 15, 1865; Macclesfield, United Kingdom

Died: April 7, 1914; Montreal, Canada

Early Life

Edith Maude Eaton was born on March 15, 1865, in Macclesfield, United Kingdom, to an English father and a Chinese mother, Grace Trefusis, who had been adopted by an English missionary in China and was educated in England. Trefusis later returned to Shanghai, China, where she met and married Edward Eaton, a silk merchant who was on a business trip in Shanghai. They started a family in Macclesfield and moved to North America in 1872. After briefly living in the United States, in the city of Hudson, New York, the Eatons settled in Montreal, Quebec, Canada.

Edith Maude Eaton, the eldest daughter and second of 14 children, witnessed her family's decline in status from middle- to working-class as her father's fortune waned. She had to leave school at the age of 11 to help support the large and growing family. Eaton suffered from ill health throughout her life, which made it difficult for her to do strenuous work; nevertheless, she continued to both work and study in her teenage years.

From her early years in England, Eaton understood her unique position as a child of an interracial couple, and she was aware of the difficulties and hardships that Chinese immigrants had experienced in Europe and North America. Eaton was devoted to her Chinese mother and influenced by her heritage; she eventually adopted Chinese culture as her own. Eaton assumed the pen name Sui Sin Far—a Cantonese name for a flower—and asserted her Chinese identity even though she could easily have passed as a full-blooded Caucasian woman. Eaton's younger sister Winnifred assumed the identity of a Japanese American woman and used the pseudonym Onoto Watanna for her writings.

Life's Work

At the age of 18, in 1883, Eaton started her literary career at the *Montreal Daily Star* newspaper, first as a typesetter and later as a journalist. She also began publishing short fiction in the 1880s in a number of Montreal journals and American magazines. Eaton traveled across the continent to find a position to support herself financially and to advance her career as a writer. In December 1896 Eaton went to Kingston, Jamaica, to work as a newspaper reporter, taking the position previously occupied by her sister Winnifred. Eaton worked on various sections of the newspaper, including social reports, short stories, and reviews. She stayed in Jamaica for a little over a year before returning to Canada. In Jamaica she contracted malaria; she never fully recovered from its effects.

In 1898 Eaton traveled to San Francisco, California, and she eventually moved to Seattle, Washington, to pursue her career as a writer and journalist. On the West Coast, she had opportunities to interact with Chinese immigrants. Eaton understood their struggles to find a sense of belonging and was able to draw on these encounters in her writings. She continued to publish articles in magazines and newspapers throughout North America, but she was never established firmly enough as a writer to have the time and money to support herself while writing a novel or any other longer work.

In 1909 Eaton settled in Boston, Massachusetts. While working there as a stenographer, she completed selections for her book *Mrs. Spring Fragrance*. A collection of novellas and short stories, the book was published in Chicago in 1912 and received positive reviews. *Mrs. Spring Fragrance* was published during a period of intense anti-Chinese sentiment; nevertheless, the book appealed to American readers because of its subject matter and its exotic expressions, designed to connote Chinese writing styles. *Mrs. Spring Fragrance* was more than a collection of previously untold stories about the lives of Chinese immigrants; it was also one of the first books that addressed the lives of the Chinese in North America and viewed their struggles with understanding and sympathy. Eaton's stories examined the marginalized groups, also investigating interracial relationships between Chinese immigrants and Caucasian Americans. Many of her protagonists were Chinese women, who had hitherto received little attention in literature. Eaton recognized the importance of these women's roles in immigrant families and communities, and she also took an interest in the issues of identity and discrimination they grappled with as they moved toward acculturation into American society.

Eaton continued to assert her Chinese heritage, introducing Chinese culture to American readers, audiences, and acquaintances she met on various occasions. Through her writings, she hoped to bridge the West and the East. Nevertheless, her work did not achieve significant influence on mainstream American society; prejudice and discrimination against Asian immigrants stubbornly persisted.

In 1913 Eaton returned to Montreal. There, ill and stricken by rheumatism, she died, on April 7, 1914.

Significance

Edith Maude Eaton was one of the first writers of Asian descent to be published in North America. She introduced American audiences to the lives of Chinese immigrants and challenged notions of discrimination against the Chinese. Eaton embraced her Chinese heritage and wrote of the experiences of marginalized Chinese immigrants, especially Chinese immigrant women. Constrained by the norms and conventions of Victorian North America, Eaton understood the struggles of those with whom she shared race and gender, and she used her voice as a writer to tell their stories.

Forgotten for decades after her death, Eaton was rediscovered in the 1970s as the field of Asian American literature and writers grew. Many of the themes Eaton examined in her short stories and novellas have remained relevant, and her works have generated scholarly discussions about interracial relationships, gender, and identity in American society.

Ji-Hye Shin

Thomas Guy

English bookseller, printer, and stock speculator

Guy was a successful bookseller, specializing in Bibles, but earned even greater wealth by speculating in the stock of the South Sea Company. Although initially regarded as somewhat miserly, he nevertheless founded one of London's most prestigious teaching hospitals, endowing it as a charity for the incurably ill.

Areas of Achievement: Bookselling, financial speculation, philanthropy

Born: 1644 or 1645; Southwark, London, United Kingdom

Died: December 27, 1724; London, United Kingdom

Early Life

Thomas Guy was the eldest of three children born to Thomas Guy, a coal merchant, carpenter, and barge operator, and Anne Vaughton. The elder Thomas was a Baptist at a time when Baptists were known as "dissenters" and were a small and despised group. He worked out of a small wharf in Southwark, near London Bridge. Young Thomas, his brother, and sister were born and lived near the wharf in a relatively poor part of London. When young Thomas was eight years old, his father died, and his mother returned with her children to her birthplace, Tamworth, in the Midlands, where her family had good standing.

It is generally believed that Guy attended Tamworth Free Grammar (high) School during the Commonwealth period (1650–1660), where he would have been taught Latin and Greek and probably math. In 1660, the year of the restoration of King Charles II, Guy returned to London to be apprenticed to John Clarke, a bookseller in Cheapside, next to St. Paul's Cathedral. At the end of his apprenticeship in 1668, Guy bought a bookstore in Cornhill and its stock of £200 worth of books. The store was situated in the financial heart of London, near Mansion House. That year Guy was admitted as a freeman of the Stationers' Company, becoming a liveryman five years later. These positions gave him the credentials to sell and print books. In 1670 he was made a freeman of the city of London, and he also served the city as an alderman.

Life's Work

One of Guy's main concerns as a bookseller was to sell Bibles. He saw the market for cheap but well-produced Bibles. But the Stationers' Company, along with the Oxford University Press, had a virtual monopoly on printing Bibles. The Bibles the Stationers' Company produced were either very poorly printed or very expensive. The university press was not interested in the Bible market, and so did nothing with its printing permit. At first, Guy tried importing Bibles from Holland, but this was technically illegal, since it broke the monopoly agreement. Guy's efforts, however, attracted the attention of two clergymen who shared his concern. They negotiated with the university press to allow Guy to print Bibles for them. This venture succeeded, and Guy was soon making a good profit of some £15,000.

Guy began to show the characteristics of his life that marked him for future fame. He remained unmarried and lived very frugally. He was accused by a rival bookseller of paying low wages and not giving money to charity. Yet Guy did engage in philanthropic ventures with his new wealth. The first such venture was providing for the extension of the grammar school at Tamworth. He next bought land in Tamworth in order to establish an almshouse for six poor women. This building was completed in 1678 at the cost of £200. The structure was enlarged in 1693 in order to provide six places for men. Guy also paid to build a workhouse for the destitute of Tamworth and a spinning school, a sort of early industrial school for women.

Selling Bibles continued to be Guy's main trade and source of income. He used the wealth derived from it in a number of ways. He started to loan out money at a time when there was no permanently established banking system in London. He tried to enter politics, running as a candidate from Tamworth in the 1690 parliamentary elections. (At the time being a member of Parliament was an unpaid position.) Guy was unsuccessful in 1690, but in 1695 he was elected as a member of the Whig (liberal) Party, remaining as one of Tamworth's two members of Parliament until 1708. In 1694 he was elected against his will as sheriff of London, and he preferred to pay a £400 fine rather than accept the office. He was defeated in the 1708 elections, and he became so embittered against Tamworth that he withdrew from performing any further philanthropy for the town.

Guy supplemented his mature wealth by engaging in two ventures, for both of which he used his bookselling profits as his capital. The first venture was trading in seamen's pay tickets during the War of the Spanish Succession (1701–1714), which Great Britain waged against France and Spain. This activity was a type of speculation in futures. The second venture was his investment in the South Sea Company. The company had been founded in 1711 by Robert Harley, first earl of Oxford, as a way of managing the national debt incurred by the War of the Spanish Succession. The company was given a monopoly to trade with the Spanish colonies of South America, in return for which the company would give the British government £10 million. The government would then pay the company a 6 percent return on this sum. The South Sea Company raised the £10 million by selling shares at £100 each. What trading the company did, however, was mainly in slaves; in fact, it did very little trading, and rather gradually took on more government debt. By 1720 the value of the company's shares skyrocketed, climbing from £128 per share in January to more than £1,000 per share by the end of August. At this time companies and stock transactions were unregulated, and the general public had little experience of the stock market. Guy, perhaps intuitively, was able to read the market, and he sold his shares at an enormous profit before the "South Sea bubble" burst—the first major collapse of a publicly traded company. The parliamentary report on the collapse implicated many politicians in a generally corrupt scheme, and a number of people were prosecuted. The profits Guy earned by selling his South Sea Company stock dwarfed the fortune he obtained by selling Bibles. It is variously estimated that he bought his shares in the company for between £42,000 and £54,000, and he sold them in 1720 for about £234,000.

By 1704 Guy had retired from active trade, and he began to take an interest in St. Thomas's Hospital, one of the main hospitals in London, located near his birthplace. That year he became one of the hospital's governors, and he looked for ways to donate some of his wealth to the facility. He gave £1,000 to build three new wards and £100 per year to fund them. A few years later, he donated an additional £3,000.

While Guy was seeking ways to benefit St. Thomas's Hospital, a leading London physician, Richard Mead, persuaded Guy to build a new hospital to care for those patients at St. Thomas's who had been pronounced incurable. In 1721 Guy leased land from St. Thomas's in Southwark, on the south bank of the Thames River, near London Bridge. The lease was for a period of 999 years. At first, Guy saw the new hospital as remaining a part of St. Thomas's, but he eventually decided to found an entirely new facility, which would be called Guy's Hospital. Construction work started in 1722, and the new buildings were roofed just before Guy's death in 1724. The facility's first matron, Ann Rainey, was from Tamworth; Guy had known her from boyhood.

Guy was buried at St. Thomas's Parish Church, Southwark. At the funeral, there were more than 40 carriages and a large number of poor people who saw Guy as their benefactor. About 50 years later, his body was reburied in the crypt of Guy's Hospital Chapel. A portrait of Guy, painted in 1706 by John Vanderbank, hangs inside the crypt.

Significance

Thomas Guy's primary legacy is the establishment of the hospital that bears his name. Guy was worth about £300,000 at his death. More than two-thirds of this sum went to the foundation of Guy's Hospital in order to maintain the upkeep of four hundred beds. A ward for 20 insane patients was also included in this bequest. The original buildings cost £18,793 to construct. Many of these first buildings erected by Guy continue to stand, including the chapel and two forecourts containing his statue. The structures are excellent examples of early eighteenth-century Georgian architecture. To mark his benevolence, a statue of Guy was erected in front of the hospital, alongside statues of Christ and the Good Samaritan.

In the twenty-first century, Guy's Hospital continues to be one of London's leading hospitals and has a worldwide reputation for excellence. The facility is administered as a part of the Guy's and St. Thomas's (Hospital) NHS (National Health Service) Foundation Trust. The facility is allied to King's College, London, as a teaching hospital for doctors, nurses, and dentists. Guy's Hospital specializes in dentistry and is the largest dental hospital in Europe.

The rest of Guy's fortune was dispersed in a number of other ways. Friends and relatives received bequests of £1,000 each. Christ's Hospital, a school for poor children in London, received funds to provide £400 worth of scholarships each year for four students. In addition, a fund was established to help release poor debtors from prison.

He is perhaps the first person from a humble background to single-handedly found such a prestigious institution, setting an example of philanthropy for self-made men for the next two centuries. His insight into handling stocks showed how others could amass personal fortunes in the stock market. He also demonstrated that self-made men do not have to live ostentatiously in order to gain social respect.

David Barratt

Hal Jackson

Radio disc jockey, media executive, sportscaster

A prominent disc jockey and radio executive, Hal Jackson was also a civil rights fundraiser and sports broadcaster. Jackson hosted Sunday Morning Classics, his popular New York City radio show presenting a mix of music from different eras and genres, from its debut in 1982 until his death. He was one of the first African American disc jockeys to reach a large white audience and was an influential presence on New York City radio for more than 50 years.

Areas of Achievement: Radio, television

Born: C. November 3, 1915; Charleston, South Carolina, United States

Died: May 23, 2012; New York City, New York, United States

Early Life

Harold Baron Jackson was the youngest of five children born to Eugene Baron Jackson, a prosperous tailor, and his wife, Laura Rivers Jackson, in Charleston, South Carolina, on about November 3, 1915. (He was born at home rather than in a hospital, and as was the case with many Southern black children at that time, his birth was never officially recorded.) Jackson's parents regarded Charleston's schools for African Americans as inferior; Jackson did begin attending the best of them, the Avery Normal Institute. His parents died when he was eight years old—his mother of tuberculosis, and his father, a few months later, of complications of high blood pressure, according to his autobiography. Jackson lived with relatives in New York City, Charleston, and Washington, D.C. He graduated from Dunbar High School in Washington and then attended (but did not graduate from) Howard University. He first broke onto the airwaves by broadcasting Howard's home baseball games. In the 1930s Jackson became a fixture at Griffin Stadium, volunteering to do trash pickup during Washington Senators games. This led to his early career as a play-by-play sports announcer for the Negro League's Homestead Grays baseball games on WOOK, making him the first African American to serve as a sports announcer.

In 1939 Jackson approached WINX, a Washington radio station owned by the *Washington Post,* and proposed an interview program. He was told by a station executive, in offensive terms, that the station would never hire an African American host. Persisting, Jackson, through white ad agencies and with the support of the African American owner of a barbecue restaurant chain, bought time on WINX for a 15-minute interview and entertainment show, neglecting to mention that he would host the program himself. He carefully chose his first guest: Mary McLeod Bethune, a close friend of Eleanor Roosevelt and an adviser to Franklin D. Roosevelt, and he arrived at the station just prior to broadcast time and began the show before anyone could stop him. After the first episode of *The Bronze Review,* as Jackson called his program, the radio station was inundated by thrilled callers, and *The Bronze Review* stayed on the air. Having broken the color line, in the 1940s Jackson hosted as many as four radio programs at once in the Washington, D.C., area, on WINX, in Washington; WOOK, in Silver Spring, Maryland; WANN, in Annapolis, Maryland; and WSID, in Baltimore. Most notable among them was a jazz and blues program, *The House That Jack Built,* which Jackson hosted on WOOK and on which he established his smooth, low-key radio persona. That approach, in contrast to the hyperkinetic, jive-talking style of other black announcers, strongly influenced later generations of disc jockeys.

While in Washington Jackson was also a civil rights fund-raiser, and he broke into television as host of a local variety show broadcast live from the Howard Theater in the spring and summer of 1949. An avid sports fan, he also became a sports entrepreneur. He organized an all–African American professional basketball team, the Washington Bears, which won the invitational World Professional Basketball Tournament in 1943.

Life's Work

Jackson first moved to New York City in 1949 but soon returned to Washington. A few years later, in 1954, he returned to New York at the urging of Nathan Strauss, who wanted Jackson to break the color barrier at WMCA. He was soon working for three stations, broadcasting three programs with distinct formats: one rhythm-and-blues, one pop, and one jazz: WABC's live midnight broadcast from the jazz nightclub Birdland. (Working for ABC, he became the first African American host on a continuing network radio show.) In the late 1950s, he also briefly had his own Sunday morning children's television show on Channel 11 featuring "Uncle Hal, The Kiddies Pal."

Jackson's career was briefly rocked by the payola scandal of 1959, when which disc jockeys were accused of accepting gifts from record companies in exchange for airtime. Jackson was arrested (in orchestrated full view of newspaper photographers) and lost his program at WLIB, although the charges against him were later dropped. Both Malcolm X and Adam Clayton Powell came to his defense, but for a time Jackson was forced to earn a living by working as a janitor and driving a cab. Many believed Jackson had been targeted because of his involvement in the civil rights movement; he had interviewed Dr. Martin Luther King Jr. and raised money for the Southern Christian Leadership Council. In the early 1960s, however, Jackson became program director at the Queens radio station WWRL.

In 1970 Manhattan borough president Percy Sutton and former *New York Amsterdam News* publisher Clarence Jones—soon joined by a group of African American entertainers, businessmen and politicians including Jackson, future New York City mayor David Dinkins, future New York State comptroller Carl McCall, and Betty Shabazz, widow of Malcolm X—launched Inner City Broadcasting Corporation. Inner City bought WLIB in 1972, making the AM-FM station New York City's first black-owned radio stations. In 1973 they created WBLS-FM from WLIB-AM's original FM sister-station. On WBLS-FM, Inner City pioneered what Frankie Crocker, the station's program director, called urban contemporary radio: a highly successful mix of rhythm-and-blues, dance music and other genres chosen for their crossover appeal. By 1979, Inner City's WBLS was the top radio station in New York City. Inner City went on to acquire other radio stations in major markets throughout the United States, and the urban contemporary format became popular all over the country. The company also engaged with two joint cable television ventures with Time Warner. During the early 1980s Jackson focused his role as a radio executive, developing programming at the stations Inner City acquired and living for a time in Los Angeles. In 1986 Jackson became Inner City's group chairman.

In 1982 Jackson decided to return to live broadcasting when a Sunday-morning slot opened up at WBLS. Jackson hosted his *Sunday Morning Classics* (later called *Sunday Classics,* and now aired on Sunday evenings) for more than 25 years. His wife, Deborah Bolling ("Debi B."), joined him on the show, as did Clay Berry. Jackson's show has been called a "history lesson in music": he played the music of classic performers such as Stevie Wonder, Miles Davis, Jackie Wilson, Billie Holiday, Ella Fitzgerald, the O'Jays, and Count Basie along with that of younger artists.

Jackson produced and hosted concerts at Harlem's Apollo Theater, which was among Inner City's holdings for a time; in Central Park; and at Palisades Amusement Park in New Jersey. He helped establish the Miss Black Teenage America pageant (later renamed Hal Jackson's Talented Teens International). He also organized fund-raising events for civil rights causes. Back in 1949 Jackson had established his familiar relaxed persona for *The House that Jack Built,* and he used the title of that radio show for his autobiography (written with James Haskins), which was published in 2001.

Hal Jackson died on May 23, 2012, in New York City. Deborah Bolling, his fourth wife, whom he married in 1987, is still, with Clay Berry, the co-host of *Sunday Classics.* Jackson's previous marriages had ended in divorce. He was also survived by his children, Jane, Jewell, and Hal Jackson Jr., as well as grandchildren and great-grandchildren. A few months after his death, Inner City was acquired by YMF Media, controlled by Ronald Burkle and Earvin "Magic" Johnson.

Significance

Jackson's wide-ranging musical interests and laid-back manner helped redefine black radio and held considerable crossover appeal, attracting both black and white mass audiences. His unassuming manner perhaps tended to obscure the formidable hurdles he faced over the course of his career, beginning in the 1930s, when it was a challenge for a black announcer to reach an audience at all. He was the first African American disc jockey to broadcast nationally on network radio, and by joining Inter City, he became one of the first African American radio station owners in New York City. In 1990 Jackson became the first African American inducted into the National Association of Broadcasters Hall of Fame, and in 1995 he was one of the first five inductees into the Radio Hall of Fame.

Kate Stern

James Y. Sakamoto

Activist and journalist

A proponent of cooperation between Japanese and non-Japanese Americans, Sakamoto edited the first English-language newspaper for the Japanese community in the United States, the Japanese American Courier. He also helped found the Japanese American Citizens League and served as president of the organization from 1936 to 1938.

Areas of Achievement: Journalism, community organizing

Born: 1903; Seattle, Washington, United States

Died: December 3, 1955; Seattle, Washington, United States

Early Life

James Yoshinori Sakamoto (yoh-shee-NOH-ree sah-kah-MOH-toh) was born in 1903 in Seattle, Washington, to Osamu and Tsuchi Sakamoto, Japanese immigrants from Yamaguchi prefecture who settled in Washington in 1894. "Jimmie" Sakamoto attended Franklin High School, where he excelled at sports, particularly football, baseball, and boxing. Patriotic from an early age, he tried to enlist in the U.S. Army when the United States entered World War I but was rejected owing to his youth. In July 1920 the U.S. House of Representatives's Committee on Immigration and Naturalization visited Seattle to hear testimony about Japanese immigration by Seattle residents. James's eldest sister, Marie, agreed to testify, and Jimmie went with her to observe the hearings. When a scheduled speaker failed to appear, Jimmie was prevailed upon to speak before the committee. In 1921 Sakamoto cofounded the Seattle Progressive Citizens League, a forerunner of the Japanese American Citizens League (JACL), which he later helped to establish.

Before graduating from Franklin, Sakamoto decided to move to the East. He finished high school in Princeton, New Jersey, and then moved to New York City, where he became the English-language section editor of the *Japanese American News*. He married Frances Imai, and the couple had a daughter. Sakamoto also pursued professional boxing, as a welterweight, but injuries sustained while boxing left him nearly blind, and after his wife's death, he returned to Seattle in 1927. In 1928 he married Misao Nishitani, an Issei, or first-generation Japanese American; they were to have three daughters, Marie, Marcia and Denise.

Life's Work

By 1910 the more than 70,000 Japanese settled on the mainland of the United States faced racially discriminatory practices in education, housing, and landownership. Nisei (second-generation Japanese Americans) began to form small political groups to cope with a growing anti-Japanese movement. Nisei leagues, of which Sakamoto's Seattle Progressive Citizens League (SPCL) was the first of its kind in terms of advocating for the Americanization of the Nisei, were organized in Washington and Oregon during the 1920s. Japanese-Americans elsewhere in the Pacific Northwest and in California contacted Sakamoto and the SPCL president, Clarence Arai, requesting advice and support in creating similar organizations. These regional groups united in 1929 to become a national Nisei organization called the Japanese American Citizens League (JACL). The first JACL national convention took place on August 29, 1930, in Seattle.

Sakamoto began publishing the *Japanese American Courier* in Seattle in 1928, at times writing editorials for the paper under the pen name Jay Esse. The newspaper, the first in the United States to be written entirely in English for a Japanese audience, encouraged *Nisei* to acculturate and become fully Americanized. In addition to disseminating news and other information, the *Courier* sponsored sports teams as a form of community outreach. The *Courier* quickly achieved circulation figures over ten thousand. In 1933, when the JACL's newspaper, the *Pacific Citizen,* faltered, Sakamoto took over its operations until 1939, doing its editing and typesetting in addition to putting out the *Courier*. His wife managed the business affairs of the newspaper and was instrumental in its survival. Although the newspaper was never a profitable venture, particularly during the Great Depression, it continued to be published until April 1942.

Meanwhile Sakamoto continued to be active in the JACL, and in 1936 he became its second president, a position he held until 1938. He strongly believed in American institutions and was conservative politically, opposing militant labor organizations and discouraging radical protest. Over the 1930s, as Japan followed an expansionist foreign policy, the *Courier* supported Japan's actions, in sharp contrast to the many U.S. publications that supported China. This stance did not survive the Japanese attack on Pearl Harbor in December 1941.

Two months after the attack on Pearl Harbor, on February 19, 1942, President Roosevelt issued Executive Order 9066 authorizing the internment of all Japanese Americans living within 50- or 60 miles of the Pacific coast of the United States. In May 1942 James and Misao Sakamoto, along with their daughters, were interned (along with thousands of other Japanese Americans from Seattle and Tacoma) at Camp Harmony in Puyallup, Washington. They spent four months at the temporary Puyallup Assembly Center, which had been hastily built on the site of a fairgrounds some 35 miles south of Seattle. Local army officials largely left administration of the camp to the JACL Emergency Defense Council, headed by Sakamoto, who was appointed chief supervisor of the internees there. Sakamoto had appeared before the Tolan Commission in February 1942 to protest internment, but he agreed to cooperate with the government, and the JACL worked to ease the transition for the Japanese American community. The JACL governing board, to which Sakamoto appointed a number of JACL colleagues, acted as a police force, enforcing curfews and issuing various rules and strict regulations for the camps. Sakamoto's accommodationist policies lost support among the camp's inmates. When Sakamoto and his family were sent on from the Puyallup camp to the Minidoka camp in southern Idaho, he did not resume a leadership role, in part because of the limitations placed on the camps' self-governance but also because the influence of the JACL had waned. Sakamoto, his youngest daughter, and his parents remained at Minidoka until the end of the war. Misao and the two elder daughters eventually were permitted to leave Minidoka to move to Indiana. After the war the family reunited in Seattle.

Without the means to relaunch the *Courier* and limited by his blindness, Sakamoto eventually found work with the St. Vincent de Paul Salvage Bureau, a Catholic-run charity, where he worked as head of the Pick-up and Telephone Solicitation Department for the rest of his life. He died of injuries sustained when he was struck by a car as he was walking to work.

Significance

Through his efforts as a journalist and activist, Sakamoto worked to break down racial barriers and build connections between Japanese Americans and other groups. Owing in part to the continued efforts of the JACL, in 1988, President Ronald Reagan authorized the payment of financial compensation to Japanese Americans interned during World War II and issued a formal apology for the event. Still active in the twenty-first century, JACL is the largest Asian American civil rights advocacy organization in the United States.

James Sakamoto's papers are held in the University of Washington Libraries' Special Collections. The collection consists of Sakamoto's personal papers and two subgroups, one devoted to the Japanese American Citizens' League (JACL) and the other to the *Japanese-American Courier*.

Judy A. Johnson

Bibliography

Abrams, Jonathan

Calacanis, Jason. "Jonathan Abrams." *This Week in Startups* #303 Nov. 6, 2012. [Full transcript available at http://thisweekinstartups.com. Consulted December 9, 2013.]

Chafkin, Max. "How to Kill a Great Idea!" *Inc.*, June 1, 2007.

Piskorski, Mikolaj Jan, and Carin-Isabel Knoop. *Friendster.* Harvard Business School Case Study, September 14, 2006. Prod. #: 707409-PDF-ENG.

Abramson, Jill

Auletta, Ken. "Changing Times: Jill Abramson Takes Charge of the Gray Lady." *New Yorker,* October 24, 2011.

Carlin, John. "The Times of Her Life: Jill Abramson on Power, Pop Culture and Puppies." *Independent,* March 3, 2012.

Grove, Lloyd. "Good Jill, Bad Jill: The Queen of the New York Times." *Newsweek,* July 31, 2013.

Kinsley, Michael. "A Q&A with Jill Abramson: The Times' Top Editor on Mean Bosses, Liberal Biases, and the Demise of the Washington Post." *New Republic,* August 19, 2013.

Pilkington, Ed. "Jill Abramson: 'I'm a battle-scarred veteran.'" *Guardian,* June 7, 2011.

Pilkington, Ed. "New York Times's Jill Abramson: 'The First Amendment is first for a reason.'" *Guardian,* October 13, 2013.

Sharp, Naomi. "Ken Auletta Questions Jill Abramson," *Columbia Journalism Review,* October 9, 2013. [Discusses the October 5, 2013, Auletta-Abramson interview at the New Yorker Book Festival; video of the full interview provided.]

Alterman, Eric

Eaves, Elisabeth. "A Liberal Sounds Off on Liberal Bias; PW Talks with Eric Alterman." *Publishers Weekly,* January 27, 2003.

Gurley, George. "The Avenging Alterman." *New York Observer,* April 14, 2003.

Moyers, Bill. "Eric Alterman on Liberalisms Past, Present and Future." Moyers and Company (TV), April 20, 2012. billmoyers.com/segment/eric-alterman-on-liberalisms-past-present-and-future/. Consulted December 10, 2013.

Arce, Julio

Barrera, Magdalena. "Of *Chicharrones* and Clam Chowder: Gender and Consumption in Jorge Ulica's *Crónicas Diabólicas*." *Bilingual Review* 29, no. 1 (January-April, 2008): 49-65.

Kanellos, Nicholas. "Recovering and Re-Constructing Early Twentieth-Century Hispanic Immigrant Print Culture in the U.S." *American Literary History* 19, no. 2 (Summer 2007): 438-455.

Tatum, Charles M. *Chicano and Chicana literature: The Mexican American Experience.* Tucson: University of Arizona Press, 2006.

Arnaz, Desi

Fidelman, Geoffrey Mark. *The Lucy Book: A Complete Guide to Her Five Decades on Television.* Los Angeles: Renaissance Books, 1999.

Gordon, John Steele. "What Desi Wrought." *American Heritage* (December, 1998): 20.

Sanders, Coyne Steven, and Tom Gilbert. *Desilu: The Story of Lucille Ball and Desi Arnaz.* Reprint. New York: It Books, 2011.

Arriola, Gus

Aldama, Frederick Luis. *Your Brain on Latino Comics: From Gus Arriola to Los Bros Hernandez.* Austin: University of Texas Press, 2009.

Harvey, Robert C. *Accidental Ambassador Gordo: The Comic Strip Art of Gus Arriola.* Jackson: University Press of Mississippi, 2000.

Whyte, Malcolm. *Great Comic Cats.* Rohnert Park, Calif.: Pomegranate Communications, 2001.

Ball, Alan

Thomas Fahy, ed. *Alan Ball: Conversations* (Univ. Press of Mississippi, 2013).

Thomas Fahy, ed. *Considering Alan Ball: Essays on Sexuality, Death, and America in the Television and Film Writings* (McFarland, 2006).

Harrington, Nancy. "Alan Ball; Writer/Producer." Archive of American Television. August 25, 2011. http://emmytvlegends.org/interviews/people/alan-ball. Consulted December 10, 2013. [Web page contains the two-hour Harrington interview via YouTube.]

Martin, Brett. *Difficult Men: Behind the Scenes of a Creative Revolution* (Penguin 2013). [Chapter Thirteen: "The Happiest Room in Hollywood."]

Beaverbrook, William Maxwell Aitken, First Baron

Chester, Lewis, and Jonathan Fenby. *The Fall of the House of Beaverbrook.* London: Deutsch, 1979.

Chisholm, Anne, and Michael Davie. *Lord Beaverbrook: A Life.* New York: Knopf, 1993.

Nowell, Iris. *Women Who Give Away Millions: Portraits of Canadian Philanthropists.* Toronto: Hounslow Press, 1996. [Discusses Christofor Dunn.]

Poitras, Jacques. *Beaverbrook: A Shattered Legacy.* Fredericton, N.B.: Goose Lane, 2007. Richards, David Adams. *Lord Beaverbrook.* Toronto: Penguin, 2008.

Taylor, A. J. P. *Beaverbrook.* New York: Simon & Schuster, 1972.

Young, Kenneth. *Churchill and Beaverbrook.* London: Eyre and Spottiswoode, 1966.

Bourdain, Anthony

Bon Appétit. "Ever Wonder How Anthony Bourdain Came to Be Anthony Bourdain? (and What He Looked Like in 1972?)" May 31, 2012. [Interview with photos.]

Geraci, Victor W., and Elizabeth S. Demers, eds. *Icons of American Cooking.* Santa Barbara, CA: Greenwood, 2011.

Jeffrey, Clara. "The Omnivore's Agenda: An Interview with Anthony Bourdain." *Mother Jones,* November/December 2010.

Morse, Gardiner. "Management by Fire: A Conversation with Chef Anthony Bourdain," *Harvard Business Review,* Vol. 80.7, July 2002.

Brûlé, Tyler

Larocca, Amy. "Planet Monocle." *New York,* December 5, 2010.

Nicoll, Ruaridh. "Tyler Brûlé The Man Who Sold the World," *The Observer,* Saturday 17 March 2012

Phillips, Patrick. "Tyler Brûlé: 'Getting Information First Is One of the Biggest Luxuries of All'." I Want Media, October 19, 2004. http://www.iwantmedia.com/. Consulted December 10, 2013. [Interview.]

Williams, Alex. "Mr. Zeitgeist." *New York Times,* January 4, 2012.

Buckley, Priscilla

Boughton, Kathryn. "Priscilla Buckley Remembered by Family Members, Sharon Residents as a Benevolent Force of Nature." *Litchfield County Times,* March 28, 2012.

Buckley, Reid. *An American Family: The Buckleys.* New York: Threshold Editions, 2009.

Hart, Jeffrey Peter. The Making of the American Conservative Mind: National Review and its Times. Wilington, DE: ISI Books, 2005.

National Review. "Remembering Priscilla Buckley," *National Review* 64, no. 7, (April 16, 2012): 25-28.

Tragakiss, Tamara. "Recalling Glory Days." *Passport Magazine/Litchfield County Times,* November 17, 2005. [A lengthy profile.]

Burri, René

BBC Radio Four. *Front Row,* with John Wilson, Apr. 23, 2013, www.bbc.co.uk. [Interview.]

Galerie Esther Woerdehoff. René Burri page. http://www.ewgalerie.com/.

Magnum Photos, "Rene Burri; Swiss, b. 1933." http://www.magnumphotos.com/.

Papst, Manfred. "The Engaged Observer." *Swiss Review* 5, October 2013: 18–21.

Vernissage TV, *René Burri/Museum für Gestaltung Zürich,* May through Oct. 2005, vernissage.tv.blog/ 2005/10/16/rene-burri-museum-fur-gestaltung-zurich/. [Three-part interview with Karolina Zupan-Rupp, with transcripts available in English.]

Burrows, James

Greenberg, Keith Elliot. *Charles, Burrows & Charles: TV's Top Producers.* Woodbridge, CT: Blackbirch Press, 1995.

Lembeck, Michael. "Visual History with James Burrows." Directors Guild of America, March 11, 2008. http://www.dga.org/craft/visualhistory. Consulted December 10, 2013. [Two-and-a-half-hour-plus interview, broken into segments; video and full transcripts.]

Rutkowski, Gary. "James Burrows; Director." Archive of American Television. December 17, 2003. http://emmytvlegends.org/interviews/people/james-burrows. Consulted December 10, 2013. [Web page contains the three-and-a-half hour Rutkowski interview via YouTube.]

Chase, David

Biskind, Peter. "An American Family," *Vanity Fair,* April 2007. [With photos by Annie Leibovitz].

Edgerton, Gary R. *The Sopranos.* Detroit: Wayne State University Press, c2013.

Gabbard, Glen O. The Psychology of the Sopranos: Love, Death, Desire and Betrayal in America's Favorite Gangster Family. New York: Basic Books, 2002.

Kashner, Sam. "The Family Hour: An Oral History of *The Sopranos*," *Vanity Fair,* April 2012. [With photo by Annie Leibovitz.]

Thomas Fahy, ed. *Considering David Chase: Essays on the Rockford Files, Northern Exposure, and the Sopranos* (Jefferson, NC: McFarland, 2008.

David Lavery, Douglas L. Howard, and Paul Levinson, eds. *The Essential Sopranos Reader.*   Lexington: University Press of Kentucky, 2011.

Brett Martin. *Difficult Men: Behind the Scenes of a Creative Revolution.* New York: Penguin, 2013.

Brett Martin. *The Sopranos: The Complete Book.* New York: Time Inc. Home Entertainment, 2007.

Polan, Dana B. *The Sopranos.* Durham, NC: Duke University Press, 2009.

Vincent, Christopher J. *Paying Respect to* The Sopranos: *A Psychosocial Analysis.* Jefferson, NC: McFarland, 2008.

Yacowar, Maurice. The Sopranos *on the Couch: The Ultimate Guide.* New York: Continuum, 2007.

Coddington, Grace

Blanchard, Tamsin. "Grace Coddington on Publishing Her Long-Awaited Memoirs." *Telegraph,* November 19, 2012. [Online edition with link to extract from Coddington's *Memoir,* November 17, 2012.]

Boodro, Michael. "Grace Notes." *Vogue,* November 1993.

Kavanaugh, Julie. "Grace Coddington: Creative Indeed." *Intelligent Life,* Spring 2011.

MacSweeney, Eve, ed. *Vogue: The Editor's Eye*, with an introduction by Hamish Bowles. New York: Abrams, 2012.

Pols, Mary. "'The September Issue': Humanizing the Devil." *Time,* August 28, 2009.

Voguepedia Editors. Grace Coddington page. Voguepedia. http://www.vogue.com/voguepedia/Grace_Coddington. Consulted December 10, 2013.

Cohen, Janet Langhart

Kozaryn, Linda D. "Meet Janet Langhart Cohen, the Secretary's Outreach Partner." U.S. Department of Defense. Dec. 8, 1999.. http://www.defense.gov/News/NewsArticle.aspx?ID=42224. Consulted December 10, 2013. [American Forces Press Service interview.]

Merida, Kevin. "In Defense of Love beyond Race." *Washington Post,* December 14, 1997.

Norment, Lynn. "Janet Langhart Cohen: First Lady of the Pentagon." *Ebony* 56.1 (2000): 154–159.

Dé, Shobhaa

Dodiya, Jaydipsinh. *The Fiction of Shobha Dé; Critical Studies.* New Delhi: Prestige Books, in association with Saurashtra University, 2000.

Dugger, Celia W. "Bombay Journal; India Relishes the Novels She Sprinkles with Spice." *New York Times,* October 15, 1998.

Gargan, Edward A. "Out There: Bombay; India's Spiciest Writer." *New York Times,* January 17, 1993.

Gupta, Shashi Kant. *Indian Ethos in Shobha Dé's Works.* New Delhi: Atlantic Publishers, 2010.

Patnaik, Bharati. *Identity and Gender: A Critical Study of the Novels of Shobha Dé.* New Delhi: Commonwealth Publishers 2013.

Shukla, B. Shobha Dé: *The Indian Feminist Icon.* Jaipur: Raj Publishing House 2010.

Singh, Monika. Feminist Approaches in the Novels of Shobha Dé. New Delhi: Vishvabhart Publications 2009.

Vats, Naresh V. *Shobha Dé: A Critical Response.* New Delhi: Creative Books, 2010.

Wanjari, Priya D. *The Fictional World of Shobha Dé.* Nagpur: Dattsons,2013.

Deutsch, Linda

Alexander, S. L. *Covering the Courts: A Handbook for Journalists.* Lanham, MD: Rowman & Littlefield, 2004.

Hayslett, Jerrianne. *Anatomy of a Trial; Public Loss, Lessons Learned from* The People vs. O. J. Simpson (University of Missouri Press, 2008)

Mills, Nancy. "Spirited Woman Q & A: Linda Deutsch." Spirited Woman Newsletter. December 2003.

Thaler, Paul. *The Spectacle: Media and the Making of the O. J. Simpson Story.* Westport, CT: Praeger, 1997.

Eaton, Edith Maude

Chu, Patricia D. *Assimilating Asians: Gendered Strategies of Authorship in Asian America.* Durham, NC: Duke University Press, 2000.

Ferens, Dominika. *Edith and Winnifred Eaton: Chinatown Missions and Japanese Romances.* Urbana: University of Illinois Press, 2002.

Huang, Guiyou. *Asian-American Autobiographers; A Bio-Bibliographical Critical Sourcebook.* Westport, CT: Greenwood Press, 2001.

Pan, Arnold. "Transnationalism at the Impasse of Race: Sui Sin Far and U.S. Imperialism." *Arizona Quarterly* 66.1 (Spring 2010): 87–114.

Spaulding, Carol V. *Blue-Eyed Asians: Eurasianism in the Work of Edith Eaton/Sui Sin Far, Winnifred Eaton/Onoto Watanna, and Diana Chang.* Ph.D. diss., University of Iowa, 1996.

Vogel, Todd. Rewriting White: Race, Class, and Cultural Capital in Nineteenth-Century America. New Brunswick, NJ: Rutgetrs University Press 2004.

White-Parks, Annette. *Sui Sin Far/Edith Maude Eaton: A Literary Biography.* Urbana: University of Illinois Press, 1995.

Gopinath, Suhas

Gopinath, Suhas. Suhas Gopinath at TEDxIITDelhi. February 19, 2013. YouTube.com.

PETA Youth. Suhas Gopinath, CEO at 17. www.PETAIndia.com.

Stünitz, Lasse, and Johannes Berchtold. "Suhas Gopinath Speaks to Lasse Stünitz and Johannes Berchtold of St Gallen Symposium ISC." April 22, 2010. Yourstory.com.

Gruber, Lilli

Cowell, Alan. The Saturday Profile: A Former Italian Journalist Lets Her Politics Show. *New York Times,* July 3, 2004.

Gruber, Micki. "Lilli Gruber (Dietlinde [Lilli] Gruber Charmelot)." www.fembio.org, January 2008. [In German; English translation available using online translation tools.]

European Parliament. Lilli Gruber. http://www.europarl.europa.eu/. [Gruber's Member of Parliament page; provides information about Gruber's political affiliations and a log of links to the texts of speeches and reports she presented as an MEP.]

Winner, Christopher P. "Lilli Gruber." *The American InItalia,* June 1, 2004.

Guy, Thomas

Bowden-Dan, Jane. "Mr Guy's Hospital and the Caribbean." *History Today* 56, no. 6 (June, 2006): 50-56. Cameron, Hector C. *Guy's Hospital, 1726-1948.* London: Longmans, Green, 1984.

Guy's Hospital Nurses League. *Guy's Hospital: History of Nursing, 1725-1968.* London: Guy's Hospital, 1968.

Handler, Clive E., ed. *Guy's Hospital 250 Years.* London : Guy's Hospital Gazette, 1976.

Lawrence, Susan C. *Charitable Knowledge: Hospital People and Practitioners in Eighteenth Century London.* Cambridge, England: Cambridge University Press, 1996.

Wilks, Samuel, and George Thomas Bethany. *A Biographical History of Guy's Hospital.* London: Ward, Lock, Bowden, 1892.

Haruka, Yoko

Dales, Laura. "Feminism and the Popular Media (Haruka Yōko's Feminism)," Chapter Five of *Feminist Movements in Contemporary Japan.* New York: Routledge, 2009.

Doi, Ayako. "Japan's Hybrid Women." *Foreign Policy,* July 12, 2010.

McLelland, Mark, and Romit Dasgupta. *Genders, Transgenderes, and Sexualities in Japan.* New York: Routledge, 2005.

Jackson, Hal

Barlow, William. *Voice Over: The Making of Black Radio*. Philadelphia: Temple University Press, 1999.

George, Martha Washington. *Black Radio ... Winner Takes All; America's First Black DJ's*. Bloomington, IN: Xlibris Corp., 2001. [Self-published.]

France, Alison. "Radio Host's Reflections on Race, Rap and Rhythm." *New York Times,*

October 23, 1993

Jones, Scott A.

Burns, Rebecca, and E. Anthony Valainis. "Mr. Jones Builds His Dream House*. " Indianapolis Monthly* 25:2 (October 2001).

Comiskey, Daniel S. "Going Public: Indy's Vibrant Startup Culture." *Indianapolis Monthly* 37:2. (October 2013).

Jordan, Robert. "Scott Jones: Boston Technology, Indiana," in *How They Did It: Billion Dollar Insights from the Heart of America* (RedFlash Press, 2010).

Morris, Jeremy Wade. "Making Music Behave: Metadata and the Digital Music Commodity," *New Media & Society* 14, no. 5 (2012): 850–866.

Shiffman, Betsy. "Digital Dream House." *Forbes,* May 17, 2002.

Van Buskirk, Eliot. "Gracenote Defends Its Evolution." *Wired,* November 13, 2006.

Kaspersky, Eugene
Kaspersky, Natalia

Bradley, Tony. "In Their Own Words: Kaspersky Lab Cofounder and CEO Eugene Kaspersky. *Forbes,* September 23, 2013.

Eleanor Dallaway. "Interview with Eugene Kaspersky, Kaspersky Labs." *Infosecurity Magazine,* May 1, 2012. www.youtube.com/watch?v=6XGKofknATg. Consulted December 11, 2013.

Dunn, John E. "Eugene Kaspersky Reacts Angrily to Alleged Kremlin Sympathies; Wired article accused of 'negative undertone.'" Techworld. July 25, 2012.

Everett, Cath. "The Russian Approach to Battling Breaches." CNET, April 30, 2008. [Includes a brief interview with Natalya Kaspersky.]

Palmer, Maija. "A Tech Tycoon Who Values Privacy." *Financial Times,* September 25, 2012.

Shachtman, Noah. "Russia's Top Cyber Sleuth Foils US Spies, Helps Kremlin Pals." *Wired* Jul. 23, 2012. November 1, 2012.

Tarzey, Bob. "Kaspersky Lab—Russia's IT Security Jewel." *Infosecurity Magazine,* October 4, 2013.

MacFarlane, Seth

Cieply, Michael, and Brooks Barnes. "Academy Award Show Raises Ratings and Hackles." *New York Times,* February 25, 2012.

Dean, John. Seth MacFarlane's $2 Billion Family Guy Empire. *Fast Company,* November 1, 2008.

Itzkoff, Dave. "Artsbeat; A Word With: Seth Macfarlane: His Star Has a Tail and a Taste for Booze." *New York Times,* June 20, 2012. [Interview focusing on *Ted.*]

Solomon, Deborah. "Family Man; Questions for Seth MacFarlane." *New York Times,* September 11, 2009. [Brief interview.]

Weinraub, Bernard. "The Young Guy Of 'Family Guy'; A 30-Year-Old's Cartoon Hit Makes an Unexpected Comeback." *New York Times,* July 7, 2004.

Messier, Jean-Marie

Briançon, Pierre. *Messier Story* (Grasset, 2002).

Chabrak, Nihel, Russell Craig, and Nabyla Daidj. "Nouveau Riche, Old Guard, Established Elite:

Kinship Networks and Control of Vivendi Universal." Proceedings, Asia Pacific Interdisciplinary Research in Accounting Conference KOBE 2013, in association with *Accounting, Auditing and Accountability Journal.* http://www.apira2013.org/proceedings/pdfs/K042.pdf. Consulted December 12, 2013.

Clark, Nicola. "In the Shadow of Vivendi Scandal, Ex-Chief Works to Clear Name." *New York Times,* June 28, 2004.

Johnson, Jo, and Martine Orange. *The Man Who Tried to Buy the World: Jean-Marie Messier and Vivendi Universal.* New York: Portfolio, 2003.

Landler, Mark. "The World; In a French Mogul's Fall, A Warning for Globalists." *New York Times,* July 7, 2002.

McQueen, Rod.   *The Icarus Factor: The Rise and Fall of Edgar Bronfman, Jr.* Toronto: Doubleday Canada, 2004.

Tagliabue, John. "His Book, His Turn: Messier Speaks Up." *New York Times,* November 15, 2002.

Ward, Vicky. "Enemies in the boardroom." *Vanity Fair* 506 (October 2002):194–213.

Omidyar, Pierre

Cohen, Adam. *The Perfect Store: Inside eBay.* Boston: Little, Brown, 2002.

Dyer, Jeff, Hal Gregersen, and Clayton M. Christensen. *The Innovator's DNA; Mastering the Five Skills of Disruptive Innovators.* Boston: Harvard Business Review Press, 2011.

Hardy, Quentin. "The Radical Philanthropist." *Forbes,* May 5, 2000.

Hill, Tiffany. "The Paperless Press in Honolulu." *Honolulu Magazine,* August 2012.

LaFrance, Adrienne. "The Omidyar Way" Reuters, October 17, 2013.

Rosen, Jay. "Why Pierre Omidyar decided to join forces with Glenn Greenwald for a new venture in news." PressThink, October 16, 2013. http://pressthink.org/2013/10/. Consulted December 12, 2013. [With updates and a generous selection of links. On November 17, 2013, Jay Rosen announced that he had signed on to the new Greenwald-Omidyar news venture as a paid adviser.]

Rushe, Dominic. "Pierre Omidyar: From eBay to Crusading Journalism?" *The Observer,* October 19, 2013.

Solomon, Lewis D. *Tech Billionaire$: Reshaping Philanthropy in a Quest for a Better World.* New Brunswick, NJ: Transaction Publishers, 2009.

Paik, Nam June

Anderson, John. "Nam June Paik: Preserving the Human Television." *Art in America,* Febrary 6, 2013.

Danzico, Matt, and Jane O'Brien. "Living Online: Visual Artist Nam June Paik Predicted the Internet Age." *BBC News,* December 17, 2012.

Judkis, Maura. "'Father of Video Art' Nam June Paik Gets American Art Museum Exhibit." *Washington Post,* December 12, 2012.

Kennikott, Philip. "Smithsonian American Art Museum Channels Nam June Paik." *Washington Post,* December 16, 2002.

Reed, Josephine. "Nam June Paik: The Artist Who Invented Video." Art NEA Arts

Rosenberg, Karen. "He Tickled His Funny Bone, and Ours; 'Nam June Paik,' at Smithsonian American Art Museum. *New York Times*, January 11, 2013.

Rice, Linda Johnson

Bengali, Shashank. "Jetsetter." (University of Southern California) *Trojan Family Magazine* Winter 2002.

Coburn, Marcia Froelke. "Valerie Jarrett & Desirée Rogers." *Chicago Magazine,* November 24, 2008. [Despite title, includes considerable material on Rice.]

Gates, Henry Louis, Jr. *In Search of Our Roots: How 19 Extraordinary African Americans Reclaimed Their Past.* New York: Crown Publishers, 2009.

Graham, Lawrence Otis. *Our Kind of People: Inside America's Black Upper Class.* New York: HarperCollins, 1999.

Hughes, Alan. "New Era for Johnson Publishing with Outside Investment." *Black Enterprise,* July 11, 2011.

Johnson, John H., with Lerone Bennett Jr. *Succeeding against the Odds.* New York: Warner Books, 1989.

Murrill, Adrienne. "New ideas, strong legacy brand, spell success for publisher Linda Johnson Rice '87." *Kellogg World* [Northwestern University], Summer 2007.

Roberts, Robin

Bozeman, Kelli. "Playing by Her Own Rules." *Mississippi Magazine,* May 1, 2007.

Caviness, Ylonda Gault. "Lessons from the Heart." *Essence* 38.1:192 (May2007).

Chappell, Kevin. "Robin Roberts: Morning Show Co-Anchor Turns Sports Dreams into Broadcast Success." *Ebony,* March 2006.

McCarthy, Tom, and Matt Wells. "How ABC and Robin Roberts Made Gay Marriage History (and Kept It a Secret)." Guardian, May 10, 2012.

Stelter, Brian. "Robin Roberts Returns to 'Good Morning America.'" *New York Times,* February 20, 2013.

Stelter, Brian. *Top of the Morning: Inside the Cutthroat World of Morning TV* (Grand Central Publishing, 2013).

Rogers, Desirée

Coburn, Marcia Froelke. "Valerie Jarrett & Desirée Rogers." *Chicago Magazine,* November 24, 2008.

Coburn, Marcia Froelke. "Desirée Rogers 'I Have Learned Who I Am.'" *Chicago Magazine,* October 21, 2010.

Dorning, Mike. "Desirée Rogers, White House social secretary, sets a new standard." *Chicago Tribune,* March 15, 2009.

Orth, Maureen. "Can Desiree Rogers Make Washington Fun Again?" *Vanity Fair,* February 2, 2009.

Norwich, William. "The Life of the Party." *Vogue,* February 2009.

Werhane, Patricia, et al. *Women in Business: The Changing Face of Leadership.* Westport, CT: Praeger Publishers, 2007.

Romenesko, Jim

Carr, David. "Romenesko's Posts Now Toast." *New York Times,* November 11, 2011.

Dumenco, Simon. "Satellite Dish." *New York,* May 8, 2000.

Lisheron, Mark. "Romenesko Roars Back." *American Journalism Review,* February/March 2012.

Mitchell, Greg. "Was Romenesko Rebuilt in a Daze?" *Editor & Publisher* 135, no. 43: 19 (November 25, 2002).

Raines, Howell. "The Romenesko Empire." *Portfolio,* June 16, 2008.

Robertson, Lori. "The Romenesko Factor." *American Journalism Review,* September 2000.

p15 Sep. 1999, p28+ Sep. 2000, Jun./Jul., 2011, Feb. 23, 2012;

Ruiz Guiñazú,, Magdalena

Molnar, Victoria. "Magdalena Ruiz Guiñazú: 'They Sold for Power or Money.'" El País (Uruguay), September 5, 2013. [Interview.]

Goyoaga, Beatriz. "Stepping Up: Magdalena Ruiz Guiñazú." Variety 373.3:58 (November 30, 1998).

Julia Talevi, Julia. "Magdalena Ruiz Guiñazú: "I Need to Feel the Love of My Family." ¡Hola! Argentina, January 13, 2012.

Waisbord, Silvio R. "A Sign of the Times: Television and Electoral Politics in Argentina, 1983–1989." Working Paper #190—January 1993. Helen Kellogg Institute for International Studies. http://kellogg.nd.edu/publications/workingpapers/WPS/190.pdf. Consulted December 12, 2013.

La Nación. "Magdalena Ruiz Guiñazú adelantó que la OEA analizará si monitorea la libertad de prensa en el país" ["Magdalena Ruiz Guinazu Had the OEA Speed Up the Analysis of Monitoring Freedom of the Press in the Country."]. 3 November 2013.

Saatchi, Charles

Booth-Clibborn, Edward, ed. *History of the Saatchi Gallery,* 2nd Ed. London: Booth-Clibborn Editions, 2011.

Fallon, Ivan. *The Brothers: The Rise and Rise of Saatchi & Saatchi.* Chicago: Contemporary Books, 1989.

Goldman, Kevin. *Conflicting Accounts: The Creation and Crash of the Saatchi & Saatchi Advertising Empire.* Simon & Schuster, 1997.

Hatton, Rita, and John A. Walker. *Supercollector: A Critique of Charles Saatchi,* 4th ed. Esher: Institute of Artology, 2010.

Kent, Sarah, Richard Cork, and Dick Price. *Young British Art: The Saatchi Decade.* London: Booth-Clibborn Editions, 1999.

Saatchi Gallery. *100: The Work that Changed British Art,* text by Patricia Ellis. London: Jonathan Cape, in association with the Saatchi Gallery, 2003.

Sakamoto, James

Daniels, Roger. *Asian America: Chinese and Japanese in the United States since 1850.* Seattle: University of Washington Press, 1988.

Fiset, Louis. *Camp Harmony: Seattle's Japanese Americans and the Puyallup Assembly Center.* Urbana: University of Illinois Press, 2009.

Hosokawa, Bill. "Blind, But with Vision." *Pacific Citizen,* December 23, 1955, A4–6, 11. http://pacificcitizen.org/digitalarchives/assets/pdf/19551223.pdf.

Hosokawa, Bill. *JACL in Quest of Justice: The History of the Japanese American Citizens League.* New York: William Morrow, 1982.

Hosokawa, Bill. *Nisei: The Quiet Americans.* New York: William Morrow & Co., 1969.

Ichioka, Yuji. "A Study in Dualism: James Yoshinori Sakamoto and the Japanese American Courier, 1928-1942." Amerasia Journal 13.2 (1986-87): 49-81.

Ichioka, Yuji. *Before Internment: Essays in Prewar Japanese American History.* Edited by Gordon H. Chang and Eiichiro Azuma. Stanford: Stanford University Press, 2006. [This compilation includes the earlier article listed above.]

Takahashi, Jere. *Nisei/Sansei: Shifting Japanese American Identities and Politics.* Philadelphia: Temple University Press, 1997

Schwartz, Gil

Benkoil, Dorian. "MB Q&A: Gil Sschwartz/Stanley Bing." Media Bistro, March 22, 2006.

Himler, Peter. "NeXT PR." The Flak [blog], November 11, 2011. [Includes audio clips.]

Landler, Mark. "CBS's Best-Kept Secret (Hint Hint)." *New York Times,* January 08, 1996.

PR Week. "Stanley Bing/Gil Schwartz, executive vice president, corporate communications, CBS Corporation." August 30, 2011.

Selected Works

Abramson, Jill

Abramson, Jill, and Barbara Franklin. *Where They Are Now: The Story of the Women of Harvard Law, 1974.* New York: Doubleday, 1986.

Abramson, Jill, and Jane Mayer. *Strange Justice: The Selling of Clarence Thomas.* Boston: Houghton Mifflin, 1994.

Abramson, Jill. *The Puppy Diaries: Raising a Dog Named Scout. New York: Times Books,* 2011.

Abramson, Jill. "Kennedy, The Elusive President." *New York Times,* October 22, 2013. [Lengthy review of the literature on the 35th president, with some recommendations.]

Alterman, Eric

Alterman, Eric. *Sound and Fury: The Washington Punditocracy and the Collapse of American Politics.* New York: HarperCollins, 1992. [Later editions subtitled The Making of the Punditocracy.]

Alterman, Eric. *Who Speaks for America? Why Democracy Matters in Foreign Policy.* Ithaca, NY: Cornell University Press, 1998.

Alterman, Eric. *It Ain't No Sin to Be Glad You're Alive: The Promise of Bruce Springsteen.* Boston: Little, Brown, 1999.

Alterman, Eric. *What Liberal Media? The Truth about Bias and the News.* New York: Basic Books, 2003.

Alterman, Eric, with Mark Green. *The Book on Bush: How George W. Bush (Mis)Leads America.* New York: Viking, 2004.

Alterman, Eric. *When Presidents Lie: A History of Official Deception and Its Consequences.* New York: Viking, 2004.

Alterman, Eric. *Why We're Liberals: A Handbook for Restoring America's Most Important*

Ideals. New York: Viking, 2008.

Alterman, Eric. *Kabuki Democracy: The System vs. Barack Obama.* New York: Nation Books, 2011.

Alterman, Eric, with Kevin Mattson. *The Cause: The Fight for American Liberalism from Franklin Roosevelt to Barack Obama.* New York: Viking, 2012.

Alterman, Eric. "Author Archive: Articles by Eric Alterman." Columbia Journalism Review. http://www.cjr.org/author/eric-alterman/. Consulted December 10, 2013.

Arnaz, Desi

Arnaz, Desi. *A Book.* New York: Morrow, 1976.

Arriola, Gus

Arriola, Gus. *Gordo's Cat. San Diego, CA: Oak Tree Publications, 1981.*

Arriola, Gus. *Gordo's Critters: The Collected Cartoons.* Berkeley, Calif.: Celestial Arts, 1989.

Baldauf, Sari

Baldauf, Sari, and Seija Kulkki. *International Divestments as the Reallocation Process of Productive Assets: A Managerial Approach.* Helsinki: Helsinki School of Economics, 1983. (Working Papers in International Business; FIBO Working Paper, 1983, no. 1.)

Bourdain, Anthony

Bourdain, Anthony. *Bone in the Throat.* New York: Villard Books, 1995.

Bourdain, Anthony. *Gone Bamboo* New York: Villard Books, 1997.

Bourdain, Anthony. *Kitchen Confidential: Adventures in the Culinary Underbelly.* New York: Bloomsbury, 2000.

Bourdain, Anthony. *A Cook's Tour: In Search of the Perfect Meal.* New York: Bloomsbury, 2001.

Bourdain, Anthony. *The Bobby Gold Stories.* New York: Bloomsbury, 2003.

Bourdain, Anthony. *Anthony Bourdain's Les Halles Cookbook.* New York: Bloomsbury, 2004.

Bourdain, Anthony. *The Nasty Bits: Collected Varietal Cuts, Usable Trim, Scraps, and Bones.* New York: Bloomsbury, 2006

Bourdain, Anthony. *No Reservations: Around the World on an Empty Stomach.* New York: Bloomsbury, 2007.

Bourdain, Anthony. *Medium Raw: A Bloody Valentine to the World of Food and the People Who Cook.* New York: Ecco Press, 2010.

Brûlé, Tyler

Brûlé, Tyler. *Fast Lane. Financial Times.* [Blog column; http://www.ft.com/arts/columnists/tylerbrule

Buckley, Priscilla L.

Buckley, Priscilla L., ed. *The Joys of National Review, 1955–1980.* New York: National Review Books, 1994.

Buckley, Priscilla L. *String of Pearls: On the News Beat in New York and Paris.* New York: Thomas Dunne Books, 2001.

Buckley, Priscilla L. *Living It Up with National Review: A Memoir.* Dallas: Spence Publishing Company 2005.

Buckley, Priscilla L. *History Writ Small: Exploring Its Nooks and Crannies by Barge, Boat, and Balloon.* New York: National Review Books, 2009.

Coddington, Grace

Coddington, Grace, Michael Roberts, and Jay Fielden, eds. *Grace: Thirty Years of Fashion at Vogue.* Edition 7L, 2002.

Coddington, Grace, Didier Malige, and Michael Roberts. *The Catwalk Cats.* Paris: Edition 7L; Göttingen, Steidl, 2006.

Coddington, Grace, with Michael Roberts. *Grace: A Memoir.* New York: Random House, 2012.

Cohen, Janet Langhart

Cohen, Janet Langhart, with Alexander Kopelman. *From Rage to Reason: My Life in Two Americas.* New York: Kensington, 2004.

Cohen, Janet Langhart, with William S. Cohen. *Love in Black and White: A Memoir of Race, Religion, and Romance.* Lanham, MD: Rowman & Littlefield, 2007.

Cohen, William S., and Janet Langhart Cohen, eds. *Race and Reconciliation in America.* Lanham, MD: Lexington Books, 2009.

Dé, Shobhaa

Dé, Shobha. *Socialite Evenings.* New York and New Delhi: Penguin Books, 1989.

Dé, Shobha. *Starry Nights.* New York and New Delhi: Penguin Books, 1991.

Dé, Shobha. *Sisters.* New York and New Delhi: Penguin Books, 1992.

Dé, Shobha. *Strange Obsession.* New York and New Delhi: Penguin Books, 1994.

Dé, Shobha. *Sultry Days.* New York and New Delhi: Penguin Books, 1995.

Dé, Shobha. *Second Thoughts.* New Delhi: Penguin Books, 1996.

Dé, Shobha. *Surviving Men: The Smart Woman's Guide to Staying on Top.* London and New Delhi: Penguin Books, 1997.

Dé, Shobha. *Speedpost: Letters to My Children about Living, Loving, Caring and Coping with the World.* London and New Delhi: Penguin Books, 1999

Dé, Shobha. *Selective Memory: Stories from My Life,* New York and New Delhi: Penguin Books, 1999.

Dé, Shobhaa. *Spouse: The Truth about Marriage.* London: Penguin Books, 2005.

Dé, Shobhaa. *Snapshots.* New Delhi: Penguin Books, 2006.

Dé, Shobhaa. *Superstar India: From Incredible to Unstoppable.* New Delhi, Penguin, 2008.

Dé, Shobhaa. *Shobhaa at Sixty.* New Delhi: Hay House India, 2010.

Dé, Shobhaa. *Sethji.* New Delhi: Penguin, 2012.

Deutsch, Linda

Deutsch, Linda, Michael Fleeman et al. *Verdict: The Chronicle of the O. J. Simpson Trial.* Kansas City, MO: Andrews & McMeel, 1995.

Deutsch, Linda. "Flash and Trash," in *Covering the Courts: Free Press, Fair Trials, and Journalistic Performance,* ed. by Robert Giles and Robert W. Snyder. New Brunswick, NJ: Transaction Publishers, 1998. [Originally published in *Media Studies Journal,* Winter 1998.]

Deutsch, Linda, and Richard Carelli. *Covering the Courts: An Associated Press Manual for Reporters.* New York: Associated Press, 1999.

Deutsch, Linda. "Dick Clark: AP Writer Linda Deutsch Remembers Teenage Appearance on 'American Bandstand.'" Huffington Post, April 19, 2012.

Eaton, Edith Maude (Sui Sin Far)

Sui Sin Far. "Leaves from the Mental Portfolio of an Eurasian." *Independent* 66 (January 1909): 125–32. [Autobiographical essay; included in the 1995 edition of *Mrs. Spring Fragrance and Other Writings.*]

Sui Sin Far. *Mrs. Spring Fragrance and Other Writings,* ed. Amy Ling and Annette White-Parks. Urbana, IL: University of Illinois Press, 1995.

Gruber, Lilli

Gruber, Lilli, and Paolo Borella. *Quei giorni a Berlin* ("Those Days in Berlin"). Turin, Nuovo ERI, 1990. [Twentieth anniversary edition, 2009, entitled *Ritorno a Berlino.*]

Gruber, Lilli. *I miei giorni a Baghdad* ("My Days in Baghdad"). Milan: Rizzoli; Rome: RAI ERI, 2003.

Gruber, Lilli. *L'altro Islam* ("The Other Islam"). Milan: Rizzoli, 2004.

Gruber, Lilli. *Chador* ("Chador"). Milan: Rizzoli, 2005.

Gruber, Lilli. *Figlie dell'Islam* ("Daughters of Islam"). Milan: Rizzoli, 2007.

Gruber, Lilli. *Streghe; La riscossa delle donne d'Italia* ("Witches: The Rescue of the Women of Italy"). Milan: Rizzoli, 2008.

Gruber, Lilli, and Paolo Borella. *Ritorno a Berlino* ("Return to Berlin"). Milan: Rizzoli, 2009. [Twentieth anniversary edition of *Quei giorni a Berlin.*]

Gruber, Lilli. *Eredità: Una storia della mia famiglia tra l'impero e il fascismo* ("Legacy; A Story of My Family between the Empire and Fascism") Milan: Rizzoli, 2012.

Haruka, Yoko

Haruka, Yoko. *Tōdai de Ueno Chizuko ni Kenka o Manabu* ("Learning How to Argue from Chizuko Ueno at Tokyo University"). Tokyo: Chikuma Shobō, 2000.

Haruka, Yoko. *Kekkon shimasen!* ("I Shall Not Marry!"). Tokyo: Kōdansha, 2001.

Haruka, Yoko. *Hataraku onna wa teki bakari* ("All a Working Woman Gets Is Enemies"). Tokyo: Asahi Shinbunsha, 2001.

Haruka, Yoko. *Kaigo to ren'ai* ("Care of the Elderly and Romantic Love"). Tokyo: Chikuma Shobō, 2002.

Haruka, Yoko. *Haiburiddo ūman* ("Hybrid Woman"). Tokyo: Kōdansha, 2003.

Haruka, Yoko. *Hataraku onna wa ude shidai* ("For Working Women, It Depends on Skill"). Tokyo: Asahi Shinbunsha, 2006.

Haruka, Yoko. *Iitokodori no onna* ("Women Who Take Only the Best Parts"). Tokyo: Kōdansha, 2006.

Haruka, Yoko. *Onna no teki* ("Women's Enemies"). Tokyo: Nikkei BP Shuppan Sentā, 2007.

Haruka, Yoko. *Onnatomodachi* ("Girlfriends"). Tokyo: Hōken, 2008.

Haruka, Yoko. *Riguretto: Ima demo anata ga koishikute* ("You Are Still Missed: Regret"). Tokyo: Seishun Shuppansha, 2009.

Haruka, Yoko. *Kimuzukashii josei tono jōzu na sesshikata* ("Positive Attitude and Hard-to-Please Women"). Tokyo: Asahi Shinbunshuppan, 2010.

Haruka, Yoko. *Shiniyuku mono no reigi* ("Courtesy of Those Dying"). Tokyo: Chikuma Shobō, 2010.

Haruka, Yoko. *Shiawase no hōsoku* ("Law of Happiness"). Koshigaya: Saiunshuppan, 2010.

Haruka, Yoko. *Honshin ga wakaranai toki ni yomu hon* ("Book to Read When You Don't Know the True Feelings"). Tokyo: Asashuppan, 2013.

Jackson, Hal

Jackson, Hal, with James Haskins. *The House that Jack Built: My Life as a Trailblazer in Broadcasting and Entertainment.* New York: Amistad Press, 2001.

Messier, Jean-Marie

Messier, Jean-Marie. *J6M.com: Faut-il avoir peur de la nouvelle économie?* ("J6M.com: Is It Necessary to Fear the New Economy?"). Paris: Hachette, 2000.

Messier, Jean-Marie, and Yves Messarovitch. *Mon Vrai Journal* ("My True Diary"). Paris: Editions Balland, 2002.

Messier, Jean-Marie. *Le jour où le ciel nous est tombé sur la tête* ("The Day the Sky Fell on Our Heads"). Paris: Seuil, 2009.

Roberts, Robin

Lieberman-Cline, Nancy, and Robin Roberts, with Kevin Warneke. *Basketball for Women: Becoming a Complete Player.* Champaign, IL: Human Kinetics, 1996.

Roberts, Robin. *From the Heart: Seven Rules to Live By.* New York: Hyperion, 2007.

Roberts, Lucimarian, with Robin Roberts, as told to Missy Buchanan. *My Story, My Song: Mother-Daughter Reflections on Life and Faith.* Nashville: Upper Room Books, 2012.

Romenesko, Jim

Romenesko, James, comp. *Death Log.* Milwaukee: Police Beat Press, 1982.

Ruiz Guiñazú, Magdalena

Ruiz Guiñazú, Magdalena. *Huésped de un verano* ("Summer Guest"). Buenos Aires: Planeta, 1994.

Ruiz Guiñazú, Magdalena. Había una vez ... la vida ("Once upon a Time … Life"). Buenos Aires: Planeta, 1995.

Ruiz Guiñazú, Magdalena, with Father Rafael Braun. *¡Qué mundo nos ha tocado!* ("What a World We Have Had! Conversations between Two Performers of Our Time). Buenos Aires: Editorial El Ateneo, 2001.

Ruiz Guiñazú, Magdalena. *Historias de hombres, mujeres y jazmines* ("Stories of Men, Women and Jasmine"). Buenos Aires: Planeta, 2002.

Ruiz Guiñazú, Magdalena, Juan Terranova. *Secretos de familia* ("Family Secrets"). Buenos Aires: Editorial Sudamericana, 2010.

Ruiz Guiñazú, Magdalena. *Héroes de un país del Sur* ("Heroes of a Southern Country"). Buenos Aires: Editorial Sudamericana, 2011.

Ruiz Guiñazú, Magdalena. *La Casa de los secretos* ("House of Secrets"). Buenos Aires: Editorial Sudamericana, 2011.

Saatchi, Charles

Saatchi, Charles. *My name is Charles Saatchi and I Am an Artoholic: Everything You Need to Know about Art, Ads, Life, God and Other Mysteries, and Weren't Afraid to Ask—.* London and New York: Phaidon, 2009.

Saatchi, Charles. *Question.* London: Phaidon, 2010.

Saatchi, Charles. *Be the Worst You Can Be: Life's Too Long for Patience & Virtue.* London and New York: Abrams, 2012.

Saatchi, Charles. *Babble.* London: Booth-Clibborn Editions, 2013.

Saatchi, Charles. *The Naked Eye.* London: Booth-Clibborn Editions, 2013.

Schwartz, Gil (writing as Stanley Bing)

Schwartz, Gil. *Biz Words.* New York: Pocket Books, 1989.

Schwartz, Gil. *Crazy Bosses: Spotting Them, Serving Them, Surviving Them.* New York: Morrow, 1992.

Schwartz, Gil. *Lloyd—What Happened, A Novel of Business.* New York: Crown Publishers, 1998.

Schwartz, Gil. *What Would Machiavelli Do? The Ends Justify the Meanness.* New York: HarperBusiness, 2000.

Schwartz, Gil. *Throwing the Elephant; Zen and the Art of Managing Up.* New York: HarperBusiness, 2002.

Schwartz, Gil. *The Big Bing.* New York: HarperBusiness, 2003.

Schwartz, Gil. *You Look Nice Today; A Novel.* New York: Bloomsbury, 2003.

Schwartz, Gil. *Sun Tzu Was a Sissy: Conquer Your Enemies, Promote Your Friends, and Wage the Real Art of War.* New York: HarperBusiness, 2004.

Schwartz, Gil. *100 Bullshit Jobs ... and How to Get Them.* New York: Collins, 2006.

Schwartz, Gil. *Rome, Inc.* New York: Norton: 2006.

Schwartz, Gil. *Executricks: How to Retire While You're Still Working.* New York: Collins, 2008. (revised and published in paperback as Executricks: *How to Relax without Getting the Axe.* 2009).

Schwartz, Gil. *Bingsop's Fables: Little Morals for Big Business.* New York: HarperBusiness, 2011.

Profession Index

Activist
Sakamoto, James Y.

Actor
Arnaz, Desi

Advertising Executive
Saatchi, Charles

Animator
Arriola, Gus
MacFarlane, Seth

Art Collector
Saatchi, Charles

Author
Haruka, Yōko

Bookseller
Guy, Thomas

Broadcast Journalist
Gruber, Lilli
Ruiz, Guiñazú, Magdalena

Business Executive
Arnaz, Desi
Kaspersky, Eugene
Kaspersky, Natalya
Messier, Jean-Marie

Cartoonist
Arriola, Gus

Chief Executive Officer (CEO)
Langhart Cohen, Janet

Chef
Bourdain, Anthony

Communications Executive
Schwartz, Gil

Corporate Director
Baldauf, Sari

Courtroom Reporter
Deutsch, Linda

Cryptologist
Kaspersky, Eugene

Director
Ball, Alan
Chase, David

Editor
Bourdain, Anthony
Buckley, Priscilla L.

Fashion Magazine Director
Coddington, Grace